OXFORD WORLD'

THE FALL OF THE R(
Roman History, BOOKS TH

LUCIUS CASSIUS DIO was born around 163 CE in the Greek city of
Nicaea (modern Iznik) in the Roman province of Bithynia in north-
west Anatolia. He followed his father into the Roman Senate, where he
enjoyed a successful career culminating in his second consulship, with
the emperor Severus Alexander as his colleague, in 229 CE, after which
he retired to Nicaea. After shorter, lost works on the dreams and portents foretelling Septimius Severus' accession as emperor and on the
civil wars which preceded it, Dio wrote his massive eighty-book
Roman History, which occupied him for over twenty-two years. Books
36 to 60, covering the years 69 BCE to 47 CE, survive largely intact, but
the rest of the work survives only in extracts and epitomes. Dio's work
follows the traditional Roman pattern of a year-by-year history of the
Roman people from the foundation of the city to his own time, but is
written in his native Greek, taking Thucydides as its chief model.

ROBIN WATERFIELD is an independent scholar and translator, and
a former university lecturer, now living in southern Greece. In
addition to over thirty volumes of translations of ancient Greek, he is
the author of numerous books, ranging from children's fiction to
Greek history.

JOHN RICH taught throughout his career at the University of
Nottingham. He is now Emeritus Professor at Nottingham and
Honorary Senior Research Fellow at the University of Bristol. He has
published widely on Roman history and historiography, with particular focuses on Roman war and imperialism, the reign of Augustus, and
the Roman histories of Appian and Cassius Dio.

OXFORD WORLD'S CLASSICS

*For over 100 years Oxford World's Classics have brought
readers closer to the world's great literature. Now with over 700
titles—from the 4,000-year-old myths of Mesopotamia to the
twentieth century's greatest novels—the series makes available
lesser-known as well as celebrated writing.*

*The pocket-sized hardbacks of the early years contained
introductions by Virginia Woolf, T. S. Eliot, Graham Greene,
and other literary figures which enriched the experience of reading.
Today the series is recognized for its fine scholarship and
reliability in texts that span world literature, drama and poetry,
religion, philosophy, and politics. Each edition includes perceptive
commentary and essential background information to meet the
changing needs of readers.*

OXFORD WORLD'S CLASSICS

CASSIUS DIO

The Fall of the Roman Republic

Roman History, Books Thirty-Six to Forty

Translated by
ROBIN WATERFIELD

With an Introduction and Notes by
JOHN RICH

OXFORD
UNIVERSITY PRESS

OXFORD
UNIVERSITY PRESS

Great Clarendon Street, Oxford, OX2 6DP,
United Kingdom

Oxford University Press is a department of the University of Oxford.
It furthers the University's objective of excellence in research, scholarship,
and education by publishing worldwide. Oxford is a registered trade mark of
Oxford University Press in the UK and in certain other countries

Published in the United States of America by Oxford University Press
198 Madison Avenue, New York, NY 10016, United States of America

British Library Cataloguing in Publication Data

Data available

Library of Congress Control Number: 2023945740

ISBN 978–0–19–882288–2

Printed and bound in the UK by
Clays Ltd, Elcograf S.p.A.

CONTENTS

INTRODUCTION

THE years 69–50 BCE saw the final crisis of the Roman Republic. In the city of Rome political violence was rife throughout, sometimes descending into anarchy. Pompey, Rome's greatest general, reached the pinnacle of his career in 67–62, when he suppressed piracy across the Mediterranean, brought Rome's long conflict with King Mithridates of Pontus to an end, and hugely extended its empire. When he returned home, Pompey found himself frustrated by conservative senators, and so allied with a rising star, Julius Caesar. As a result, Caesar won a great command in his turn, and used it to conquer Gaul in 58–50 and so make himself Pompey's equal. By 50 Caesar's alliance with Pompey had collapsed, and civil war broke out between them in January 49. Twenty years of nearly continuous civil war followed, ended only by the final victory in 31–30 of Caesar's heir Octavian, who went on to take the name Augustus and establish the monarchy of the emperors.

Cicero's speeches and letters provide vivid contemporary evidence for Roman politics in these last years of the Republic, and Caesar's *Gallic War* is a brilliant account of his campaigns in Gaul. (Both writers, of course, are far from objective.) For much of our information on the period, however, we depend on later writers, and by far the fullest surviving account is given by a historian writing over 250 years later, Cassius Dio. Dio's vast eighty-book *Roman History* began with the foundation of the city and took the story down to his own time, but he devoted most space to the transition from the Republic to the imperial system under which he still lived. His account of the years 69–50 in Books 36–40 (to which we have given the title *The Fall of the Roman Republic*) provides our fullest and sometimes our only account of important developments, and, although there are plenty of errors and misinterpretations, its overall standard of accuracy is high. It is also a fascinating and idiosyncratic narrative in its own right, vividly evoking the turbulent events of the time and offering quirkily original interpretations of motives and actions.

Lucius Cassius Dio, to give him his full name,[1] was born around 163 at Nicaea (modern Iznik) in the province of Bithynia in north-western

---

[1] Dio's *praenomen* Lucius is supplied by a veteran's discharge tablet, dated by his second consulship.

Anatolia. His family had long been prominent there, and will have held the Roman citizenship for several generations. By the mid-second century CE, it had become not uncommon for aristocrats from the Greek-speaking eastern provinces to gain entry to the Roman Senate. Dio's father, Marcus Cassius Apronianus, was one of these, and went on to govern several provinces. His father's senatorial duties will have meant that Dio spent much of his early years in Rome and Italy rather than at Nicaea. He will have grown up as fluent in Latin as in his native Greek and educated in both cultures.

Dio followed his father into the Senate, entering it by holding the quaestorship around 189. In 194 he was praetor, and his subsequent career included a first consulship and several provincial governorships. In 229 it was crowned by the rare distinction of a second consulship, with the emperor Severus Alexander as his colleague, after which Dio retired to his native Bithynia. Dio identified completely with the Senate and its values, and his account of his own times is full of the tensions of senatorial life under oppressive emperors such as Commodus, Septimius Severus, and Caracalla.

Dio himself tells us how he came to write his history (73[72].23.1–5). He had written a little book about the dreams and portents which led Septimius Severus to hope that he might become emperor and had sent it to Severus. The emperor replied with a long, favourable letter, and the night after he received this Dio had a dream which he took to be a divine command to write history. He obeyed by composing a history of the 'wars and civil strife' which followed Commodus' death in 192. When this too was well received, he decided to write an account of 'everything else that concerned the Romans', incorporating the work he had just written. Throughout this great task he was, he assures us, supported by his guardian goddess Fortune, who sent him encouraging dreams. He then tells us that 'I spent ten years in collecting all the achievements of the Romans from the beginning to the death of Severus, and another twelve in writing my history; subsequent events will be recorded for as long as possible'. The chronological implications of these statements have been disputed, but the twenty-two-year period devoted to the composition of the history up to Severus' death in 211 is best identified as *c.*201–23.[2] Dio subsequently continued the work up to 229.

---

[2] See P. M. Swan, *The Augustan Succession: An Historical Commentary on Cassius Dio's Roman History Books 55–56 (9 BC–AD 14)* (New York, 2004), 28–36; C. T. Mallan,

The second and early third centuries CE saw a brilliant flourishing of Greek prose literature across a wide range of genres, a development sometimes known as the Second Sophistic. Two of these writers, both working in the early second century, dealt at length with the Roman past, namely Plutarch, in his comparative biographies of eminent Greeks and Romans, and Appian, whose Roman history was organized innovatively by regions and wars. Dio, however, was the first of these Greek writers under the empire to undertake a comprehensive account of all of Roman history, organized in the main annalistically, by consular years.

In writing a history of Rome on this pattern, Dio was conforming to the original model established by the first historian of Rome, Fabius Pictor, writing at the end of the third century BCE. From the later second century BCE some historians of Rome had dealt only with more limited periods or with individual wars, although these too had mostly opted for year-by-year organization. However, annalistic histories of Rome from the beginning to the author's own time had continued to be written and had culminated in the vast work of Livy, written mostly under Augustus, which covered the period from the foundation to 9 BCE in 144 books and achieved the literary mastery which its predecessors had lacked. Fabius Pictor and his immediate successors had written in Greek, then the established language for historical writing, but all the comprehensive annalistic histories of Rome composed from the later second century BCE on had been in Latin. Dio's work was thus at once traditional and innovative: he was writing the history of Rome on the standard annalistic pattern from the foundation to his own day, but he was doing so in his native language, as a provincial from the Greek East. Dio's history, like Dio himself, was thus a fusion of Roman and Greek.

Like the other Greek writers of the imperial period, Dio aspired to the highest literary standards. He composed his history in an Attic Greek modelled on the language of the great Athenian writers of the fifth and fourth centuries BCE. Like all members of the Greek and Roman elites, his education had been dominated by rhetoric, and this training had a pervasive influence on his style, especially in speeches

Cassius Dio, Roman History Books 57 and 58 (The Reign of Tiberius) (Oxford, 2020), 353–5. For other views, see A. M. Kemezis, *Greek Narratives of the Roman Empire under the Severans* (Cambridge, 2014), 282–93; M. O. Lindholmer, 'The Time of Composition of Cassius Dio's Roman History: A Reconsideration', *Klio* 103 (2021), 133–59.

and dramatic narrative episodes. He also frequently imitates the wording of classical predecessors. Chief among these models was the historian Thucydides, and here his debt is not merely stylistic. Dio shared Thucydides' cynical outlook on human affairs, and, like him, loved to point the contrast between men's claims and their true motives. It is often in Thucydides' terms that he formulates his antitheses between appearance and reality and his reflections on human nature.[3]

Dio's work is only partially preserved. The main part of his original text to survive runs from Book 36 to Book 60, covering the years 69 BCE to 47 CE, with frequent gaps at the start and from Book 55. For the rest of the work we are mainly dependent on extracts in various Byzantine collections and summaries by two Byzantine writers: John Zonaras, who in his *Epitome of Histories* used Dio as his main source on Roman history down to 146 and again from 44 BCE, and Xiphilinus, who produced an epitome of Dio's Books 36–80.

Dio organized his eighty books (each originally a papyrus roll) into ten-book groups (decads). He assigned the first forty books to the period before the outbreak of the war between Caesar and Pompey, Books 41–50 to the civil wars from 49 to the decisive Battle of Actium in 31 BCE, and the remaining thirty books to the reigns of the emperors from Augustus on.

In Books 1–2 Dio narrated the foundation of Rome and the rule of its early kings, and Books 3–10 were then devoted to the early centuries of the Republic. Books 11–20 covered the years *c.*264–150, dealing with Rome's initial expansion outside Italy and in particular with the first two great wars against Carthage and the wars with successive eastern kings. Books 21–30 began with the outbreak of Rome's third and last war with Carthage and probably continued down to the Social War in 91–89, so covering the early phase of the upheavals which destabilized the Republic. Books 31–35 probably began with the year 88, which saw the outbreak of both the first war with Mithridates and the first of the civil wars between Marius and his supporters and Sulla, and concluded with the first consulship of Pompey and Crassus in 70.[4]

---

[3] Human nature: e.g. 36.1.2, 20.1, 31.4; 38.7.2, 18.3, 36.3; 39.6.1. For other imitations of Thucydides, see notes to 38.36–44; 39.40–3; 40.34.2.

[4] Sadly, very little has survived of Dio's account of the years 146–70 BCE, but fragments show that Dio was sharply critical of the radical tribunes Tiberius and Gaius Gracchus and the populist general Marius and deplored the brutality with which the victorious Sulla purged his opponents (frgs. 83, 85, 89, 109).

Thus, overall, Books 31–40, Dio's fourth decad, probably began with the first civil war, and then brought the narrative down to the point when the second civil war was about to break out.

Sources

How did Dio work in the long years devoted to his history? He gives us a valuable indication with his claim (cited above) that he spent ten years collecting material for the bulk of his history and then twelve years writing it up. During the initial ten years he must have accumulated copious notes, extracts, and drafts (doubtless with the help of slave or freedmen assistants), and in the writing-up stage he probably worked mainly from these materials, only occasionally consulting the original texts. For some sections of his work his notes will have come chiefly from one source, but for much of the history Dio probably had to make a coherent account of his own from notes drawn from a variety of sources. This way of working may account for some of Dio's errors, but it probably also helps to explain his independence of treatment—the freedom with which he selected and shaped his material and developed his own interpretations and explanations.

On events in his own time or the recent past Dio drew on his own experience and oral testimony, but for the rest of his work he was entirely dependent on earlier writers. It is unlikely that for our period he made any use of documentary evidence from inscriptions or archives.

Dio tells us little about what he read: he occasionally notes the existence of more than one version or indicates uncertainty by phrases like 'as some say', but the only sources he names are the autobiographies of the emperors Augustus and Hadrian.[5] He cannot, as he boasts in a fragment from his lost preface (frg. 1.2), have read 'virtually everything written about the Romans', but he will have read widely in the works he regarded as relevant for his purpose. His principal sources must have been earlier histories, and two major works of this kind which he surely drew on in Books 36–40 are Asinius Pollio's history of the civil wars and the relevant part of Livy's comprehensive Roman history, both written mainly under Augustus and almost

[5] Multiple versions: 40.27.2–3, 59.4. Uncertainty: 36.11.1–2; 37.36.4; 38.13.5; 39.23.4, 38.4–6; 40.43.2. Imperial autobiographies: 44.35.3; 66.17.1; 69.11.2.

entirely lost to us. Dio probably also exploited memoirs and biographies, but he made little use of other types of literature. Although he drew on Cicero's published speeches for some of the speeches in his history (see p. xxv and note to 36.25.1), for his narrative Dio seems to have made no use of Cicero's speeches or letters.

The earliest Roman historical work to survive intact is Sallust's account of Catiline's conspiracy, composed after his retirement from political life around 42 BCE. This was clearly not one of Dio's main sources for that topic, in view of the extensive divergences between their accounts, but Dio did make some use of the work, as is shown by one passage where the similarities between their versions are so close that Sallust must have been Dio's source (see note to 37.35.1). After writing his innovative monographs on Catiline and Jugurtha, Sallust reverted with his *Histories* to the more traditional pattern of an annalistic account of recent Roman history, covering the years 78–67 BCE. Dio must have made substantial use of this work in his lost account of events down to 70, and close correspondences between fragments of Sallust's *Histories* and several passages in the opening chapters of Book 36 show that Dio was still making extensive use of it for his account of the final phase of Lucullus' campaign against Mithridates (see notes to 36.1.2, 9.5, 17.2).

For Caesar's campaigns in Gaul Dio's main source was Caesar's own *Gallic War*. Dio's account is so close to Caesar's in its structure and in much of the narrative detail that he is much more likely to have been using Caesar's work directly than via a later writer (as some scholars have argued). Dio's account is much more compressed than Caesar's, and there are also numerous divergences, many noted in the Explanatory Notes. Some of these must be due to Dio's use of other sources, for example his radically different accounts of the defeat and death of Cotta and Sabinus and of Vercingetorix's surrender (see notes to 40.5–6, 41). For many of the divergences, however, Dio himself was probably responsible: sometimes this will have been by deliberate choice, but in other cases changes will have slipped in, often as simple errors, as he made his notes or later when he wrote them up. Two changes which must be Dio's own are echoes of Thucydides (see notes to 39.40.5 and 40.34.2).[6]

---

[6] C. Pelling, in *Classical Review* 32 (1982), 146–8, attributes most of the divergences to Dio himself. Greater use of another source or sources is postulated by I. McDougall, 'Dio and His Sources for Caesar's Campaigns in Gaul', *Latomus* 50/3 (1991), 616–38,

Caesar's account consistently portrays himself in the best possible light—his actions as invariably motivated solely by his judgement of the Romans' public interest, and his conduct of the war as impeccable throughout. Dio's version is often (but not always) less positive: what Caesar portrays as prudent restraint here sometimes becomes fear, and the achievements of individual campaigns are sometimes minimized.[7] At two points Dio makes Caesar appear to have acted treacherously in diplomatic dealings with enemies (see notes to 38.32.1 and 39.48.1).

Dio's most notable divergence concerns Caesar's motivation. Already in his account of Caesar's earlier campaign in Further Spain, he had portrayed him as driven by ambition and the desire for glory and so making demands just in order to get a pretext for war (37.52.1–3). Now he tells us that in Gaul too Caesar was impelled by the desire for glory and the power to which it would lead, and in particular that he made demands of Ariovistus just 'to get a good and plausible excuse for war' against him (38.31.1, 34). The topic does not recur in Dio's accounts of Caesar's Gallic campaigns from 57 on but, when he comes to Caesar's two crossings to Germany and Britain, Dio asserts that his chief motive was the glory to be won from these unprecedented feats (39.48.3–4, 51.1, 53.1; 40.1.2, 32.2). Dio will have found at least some of this material in his sources, but it was his own choice to insist on the theme and give it such prominence, and, as we shall see, it coheres with his overall conception of Caesar's character.

Subject Matter and Arrangement

'I have compiled the deeds of the Roman people in war and at home [*militiae et domi*] in the consulship of Marcus Lepidus and Quintus Catulus and thereafter.' Thus Sallust announced his theme at the start of his *Histories*, placing the work explicitly in the tradition of Roman annalistic historical writing. The subject matter of such histories, from Fabius Pictor on, had always been conceived as the domestic and military achievements of the Romans, arranged by the consular year. The pattern can be seen most clearly in the surviving

and M. O. Lindholmer, 'Caesar's Campaigns in Cassius Dio's Late Republic', in C. H. Lange and A. G. Scott (eds.), *Cassius Dio: The Impact of Violence, War and Civil War* (Leiden, 2020), 92–119.

[7] e.g. 38.33.3; 39.1.3–2.1, 44.2, 48.5, 51.1, 53.1; 40.1.2, 32.1–2.

parts of Livy's history, and Livy ends many of his year-narratives with formulas like, 'These were the events of that year at home and in war [*domi militiaeque*]'.

This was the tradition within which Dio was working, and throughout he followed this conception of his subject matter, as is shown by the analysis of the structure of these books (pp. xxxvi–xxxviii). Over 40 per cent of Books 36–40 is taken up by Dio's accounts of the major wars of the time—the campaigns of Lucullus and Pompey against Mithridates and others in the East, Caesar's Gallic Wars, and Crassus' disastrous Parthian expedition—and he also includes brief sections on a few minor wars.[8] The content of Dio's domestic sections is more diverse, but the bulk of them is devoted to what he regarded as the chief political events of the day, often centring on leading figures like Pompey, Caesar, and Cicero, and sometimes on key themes such as political corruption or violence.

Dio's sources provided much more detail than he could use, and he recognized that he had to be selective (frg. 1.2). Occasionally he remarks that he has omitted information unnecessary for his history (37.17.4; 38.7.6; 39.17.1; 40.15.1, 31.1), and he permits himself only a few digressions, mostly on Roman institutions.[9] His domestic sections, however, sometimes include apparently minor and even trivial events, informing us, for example, that spectators at a gladiatorial show were given a lunch-break for the first time in 61, that Faustus Sulla gave a particularly brilliant show the following year, and that in 57 the consul Lentulus Spinther succeeded in evading the rules on the membership of priestly colleges to get an augurship for his son.[10] Such routine items were a traditional feature of Roman annalistic histories, and including such material was one of the ways in which Dio evoked this tradition. They also sometimes served to bulk out a thin section, or to illustrate the overriding of conventions which Dio saw as an endemic feature of the Late Republic.

Another feature of the Roman annalistic tradition taken over by Dio is reports of prodigies and portents. Such reports in Livy include

---

[8] See 36.18–19; 37.47–48, 52–53; 39.54. Accounts of further overseas commands are worked in incidentally: 38.12.1–3; 39.22, 56–58.

[9] e.g. 37.24.1–3, 28.1–3; 38.13.3–5; 39.35.1–2. Other digressions: 37.17–19; 39.49–50; 40.14–15.

[10] See 37.46.4, 51.4; 39.17. For other such reports, see 36.40.4–41.2; 37.9.3–5, 45.3, 51.3; 39.65.

not just the prodigies themselves, but also the measures taken by the Roman authorities to expiate the divine anger of which they were held to be evidence. Dio mentions such measures only when they had wider political implications (37.9.1–2, 34.3–4; 39.15–16, 20), and his own interest is rather in what these prodigies portended. He repeatedly makes clear his belief that prodigies and the like were signs from 'divinity' (*to daimonion* or *to theion*, the neutral terms he generally uses in respect of divine interventions).[11] In several passages he points ahead to forthcoming disasters through prominent reports of the phenomena which he takes to portend them,[12] and sometimes it seems to be Dio himself who has made the connection.[13]

Like the earlier annalistic historians, Dio organized his material carefully by consular years. He notes the start of each year by naming the new consuls and repeats this information later when necessary. Most events are mentioned under an identified year, and Dio rarely gets the year wrong.[14] However, he deploys his annalistic structure with considerable flexibility, much more so than Livy and Tacitus in what survives of their histories.[15] Flashes back or forward in time occur quite often, usually brief, but occasionally more extended, with the return to the main narrative commonly signalled by phrases like 'but then'. Rather than adhering to a strict year-by-year arrangement, Dio in Books 36–40 generally seeks to maintain narrative continuity by covering events in the same sector in sequence for two and sometimes for three or more years, as the structural analysis below brings out.[16] Awkward consequences sometimes result, and some scholars have criticized Dio for chronological incompetence,[17] but recent

---

[11] e.g. 37.25.2, 35.4, 58.2; 39.15.1, 61.1; 40.17.2–3, 18.5.

[12] e.g. 37.9.1–2, 25.1–2, 58.2–4; 40.17–19, 47.   [13] So esp. 37.58; 40.47.

[14] For episodes dated to the wrong year, see 39.47–9 (Caesar's activity in summer 55 misdated to winter 56) and 39.54 (Metellus Nepos' command in Spain).

[15] See further J. Rich, 'Structuring Roman History: The Consular Year and the Roman Historical Tradition', *Histos* 5 (2011), 1–41, on earlier Roman historians' use of annalistic structure, and 'Annalistic Organization and Book Division in Dio's Books 1–35', in V. Fromentin et al. (eds.), *Cassius Dion: Nouvelles lectures* (Bordeaux, 2016), 271–86, on Dio's likely use of such structure in Books 1–35.

[16] Continuous sections of three or more years: Lucullus' eastern campaigns in 69–67 (36.1–17) and Pompey's in 66–64 (36.45–47); domestic events, 57–55 (39.6–39); the Parthian war, 54–51 (40.12–30); Caesar's final Gallic campaigns in 53–51 (40.31–44).

[17] e.g. A. W. Lintott, 'Cassius Dio and the History of the Late Roman Republic', in W. Haase and H. Temporini (eds.), *Aufstieg und Niedergang der römischen Welt*, 2.34.3 (Berlin, 1997), 2503–11.

discussions have rightly stressed the way in which these techniques serve his artistic purposes.[18]

One of Dio's most remarkable anticipations occurs at the end of his account of Pompey's eastern campaigns. After narrating the death of Mithridates and Pompey's final campaign in 63, he continues down to Pompey's return to Italy and triumph (37.20–3). Pompey in fact only reached Italy in late 62 and held his triumph in 61, but Dio leaves these events undated. He only indicates that he has run ahead in time when he turns back to the domestic events of 63 (37.24.1), and later notes Pompey's return at the appropriate point (37.49.1). Despite this awkwardness, the anticipation serves an important purpose, permitting Dio to continue his Pompeian narrative to the climax of his career and also, as we shall see, to point ahead to his subsequent inability to avoid others' envy and resulting political frustration.

In Book 40 Dio makes his most radical departure so far from annalistic ordering. The book opens with Caesar's activity in Gaul in 54 (40.1–11), but the rest of the book comprises three sections dealing successively with events down to 50 BCE in Parthia (40.12–30), Gaul (40.31–43), and Rome (40.44–66). Consular dates are not clearly marked in the final part of the Parthian narrative (40.28–30) and not at all in the Gallic section. Switching to this completely regional organization at this point enables Dio to give extended treatment to dramatic events in the two war zones—Crassus' catastrophe in 53 and Caesar's hard-won victory over the Gallic rebels in 52—and then devote himself exclusively to the critical developments at Rome leading up to the outbreak of civil war.

Dio showed similar flexibility in handling annalistic structure over the rest of his work: thus for the civil-war period he devoted single, continuous sections to the activity of Brutus and Cassius in 44–42 (47.20–34) and of Antony in the East in 38–35 (49.19–33), and he generally set his year-by-year accounts of emperors' reigns in a biographical frame, expanding the accounts of their accession and death into assessments of their rule.

Dio only occasionally mentions seasons and makes little further attempt to indicate chronology within individual years. Individual episodes are often narrated in broadly chronological sequence, but

---

[18] e.g. C. Baron, 'Wrinkles in Time: Chronological Ruptures in Cassius Dio's Narrative of the Late Republic', in J. Osgood and C. Baron (eds.), *Cassius Dio and the Late Roman Republic* (Leiden, 2019), 50–71.

sometimes he prefers a thematic organization, and this can produce chronological distortion.[19] Switches between military and domestic sections or between discrete episodes within domestic sections are often made just by loose connections like 'meanwhile', and this can lead to distortions of interpretation as well as of chronology. Thus postponing his mention of Caesar's election as Pontifex Maximus to the end of his account of the year 63 enabled Dio both to avoid interrupting his narrative of Catiline's conspiracy and to draw a contrast between the relative popularity of Cicero and Caesar (see note to 37.37.2), but his implication that Caesar owed his success in part to his opposition to the execution of the Catilinarians (in December) overlooked that the election had in fact been held several months earlier (around October). A particularly bad distortion results from the switch of focus in Dio's domestic narrative for 59 from Caesar's consulship (38.1.1–9.1) to Cicero and the events leading up to his exile (38.9.2–12.7). Wrongly accepting Cicero's involvement in the conspiracy alleged by Vettius, Dio dates it before his outburst at the trial of Antonius, although in fact the trial took place in March and Vettius made his allegations around August (see notes to 39.9.4, 10.3).

Dio shaped his books into groups as artistic units, with each group starting and/or ending with key events. Books 36–40 form two such groups, each covering ten years, with Pompey and Caesar providing central themes throughout. Books 36–37, covering the years 69 to 60, recount the culmination of Pompey's career in his eastern campaigns and the beginnings of Caesar's rise, and conclude with the alliance between Caesar, Pompey, and Crassus. Books 38–40, covering 59 to 50, trace the continuing ascent of Caesar to equality with Pompey through his consulship and subsequent conquest of Gaul, the elimination of Crassus, and the tensions at Rome which bring the Republic to the point of civil war.

Speech

Speech figured extensively in most ancient historical works, ranging from one-liners and other short utterances to extended orations, in either direct or reported speech or a mixture. A number of short utterances feature in Dio's Books 36–40, as in the rest of his work. He

---

[19] e.g. on activity against corruption in 67 (36.38–41, with note to 36.39.2).

will have drawn at least some of these from his sources, as is confirmed by similar accounts in other authors.[20] In these books he also reports two speeches a little more fully, in a mixture of direct and reported speech, namely Pompey's speech in favour of Caesar's agrarian bill (38.5.1–4) and Crassus' ill-omened speech to his army at the start of his Parthian campaign (40.19.1–3): these were opportunities to compose extended orations which Dio chose not to take up.

Dio includes fourteen extended speech episodes in Books 36–56, covering the period from 69 BCE to the death of Augustus in 14 CE. Such episodes were at least as frequent in the fragmentary early books, but played much less part in Dio's account of Augustus' successors. All are in direct speech and they include single speeches, multi-speech debates, and dialogues. The settings include the Senate and assembly at Rome, Roman army camps, and private meetings. Although some of the private conversations were completely invented by Dio, for the remainder of these episodes he had at least some indication that speeches were given, and sometimes made some use of earlier evidence about what had been said. However, for the greater part of his speeches Dio felt free to invent, and often departed radically from earlier accounts, where they existed.

One purpose which the extended speech episodes served for Dio was the display of his literary and rhetorical skills. Some conform to standard patterns which served as exercises in the rhetorical schools, and they make extensive use of moral maxims and echoes of classical Greek authors. However, they were not, as has sometimes been claimed, mere showpieces, detachable from their context. These speech episodes are embedded in their narrative context, and Dio uses them both for dramatic purposes and to explore historical issues he regarded as important.[21]

The occasion for the first extended speech episode in Books 36–40 is the assembly debate in 67 BCE over Gabinius' law appointing Pompey to a great command against the pirates, evidently chosen by

---

[20] Thus 36.36.a; 37.46.3; 38.5.4, 16.6; 39.19.1–2, 30.1–2; 40.16.3, 19.2.

[21] On Dio's speeches, see esp. C. Burden-Strevens, *Cassius Dio's Speeches and the Collapse of the Roman Republic* (Leiden, 2020), and J. Rich, 'Speeches in Cassius Dio's *Roman History* Books 1–35', in C. Burden-Strevens and M. O. Lindholmer (eds.), *Cassius Dio's Forgotten History of Early Rome: The* Roman History *Books 1–21* (Leiden, 2019), 217–84. In general on speeches in ancient historians, see J. Marincola, 'Speeches in Classical Historiography', in Marincola (ed.), *A Companion to Greek and Roman Historiography* (Malden, MA, 2007), 118–32.

Dio because of both its significance in Pompey's own career and the important contribution made by the special commands, of which this was the first, to the Republic's fall. First comes a short speech by Pompey himself declining the appointment, claiming to be worn out by his long series of commands and fearful of the jealousy which such an honour would bring (36.25–26). Gabinius responds with a second short speech, arguing that only Pompey could carry out the assignment, and urging the people to grant the command and Pompey to accept it (36.27–29).[22] The dramatic irony with which both speeches are to be read is clearly signposted, with introductory remarks bringing out each speaker's disengenuousness: Pompey, Dio tells us, was in fact greedy for the command, but characteristically dissembled his desire in the hope of avoiding jealousy (36.24.5–6), while Gabinius was acting merely from self-interest rather than the public good (36.23.4). The speeches serve to stress individual ambition and others' jealousy, themes which, as we shall see, Dio regarded as crucial both in Pompey's career and in the Late Republic more broadly.

The last speech in Dio's debate, by the respected senior senator Catulus, is much longer and its conclusion is lost (36.31–36). That Catulus had spoken against Gabinius' law was well known, particularly its closing incident (36.36a), but Dio may have been the only historian to provide a full version. He uses arguments which Catulus and other opposition speakers were known to have deployed, that Pompey alone should not be given such great and repeated power and that constitutional innovation should be avoided,[23] but develops the speech into an elaborate disquisition on the Republic's command institutions. This points ahead to the danger that special commands were to pose, but also brings out the inadequacy of the alternatives which the conservative opposition could offer: Dio makes Catulus propose that multiple commands should be created against the pirates (36.35–36), but this would have been manifestly impractical, and his claim that a single commander could not defeat them is refuted by Dio's rapid narrative of the course of the campaign (36.37).

The two remaining extended speech episodes in these books both occur in Book 38 under the year 58 BCE. The first is a dialogue which Cicero purports to have held with a Greek acquaintance, Philiscus,

[22] For the sources which Dio probably drew on for these speeches, see note to 36.25.1.

[23] For the opposition's use of these arguments, see Cicero, *On the Command of Gnaeus Pompeius* 52; Velleius 2.32.1.

who seeks to convince him that there is nothing to regret about his exile (38.18–29). The whole dialogue is Dio's own free invention, including the otherwise unknown Philiscus. It is a display piece, showing off Dio's skill at an established literary genre, consolation for exile, and some scholars have dismissed it as a mere exercise. It does, however, relate to its narrative context: Philiscus presents an ideal-ized view of Cicero's achievements, which takes him at his own exalted valuation and makes an ironic contrast with Dio's often more critical portrayal, and he points ahead to Cicero's grim end (38.29.2) and suggests that by retiring from the political struggle Cicero might have avoided his fate.

Next comes one of the most remarkable of all Dio's speeches, his version of Caesar's speech at Vesontio to quell the panic in his army as he advanced against the German ruler Ariovistus (38.36–46). Caesar's own indirect-speech version (*Gallic War* 1.40) deals mainly with the troops' fears about the enemy soldiers, the route and sup-plies, but these occupy only the last part of Dio's long direct-speech oration (38.45–46). The rest responds to other concerns which Dio had already alleged, namely that they were embarking on a war which was none of their business and had not been voted and doing so just to further Caesar's personal ambition (38.35.2). Dio's Caesar starts by insisting that all should now be thinking just of 'what is proper and advantageous for all Romans collectively' and goes on to argue that the safety of Rome and its empire requires them to fight Ariovistus, on the grounds that the empire could only be preserved, as their fore-fathers had done, by continued expansion and resistance to enemies' attacks (38.36–40). This is followed by sections arguing that a war vote by the Senate and in the popular assembly was not required, and that Ariovistus' conduct in their negotiations constituted a breach of friendship with Rome and so the war would be just (38.41–43). Dio supplies an effective case that a war vote was not required (see note to 38.41.1), but his introductory narrative has undermined the other arguments just as effectively as it did for the speeches of Pompey and Gabinius, asserting clearly, as we saw above (p. xiii), that Caesar fought this and many other campaigns chiefly out of personal ambition and that his diplomatic dealings with Ariovistus had been designed to provoke him into supplying a pretext for war.

The speech includes numerous echoes of Demosthenes' speeches urging the Athenians to act against the threat from Philip II of Macedon

and of speeches in Thucydides' history, and these Thucydidean
echoes reinforce Dio's demonstration of Caesar's hypocrisy. The
speech draws heavily on the language of Pericles, whom Thucydides
presents as a disinterested servant of the state, seeking merely to
ensure the safety of Athens and its empire and the retention of what the
Athenians already held. However, the overall thrust of Caesar's argument for continued expansion derives rather from the by no means
disinterested Alcibiades, who perverts Pericles' case to argue instead
for a great new conquest in Sicily, with disastrous consequences (see
note to 38.40.3).

Thus the speech Dio writes for Caesar here, like those for Pompey
and Gabinius earlier, helps to develop his portrait of the central part
played by individuals' ambition and its involvement in Rome's external wars in the downfall of the Republic. Another issue is at play here
as well. Since Caesar's motivation is shown so ironically here, Dio
certainly cannot be taken (as some scholars have claimed) as arguing
himself for the imperial doctrine which he has put into Caesar's
mouth. Nonetheless, enough survives of Dio's account of Rome's
early expansion to show that he was to a considerable extent in agreement with the analysis of the forefathers' policies which he attributes
to Caesar. A notable instance is his account of the origins of the first
war between Rome and Carthage, where he tells us, with another
Thucydidean echo, that the true reason was each side's 'desire of con-
tinually acquiring more' and their fear of their opponent.[24]

Dramatic irony is exploited again in several of Dio's later speeches
to expose the contrast between the claims made by or on behalf of
individuals and their true, self-interested motivation. Notable instances
are Caesar's address to his mutinous army in 49 (41.27–35) and the
disingenuous resignation speech which Dio composed for Octavian
in 27 (53.3–10), which Dio represents as a successful device to secure
consent to his monarchy (53.2.6, 11.1–5), and which echoes the themes
of Pompey's speech pretending to decline the pirate command.

---

[24] Frg. 43.1–3, echoing Thucydides 1.23.5–6 on the 'truest reason' for the
Peloponnesian War. See further J. Rich, 'Causation and Morality: Cassius Dio on the
Origins of Rome's External Wars under the Republic', in Lange and Scott (eds.), *Cassius
Dio: The Impact of Violence, War and Civil War*, 65–91. On Dio's speech for Caesar
at Vesontio, see also esp. A. Kemezis, 'Caesar's Vesontio Speech and the Rhetoric of
Mendacity in the Late Republic (Dio 38: 36–46)', in C. H. Lange and J. M. Madsen
(eds.), *Cassius Dio: Greek Intellectual and Roman Politician* (Leiden, 2016), 238–57.

Cassius Dio and the Fall of the Roman Republic

At the start of Book 52, Dio asserts that it was at that point, in 29 BCE, following Octavian's victories over Antony and Cleopatra, that the Romans reverted to monarchical government, after 725 years 'under the kingship [*basileia*], the *demokratia* and the *dynasteiai*' (52.1.1). By *demokratia*, rule by the people (*demos*), Dio here and elsewhere means merely republican government as opposed to monarchy, a usage which had become standard for Greek writers of the imperial period.

He makes frequent usage of the word *dynasteia* to denote personal power, often (though not always) autocratic power. By 'the *dynasteiai*' here he probably meant primarily the civil-war period 49–30, dominated by the autocracies first of the dictator Caesar and later of the triumvirs Antony, Octavian, and Lepidus.[25] Dio repeatedly asserts that, apart from Brutus and Cassius, who were fighting for freedom and *demokratia*, all the leaders in those civil wars were impelled by the desire for *dynasteia*.[26] By implication, then, the years 69–50, covered by Books 36–40, were for Dio the last years of *demokratia*, although already deeply flawed.

Dio shared the preference for monarchy over republican government which by his day had long been conventional, but in what survives of his history it is not until Caesar's death that he makes this view explicit. Condemning Caesar's murder, he tells us that '*demokratia* has a fair name . . . but monarchy, although sounding unattractive, is the best form of government', that *demokratia* has only ever flourished in states in states small enough not to generate 'excesses from prosperity or jealousies from ambition', and that for Rome, ruling the largest and finest part of the world, moderation and concord would be unattainable under *demokratia* (44.2.1–4). The claim that Rome had grown too powerful for *demokratia* to be viable is repeated several times later in his work.[27]

In the course of Books 36–40 Dio highlights various ways in which the republican system was malfunctioning. Breaches of constitutional

---

[25] Dio may also have had in mind the brief autocracies of Marius, Cinna, and Sulla in the 80s BCE. For different interpretations, see Kemezis, *Greek Narratives*, 104–12; M. Lindholmer, 'Cassius Dio and the "Age of Δυναστεία"', *Greek, Roman and Byzantine Studies* 58 (2018), 561–90.

[26] See 41.17.3; 53.2, 57.4; 42.8.2; 43.25.3; 46.34.4; 47.39.1–2.

[27] See 47.39.4–5; 53.19.1; 54.6.1; cf. 52.15.5–16.4.

convention (real or alleged) are carefully noted.[28] The prevalence of electoral and other corruption is illustrated by, for example, Dio's account of domestic events in 67 and of the activity of Ptolemy Auletes (36.38–41; 39.12–16, 55–63). The by then endemic political violence is vividly portrayed in many of Dio's accounts of urban events in these books.

Dio, however, saw the primary cause of the fall of the *demokratia* not in such institutional developments but in moral failings: *philotimia* (ambition, rivalry), *ephithymia* (desire), *pleonexia* (greed for more), and their invariable consequence, *phthonos* (jealousy).[29] He viewed these qualities as constants of human nature, identifying them as already in operation in his imperfectly preserved account of the Early and Middle Republic, but he nonetheless regarded the great Romans of that time as motivated by concern for the public good, and believed that, at its best, as at the start of the Second Punic War, Rome had enjoyed moderation and concord (frg. 52).[30] In the Late Republic, however, Dio held that, despite their protestations, almost all politicians sought just their own advantage.[31] He names only Cato, Catulus, and later Brutus and Cassius as exceptions, concerned not for their own interest, but for that of the community (37.22.3, 46.3, 57.3; 47.38.3).

Like other Greek writers of the imperial period, Dio is usually crude in describing Roman political groupings, representing conflict as between the plebs or common people (*plethos*, *homilos*) and the Senate or 'leading men' (*dynatoi*, see note to 36.24.3). He also does little to bring individuals to life as personalities. Secondary figures usually get no more than an introductory phrase in characterization', and even for key individuals little detail is given: the excursuses on Caesar's use of code (40.9.3) and personal vanity (43.43) are exceptional departures. Dio does, however, devote much space to individuals'

[28] See 36.39.2; 37.6.2, 21.1, 22.4, 27.2, 40.2, 51.2; 39.11.2, 17.2, 56.4, 64–65; 40.54.2.

[29] On the part played by these concepts in Dio's work, see Burden-Strevens, *Cassius Dio's Speeches*, 192–247.

[30] See C. Burden-Strevens and M. Lindholmer (eds.), *Cassius Dio's Forgotten History of Early Rome* (Leiden, 2019), esp. M. Coudry, 'The "Great Men" of the Middle Republic in Cassius Dio's *Roman History*', 126–64, and M. Lindholmer, 'Breaking the Idealistic Paradigm: Competition in Dio's Earlier Republic', 190–214.

[31] See 37.57.2–3; 41.17.3. Sallust had expressed a similar sentiment (*Catiline* 38.3: 'whoever stirred up the state with honourable claims . . ., under pretence of the public good, strove for their own power').

motivation, providing frequent explanations of their actions, often evidently his own conjectures. For key figures these explanations can be very elaborate, providing speculative accounts of their thought processes in which they weigh up their own or others' plans in terms of the general considerations about human nature which Dio himself loves to deploy.

Dio often envisages secondary characters as acting just as the agents of principal figures. A notable instance is Clodius, whom Dio regards as acting for Caesar and Pompey in his persecution of Cicero (38.12.1, 14.3, 15.1). In fact, in driving Cicero into exile Clodius was pursuing a personal vendetta, which originated in Cicero's exploding of Clodius' alibi at his trial for the profanation of the Bona Dea rite, a crucial detail overlooked by Dio (see note to 37.46.2).

Three individuals get Dio's closest attention in these books: Cicero, Pompey, and Caesar. As we saw above, each is accorded a speech episode, and each provides the narrative focus for substantial passages. Crassus has less prominence, except for his disastrous Parthian campaign.

The extensive coverage given to Cicero in part reflects his literary pre-eminence, but Dio's view of him is predominantly hostile and draws heavily on the established anti-Ciceronian tradition. As an assessment of Cicero, Dio's account is unsatisfactory and sometimes perverse, but it does present a coherent interpretation of him as a flawed personality whose self-centredness was characteristic of his age.[32]

Cicero's first appearance in the extant books comes in 66, the year of his praetorship, when Dio tells us of his support for Manilius' law conferring the Mithridatic command on Pompey and his involvement in Manilius' subsequent trial (36.43.2–44.2). Coupling Cicero with Caesar, Dio claims that they both supported Manilius' law not in the public interest or Pompey's, but for their own advancement, that Cicero was seeking to win the favour of both the plebs and the leading men and so switched between the two, and that as a result he was criticized as a 'defector' (a traditional charge in the anti-Ciceronian tradition).

Dio's account of Cicero's consulship in 63 does bring out his effectiveness in suppressing the conspiracy of Catiline and his associates

---

[32] For a recent discussion, see R. Porod, 'Dio and the Failed Politician Cicero', in A. Kemezis et al. (eds.), *The Intellectual Climate of Cassius Dio* (Leiden, 2022), 373–99.

and stresses how fortunate it was for the Romans that he had remained at Rome (37.34.3). However, Dio plays down Cicero's achievement by claiming that Catiline 'is better known than his accomplishments deserved, owing to Cicero's fame and the speeches he delivered against him' (37.42.1). He also includes some unfavourable hints which get expanded later: the political influence Cicero had won by his speeches was based on fear as well as goodwill (37.33.1, 35.4), and he enjoyed both others' praise and praising himself (37.38.2). Dio closes his account of the year by claiming that the execution of the conspirators had made Cicero hated by the common people, by contrast with Caesar's enhanced popularity (37.38).

From 59 to 57, a substantial part of Dio's domestic narrative is focused on Cicero's exile and restoration (38.9.2–30.4; 39.6–11). Cicero's exile, as we have seen, is attributed to his having provoked Caesar, who responded by deploying Clodius against him, and Pompey and Caesar are implausibly said to have collaborated in tricking him into resisting (see note to 38.15.1). Cicero's fall is also attributed in part to the vulnerability for which he himself was to blame: his speeches had caused much resentment, and he had made bitter enemies by regarding himself as superior to everyone, by his boasting, and by speaking to all with 'intemperate and immoderate frankness' (38.12.5–7). Here Dio sums up the case against Cicero, drawing on the anti-Ciceronian tradition in terms similar to those used at some points by Plutarch, in his overall much more favourable biography.[33]

Cicero plays much less part in Dio's account of the late fifties, but occasional references continue to show him in a poor light, over the trials of Gabinius (39.59–63), when Dio claims that he was again stigmatized as a 'defector', and over those of Milo and Plancus, when Dio exaggerates his courtroom failure (notes to 39.54–55). Cicero comes centre stage again in the period after Caesar's death, when Dio accords him two Senate speeches. In the immediate aftermath of Caesar's murder, Cicero successfully proposes an amnesty, making a powerful case for a return to ancestral concord (44.23–33): the occasion is historical, but the speech Dio's free composition. In the event, Cicero does not conform to its noble sentiments. At the start of 43, he urges the Senate to war against Antony, attacking him bitterly in a huge speech for which Dio drew on several of Cicero's extant *Philippics*

---

[33] Plutarch, *Cicero* 5–6, 24, 27.

(45.18–47), but he is answered in a similarly long and bitter attack by Quintus Fufius Calenus (46.1–28). At its close, Dio comments that 'while he always spoke with intemperate and immoderate frankness to everyone alike, he could not bear to receive the same from others' (46.29.1). In the sequel, Cicero suffers the fate which Dio had made his invented Philiscus prophesy (38.29.2; 47.8.3–4).

Pompey's rise will have occupied much of the immediately preceding lost books, and, as we have seen, his culminating successes in the East take up much of Books 36–37. Dio stresses both Pompey's desire for the commands against the pirates and Mithridates and his pretended reluctance in the hope of avoiding jealousy (36.24.5–6, 26.1–2, 45.1–2). This narrative concludes with Pompey's return and triumph, but Dio's main emphasis there is on his dismissal of his army on arrival in Italy and his avoidance of further honours (37.20.4–21.1, 23.1–4). Other sources report fears that Pompey might seize power, and it was probably to disarm such claims that he disbanded his army early, but only Dio makes the unlikely claim that he could have taken autocratic power easily but chose not to do so to avoid hatred. He goes on to attribute the lack of further honours (in fact probably not mooted at this point) to elaborate calculations on Pompey's part about avoiding jealousy.[34] When, in 60, Pompey's wishes to get land for his veterans and his eastern settlement ratified were frustrated by senatorial opposition, Dio tells us that Pompey realized that 'he did not have real power, but only the title and jealousy that his former power had earned him', and claims that he now regretted dismissing his army early (37.50.6).

Dio's mention of Caesar's support for Manilius' law giving Pompey the Mithridatic command seems to have been his first appearance in Dio's work, but thereafter his progress is regularly treated from his aedileship in 65 on. Caesar is presented throughout as the master manipulator: he seeks to win the populace over from Pompey to himself; he promotes measures in Pompey's honour not for Pompey's sake but because they were popular, and he aims to weaken Pompey and expose him to jealousy; he is ready to fawn on anyone in his pursuit of power (36.43.3–4; 37.22.1, 37.2–3, 44.2). When Dio reaches Caesar's command in Further Spain after his praetorship, he dilates on Caesar's wider ambitions: his desire was for glory, he was emulating

---

[34] See further notes to 37.20.3, 23.4.

Pompey and others who had held great power, and he was hoping to follow military success in Spain with immediate election to the consulship and then 'do extraordinary things'. Only at this point does Dio backtrack to the incidents during his earlier term in Further Spain, as quaestor, which were traditionally believed to have impelled Caesar to seek greatness (see note to 37.52.2).

On his return from Spain, Caesar proceeded directly to win the consulship, dispensing with a triumph on the grounds that the consulship would pave the way to far greater successes (37.54.2). Dio rightly regards it as a mark of his cleverness that he won the support of both Pompey and Crassus for his election and then reconciled them to collaborate as his allies (37.54.4). He then provides one of his most elaborate speculations on motive, setting out the considerations which he believes led each of the three to conclude that joining the alliance would be to their advantage (37.55–56).

As consul, Dio tells us, Caesar completed the process of winning over the plebs by his land laws and by remitting tax contracts won over the *equites* as well (38.1.1, 7.4), while from 58 his command in Gaul enabled him to realize all his hopes of glory (see p. xiii). Under the year 56, Dio explores the reactions of his allies: Pompey, he tells us, bitterly resented Caesar's increased strength and the enthusiastic reception his achievements had received, and, with further subtle reconstruction of their calculations (39.25–26), Dio explains that he and Crassus then decided to work against Caesar, getting a joint consulship for 55, followed by extended commands in respectively Spain and Syria. Dio has some difficulty in explaining their granting a parallel extension of Caesar's command (39.33.3–4), and in any case other sources show that Dio's interpretation is here altogether mistaken. Suetonius, Plutarch, and Appian all tell us that Caesar, Pompey, and Crassus met at Luca in 56 and agreed to collaborate again to obtain the consulships and commands which followed in 55. This may anticipate decisions only reached later, but Cicero's evidence shows that the three renewed their alliance at meetings in spring 56 and thereafter succeeded in imposing their wishes.[35]

Dio must have encountered the version preserved for us by Suetonius and others in his reading. How he came to opt for such a radically different account of the events of 56–55 we can only speculate. A source

[35] See further note to 39.25.1.

may perhaps have given some support to his version. Dio may simply have overlooked the opposing account when writing up, but it is perhaps more likely that he deliberately rejected it in the belief that his alternative version of the protagonists' motivations was more plausible.

By 52, the situation had changed dramatically: Crassus had died at the Parthians' hands, and the crisis over Clodius' murder led to Pompey's appointment as sole consul and the extension of his Spanish command. According to Dio, this amounted to Pompey's being won over to the Senate's side (40.50.5), and from 50 Pompey 'openly worked against Caesar in all he said and did' (40.63.1). This gives the impression that Pompey was to blame for the outbreak of the civil war, but in his war narrative Dio is explicit that Pompey and Caesar alike were now fighting for supreme power.[36] Lucan had claimed that 'Caesar could not endure a superior or Pompey an equal',[37] but Dio's view of their motivations leads him to reverse the assessment, saying that 'Pompey wished to be second to no man and Caesar to be first of all', and adding that 'Pompey was anxious to be honoured by men of their own free will, to be their leader by their consent, and to be loved by them, whereas Caesar did not mind if he ruled over the unwilling, issued orders to men who hated him, and conferred his honours himself' (41.54.1).

By contrast with Pompey, whom Dio had portrayed as doing his best to avoid the jealousy that great honours could provoke, Caesar allows himself to be decreed extravagant honours, and Dio regards this as his fatal weakness, leading to his murder (44.3 ff.). There is, however, another strand to his treatment of the dictator Caesar. He approves of his clemency, and, on his victorious return to Rome in 46, has Caesar address the Senate in a speech in which he promises to be not a tyrant and master, but their leader (43.15–18). At first reading we naturally assume that, as with Caesar's earlier speeches, Dio intends us to take this too as hypocritical, but this turns out not to be the case: after the speech, Dio comments that this and a similar speech to the people relieved some of their fears, and they were fully reassured when 'he confirmed his promises by his actions' (43.18.6). He subsequently condemns Brutus and Cassius for killing the city's 'leader and protector' (44.2.5).

---

[36] See 41.17.3, 53.2, 57.4.
[37] Lucan, *Pharsalia* 1.125–6, followed by Florus 2.13.14.

The same tension can be observed in Dio's treatment of Caesar's heir, the future Augustus. Dio the realist portrays his rise as the consistent and ruthless pursuit of power and the resignation speech to the Senate in 27 which led to his constitutional settlement as a disingenuous device 'to get men to confirm his monarchy apparently of their own free will' (53.2.6–12.1). However, Dio the monarchist presents Augustus as an ideal ruler and at his death praises him for having mixed monarchy and 'democracy' and for enabling the Romans to live at once under freedom with moderation and monarchy without fear (56.43.4).[38]

---

[38] See further J. Rich, 'Dio on Augustus', in A. Cameron (ed.), *History as Text* (London, 1989), 86–110.

TRANSLATOR'S NOTE

THIS book is very much the product of collaboration between translator and editor. As translator, I would like to thank John Rich warmly for correcting errors and improving the translation in many respects.

The Greek text taken as the basis for this translation is that of the recent edition by Guy Lachenaud and Marianne Coudry. We have deviated from this text only in a few cases, which are marked in the translation by an obelus or dagger (†), as follows:

36.36.3:	Deleting καὶ στρατηγοὺς (Rich).
37.53.2:	Retaining γῇ with L (the principal manuscript).
38.11.6:	Reading πάντως <οὐκέτι> (Leunclavius).
38.12.7:	Reading λόγοις ὁμοίως (Reiske).
38.17.1:	Reading δι' αὐτόν with L.
39.9.2:	Reading οἵῳ (with L), γε (with R and Stephanus), and θεάτρῳ (with L).
39.45.3:	There seems no reason to posit a lacuna.
40.17.2:	Boissevain's supplement omitted.
40.25.2:	Reading διαπεφευγότων (Bekker).
40.39.3:	Reading ὁρμαῖς ἄπληστοι ὄντες καὶ (Reiske).
40.59.1:	Reading καὶ τοῖς πολλοῖς ὅτι (Madvig).

The translation omits the contents summary and lists of consuls for the years covered that are included in our manuscripts before each book (lost for Book 36). On this material, see C. T. Mallan, 'The Book Indices in the Manuscripts of Cassius Dio', *Classical Quarterly* 66 (2017), 705–23.

RAHW

SELECT BIBLIOGRAPHY

Cassius Dio

EDITIONS

Dio's Roman History, ed. and trans. E. Cary, Loeb Classical Library, 9 vols. (1914–27) (Greek text and English translation).

Dion Cassius, Histoire romaine, Livres 36 & 37 , ed., trans. and comm. by G. Lachenaud and M. Coudry, Les Belles Lettres (Paris, 2014) (Greek text and French translation and commentary).

Dion Cassius, Histoire romaine, Livres 38, 39 & 40, ed., trans. and comm. by G. Lachenaud and M. Coudry, Les Belles Lettres (Paris, 2011) (Greek text and French translation and commentary).

OVERVIEWS

Millar, F., *A Study of Cassius Dio* (Oxford, 1964).

Madsen, J. M., *Cassius Dio* (London, 2020).

COLLECTIONS OF ESSAYS (each including studies bearing on Books 36–40)

Fromentin, V., Bertrand, E., Coltelloni-Trannoy, M., Molin, M., and Urso, G. (eds.), *Cassius Dion: Nouvelles lectures* (Bordeaux, 2016); 48 studies, mostly in French.

Kemezis, A., Bailey, C., and Poletti, B. (eds.), *The Intellectual Climate of Cassius Dio* (Leiden, 2022).

Lange, C. H., and Madsen, J. M. (eds.), *Cassius Dio: Greek Intellectual and Roman Politician* (Leiden, 2016).

Lange, C. H., and Scott, A. G. (eds.), *Cassius Dio: The Impact of Violence, War, and Civil War* (Leiden, 2020).

Madsen, J. M., and Lange, C. H. (eds.), *Cassius Dio the Historian* (Leiden, 2021).

Madsen, J. M., and Scott, A. G. (eds.), *Brill's Companion to Cassius Dio* (Leiden, 2023).

Osgood, J., and Baron, C. (eds.), *Cassius Dio and the Late Roman Republic* (Leiden, 2019).

OTHER STUDIES ON BOOKS 36–40

Burden-Strevens, C., *Cassius Dio's Speeches and the Collapse of the Roman Republic* (Leiden, 2020).

Kemezis, A. M., *Greek Narratives of the Roman Empire under the Severans: Cassius Dio, Philostratus and Herodian* (Cambridge, 2014).

Lindholmer, M. O., 'Reading Diachronically: A New Reading of Book 36 of Cassius Dio's *Roman History*', *Histos* 12 (2018), 139–68.

Lindholmer, M. O., 'The Fall of Cassius Dio's Roman Republic', *Klio* 101 (2019), 473–504.

Lintott, A. W., 'Cassius Dio and the History of the Late Roman Republic', in W. Haase and H. Temporini (eds.), *Aufstieg und Niedergang der römischen Welt* 2.34.3 (Berlin, 1997), 2497–2523.

Pelling, C., 'Breaking the Bounds: Writing about Julius Caesar', in B. McGing and J. Mossman (eds.), *The Limits of Ancient Biography* (Swansea, 2006), 255–80.

Pelling, C., 'Seeing through Caesar's Eyes: Focalization and Interpretation', in J. Grethlein and A. Rangakos (eds.), *Narratology and Interpretation* (Berlin, 2009), 507–26.

Pitcher, L., 'Cassius Dio', in K. De Temmerman and E. van Emde Boas (eds.), *Characterization in Ancient Greek Literature* (Leiden, 2018), 221–35.

Rees, W., 'Cassius Dio, Human Nature and the Late Roman Republic', DPhil. thesis (Oxford, 2011), online at https://ora.ox.ac.uk/objects/uuid:75230c97-3ac1-460d-861b-5cb3270e481e.

Other Sources for the Late Roman Republic

Appian, *Roman History*, ed. and trans. B. McGing, Loeb Classical Library, 6 vols. (Cambridge, MA, 2019–20).

Appian, *The Civil Wars*, trans. J. Carter, Penguin Classics (Harmondsworth, 1996).

Asconius, *Commentaries on Speeches by Cicero*, trans. and comm. R. G. Lewis, Clarendon Ancient History Series (Oxford, 2006). A replacement for this edition is in preparation by J. T. Ramsey.

Caesar, *The Landmark Julius Caesar*, trans. and comm. K. A. Raaflaub (New York, 2017).

Cicero, *Catilinarians*, ed. and comm. A. Dyck, Cambridge Greek and Latin Classics (Cambridge, 2008).

Cicero, *Defence Speeches*, trans. D. H. Berry, Oxford World's Classics (Oxford, 2000).

Cicero, *Letters to Atticus*, ed. and trans. D. R. Shackleton Bailey, 4 vols., Loeb Classical Library (Cambridge, MA, 1999).

Cicero, *Letters to Friends*, ed. and trans. D. R. Shackleton Bailey, 3 vols., Loeb Classical Library (Cambridge, MA, 2001).

Cicero, *Letters to Quintus and Brutus . . .*, ed. and trans. D. R. Shackleton Bailey, Loeb Classical Library (Cambridge, MA, 2002).

Cicero, *Political Speeches*, trans. D. H. Berry, Oxford World's Classics (Oxford, 2006).

Cicero, *Pro Milone*, ed. and comm. T. J. Keeline, Cambridge Greek and Latin Classics (Cambridge, 2021).

Cicero, *Speech on Behalf of Publius Sestius*, trans. and comm. R. A. Kaster, Clarendon Ancient History Series (Oxford, 2006).

Plutarch, *Roman Lives*, trans. R. Waterfield, Oxford World's Classics (Oxford, 2006).

Plutarch, *Caesar*, trans. and comm. C. Pelling, Clarendon Ancient History Series (Oxford, 2011).

Sallust, *Catiline's Conspiracy, The Jugurthine War, Histories*, trans. W. W. Batstone, Oxford World's Classics (Oxford, 2010).

Sallust, *Fragments of the Histories*, ed. and trans. J. T. Ramsey, Loeb Classical Library (Cambridge, MA, 2015).

Suetonius, *Lives of the Caesars*, trans. C. Edwards, Oxford World's Classics (Oxford, 1999).

Velleius Paterculus, *The Roman History*, trans. J. C. Yardley and A. A. Barrett (Indianapolis, 2011).

Santangelo, F. (ed.), *Late Republican Rome, 88-31 BC*, LACTOR Sourcebooks in Ancient History (2nd edn., Cambridge, 2023).

The Late Roman Republic

OVERVIEWS

Steel, C., *The End of the Roman Republic, 146 to 44 BC* (Edinburgh, 2013).

Wiseman, T. P., 'The Senate and the *populares*, 69–60 B.C.', in J. A. Crook, A. Lintott, and E. Rawson (eds.), *The Cambridge Ancient History*, vol. 9: *The Last Age of the Roman Republic, 146–43 B.C.* (2nd edn., Cambridge, 1994), 327–67.

Wiseman, T. P., 'Caesar, Pompey and Rome, 59–50 B.C.', in J. A. Crook, A. Lintott, and E. Rawson (eds.), *The Cambridge Ancient History*, vol. 9: *The Last Age of the Roman Republic, 146–43 B.C* (2nd edn., Cambridge, 1994), 368–423.

STUDIES OF INDIVIDUAL POLITICIANS

Caesar:

Billows, R., *Julius Caesar: The Colossus of Rome* (London, 2009).

Gelzer, M., *Caesar: Politician and Statesman*, trans. P. Needham (Oxford, 1968).

Goldsworthy, A., *Caesar: The Life of a Colossus* (London, 2006).

Griffin, M. (ed.), *A Companion to Julius Caesar* (Chichester, 2009).

Meier, C., *Caesar*, trans. D. McLintock (London, 1995).

Morstein-Marx, R., *Julius Caesar and the Roman People* (Cambridge, 2021).

Osgood, J., *Uncommon Wrath: How Caesar and Cato's Deadly Rivalry Destroyed the Roman Republic* (Oxford, 2022).

Stevenson, T., *Julius Caesar and the Transformation of the Roman Republic* (London, 2015).

Catiline:

Berry, D. H., *Cicero's Catilinarians* (New York, 2020).

Levick, B., *Catiline* (London, 2015).

Urso, G., *Catilina: Le Faux populiste* (Bordeaux, 2019).

Cato:

Drogula, F. K., *Cato the Younger* (New York, 2019).

Osgood, J., *Uncommon Wrath: How Caesar and Cato's Deadly Rivalry Destroyed the Roman Republic* (Oxford, 2022).

Cicero:

Habicht, C., *Cicero the Politician* (Baltimore, 1990).

Lintott, A. W., *Cicero as Evidence* (Oxford, 2008).

Mitchell, T. N., *Cicero: The Ascending Years* (New Haven, 1979).

Mitchell, T. N., *Cicero: The Senior Statesman* (New Haven, 1991).

Tempest, K., *Cicero: Politics and Persuasion in Ancient Rome* (London, 2011).

Clodius:

Tatum, W. J., *The Patrician Tribune: Publius Clodius Pulcher* (Chapel Hill, NC, 1999).

Crassus:

Marshall, B. A., *Crassus: A Political Biography* (Amsterdam, 1976).

Stothard, P., *Crassus: The First Tycoon* (New Haven, 2022).

Ward, A. M., *Marcus Crassus and the Late Roman Republic* (Columbia, MO, 1977).

Lucullus:

Keaveney, A., *Lucullus* (London, 1992).

Pompey:

Seager, R., *Pompey the Great* (2nd edn., Oxford, 2002).

ROMAN POLITICAL LIFE

Arena, V., and Prag, J. (eds.), *A Companion to the Political Culture of the Roman Republic* (Chichester, 2022).

Broughton, T. R. S., *The Magistrates of the Roman Republic*, vols. 1–2 (Cleveland, OH, 1951–2); vol. 3 (Atlanta, GA, 1986).

Brunt, P. A., *The Fall of the Roman Republic and Related Essays* (Oxford, 1988).

Gruen, E. S., *The Last Generation of the Roman Republic* (Berkeley and Los Angeles, 1974).

Hölkeskamp, K.-J., *Reconstructing the Roman Republic* (Princeton, 2010).

Lintott, A. W., *The Constitution of the Roman Republic* (Oxford, 1999).

Millar, F., *The Crowd in the Roman Republic* (Ann Arbor, 1998).

Morstein-Marx, R., *Mass Oratory and Political Power in the Late Roman Republic* (Cambridge, 2004).

Mouritsen, H., *Politics in the Roman Republic* (Cambridge, 2017).

Rosenstein, N., and Morstein-Marx, R. (eds.), *A Companion to the Roman Republic* (Malden, MA, 2006).

ROMAN GOVERNMENT AND ADMINISTRATION

Brunt, P. A., *Italian Manpower 225 BC–AD 14* (Oxford, 1971).

Kallet-Marx, R. M., *Hegemony to Empire: The Development of the Roman Imperium in the East from 148 to 62 BC* (Berkeley and Los Angeles, 1995).

Lintott, A. W., *Imperium Romanum: Politics and Administration* (London, 1993).

Morrell, K., *Pompey, Cato, and the Governance of the Roman Empire* (Oxford, 2017).

EXTERNAL WARS AND RELATIONS

de Souza, P., *Piracy in the Graeco-Roman World* (Cambridge, 1999).

Fitzpatrick, A. P., and Haselgrove, C. (eds.), *Julius Caesar's Battle for Gaul: New Archaeological Perspectives* (Oxford, 2019).

Raaflaub, K. A., and Ramsey, J. T., 'Reconstructing the Chronology of Caesar's Gallic Wars', *Histos* 11 (2017), 1–74, with chronological tables at 162–217.

Roller, D. W., *Empire of the Black Sea: The Rise and Fall of the Mithridatic World* (Oxford, 2020).

Sampson, G. C., *The Defeat of Rome: Crassus, Carrhae and the Invasion of the East* (Barnsley, 2015).

Schlude, J. M., *Rome, Parthia and the Politics of Peace* (London, 2022).

Sherwin-White, A. N., *Roman Foreign Policy in the East 168 BC to AD 1* (London, 1984).

Further Reading in Oxford World's Classics

Caesar, Julius, *The Civil War*, trans. with an introduction and notes by J. M. Carter.

Livy, *The Rise of Rome: Books One to Five*, trans. with an introduction and notes by T. J. Luce.

Livy, *Rome's Italian Wars: Books Six to Ten*, trans. J. C. Yardley, introduction and notes by Dexter Hoyos.

Livy, *The Dawn of the Roman Empire: Books Thirty-One to Forty*, trans. J. C. Yardley, introduction and notes by Waldemar Heckel.

STRUCTURE

D   Domestic events
M   Military operations
*   Lost material at the start or end of a section
Bold New consular years indicated by Dio

Book Thirty-Eight

Book Thirty-Nine

Book Forty

A CHRONOLOGY OF EVENTS

BCE

146 End of the Third Punic War; destruction of Carthage

133 Tribunate and death of Tiberius Gracchus

123–122 Tribunates of Gaius Gracchus

121 Death of Gaius Gracchus

107 First consulship of Marius

104–100 Marius consul for five successive years

91–87 Social War (rebellion of Rome's Italian allies)

88–87 First Roman civil wars

88–85 First war with Mithridates, king of Pontus

83–82 Sulla returns from the East and wins civil war

82–81 Sulla dictator; proscriptions; constitutional reforms

79 Death of Sulla

78–77 Rebellion of Lepidus

77–71 Pompey commanding in Spain against Sertorius

74 or 73 Outbreak of final war with Mithridates, with Lucullus as Roman commander

73–71 Slave rebellion of Spartacus

70 First consulship of Pompey and Crassus

67 Tribunates of Cornelius and Gabinius; Lucullus superseded as commander against Mithridates; Pompey's command against the pirates

66 Manilius' law gives Pompey the command against Mithridates; Pompey drives Mithridates out of Pontus and receives surrender of Tigranes, king of Armenia

65 Mithridates flees to the Bosporus

64–63 Pompey in Syria

63 Death of Mithridates. Consulship of Cicero; conspiracy of Catiline

62 Defeat and death of Catiline; Pompey returns to Italy (Dec.)

61 Clodius acquitted of sacrilege (May); triumph of Pompey (Sept.)

61–60 Caesar's campaigns in Further Spain

60 Pompey and Crassus ally with Caesar to support his consulship

59 Caesar, consul for the first time, carries agrarian and other laws, and obtains five-year command of Cisalpine and Transalpine Gaul and Illyricum; Clodius adopted as a plebeian

58 Tribunate of Clodius; Cicero flees into exile (Mar.). Caesar in Gaul defeats Helvetii and Ariovistus

58–56 Cato carries out annexation of Cyprus

57 Cicero returns and Pompey given grain commissionership (Sept.). Caesar conquers the Belgae

56 Caesar, Pompey, and Crassus renew their alliance (Apr.). Caesar completes conquest of Gaul

55 Second consulship of Pompey and Crassus; they obtain five-year commands in Spain and Syria and extension of Caesar's command.

Gabinius restores Ptolemy Auletes in Alexandria. Massacre of Usipetes and Tencteri; Caesar's first crossing of the Rhine and expedition to Britain

54 Caesar's second expedition to Britain

54–53 Rebellion of the Eburones and others in north-eastern Gaul

53 Defeat and death of Crassus at Carrhae. Consuls not appointed until July/Aug.

52 Clodius killed (Jan.); Pompey made sole consul to restore order. Vercingetorix leads great Gallic rebellion, crushed at Alesia

50 Tribunate of Curio; breakdown of negotiations over Caesar's return

49 Outbreak of civil war; Pompey withdraws to Greece; Caesar appointed dictator

48 Caesar defeats Pompey at Pharsalus (Aug.); Pompey murdered in Egypt (Sept.)

46 Caesar defeats Pompeians at Thapsus in Africa; Cato commits suicide

45 Caesar defeats Pompey's sons at Munda in Spain

44 Caesar assassinated (15 Mar.)

43 Antony, Octavian, and Lepidus ally and are appointed 'triumvirs to establish the republic' (Nov.); proscriptions, in which Cicero killed

42 Antony and Octavian defeat Brutus and Cassius at Philippi

32 Outbreak of war between Antony and Octavian

31 Octavian defeats Antony and Cleopatra in sea battle at Actium (2 Sept.)

30 Death of Antony and Cleopatra at Alexandria

27 Constitutional settlement, and Octavian takes the name Augustus

CE

14 Death of Augustus

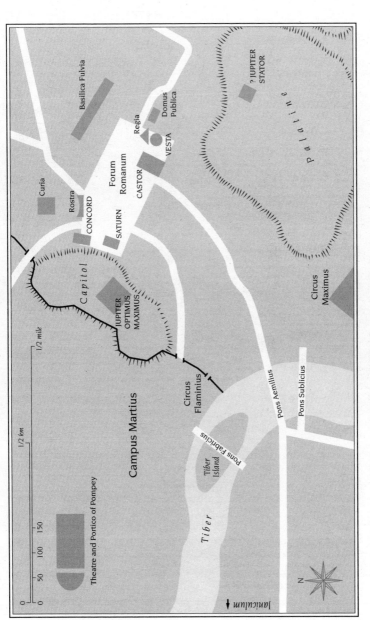

Central Rome in the Late Republic

The East at the time of the campaigns of Lucullus, Pompey, and Crassus

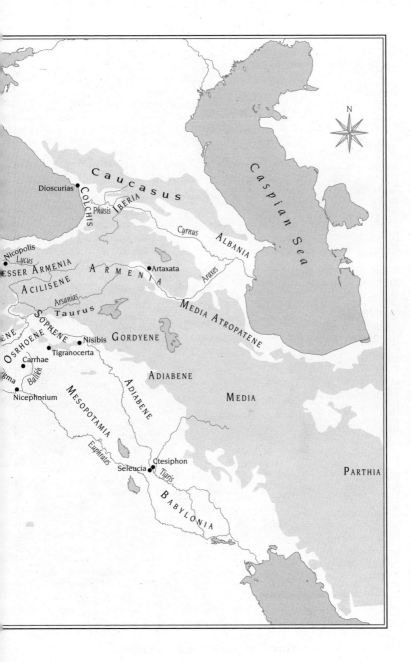

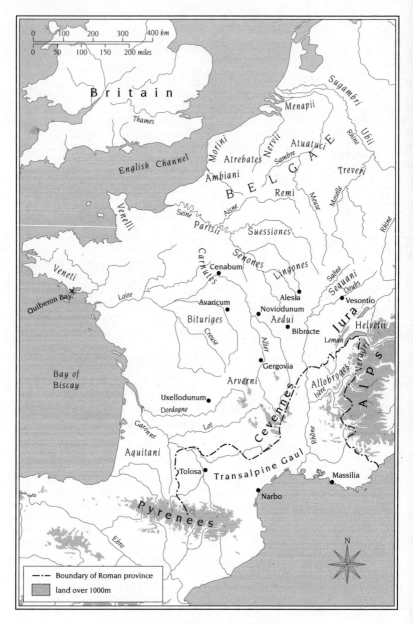

Gaul at the time of Caesar's campaigns

THE FALL OF THE
ROMAN REPUBLIC

Roman History, Books Thirty-Six to Forty

THE FALL OF THE
ROMAN REPUBLIC

Roman Lives; Book Thirty-Six 1911

BOOK THIRTY-SIX

[From Xiphilinus' epitome]* 1a. *When the consuls drew lots, Hortensius* obtained the war against the Cretans.* But because he liked living in the city, and because he had greater standing in the courts than anyone else at the time apart from Cicero, he voluntarily gave up the campaign in favour of his colleague and stayed at home himself. Metellus therefore set out for Crete . . .**

    1b. *At this time, Lucius Lucullus, after defeating the dynasts of Asia, Mithridates and Tigranes of Armenia,* and forcing them to avoid battle, was laying siege to Tigranocerta.* But the barbarians inflicted heavy casualties on him with their archers, and also with the naphtha* which they poured down on to the siege engines. [2] This substance, which is rich in bitumen, is so inflammable that it burns to ashes everything it touches and cannot easily be extinguished by any liquid. Tigranes' confidence therefore increased and he advanced* with such a large force that he even laughed in scorn at the Romans who were there. In fact, he is said to have remarked that they came in small numbers to fight, but in large numbers to negotiate. [3] But he did not remain cheerful for long, and he very quickly discovered the degree to which courage and skill are superior to any body of men, no matter how numerous. After he had fled, the soldiers found his tiara and the diadem* that went around it and gave them to Lucullus; Tigranes had torn them off and thrown them away, out of fear that they would give him away and lead to his capture.*

1. [. . .] and seeing that Mithridates was familiar with being buffeted by Fortune for both better and worse, Tigranes entrusted the supreme command to him, in the belief that his many defeats and just as many victories had made him the better general. So they were making their arrangements as if this were the outbreak of a new war, and they sent embassies to their neighbours, including Arsaces of Parthia,* even though he had fallen out with Tigranes over some disputed territory.* [2] They offered to cede this territory to him, and they alleged that, if they were left unsupported and the Romans defeated them, the very next campaign the Romans launched would be against him.* It was not just, they said, that every conquering force by its nature has an

insatiable appetite for success and sets no limits on its greed for more, but also that, with so many places already in their power, the Romans would not be willing to leave him alone.

2. So this is what Mithridates and Tigranes were doing. Lucullus did not pursue Tigranes,* but let him reach safety without harassing him at all. This led a number of people, and not least his fellow citizens, to accuse him of being unwilling to conclude the war,* in order to have his command extended. [2] That was why they not only returned the province of Asia to the praetors then,* but also later, when Lucullus was thought to have done the same thing again, they sent the consul of that year to succeed him.* [3] But he did capture Tigranocerta, when the foreigners who lived in the city alongside the Armenians rose up against them. Most of them were Cilicians who had been deported there at some point, and they let the Romans in one night. [4] The Cilicians' property was therefore spared the general plundering of the city that took place, and Lucullus also protected many of the wives of the leading men from outrage—an action which won him the allegiance of their husbands as well. [5] He also received Antiochus, the king of Commagene (a country which forms part of Syria and abuts both the Euphrates river and the Taurus mountains), and others who had made overtures to him, including an Arab dynast called Alchaudonius.*

3. Lucullus heard from them of Tigranes' and Mithridates' embassy to Arsaces, so he in his turn sent some of the allies to Arsaces,* bearing both threats, if he helped Tigranes and Mithridates, and promises, if instead he chose the Roman cause. [2] At that time Arsaces was still angry with Tigranes and had no reason to doubt the Romans, so he sent ambassadors back to Lucullus and entered into a treaty of friendship and alliance with him. Later, however, in view of the fact that it was Sextilius* who went to him, he began to suspect that he was there to spy out his land and forces, [3] and that this was why such an eminent military man had been sent—that his presence had nothing to do with the treaty, which had already been agreed—and he cut off all his support for Lucullus. Not that he actually opposed him, but he remained neutral, out of a natural desire to increase the strength of neither side. His thinking was that his best hope of safety lay in their being evenly matched in their war. These were the achievements of Lucullus in this year, while winning over much of Armenia.*

4. In the consulship of Quintus Marcius*—for he served as con-   68 BCE
sul alone, even though he was not appointed alone, since Lucius
Metellus,* the man elected with him, died right at the start of the
year, and the man chosen to replace Metellus* died before taking
office, and consequently no one else was appointed—[2] in this year,
then, by the time Lucullus set out on campaign it was already midsummer, since the cold ruled out an invasion of the enemy's territory
in the spring. He ravaged some of the land, with the intention of
drawing the barbarians into battle when they came to defend it, and
when, despite this, they still made no move, he advanced against
them.*

5. While he was on the march, the enemy cavalry made things difficult for the Roman horsemen, but none of them engaged the Roman
infantry. In fact, whenever Lucullus' foot soldiers came to the assistance of the cavalry, the enemy turned to flight. They still came off
unscathed, however: they shot back at their pursuers, killing many of
them straight away and wounding them in very large numbers.
[2] The wounds were serious and not easily healed, since the arrows
they used had heads with two sets of barbs, and were also made in
such a way that whether the arrows remained embedded in any part
of a body or were drawn out, they would still cause rapid death, in the
latter case because the second of the two iron heads remained inside,
with no way of extracting it.

6. Seeing that many of his men were being injured, and either
dying from their wounds or at least being disabled, and since at the
same time they had run short of provisions, Lucullus withdrew from
there and marched against Nisibis.* [2] This city is situated in the
land called Mesopotamia, the name given to all the territory between
the Tigris and the Euphrates; it is now one of our possessions and has
the status of a colony of ours,* but at the time in question Tigranes,
who had taken it from the Parthians, had made it the location of his
treasury and had left most of the rest of his property there as well,
entrusting its protection to his brother.* [3] So Lucullus came up to
the city in the summer, but despite his fierce assaults he made no
progress at all. The fortifications consisted of two surrounding walls
made of brick, which were not only very thick, but were separated by
a deep moat, and there was no point at which they could either be
battered down or undermined. Even Tigranes was therefore not
bothering to come to the assistance of the besieged.

7. When winter set in, however, the barbarians grew careless, since they had the upper hand and were expecting the Romans to leave at any moment. Lucullus waited for a stormy, moonless night of driving rain and thunder, [2] which meant that the enemy could see and hear nothing, and had virtually abandoned the outer wall and the intervening moat. He approached the wall at many points, ascended it without much difficulty thanks to the embankments, and easily killed the guards who had been left to defend it, since there were only a few of them. [3] This made it possible for him to fill in a stretch of the moat (the barbarians having earlier destroyed the bridges), because the rain was too heavy for archery or fire to be effective against him; and as soon as he had crossed the moat he captured everything else, because the inner circuit wall was not very strong, since the enemy had relied on the outer defences. [4] Some of the defenders fled to the citadel, however, including Tigranes' brother, but Lucullus later got them to surrender. He gained a great deal of money, and spent the winter there.

8. So Nisibis fell to Lucullus, but he lost much of Armenia and the Pontus region.* What happened was that Tigranes attacked these places instead of sending troops to relieve Nisibis, which he believed to be impregnable, to see if he could gain them while Lucullus was occupied with Nisibis. [2] He sent Mithridates back to his homeland, while he went to his Armenia, where Lucius Fannius* was his opponent. He caught Fannius unawares and put him under siege, until Lucullus found out about it and came to help.

9. Meanwhile, Mithridates invaded the other Armenia and the rest of his former territory,* where he fell unexpectedly on the Romans he found at large in the countryside and killed a lot of them. He took more Roman lives in battle as well, and this enabled him rapidly to recover most places, [2] because the general populace was well disposed towards him thanks to their kinship and the fact that he was the hereditary king, and hated the Romans as foreigners and because of the abuses of those who had been set over them. So they sided with Mithridates, and subsequently defeated Marcus Fabius,* who was the Roman commander there, [3] when the Thracian mercenaries (who had previously served Mithridates but were then with Fabius) and the slaves who were in the Roman camp gave them valiant assistance. What happened was that when the Thracians were sent out by Fabius as scouts, they brought him back a false report, [4] and then later, when he was advancing without adequate protection and Mithridates suddenly fell on him, they joined in the attack on the Romans—and then, once the barbarian king had a herald proclaim his promise of their freedom, the slaves pitched in as well. [5] The Romans would have been wiped out to a man if Mithridates himself had not been struck by a stone while engaging the enemy—he took part in the fighting even though he was over seventy years old*—and if the barbarians had not become afraid that the injury was fatal. They therefore called a halt to the fighting, and Fabius and the rest were able to escape to safety.

10. Later, Fabius was pinned inside Cabira* and endured a siege, but he was saved by Triarius, who was passing through the region on his way from Asia to Lucullus.* When Triarius found out what had happened, he gathered as large a force as he could in the circum-stances,* [2] and Mithridates, who supposed that Triarius was advancing with the bulk of the Roman army, was frightened into retreating before he even caught sight of him. Triarius' confidence increased because of this and he pursued Mithridates as far as Comana,* where he defeated him in battle. [3] Mithridates was encamped on the opposite side of the river from the point at which the Romans were approaching, and he wanted to engage them while they were still tired from the march. He therefore advanced to meet them himself, while also ordering others of his officers to cross the river by another bridge and launch an attack at the critical moment of the battle. Although he held his own for a very long time, the bridge collapsed under the weight of the mass of men who were hurrying across, and this deprived him of reinforcements and unnerved him as well.

11. Subsequently, since it was now winter, both sides withdrew to their own strongpoints and remained inactive. Comana, which is now in Cappadocia, was said to have always (up until then) had the famous Taurian statue of Artemis and Agamemnon's family. To the question how this statue group reached them or came to be lodged there, I have not been able to find a clear answer, because there are many different accounts. [2] But what I can state with certainty is that there are two cities in Cappadocia with this name which are situated not very far from each other and lay claim to the same traditions.* The stories they tell and the relics they display are all identical, including what is supposed to be Iphigenia's sword, which they both possess.

12. So much for that topic: the following year, when Manius Acilius and Gaius Piso were consuls,* Mithridates set up camp near Gaziura,* close to Triarius, as a way of challenging him to battle and nettling him. [2] One of his many provocations was that he did his own training exercises and had his men drill within sight of the Romans. He hoped to bring Triarius to battle and defeat him before Lucullus arrived, and thereby to recover the rest of his kingdom. Triarius stayed where he was, however, so Mithridates sent some men to Dadasa,* a fortress where the Romans had deposited their baggage. His intention was to draw Triarius into conflict when he went to its defence. [3] And that is what happened. For a while, Triarius did nothing; he was alarmed by the size of Mithridates' army and was waiting for Lucullus, whose help he had requested. But then he found out that Dadasa was under siege, and his men were becoming mutinous out of concern for the safety of the place; they were starting to threaten to take the initiative themselves and go to the relief of Dadasa if no one led them out into the field, and so Triarius reluctantly set out.* [4] But as he was advancing, the barbarians fell on him. With the help of their superior numbers, they surrounded the nearest Romans and overwhelmed them, and then they rode around them and set about killing those who had fled down on to the plain, not knowing that the river had been diverted into it.

13. The Romans would have been completely annihilated, if one of them, pretending to be one of Mithridates' auxiliaries (as I have already said,* many of his men were equipped in the Roman fashion), had not approached him as though he wanted to tell him something, and wounded him. The man was immediately seized and killed, but the barbarians were unnerved by what had happened and many of the Romans managed to escape. [2] While Mithridates was undergoing treatment for his wound, he conducted a review of his troops, because (although he did not let on that this was the reason) he suspected that there were more enemy soldiers in the camp. After the review he ordered his men to make their way at the double to their own tents, which left the Romans exposed, and he killed them while they were isolated.

14. Just then Lucullus arrived, and some people thought that he would easily defeat Mithridates and would need little time to regain everything that had been lost. But in fact he achieved nothing, [2] because, first, Mithridates, entrenched in high ground near

Talaura,* refused to come out against him; then the other Mithridates, from Media,* the son-in-law of Tigranes, fell on the Romans without warning at a time when they were out of formation and took a lot of lives; then the news arrived that Tigranes himself was on his way, and there was a mutiny in the army. [3] The Valerians,* who had enlisted again after being discharged from service,* had been restive in Nisibis* as well, as a result of their victory and the following period of inactivity, and also because they had no shortage of provisions and were left to their own devices most of the time, since Lucullus often had to be elsewhere. [4] But the main cause of their restiveness had been a certain Publius Clodius* (called Claudius by some*), who had incited them to mutiny out of an innate desire to make mischief, even though one of his sisters was married to Lucullus. On the occasion in question, however, the particular trigger for their restiveness was the news that the consul Acilius was drawing near; he was the one who had been sent out, as I have already explained, as Lucullus' replacement.* This made them despise Lucullus, as though he were already just a private citizen.

15. Lucullus was confounded not just by the mutiny, but also by the refusal of Marcius, Acilius' predecessor in the consulship, who was on his way to Cilicia to take up his post there as governor, to send the help he asked for.* [2] Lucullus was reluctant to break camp pointlessly, but he was also afraid to stay where he was, so he set out against Tigranes, to see if he could catch him off guard while he was weary from the road and drive him back, and also to see if this would somehow help to quell the mutiny in his ranks. But he succeeded at neither of these objectives. [3] The army accompanied him as far as a point where the road branched off for Cappadocia, and with one accord—and without saying a word—they all turned off in that direction.* And the Valerians, who had found out that they had been discharged from service by the authorities at home, withdrew altogether.*

16. It should occasion no surprise that as outstanding a general as Lucullus—the first Roman to cross the Taurus* with an army and for war, and the conqueror of two powerful kings (whom he would have captured if he had been willing to bring the war to a rapid end)*—was unable to control his men,* and that they were constantly mutinous and eventually deserted him. [2] It was not just that he asked a lot of them, but also that, since he was aloof, rigid in his insistence on results, and implacable when it came to punishment, he lacked the ability to

win men over by persuasion or mildness, and did not know how to gain
their friendship by awarding them honour or rewarding them finan-
cially—all abilities which are essential when dealing with a large body
of men, especially out on campaign. [3] The upshot was that his soldiers obeyed him as long as things were going well for them and they
were gaining booty that adequately compensated them for the dangers
they faced, but when they met with setbacks and fear replaced hope, their
loyalty came to an end. The proof of what I have been saying is that
when Pompey took over the command of these same men (he even
enrolled the Valerians again),* he met with not the slightest hint of
mutiny. This just shows how different two men may be.

17. After the Roman soldiers had done this, Mithridates recovered almost all his kingdom and wreaked havoc on Cappadocia,*
which was left undefended not just by Lucullus (who had the excuse
that Acilius was now close), but also by Acilius. Earlier, Acilius had
hurried in order to deny Lucullus victory as quickly as possible, but
now, when he saw what had happened, he lingered in Bithynia rather
than join Lucullus' legions. [2] And Lucullus received no help from
Marcius either, whose pretext was that his soldiers refused to follow
him.* Marcius went to Cilicia instead,* where he was joined by a man
called Menemachus,* who had deserted from Tigranes, and he gave
command of the fleet to Clodius, who had left Lucullus out of fear
about what he had done in Nisibis. (Marcius too had one of Clodius'
sisters as his wife.) [3] Clodius was captured by pirates,* and after
they let him go (out of fear of Pompey*), he went to Antioch in Syria,*
proposing to help them in their conflict with the Arabs, their enemies
at the time, and while he was there he again started an uprising, and
came close to losing his life.

[From Xiphilinus' epitome]* 17a. *Metellus subsequently subjugated
all of Crete, even though Pompey the Great,* who now had command of
the entire sea and of land up to three days' march from the sea,* obstructed
and hindered him on the ground that the islands too were under his authority. Nevertheless, despite Pompey's opposition, Metellus brought the
Cretan war to an end* and consequently celebrated a triumph* and gained
the additional name 'Creticus'.**

18. [. . . Metellus did not] spare. In his lust for power* he attacked
even the Cretans who had come to terms with Pompey. He was oblivious

to their claim that an accord had been reached, and was in a hurry to subdue them before Pompey arrived. Octavius* had come, but he had no army, so he did nothing. He had been sent out not to make war, but to accept the cities' surrender. Cornelius Sisenna,* the commander in Greece, went to Crete when he found out what was happening, and advised Metellus to leave the cities alone, but when his advice fell on deaf ears he did nothing actually to oppose him. [2] Among many cases of Metellus' mistreatment of the islanders were his capture of Eleutherna by treachery and his subsequent extortion of money from the city. What happened was that, under cover of darkness, the traitors used repeated applications of vinegar to soak and weaken one of the towers—a very tall and almost impregnable one, which was made out of bricks. After that, Metellus assaulted and took Lappa, despite the fact that it was occupied by Octavius, and, although he did Octavius no harm, he killed the Cilicians he had with him.

19. This made Octavius furious and he threw off his inactivity. At first, he made use of Sisenna's army—Sisenna having fallen ill and died—and went around the island bringing help to Metellus' victims, and then, when these troops were recalled, he went to Aristion* in Hierapytna and fought alongside him. Aristion had recently been driven from Cydonia, and after defeating a certain Lucius Bassus* who had put to sea against him, he had occupied Hierapytna. [2] Octavius and Aristion held out for a while, but when Metellus came against them they abandoned the fortress and put to sea, where they met with a storm which drove them on to land with considerable loss of life. After this, Metellus conquered the whole island. [3] So that is how the Cretans lost their liberty.* There had never been a time before when they were not free; they had never had a foreign master. Metellus was named 'Creticus' after them, but his desire to have Panares and Lasthenes,* whom he had captured, take part in his triumph was foiled when Pompey persuaded one of the tribunes that the men had surrendered to him, not Metellus, and stole them away.

20. I shall now give an account of how things stood with Pompey.* Pirates had always been a hazard for those who sailed the sea, just as brigands were on land. There was never a time when this was not the case, nor will it ever cease to be as long as human nature remains the same.* [2] In former times, however, only small bands of robbers plied their trade on land and sea, and only in certain areas and at the suitable season. But at the time in question, since wars had been

fought year after year in many parts of the world at once, and since many towns had been laid waste and punitive measures threatened all those who escaped from them, and everyone lived in constant fear, people turned to brigandage and piracy in large numbers.

[3] It proved fairly easy to put an end to land-based brigandage, because it took place more or less within sight of the towns; the injury was perceived from close at hand and it was not particularly hard to capture the perpetrators. But sea-based piracy increased until it became a major problem. [4] While the Romans were occupied with their wars, the pirates went from strength to strength; they sailed everywhere and recruited all those who were similar to themselves. Some of them even provided help to many others, as though they were in alliance.

21. I have, in fact, already given an account of what they achieved in league with others,* but the pirates did not stop even after those wars came to an end, and, acting on their own, they did a great deal of harm to both the Romans and their allies. They no longer sailed in small numbers, but with large fleets and with admirals in command, so that they acquired a fearsome reputation. [2] At first, the main targets of their plundering were other seafarers—and they did not let them sail in peace even in winter, since their daring, their experience, and their ascendancy made it possible for them to take to the sea even then with impunity—but subsequently the inhabitants of harbour towns became their victims as well. [3] Anyone who was bold enough to put to sea against them was generally defeated and killed, and even if he came off best, the speed of the pirate ships still made it impossible for him to capture any of them. The pirates would therefore turn up again before long, just as if it was they who had won, and would set about destroying and burning not just villages and fields, but even whole towns. Some places they got on good terms with, however, so as to gain winter quarters and bases for themselves in something like friendly territory.

22. As a result of these successes, they began to move inland as well, and to harass even people who had nothing to do with the sea. What is more, these raids were not confined to allied territory abroad, but took place even in Italy. [2] The pirates' thinking was not just that their profits would be greater from Italy, but also that people in other countries would be even more terrified of them if their reach extended to there, and so they sailed even into Ostia,* let alone other Italian towns, setting fire to ships and stealing everything. [3] In the end, since there were no repercussions, they began to live on the land and to dispose with impunity of both people (those they left alive) and the booty they gained, just as if they were in their homeland.

[4] Although the raiders operated in different regions, since, of course, the same men could not make mischief over the whole sea at once, the ties of friendship between them were so strong that they used to send both money and auxiliaries even to men who were completely unknown to them, as though they were immediate family. [5] This, in fact, was one of the chief sources of their strength—that men who extended the hand of friendship to any of them were honoured by all of them, while men who opposed any of them were preyed on by all of them.

23. So the pirate menace grew, until combating it required major, continuous warfare, permitting neither precautions nor truces. Naturally, the Romans heard about what was going on, and even saw some of it, since their grain supply was thoroughly interrupted and none of their other imports could get through to them either, [2] but they failed to take it seriously when they should have, and instead merely dispatched fleets and generals when they were disturbed by some news.* So far from accomplishing anything by this, they made their allies much worse off than they were before, and in the end found themselves in extreme danger. Only then did they meet and deliberate, over the course of many days, about what to do. [3] They were exhausted by the constant dangers and saw that they were engaged in a great and wide-ranging war. They thought that fighting all the pirates at once and dealing with them one by one were both equally impossible, since they tended to help one another and there was no way to repel them everywhere at once. For a long time they were therefore at a loss, with no hope of success.

[4] Eventually, however, a man called Aulus Gabinius, a tribune, made a proposal.* Perhaps he had been put up to it by Pompey, or perhaps he just wanted to do him a favour, but he was certainly not thinking of the common good, because he was a man of the worst sort.* His proposal was that a single general should be chosen from among the ex-consuls and given full powers to tackle all the pirates, holding the command for three years with a huge force and assisted by a large number of legates. [5] He did not actually name Pompey,* but there could be no doubt that, as soon as the populace heard such a proposal, their choice would fall on Pompey.

24. And that is exactly what happened. Gabinius' proposal won approval and everyone—everyone except the Senate—immediately thought of Pompey. The Senate would rather the pirates had a free hand than entrust such a great command to Pompey, and in fact they even came close to killing Gabinius right there while the Senate was in session.* [2] He managed to escape, however. When the people learnt of the senators' attitude, they rioted and rushed in on them as they sat in session, and if they had not withdrawn they would certainly have been killed. [3] The rest of the senators scattered and hid themselves, but Gaius Piso, the consul (this happened in the year when he and Acilius were consuls), was seized* and would have been killed as a stand-in for his fellow senators if Gabinius had not interceded and saved his life. After this, the leading men* kept quiet, content to be allowed to live, but they did try to persuade the nine other tribunes to oppose Gabinius. [4] Most of them, however, were too afraid of the plebs to argue against Gabinius; only two of them, Lucius Trebellius and Lucius Roscius,* had the necessary courage, but they were unable to speak or act as they had promised.* On the day that had been designated for voting the proposal into law, this is what happened.*

[5] Pompey coveted the command. In fact, under the combined influence of his ambition and the enthusiastic support of the people, he had stopped regarding the appointment as an honour and was inclined only to think that it would reflect badly on him if he failed to get it. But, knowing that the leading men were against him, he wanted to make it look as though he was being forced to accept the command against his will.* [6] He was in any case generally inclined to pretend that he had absolutely no desire for the things he wanted, and on this occasion he dissembled even more than usual, not just because of the jealousy* that would ensue if he deliberately sought the appointment, but also because of the glory that would ensue if, even despite his reluctance, he gained the command on the grounds that there was no one else so well fitted for it.

25. He stepped forward and spoke as follows:* 'Quirites,* it pleases me to be honoured by you. After all, it's only natural for anyone to feel proud when his fellow citizens show their appreciation of him, and on this occasion, speaking for myself, although I have often enjoyed honours from you, the great delight I take in this distinction is still less than it merits. Nevertheless, I don't think it right either for you to behave as though you can't get enough of me or for me constantly to be in a position of command. I've worked tirelessly from a very early age, and you should bestow your favours on others too. [2] Have you perhaps forgotten all the hardships I endured in the war against Cinna, even though I was still very young?* And what about all my hard work in Sicily and Africa, at a time when I did not yet fully count as a youth,* or all the dangers I faced in Spain, when I was not yet a senator?*

'Now, I'm not saying that you didn't express your gratitude for all these labours of mine. [3] How could I, when that's far from being the case? In addition to all the notable ways in which you've dignified me, the very fact that you entrusted me with the command against Sertorius, when no one else was either willing or able to take it on,* and that I was granted a triumph for it, contrary to custom,* was a signal honour for me. [4] But all the stress and danger I've endured have left me physically drained and mentally exhausted. Figuring out that I'm still young or calculating my age in years is pointless, [5] because if you add up the campaigns I've fought and the dangers I've faced, you'll find that they easily surpass the tally of my years, and then you'll be more likely to believe me when I say that I can no longer endure either the effort or the stress.

26. 'If any of you is inclined to resist even these arguments, you should bear in mind also that all such appointments provoke jealousy and hatred in others. You may be able to discount such feelings, and indeed it isn't right for you even to pretend to take any of them into consideration, but they would make things very difficult for me. [2] In fact, I confess that not one of the horrors of war disturbs or upsets me as much as these emotions in others. I mean, how could any sensible man be happy to live among people who were jealous of him? Why would anyone actively seek a public role when that meant that he'd be taken to court if he failed, and would be the object of envy if he succeeded? [3] For all these reasons, and others, leave me to enjoy my leisure and mind my own business, so that at long last I can look after my household and not die of exhaustion. Choose someone else to tackle the pirates. There are plenty of men, both younger and older, who are willing and able to take command of the fleet, and with such a large pool to pick from the decision will be easy. [4] I'm not the only man who cares for you, nor am I the only one with skill at warfare. Any number of men may be found with these qualities—I mention no names only so as not to seem to favour anyone.'

27. The response to Pompey's speech came from Gabinius. 'Quirites,' he said, 'this behaviour from Pompey, neither seeking the command nor rushing to accept it when it's offered to him, is only what you'd expect from a man like him. [2] The desire to command and to manage state business is in general not an attribute of a good man. Besides, in the present case he's right to think before consenting to everything that's being asked of him, so that, when it comes to action, he'll be equally safe then too. Rushing into making promises generates excessive haste when it comes to action as well and has caused many a blunder, but scrupulousness at the start leads to the same in action too, and serves everyone well. [3] Now, your job isn't to choose the course that's agreeable to Pompey, but the one that's good for Rome. Positions of public responsibility should, I suppose, go to men who are capable, not to those who are hungry for power, and while there are very many of the latter, you won't find another Pompey. [4] You should remember how often and how terribly we suffered in the war against Sertorius when we lacked a general, and that we found no one else of any age suitable for the job except him.* Despite his youth and lack of senatorial status, it was him we dispatched to the war rather than the two consuls.

[5] 'Naturally, I'd be happy if you had large numbers of good men at your disposal, and if that is something one should pray for, I would certainly offer up such prayers. But the necessary competence isn't a matter of prayer and doesn't come without effort either. First, a man must be born with a natural gift for it, and then he has to master all the relevant topics and gain appropriate practical experience, and above all he must be blessed with good luck. But these are qualities which, as you know, very rarely coincide in a single individual. [6] It follows that, when such a man appears, all of you, with one accord, must back him and make use of him, even if he's reluctant. This kind of force is perfectly honourable both for the person applying it and for the one at the receiving end of it—to the former because it will save his life, and to the latter because he will save his fellow citizens. And any truly good and patriotic man would gladly sacrifice both body and soul to save his fellow citizens.

28. 'This is the same Pompey who was capable in his youth of launching military operations, holding commands, increasing your possessions, protecting those of your allies, and acquiring those of your enemies.* Do you really think that he would not be of the greatest use to you now, when he's in his prime (which is to say that he has reached the age when everyone is at his best) and when he has immense experience of warfare under his belt? [2] Will you reject the man you chose for command in his youth now that he's an adult? Will you refuse to entrust this campaign to a man who has by now joined the Senate, when you consigned those earlier wars to him while he was still only an *eques*?* [3] He was the only one you turned to when you were faced with those earlier crises, and that was before he had been thoroughly tested, so now that you have ample proof of him won't you entrust the current emergency to him, which is no less of a threat than those earlier ones? When you chose him as general to combat Sertorius even though at the time he was not yet really of an age even to hold office, won't you send him against the pirates now that he has served as a consul?

[4] 'Your course is clear—and as for you, Pompey, listen to me and your country. It was she, after all, who gave you birth and brought you up. You are obliged to serve her interests and to shrink from no hardship or danger in order to secure them. Even if it becomes necessary for you to die, you must not wait for the end of your natural span, but face death in whichever form it presents itself to you.

29. 'I suppose I'm making a fool of myself in offering you advice when you've demonstrated your courage and your goodwill towards your country so often, in so many notable wars. [2] So listen to me and to those here today, and don't worry about the odium you'll face from some quarters, but make that in itself a reason to be more resolute. Focus on the affection the majority feel for you and on what will benefit all of us in common, and scorn your detractors. [3] In fact, if the idea of annoying them attracts you at all, make that a reason for accepting the command. You'll not only irritate them by confounding their expectations and commanding in a way that brings you credit, but by freeing us of a great many serious troubles you will set a crown worthy of yourself on your earlier achievements.'

30. After this speech by Gabinius, Trebellius wanted to reply, but he failed to gain permission to speak,* so instead he opposed the taking of the vote.* [2] This made Gabinius angry, and he postponed the vote about Pompey and instead introduced a fresh motion about Trebellius himself.* The decision of the first seventeen tribes to cast their vote was that Trebellius was in the wrong and should no longer be tribune, so when the eighteenth tribe was about to cast its vote in the same way, Trebellius resigned himself to holding his tongue. [3] Seeing this, Roscius did not dare to speak, but he managed to suggest by signalling with his raised hand that they appoint two men to the command, so as to deny Pompey some of his power.* As he was making these gestures, then, the people gave a great menacing shout—so loud that a crow that was flying over their heads was stunned and fell as if struck by a thunderbolt. [4] After that, Roscius kept quiet not only with his tongue, but with his hands as well. As for Catulus, although he would otherwise have stayed silent, Gabinius urged him to speak,* because Catulus was the most eminent of the senators and it seemed likely that the rest too would follow his lead, [5] and because Gabinius expected Catulus to join in approving the bill in view of what was happening to the tribunes. So Catulus was granted permission to speak, since everyone respected and honoured him as one who always said and did what was in their best interests,* and he addressed them somewhat as follows:*

31. 'You are, of course, perfectly well aware, Quirites, that my devotion for you, the people, knows no bounds. This being so, it is up to me to give a full and open account, speaking freely, of what I know to be in the best interests of the city, and it is your job to listen in silence to what I have to say and then afterwards to deliberate about what to do. [2] If you create a disturbance, the chances are that you will miss a useful piece of information, while the way to ensure accurate reception of advice that is in your best interests is to pay attention to what's being said.

[3] 'The first and most important thing I have to say is that no one man should be assigned so many positions of command one after another. It's not just that this is illegal,* but also that experience has shown how risky it is. Almost the only thing, for instance, that made Marius turn out as he did was that he was entrusted with so many wars in the shortest period of time and was made consul six times in rapid succession.* [4] The same goes for Sulla too.* Again, the chief factor was that he had command of the legions for so many years in succession, and was subsequently made dictator and then consul. Given human nature, it's impossible for anyone, young or old, to hold positions of power for a long time and still be willing to abide by traditional ways.

32. 'I'm not in the slightest motivated to say this by a desire to denigrate Pompey,* but because it's clear that this policy has never

done you good, as well as being against the law. And in fact, if this command represents an honour for those on whom it is conferred, then everyone, or at any rate all the possible contenders, ought to share that honour, because that is democracy; and if it entails hard work, they should all play their part proportionately, because that is equality.* [2] Besides, if you do as I suggest, many people gain practical experience, and the fact that you can appraise them makes it easy for you to choose those whom you can trust to do everything that needs to be done. But if you follow the other course, it's absolutely certain that there will be a considerable shortage of men with the relevant experience to be entrusted with command. [3] In fact, that's the main reason why you were unable to find a general for the war against Sertorius*—because previously you had been using the same men for many years. In other words, even if in all other respects Pompey deserves to be voted the command against the pirates, the fact that to choose him would infringe both what has been decreed by law and what has been determined by experience means that this is the last thing that is appropriate for either you or him.

33. 'That is the first and most important point I want to make, but the second is this, that as long as consuls, praetors, and those who act on their behalf are being assigned offices and commands in an orderly and legal fashion, it is neither right nor advantageous for you just to ignore them and introduce some new office. [2] I mean, why hold the annual elections of magistrates if you make no use of them in situations like this one? It's not, I suppose, so that they can strut around in purple-bordered togas* or be invested just with the name of their office while being denied the actual work it involves. [3] How could you fail to make enemies of these men, and of anyone else who elects to play a part in public life, if you abolish the traditional magistracies and refuse to entrust the legally appointed officers with the slightest responsibility, and instead confer some novel and unprecedented command on a private citizen?

34. 'As a matter of fact, if it's ever necessary to choose another officer, over and above those that are annually elected, there's an ancient precedent for this too. I'm talking about the dictatorship.* But, given the nature of this post, our fathers did not appoint a dictator for all occasions or for a term of more than six months. [2] So, if you feel in need of officer of this kind, you can, without breaking the law or acting in a cavalier fashion over a decision that affects the public

interest, appoint Pompey or anyone else you like to a dictatorship, as long as he holds office for no longer than the prescribed term and does so within Italy. I'm sure you're aware that this second restriction was also scrupulously observed by our fathers, so that no instance exists of any dictator chosen to work outside Italy, except for just one, who was sent to Sicily and achieved nothing.* [3] But since Italy has no need of a dictator, and since from now on (as you made plain by your furious reaction to Sulla) you won't tolerate even the title of dictator, let alone the reality of it, does it make sense to create a new command, especially one with a three-year term and with a virtually universal scope, since it covers both Italy and the regions outside it? [4] Every single one of you is aware of the many terrible effects such a policy has on cities, and you know how often men, impelled by a lawless lust for power, have made trouble for our people and brought disaster down on their own heads.*

35. 'I shall say no more about this, since it's clear to everyone that in no way is it advisable or advantageous for a single individual to be given sole responsibility for our affairs and for all our current assets to be in the hands of just one man. He may be the most virtuous person in the world, but great honours and excessive power turn the heads of even good men and corrupt them. [2] But there's another point that I want you to consider, namely that it isn't even *possible* for a single person to have authority over the entire sea and to properly manage this war as a whole. I mean, if you're to make any significant progress at all, you have to make war on the pirates everywhere at once; otherwise they'll either join forces or find refuge with those who aren't involved in the war, and in either case they'll become unassailable. [3] But it's completely out of the question for a single commander to do this. How could he fight on the same days in both Italy and Cilicia, Egypt and Syria, Greece and Spain, in the Ionian Sea and among the Aegean islands? It follows that large numbers of both soldiers and generals will be required to win; smaller numbers will be no use to you.

36. 'Now, someone might argue that even if you did make a single individual responsible for the entire war, he would, of course, certainly have a large staff of naval commanders and adjutants. But is the following not far more fair and advantageous, or so I would claim? What's to stop you from picking them too, the men who are going to serve as his adjutants—picking them for the specific job at hand and commissioning them as officers with their own independent commands? [2] If

you do that, the war will be of more concern to them, because each of them will have his own sphere of responsibility and will be unable to blame anyone else for any neglect of it. Moreover, the rivalry among them will be sharper, because they'll be independent agents and will themselves gain the glory of their achievements.

'But if you follow the other course, do you imagine that any of them will be that assiduous if he's subordinate to someone else? Do you think that any of them will do anything unreservedly when victory will be credited not to him but someone else? [3] That it would be impossible for a single individual to manage such a great war has also been admitted by Gabinius himself, when he asks for whoever is chosen for the command to be given numerous assistants. The only remaining question, then, is whether these men should be sent out as commanders or as subordinates,† and appointed with an independent power by the whole people or by him alone for his assistance.*

[4] 'All of you, then, will admit that my proposal is both more lawful and more advantageous, not only where the pirates are concerned, but in general. Besides, there's another point for you to consider. Think how serious it would be for all your other magistracies to be abolished* on the pretext of the pirates, and none of them, whether their duties lay in Italy or in the subject territory at that time [. . .]'*

[Possible fragments of Catulus' speech]

1. Moreover, his sole rule over all your possessions is bound to attract jealousy.
2. It is of course important for an intelligent man to provide for such a possibility.

[From Xiphilinus' epitome] 36a. *One of the aristocrats, a man called Catulus, said to the people: 'If he is sent out on this mission and fails, as happens in a great many conflicts, especially those fought at sea, who else will you find to replace him and deal with the increasing crisis?' And the whole multitude, as if by prior agreement, shouted out 'You!'* This was how Pompey gained the command of the sea, and of the islands and mainland for a distance of four hundred stades from the sea.**

37. [. . .] and of Italy, as proconsul, for a period of three years. They also assigned him fifteen legates and the entire navy, and decreed that he should take as much money and manpower as he might want.* And the Senate, despite its reluctance, ratified these provisions, and likewise from time to time decreed all the other measures that were entailed by them, [2] not least when Piso* refused Pompey's officers permission to recruit troops in Narbonese Gaul, of which he had command, and the people were furious. In fact, they would immediately have removed him from office* if Pompey had not pleaded on his behalf.

[3] So, having made his preparations, as dictated by the situation and his judgement, he patrolled—in person or through his legates—the entire stretch of sea that was being plagued by the pirates, and pacified most of it within a single year.* [4] He had such a huge fleet and army at his disposal that he was irresistible on both sea and land, and by displaying clemency towards those who came to terms with him he was able to win a great many over, [5] as people who were defeated by his forces and experienced his decency enthusiastically gave him their allegiance. He took care of them in a number of ways, especially by ensuring that they would never again be forced by poverty to turn to criminal activities. What he did was give them any uninhabited land he found and any towns that were in need of repopulating. [6] Among the towns that were refounded by him was the one called Pompeiopolis, which is situated on the Cilician coast and had been sacked by Tigranes.* Its former name was Soli.

38. These were not the only events that took place in the year of the consulship of Acilius and Piso.* On the proposal of the consuls themselves, a law was passed forbidding those who had been convicted of electoral bribery from holding office or serving in the Senate, and making them also liable to a fine.* [2] The context was that, since the tribunate had regained its ancient power,* and since many men who had been struck off by the censors* were keen to get back into the Senate by fair means or foul, a great many coalitions and cliques were being formed to influence the elections to all offices. [3] The consuls did not do this because they found the practice offensive; after all, they themselves had been appointed after running corrupt campaigns, and Piso had even been indicted for it, but by bribing one man and another he made sure that the case did not come to court.* They did so, rather, because the Senate left them no choice.

[4] This is how it came about. One of the tribunes, a certain Gaius Cornelius,* proposed very harsh penalties for such offenders, and the

people were in favour. The Senate, however, realized that, while excessive punishments may have a deterrent effect, their utterly ruinous nature makes it difficult to find men either to bring charges or condemn the guilty; [5] moderation, on the other hand, often actively encourages men to bring charges and does not discourage them from condemning the guilty, and so they ordered the consuls to pass a modified version of Cornelius' proposal into law.

39. The elections had already been proclaimed, making it illegal for any law to be carried before they had taken place,* but in the intervening period misconduct from the candidates was rife, with even murders taking place, so the senators voted that the consuls were to introduce the law before the elections, and were to be granted an armed guard.* [2] This was not good enough for Cornelius, and he brought forward a proposal* that the senators should not be allowed to grant an office to anyone seeking it contrary to the laws, or to vote on any other issue that was the people's prerogative—which had been the law from very ancient times, but was not being observed in practice. [3] When many of the senators, and not least Piso, opposed Cornelius' proposal, a riot ensued, and the mob broke Piso's fasces and seemed determined to tear him limb from limb. [4] Seeing the way things were going, then, Cornelius dismissed the assembly for the time being without holding a vote,* and later he added a rider to the law,* to the effect that the Senate should pass a preliminary decree on such matters and that it would be obligatory for this decree to be ratified by the people.

40. So that is how Cornelius got this law passed,* and another one as well. All the praetors used to compose and publish the principles according to which they were going to judge court cases,* because not all the regulations relating to contracts had yet been finalized.* [2] But this was not something they did once and for all, and in fact they did not adhere to their own written regulations, but often altered the wording, and many of these changes, as was only to be expected, were made in order to oblige or harm certain people. So Cornelius proposed that at the start of their term the praetors should immediately publish the principles they were going to follow, and should not depart from them at all.

[3] Generally speaking, the Romans were so concerned at that time to stamp out corruption* that, in addition to punishing those who were convicted, they rewarded those who brought charges

against them. At any rate, after Marcus Cotta,* despite having dismissed the quaestor Publius Oppius* for bribery and suspicion of conspiracy, had himself hugely profited from Bithynia,* [4] they elevated the man who accused him, Gaius Carbo, to consular rank,* even though he had previously only been a tribune. And when Carbo himself later became governor of Bithynia and behaved no less reprehensibly than Cotta, he was accused in his turn by Cotta's son and found guilty.* [5] But it is clear that some people find it much easier to censure others than to admonish themselves, and have not the slightest hesitation about behaving in ways for which they think others deserve to be punished. In other words, it is impossible to believe that they do actually find reprehensible the behaviour for which they find others at fault.

41. However, Lucius Lucullus* served as praetor at Rome, but, when allotted the governorship of Sardinia, refused to take it up.* The unscrupulous behaviour of many men when serving in the provinces had made the role repulsive to him. This was not the only occasion when he gave excellent proof of his mild nature: [2] when, because he had failed to acknowledge his presence by standing up, Acilius* ordered the chair* to be broken on which he sat to hear cases, he did not lose his temper, but both he and his colleagues, who followed his example, went on to deliver their verdicts on their feet.

42. Roscius also introduced a law, and so did Gaius Manilius when he was tribune.* Roscius was praised for his law,* which clearly distinguished the seats in the theatres that were reserved for *equites* from everyone else's. [2] Manilius, however, came very close to standing trial, because on the last day of the year, and late in the day, he won over some elements of the people and gave the class of freedmen the right to vote alongside the men who had freed them.* [3] Immediately on the following morning, on the first of the month, the day on which
66 BCE Lucius Tullus and Aemilius Lepidus took up their consulships,* the Senate rejected his law.* Manilius, terrified by the ferocious anger of the plebs, first laid responsibility for the proposal on Crassus and some others,* [4] but no one believed him, so he curried favour with Pompey instead,* even though he was not there, especially because he could see that Gabinius had a great deal of influence with him. What he did was assign Pompey the command of the war against Tigranes and Mithridates, and at the same time the governorship of both Bithynia and Cilicia.*

43. At that, the leading men became angry, and they argued against the proposal,* especially because Marcius and Acilius* were being made to step down before their term of office had come to an end. [2] But even though the people, concluding that the war was over from what Lucullus had told them in his letters, had a little earlier sent out commissioners to set the captured territories in order,* they still voted in favour of Manilius' proposal.

They were urged to do so above all by Caesar and Marcus Cicero.* [3] These men were moved to support the proposal not by the thought that it was in Rome's best interests, nor because they wanted to ingratiate themselves with Pompey. Since it was going to happen anyway, Caesar was simultaneously courting the favour of the masses because he could see how much stronger they were than the Senate, [4] and preparing the ground for a similar vote to be passed in his favour at some point.* At the same time, Caesar also wanted Pompey to have honours heaped on him, so that he would become more of an object of jealousy and hatred, and it would take less time for the people to have had enough of him. As for Cicero, he aspired to political leadership in Rome, and he was making it plain to both the people and the leading men that he was certain to increase the strength of whichever side he joined. [5] He was playing a double game, acting in the interests now of one side and now of the other, in order to win support from both.* At any rate, he had earlier claimed to be on the side of the better sort, giving that as his reason for wanting to be an aedile rather than a tribune, but he now switched allegiance to the riff-raff.*

44. Later, however, when the leading men arranged for Manilius to be taken to court and Manilius wanted the hearing to be delayed, Cicero set about trying to thwart him in various ways and, since he was a praetor and president of the court, reluctantly postponed it until the following day, giving as his excuse for doing so that the year was coming to an end. [2] This infuriated the people, and when Cicero presented himself before them in assembly (claiming to be forced to do so by the tribunes), he castigated the Senate and promised to speak in support of Manilius.* The upshot of this was that he gained a bad reputation, and in particular came to be called a defector.* However, the tumult that immediately ensued prevented the court from being convened.*

[3] Publius Paetus and Cornelius Sulla (a nephew of the famous Sulla), who had been elected consuls for the following year and then

found guilty of corruption,* plotted to kill their accusers, Lucius
Cotta and Lucius Torquatus, especially because they had been chosen
to replace them.* [4] Others were prevailed upon, including Gnaeus
Piso* and Lucius Catilina, a presumptuous hothead who had canvassed for the consulate himself and was therefore resentful,* but
they were unable to do anything because the plot was discovered,*
and Cotta and Torquatus were granted a bodyguard by the Senate.*
[5] A decree would have been pronounced against them, if it had not
been vetoed by one of the tribunes.* Even so, Piso remained a trouble-
maker, and the Senate, concerned about the possibility of some disturbance, bundled him off straight away to Spain, ostensibly to take
up some command.* And while he was there he was murdered by the
inhabitants, who had been suffering under his abuses.*

45. Pompey, meanwhile, had been getting ready to sail to Crete
against Metellus,* which was his original plan, and when he found
out about Manilius' decree he repeated the ploy of pretending to be
annoyed,* and accused his political opponents of constantly making
trouble for him and trying to trip him up. [2] In fact, however, he
received the news with the greatest pleasure, and he stopped regarding Crete or any other Mediterranean business that had yet to be
settled as of the slightest importance, and prepared for war against
the barbarians.

While he was occupied with this, he wanted to find out Mithridates'
intentions and he sent Metrophanes to him with words of friendship.* [3] Now, at the time Mithridates regarded Pompey as no threat;
Arsaces, the Parthian king, had recently died, and Mithridates was
confident that he could win Phraates, Arsaces' successor, over to his
side. But Pompey got in first, quickly agreeing a pact of friendship
with Phraates on the same terms,* and persuading him to launch an
invasion of Tigranes' Armenia.* The news worried Mithridates, and
he lost no time in sending an embassy to seek an agreement. [4] But
Pompey demanded that he lay down his arms and surrender the
deserters, and Mithridates had no time to think what it was best for
him to do, because when the men in his camp heard what was going
on, the deserters, of whom there were many, became afraid that they
would be handed over, and the barbarians that they would be forced
to fight without the deserters, and they rioted. [5] They would have
taken it out on Mithridates if he had not lied and told them that he
had sent the envoys not to make a treaty, but to spy out the disposition

of the Roman forces. It was a close call, but he managed to check them with this ploy.

46. Pompey therefore decided that war was unavoidable and took the appropriate steps, which included re-enlisting the Valerians.* He had reached Galatia when Lucullus met him* and told him that there was nothing left for him to do—that the war was over, there was no need of a further campaign, and that was why the commissioners who had been sent by the Senate to arrange a settlement for the region* had already arrived. [2] Lucullus failed to persuade Pompey to withdraw, however, and he turned instead to abuse, accusing him, among other things, of being meddlesome and greedy for war and command. But Pompey scarcely listened to him. He told everyone to stop taking orders from Lucullus and he set out at speed against Mithridates, since he wanted to engage him as soon as possible.

47. For a while, Mithridates fled before him, since his forces were smaller.* Wherever he found himself, he laid waste to the farmland, forcing Pompey to stray from his route and depriving him of provisions. But then Pompey entered Armenia,* not just because of Mithridates' tactics, but also because he hoped to take it over while it was defenceless. [2] Mithridates, worried about the country's vulnerability, went there as well. He occupied a defensible hill near the Roman position, and stayed there with his entire army, doing nothing. He was expecting to wear the Romans down by denying them food—he himself was receiving plenty of supplies from all quarters, since he was in subject territory—so he kept sending cavalry detachments down to the open plain. They wreaked havoc on everyone they came across, and the upshot was that deserters poured into his camp.

[3] Pompey did not dare to attack the enemy where they were, so he moved camp to a spot where, since the surrounding countryside was wooded, he would be less troubled by their cavalry and archers. [4] Then he seized an opportunity to lay an ambush and openly approached the barbarians' camp at the head of a small number of troops. At this, the barbarians' discipline broke down, and he lured them out to where he wanted and inflicted heavy casualties on them. Encouraged by this success, he also began to send troops here and there in the countryside to forage for provisions.

48. So Pompey was able to supply himself safely and, with help from certain quarters, he gained control of the region of Armenia called Anaïtis,* which is sacred to a goddess with the same name.

[2] As a result of this, many others began to come over to him, and he was also reinforced by Marcius' troops.* All this made Mithridates afraid and he decided to move.* He immediately and stealthily broke camp under cover of darkness, and then he marched through the night towards Tigranes' Armenia. [3] Pompey followed him, since he wanted to bring him to battle, but he did not dare to do so either by day (because the enemy refused to emerge from their camp) or by night (because he was worried about his ignorance of the terrain), until they were close to the border. At this point, knowing that the enemy was about to escape, he had no choice but to fight, and it had to be a night battle.

[4] Having come to this realization, Pompey set out ahead, on the route the barbarians were going to take, giving them the slip while they were taking their siesta. When he came to a valley surrounded by hills, he had his army climb up to the heights and wait for the enemy. [5] They entered the valley confidently and without taking any precautions, because nothing bad had ever happened to them before and now they were at last heading for safety. They were even expecting the Romans to stop following them. It was pitch-black when Pompey launched his attack, because there was no illumination coming from the sky and the enemy had no other source of light either.

49. The battle went as follows. First, at a signal, all the Roman trumpeters together sounded the attack, then the soldiers and all the camp followers roared out the war cry, and while the soldiers beat on their shields with their spears, the rest struck stones against their bronze vessels and implements. [2] Since the mountains formed a depression, they received and returned this terrifying sound, with the result that the barbarians, unexpectedly hearing these noises in the dark and the wild, were frightened out of their wits and thought they were in the presence of some supernatural phenomenon. [3] Meanwhile, from all directions the Romans were firing stones, arrows, and javelins down from the heights. There were so many of the enemy that their missiles were bound to find a mark, and the barbarians found themselves in the direst straits. They were drawn up for marching, not battle; men, women, horses, camels, and all sorts of baggage were all occupying the same space. [4] Some people were on horseback, others were riding on chariots, or in covered wagons and carriages all jumbled up together and, with some of them being wounded and others expecting to be wounded, they were in disarray, and it became easier to kill them because they kept bunching up.

[5] This was the situation while they were being shot at from a distance, but when the Romans exhausted their long-distance weaponry and charged down the slopes at them, those on the fringes of the column began to be slaughtered (and a single blow was enough to cause death, since most of them were wearing no armour), while those in the middle were being pressed close together, because everyone was tending in that direction out of fear of the danger surrounding them. [6] And that was how they died, shoving and trampling one another, with no way to defend themselves or take the fight to the enemy, because most of them were horsemen and archers, and they were incapable of seeing anything in the darkness, and just as incapable of manoeuvring in the confined space.

Finally the moon rose, to the delight of the barbarians, who felt certain that they would be able to repel some of the enemy now that there was light. [7] And it would have done them some good, if the Romans had not had the moon behind them; by attacking now from this direction and now from that, they made it very difficult for the enemy to see clearly or act precisely. There were so many of them, and together they cast such a solid shadow, that they bewildered the barbarians, even before they had made contact with them. [8] The barbarians, thinking that the Romans were within range, struck uselessly at empty space, and even when they were at close quarters they were being wounded by blows the shadows made them unable to anticipate. And so they died in large numbers,* and just as many men were taken prisoner. But a great many escaped as well, including Mithridates.

50. Mithridates' first thought was to join Tigranes* as quickly as possible, and he sent envoys on ahead to him—but he was received coldly. The younger Tigranes had risen up against his father, and the elder Tigranes suspected that Mithridates, who was the younger Tigranes' grandfather,* was responsible for their falling-out. That was why he refused to give him shelter;* in fact, he even arrested and imprisoned the envoys. With his hopes frustrated, Mithridates turned aside and headed for Colchis instead.* [2] From there he travelled overland to the Maeotis and the Bosporus,* winning places over on his way by either diplomacy or force. He recovered the Bosporan region too; it was currently ruled by Machares, his son, who had gone over to the Roman side.* Machares was so frightened of his father that he did not dare even to meet him, and Mithridates had him killed by some of his own courtiers,* to whom he promised both immunity and money. [3] Meanwhile, after Mithridates escaped across the Phasis* from the force Pompey had sent to pursue him, Pompey founded a city at the site of his victory and gave it to the injured soldiers and the veterans. Many of the locals also volunteered to join Pompey's men in the new settlement, and their descendants live there still. They are called the people of Nicopolis,* and they pay their taxes to the province of Cappadocia.*

51. While Pompey was occupied with this, Tigranes, the son of Tigranes, fled to Phraates,* taking with him some of the leading men of Armenia, who were discontented with the elder Tigranes' rule. Phraates, who was considering what he ought to do in view of his treaty with Pompey, was persuaded by the younger Tigranes to launch an offensive in Armenia. [2] They got as far as Artaxata,* subduing all the territory on the way, and attacked the city itself, since the elder Tigranes had fled to the mountains in fear of them. But once it became clear that it was going to be a protracted siege, Phraates left a division of his army with the younger Tigranes and went back home. At that point, the elder Tigranes launched an attack in his turn on his son, who was now on his own, and defeated him. [3] The younger Tigranes turned to flight. His original plan was to go to Mithridates, his grandfather, but when he found out that Mithridates had been defeated and was more in need of help himself than in a position to help others, he went over to the Romans. Pompey, using him as his guide, launched a campaign in Armenia against his father.

52. The news of the offensive alarmed Tigranes, and he immediately made overtures to Pompey and handed over Mithridates' envoys. His son's opposition made it impossible for him to obtain moderate terms, and moreover Pompey had crossed the Araxes and was near Artaxata, [2] so under these circumstances Tigranes surrendered the city to him and voluntarily came to his camp.* He did his best to make himself seem deserving of both respect and pity, by dressing halfway between his former majesty and his current abasement. [3] That is, he shed his tunic of purple shot with white and his candys of pure purple, but retained his tiara and diadem.* However, when he made as though to enter the fortress itself on horseback, according to the custom of his people, Pompey sent a lictor to him and had him dismount.

But when Pompey saw him enter on foot, cast aside his diadem, drop to the ground and prostrate himself,* he felt sorry for him. [4] He jumped up, raised Tigranes to his feet, tied his diadem back on, and sat him down by his side. He tried to reassure him about his situation, saying, in particular, that he had not lost the kingdom of Armenia, but gained the friendship of Rome. Once he had consoled him in this way, he invited him to dinner. **53.** However, the younger Tigranes, who was sitting on the other side of Pompey, had remained sitting down when his father arrived and had not acknowledged his presence in any other way; in fact, even though he too had been invited to dinner, he did not turn up, which earned him Pompey's hatred.

[2] The next day, at any rate, after Pompey had heard what they had to say, he let the elder Tigranes have his ancestral kingdom back in its entirety, but stripped him of his more recent acquisitions* (the most important of which were parts of Cappadocia and Syria, namely Phoenicia and Sophanene,* a large region bordering Armenia), and also required him to pay money.* To the younger Tigranes he gave only Sophanene. [3] Now, this was where the treasuries were, and the young man claimed them as his own. When he lost the argument (after all, there was nowhere else from where Pompey could get the funds specified in the agreement), he was furious and planned to escape. But Pompey got wind of this and put him under guard, while ordering the treasurers by letter to give all the money to his father. [4] When they refused, claiming that it was the young man's job to give them such an order, since the country was now regarded as his, Pompey sent him to the strongholds. Finding them barred, he drew near and, albeit reluctantly, ordered the gates opened. But the treasurers still disregarded him, on the grounds that he was giving the order under compulsion rather than of his own free will, and in exasperation Pompey put Tigranes in chains.

[5] So the elder Tigranes regained his treasuries. Pompey spent the winter in Anaïtis* by the river Cyrnus,* with his army in three divisions. Tigranes kept him amply supplied and, in particular, gave him far more money than had been stipulated in their agreement. [6] This was the chief reason why, not much later, Pompey enrolled Tigranes among the friends and allies,* and brought his son to Rome under guard.*

54. The winter did not pass without incident for him, however. Oroeses, the king of the Albanians, who live north of the Cyrnus, took to the field against the Romans at the time of the Saturnalia.* He did so partly because he wanted to help the younger Tigranes, with whom he was on good terms, but mainly because he was afraid that the Romans might invade Albania; he also thought that, if he attacked them during the winter when they would not be expecting it and were split up among different camps, he was bound to achieve some success. [2] He himself marched against Metellus Celer, who had Tigranes in his keeping, while he sent others against Pompey and yet others against Lucius Flaccus,* the commander of the third division of the army, so that everyone would be in turmoil at the same time and they would not come to one another's aid.

[3] Nevertheless, he was entirely unsuccessful in all three places. He himself was forcefully repulsed by Celer. Flaccus, seeing that the entire circuit of his entrenchments was too large for him to be able to keep it all safe, had dug another one inside the camp. This gave the enemy the impression that he was afraid of them, and he lured them inside the outer trench. [4] He then charged out at them when they were not expecting it and took many lives, either in the course of the fighting or as they fled.

Meanwhile, Pompey, who had heard about the barbarians' attempts on the other two camps, marched out to meet the force that was advancing against him, much to their surprise. He defeated them and, without pausing, set out immediately against Oroeses. He was too far ahead, however, since he had fled as soon as he had been repulsed by Celer and had learnt that his other forces had been defeated as well, [5] but Pompey did catch a large number of Albanians at the Cyrnus crossing, whom he killed. Afterwards, he granted them a truce, at their request. There was little he wanted more than to invade their country, but because of the winter he was happy to postpone the war.

BOOK THIRTY-SEVEN

1. So much for Pompey's exploits that year. In the following year, 65 BCE when Lucius Cotta and Lucius Torquatus were consuls, he made war on both the Albanians and the Iberians.* He was obliged to fight the Iberians first, and against his wishes. [2] Iberian territory straddles both banks of the Cyrnus, bordering Albania on one side and Armenia on the other,* and Artoces, the Iberian king, was afraid that Pompey would turn his attention their way. He therefore sent envoys to him, on the pretence of seeking his friendship, but in fact he was getting ready to attack him while he was confident and therefore off guard. [3] When Pompey found out what Artoces was up to, he launched a pre-emptive invasion of Iberia, before Artoces' preparations were complete and before he had occupied the pass, which would have presented a major challenge. He got as far as Acropolis,* as it is called, before Artoces knew he was there. [4] This fortress is situated right in the narrows, with the Cyrnus flowing past it on one side and the flanks of the Caucasus mountains on the other side, and had been built there to guard the pass. Artoces was frightened. With no time to marshal his forces, he crossed the river and burnt the bridge, and in view of his flight, [5] and also once they had been defeated in a battle, the troops in the fortress surrendered. Once he had gained control of the pass, Pompey installed a garrison to secure it, and then he set out from there and subdued all the territory south of the river.

2. But just as he too was about to cross the Cyrnus, Artoces got in touch with him. He asked for peace and promised to provide him with a bridge and supplies. [2] He fulfilled both of these promises, as though he were planning to come to terms, but when he saw Pompey on his side of the river, he became afraid and fled to the Pelorus,* another river that flowed through his kingdom. In other words, first he invited him in, when he might have prevented him from crossing the river, and then he ran away from him. [3] Seeing this, Pompey went after him, caught up with him, and defeated him in battle. He had his men sprint forward and come to close quarters before Artoces' bowmen could make use of their skill, and then it took hardly any time for the enemy to be routed.

[4] After this defeat, Artoces crossed the Pelorus, burnt the bridge over that river as well, and fled. As for his men, some died fighting and others while fording the river. [5] Many others scattered into the forest and survived for a few days by firing arrows from the trees, which were exceedingly tall, but once the trees were cut down they were killed as well. Under these circumstances, Artoces approached Pompey yet again to sue for peace, and sent him gifts. [6] Pompey accepted the gifts, so that the prospect of a treaty would make Artoces stop running away, but he refused to agree to peace unless the king first sent him his sons as hostages. Artoces hesitated for a while, [7] but then, in the summer, the Pelorus became fordable and the Romans crossed it without any difficulty, especially since no one tried to stop them. Then Artoces sent Pompey his sons, and later a treaty was concluded.

3. Next, finding out that the Phasis was quite close,* Pompey thought he would march alongside it down into Colchis, and then go from Colchis to the Bosporus against Mithridates. He set out according to this plan,* [2] and marched through the territory of the Colchians and their neighbours, either winning them over by diplomacy or cowing them into submission. But then he realized that the overland route would take him through the territory of many unfamiliar and aggressive tribes, and that the sea journey would be particularly difficult because of the lack of harbours in that part of the world and the hostility of the local inhabitants. [3] He therefore ordered his fleet to blockade Mithridates, to stop him sailing off anywhere and to prevent him from bringing in provisions, while he went against the Albanians. He went to Albania via Armenia,* rather than taking the shortest route, because he hoped by this tactic, and because of the truce, to take them by surprise.

[4] He crossed the Cyrnus by foot at a point where the summer had made this feasible. He ordered the cavalry, then the pack animals, and then the infantry to cross downstream from one another in that order, so that the horses would break the force of the stream with their bodies, and so that any pack animal that was still swept off its feet would collide with the men who were on the other side of them and would not be swept further downstream. [5] Next, he marched to the Cambyses,* and although the enemy gave him no trouble, he and the entire army suffered very badly from the heat and the thirst induced by the heat. They suffered like this even though they mostly travelled

at night, because their guides, who were drawn from the prisoners, did not take them on the best route. [6] Even the river was no help, because the water was bitterly cold and a lot of the people who gulped it down were badly affected. Since they met no resistance at the Cambyses either, they continued on to the Abas.* They took with them only water, because they were being given everything else by the natives, who were glad to supply them, and in return the Romans did them no harm.

4. They had already crossed the Abas when news arrived that Oroeses was advancing towards them. Now, Pompey wanted to bring him to battle before he learnt the size of the Roman forces, because he was worried that he would pull back if he caught sight of them. [2] He therefore posted his cavalry out in front, primed with orders he had given them beforehand, and he had the rest of his troops kneel behind the cavalry and cover themselves with their shields, keeping perfectly still, so that Oroeses would not know they were there until battle had been joined. [3] Since he assumed that the cavalry was unsupported, Oroeses expected them to give him no trouble; he attacked them, and when after a short while they deliberately turned to flight, he pursued them vigorously. Then the infantry suddenly stood up. They opened their ranks so that their comrades could escape safely through their centre, but then absorbed the incautious charge of the enemy and surrounded a large number of them. [4] And while these troops were cutting down those of the enemy who were caught in their trap, the cavalry wheeled round, some to the right and some to the left, and fell on the rear of those who remained outside the trap. Both the infantry and the cavalry took many Albanian lives there, and they burnt to death others who had taken refuge in the forest, chanting 'Io Saturnalia, Saturnalia!', with reference to the earlier attack the Albanians had made at the time of the festival.*

5. After having won this battle and overrun the countryside, Pompey granted peace to the Albanians, and when he was approached by some of the other peoples who live alongside the Caucasus range up to the Caspian Sea, where these mountains end after starting from Pontus, he agreed terms with them too. [2] Phraates also sent to him, because he wanted to renew their treaty.* He could see how well things were going for Pompey; he could also see that Pompey's leg-ates were subduing the rest of Armenia and the nearby part of Pontus, and that Gabinius* had even crossed the Euphrates and advanced as far as the Tigris. All this made him afraid of the Romans, and he wanted to confirm the treaty. He was completely foiled in this, however, [3] because, in view of his present successes and the hopes they aroused in him, Pompey felt contempt for Phraates. He spoke arrogantly to his envoys and demanded the return of Gordyene, the territory which Phraates was disputing with Tigranes.* [4] But the envoys had received no instructions on this matter, so they made no response. Pompey wrote to Phraates, but he sent Afranius* to Gordyene straight away, without waiting for a reply, took it over without a fight, and gave it to Tigranes. [5] As Afranius passed through Mesopotamia on his way to Syria (which contravened the terms of the treaty with the Parthian), he lost his way and suffered badly from winter cold and shortage of provisions. In fact, there would have been great loss of life if the Carrhaeans* (originally Macedonian colonists who lived in the region) had not taken him in and helped him on his way.

6. That was the use Pompey made, in his dealings with Phraates, of the power he currently enjoyed, making it perfectly clear to those greedy for more* that everything depends on armed force, and that the man who wins with its help inevitably lays down the law according to his wishes. Moreover, he also used Phraates' title to insult him—the title in which Phraates gloried before all the world, including the Romans, and which they in their turn had always used when addressing him. [2] What Pompey did was eliminate 'of Kings' from Phraates' title 'King of Kings', and in his letter address him only as 'King'.* (Later, however, he gave the title, contrary to custom, to his prisoner Tigranes, when he celebrated his triumph over him in Rome.*) [3] Although Phraates was frightened of Pompey and was paying court to him, this made him angry and he felt that his kingship had been denied. He sent envoys to Pompey, reproving him for all the wrongs he had suffered and forbidding him from crossing the Euphrates.*

[4] Pompey's response was far from conciliatory, however, and before very long Phraates launched a campaign against Tigranes, in which he was supported by Tigranes' son,* who was married to one **64 BCE** of his daughters. This was in the spring of the year when Lucius Caesar and Gaius Figulus were consuls.* He lost one battle, but later it was his turn to inflict a defeat on Tigranes. [5] When Tigranes asked for help from Pompey, who was in Syria, Phraates again sent envoys to Pompey, bringing many charges against Tigranes and making

many insinuations against the Romans as well, and the upshot was that Pompey felt ashamed and alarmed.

7. Pompey therefore sent no help to Tigranes and took no further hostile action against Phraates, on the grounds that he had not been assigned such a campaign and that Mithridates was still in arms.* He said that he was satisfied with what he had accomplished, and he did not want more because he was afraid that, if he aimed for more, he might come to grief and compromise even the successes he had already won, as Lucullus had.* [2] Thus he philosophized, and he condemned greed for more as dangerous and desiring others' possessions as unjust—or so he said, now that these were no longer viable options for him since he was refusing to go to war. He was being urged to do so, but the Parthian's strength worried him and the instability of the situation frightened him.

He also shrugged off Phraates' complaints about Tigranes. [3] Rather than addressing them, he said that since Phraates' dispute with Tigranes was over borders, a commission of three should decide the issue for them. He arranged for these commissioners to be sent, and once they had been officially acknowledged by the kings as bona fide arbitrators, they resolved all the complaints they had against each other.* Tigranes was angry about being denied the help he had asked for, [4] and Phraates wanted the Armenian to survive so that he could have him as an ally, if the need arose, against the Romans. They both understood perfectly well that the victory of one of them over the other, whichever it was, would help the Roman cause, and that the winner would himself become easier for the Romans to subdue.* [5] These were the kings' reasons for becoming reconciled.

Pompey also wintered then in Aspis,* winning over the remaining places that still held out against him, and not least the fortress called Symphorium, which was betrayed to him by Stratonice. She was married to Mithridates, but she was angry with him for having abandoned her there, so she sent the soldiers of the garrison out of the fortress to forage for food and then let the Romans in, even though her son* [. . .]

7a. [From Xiphilinus' epitome]* *On his way back from Armenia, Pompey arbitrated disputes and managed affairs for the kings and dynasts who approached him.* Some were confirmed in their kingdoms or had the territory under their rule increased, but he also curbed the excessive power*

of some and humbled them. He settled Coele Syria and Phoenicia, which
had in recent years rid themselves of their kings and been ravaged by the
Arabians and Tigranes. Antiochus* dared to ask for them to be returned to
him, but he did not get them; they were classed as a single province and
were given laws so that they were governed in the Roman fashion.**

65 BCE 8. [. . .] Caesar earned praise during his aedileship not only for this,*
but also because of the enormous amount of money he spent putting
on both the Roman and the Megalensian Games,* and also because
he arranged gladiatorial contests to commemorate his father* in the
most magnificent style. It is true that some of the expense of these
celebrations was shared with his colleague Marcus Bibulus,* and only
some came just out of Caesar's own pocket, [2] but his spending was
so lavish that he gained the glory of the rest too and was thought to
have taken on all the costs himself. Bibulus even used to joke about it,
saying that he was in the same position as Pollux, who shares a temple
with his brother Castor, but the temple is named after Castor alone.*

9. The Romans enjoyed these festivals, but portents occurred that
caused them a great deal of anxiety. On the Capitol, many statues of
men and gods were melted by thunderbolts, including one of Jupiter
which was set on a pillar; a statue group of a she-wolf along with
Remus and Romulus* fell down from its pedestal; [2] and the writing
on the tablets on which the laws were inscribed* melted and became
indistinct. On the advice of the *haruspices** they therefore performed
various sacrifices, and above all they voted to put up a larger statue of
Jupiter, facing east and towards the Forum, so that the conspiracies
which were the cause of the turmoil might be exposed.*

[3] These were the events of that year. In addition, the censors*
fell out over the question of the people who lived north of the
Po*—one of them thinking they should be admitted to citizenship,
the other not—and they resigned without having achieved anything
else either. [4] For this reason their successors* also did nothing the
following year, since the tribunes prevented them from drawing up
the list of senators because they were afraid of being expelled from
the Senate themselves.* [5] Also at that time* all those residing in
Rome who were not inhabitants of what is now Italy were expelled
from the city, on the proposal of a tribune called Gaius Papius, on the
grounds that there were too many of them and they were not suitable
co-inhabitants.*

10. In the following year, when Figulus and Lucius Caesar were in   64 BCE
office, little happened, but the little is worth recording because of
what it tells us about the unpredictable aspects of human life. [2] Largely
through the efforts of Julius Caesar,* the trial took place of the man
who had killed Lucretius on Sulla's orders,* and also of another man,
who had killed many of those who had been proscribed by Sulla,* and
they were both punished. [3] This just goes to show that men who
once wielded great power often lose it all when political circumstances
change. This affair turned out quite differently from what people had
expected, then, and they were no less surprised by the acquittal of
Catiline,* who was charged with the same crime as these two men,
since he too had killed many men who were similarly proscribed.
Moreover, after this he became far worse, and as a result ultimately
lost his life. [4] What happened was that, in the year when Marcus   63 BCE
Cicero was consul, with Gaius Antonius as his colleague,* at a time
when Mithridates was no longer a threat to Roman interests and in
fact had destroyed himself, Catiline tried to overthrow the government.
He recruited others for the attempt, and made the Romans terrified
by the prospect of a major war. I shall explain what happened with
both Mithridates and Catiline.*

11. So far from giving up in the face of his setbacks, Mithridates
took more account of his desires than his resources, and, emboldened
by Pompey's staying in Syria, was planning to march through Scythia
to the Danube, and from there to invade Italy.* [2] Mithridates was by
nature inclined to grand projects, and his considerable experience of
both failure and success had led him to believe that there was no
enterprise that he could not undertake and no goal that was out of his
reach. If he was to fail, he preferred to perish along with his kingdom,
with his pride intact, rather than lose his kingdom and live on in
humble obscurity. [3] He himself was confident that his plan would
succeed. The weaker and more feeble he became physically, the
stronger his determination grew, so that his mental power compensated for his bodily failings. [4] However, as the Romans' strength
increased and Mithridates' decreased—apart from anything else, the
worst earthquake they had ever experienced destroyed many of the
cities*—his associates began to drift away from him. The army was
restive and some of his children were kidnapped and taken to Pompey.

12. In some cases, Mithridates had conclusive proof of men's guilt
in this affair, and they were duly punished, but others were seized in

a pre-emptive strike dictated by his anger, just because he was suspicious of them. He no longer trusted anyone, and even killed some of his remaining children whose loyalty he doubted. Seeing this, Pharnaces, one of his sons, plotted against him; he was motivated not only by fear of his father, but also by the expectation that he would be given the kingdom by the Romans, now that he had come of age. [2] The plot was found out, however, because plenty of people were overtly or covertly concerning themselves with everything Pharnaces did, and he would have been punished on the spot if the palace guard had felt the slightest loyalty towards the old king. As things were, however, even though Mithridates was a very intelligent ruler in all other respects, he failed to understand that neither men-at-arms nor plenty of subjects are the slightest good to a person unless he has their affection. In fact, the more of them there are, the more they are a cause for anxiety, if he cannot trust them.

[3] At any rate, Pharnaces lost no time in setting out against his father, and he was accompanied not only by those he had previously recruited, but also by the men his father had sent to arrest him, whom he won over without the slightest difficulty. The old king was in Panticapaeum,* and when he found out what was going on he sent a few soldiers on ahead to deal with his son, intimating that he would be right behind them. [4] But Pharnaces quickly changed their minds, since they too had no love for Mithridates. Then the city voluntarily surrendered to him, and he killed his father, who had taken refuge in the palace.

13. Mithridates had tried to commit suicide. He first used poison to do away with his wives and remaining children, and then drank what was left, but neither poison nor sword brought him the death at his own hands that he sought. [2] The poison was deadly, but it failed to kill him because he had been strengthened by substantial daily doses of antidotes, taken as a precautionary measure;* and the arm which wielded the sword had been enfeebled by old age, the parlous state of his affairs, and the fact that he had taken the poison, such as it was. [3] He failed to die by his own hands, then, and since it looked as though he was going to linger for some time, the men he had sent against his son fell on him and sped him on his way with their swords and spears.* [4] So Mithridates, who had always experienced great and varied changes of fortune in life, met with a death that was not straightforward either. He desired death, but he did not want it; he

wanted to kill himself, but was unable to do so; and he was at one and the same time a suicide, by a combination of poison and sword, and a murder victim, killed by his enemies.

14. Pharnaces embalmed the body and sent it to Pompey as proof of what he had done, and surrendered himself and his kingdom. Pompey did not dishonour or desecrate the corpse in any way, and in fact it was on his orders that Mithridates was buried among the tombs of his ancestors.* In his opinion, the king's enmity had been extinguished along with his life, making it pointless for him to vent his anger on the corpse. [2] Nevertheless, he did grant the Bosporan Kingdom to Pharnaces, as the wages of his murder, and enrolled him among the friends and allies.* [3] After Mithridates' death, almost all his empire was subjugated. His garrisons still continued to hold some fortresses outside the Bosporus, without immediately coming to terms, but this was not so much because they were intending to offer Pompey any resistance, as because they were afraid that, if the money they were guarding was stolen, the thieves might lay the blame on them. They hung on, then, because they wanted to show Pompey himself that it was all there.

15. Once these regions were under control,* Phraates was keeping quiet, and Syria and Phoenicia had been settled, Pompey turned his attention to Aretas. He was the king of the Arabians—now subjects of Rome—who occupy the land up to the Red Sea.* Earlier, he had wreaked havoc on Syria and this had involved him in a battle with the Romans who were defending it. He lost the battle, but he was still at war.* [2] So Pompey marched against Aretas and his neighbours; they surrendered without offering any resistance, and Pompey put them under a garrison.*

Then he set out for Syria Palaestina,* because its inhabitants had ravaged Phoenicia. They were ruled by two brothers, Hyrcanus and Aristobulus,* and it so happened that they had fallen out and stirred up factional strife in the cities over the priesthood (as they call their kingship) of their god, whoever he may be. [3] Pompey therefore immediately gained the allegiance of Hyrcanus, who had no force of any strength and did not put up a fight, and he pinned Aristobulus in a fortress and forced him to come to terms. When Aristobulus failed to surrender either the money or the fortress, however, Pompey put him in chains.* After that it was easier for him to win over the rest of the people, but the siege of Jerusalem proved troublesome.

16. The rest of the city fell to him without any trouble, when Hyrcanus' supporters let him in, but Aristobulus' men had occupied the temple itself and it was a struggle to take it, [2] since it was situated on a hill and had its own defensive wall. If the defenders had resisted equally well every day, Pompey would never have taken it. But in fact, because they took a break every Saturn-day, as it is called, when they undertook no activity whatsoever, it became possible for the Romans to take advantage of this lapse and batter down the wall. [3] What happened was that when the Romans found out about this devotional practice of theirs, they put no effort into their attempts the rest of the time, but whenever those days came around they attacked with maximum force.* [4] So the defenders were captured one Saturn-day* without even putting up a fight, and all their wealth was plundered.* The kingship was given to Hyrcanus, and Aristobulus was taken away to captivity.*

[5] So much for events in Palestine in this year. The name 'Palestine' has been given since ancient times to the whole region extending along the coast from Phoenicia to Egypt, but it has another name as well, a more recent acquisition: it is called Judaea, and the people are known as Jews.* **17.** I have no idea what the origin of this name is, but it is also used for everyone else who follows their customs, even those of a different ethnicity. There are also Jews living among the Romans* and, although they have often been repressed, they have made great progress and have even won the right to practise their form of worship openly.

[2] The Jewish way of life is different from that of the rest of mankind in almost every respect, and especially because they do not worship any of the other gods, but passionately revere just one god. There is no statue of him at all, even in Jerusalem, and never has been; they believe that he is unnameable and formless, and so they worship him in the most extraordinary fashion. [3] They made an enormous temple for him, which was exceptionally beautiful, except that it was open and roofless,* and they dedicated to him the day known as Saturn-day. And on that day, besides many other distinctive observances, they engage in no work of any importance.

[4] Anyway, as far as their god is concerned, there are plenty of accounts available of who he is and how he came to be worshipped in this way, and why the Jews feel such devotion to him, and in any case such an account has no relevance to this history of mine. **18.** But the

custom of assigning days to the seven heavenly bodies known as planets* was instigated by the Egyptians,* and has spread all over the world, although this is a quite recent development. At any rate, no ancient Greeks anywhere knew of the system, as far as I am aware. [2] But since it is now a firm custom everywhere, including in Rome, and is in a sense already even an ancestral tradition, I would like to say a few words about it—about the system that it follows and the principles of its organization.

I have heard two explanations, neither of which is particularly difficult to follow, although there is some theory involved in both of them. [3] Suppose one were to bring in what is called the tetrachord* (which is held to constitute the foundation of all music), and apply it to the heavenly bodies which are spaced at intervals throughout the entire cosmos, following the order of each of their orbits. Now, begin with the most remote orbit, the one which is assigned to Saturn, [4] and then, omitting the next two, name the master of the fourth, and then pass over two more and arrive at the seventh. Next, continuing to employ the same procedure of omitting two, carry on cycling around through them, and apply the names of their presiding deities to the days. If one does this, one finds that all the days bear a relationship that one could call musical to the structure of the heavens.*

19. That is one of the explanations, and the second is as follows. Starting with the first hour, count the hours of the day and the night, and assign the first hour to Saturn, the second to Jupiter, the third to Mars, the fourth to the Sun, the fifth to Venus, the sixth to Mercury, and the seventh to the Moon [2] (that is, following the order of the orbits which the Egyptians observe). Repeat the process until you have in this way covered all twenty-four hours, and you will find that the first hour of the following day falls to the Sun. [3] If you then do the same for the twenty-four hours of the new day, following the same principle as before, you will find that the first hour of the third day belongs to the Moon, and if you carry on and do the same for the rest of the days, each day will receive its appropriate god. Anyway, these are the two explanations that have come down to us.

20. After the achievements narrated above,* Pompey returned to Pontus, and, once he had received the surrender of the fortresses* there, he went back via Asia and Greece to Italy. [2] He had won many battles, gained the allegiance of many dynasts and kings by either war or diplomacy, founded eight cities,* acquired much land* and revenue* for the Romans, and established and organized most of the peoples of the continent of Asia who were then subject to Rome under their own laws and constitutions. In fact, even today they use the regulations that were established by him.*

[3] Now, although these were important achievements, which eclipsed those of any earlier Roman, they might be ascribed to Fortune and those who served under him. There was one thing he did, however, that was certainly all his own; it deserves to be admired for ever, and I shall now give an account of it.* [4] He had unrivalled strength both at sea and on land; he had huge wealth at his disposal from booty; he counted numerous dynasts and kings among his friends; his benefactions had assured him the goodwill of almost all the inhabitants of the regions where he held sway.* [5] He could have used all this to make himself master of Italy and to take for himself complete power over the Romans, since he would have met little opposition, and any men who did resist him would be too weak to do anything but come to terms. But he refused to do this. [6] Instead, as soon as he reached Brundisium,* he dismissed all his forces on his own initiative, without any vote on the matter from either the Senate or the people, and without concern even for having his troops take part in his triumph. He understood the hatred that Marius and Sulla had aroused in people,* and he did not want make them afraid, even for a few days, that the same kind of thing might happen again.

21. He did not take any new name, although there were many to which he would have been entitled by his achievements.* As for his triumph* (it was, I need hardly say, the kind regarded as greater*), although it was not sanctioned by strict tradition for a triumph to be celebrated by anyone without the troops who had shared in his victory,* it was still decreed, and he accepted it. [2] The triumph was held in honour of all his wars at once,* and a great many beautifully decorated trophies were on display, one for each of his achievements, even the slightest. Right at the end of the parade came a majestic trophy, fabulously decorated, with an inscription saying that it was for victory over the inhabited world.* [3] Nevertheless, he awarded himself no additional name, but was content with just 'Magnus', which, of course, he had in fact gained earlier, before these successes.* Nor did he push for any other extravagant distinction, and he only once made use of the honour which had been voted to him in his absence. [4] This was the right, granted in perpetuity, to wear a laurel wreath

at all the games, and also the right to wear a *toga praetexta* at all the games and the triumphal toga at the chariot-races.* These privileges were granted to him thanks above all to the support of Caesar, and despite the objections of Marcus Cato.*

22. I have already introduced Caesar.* I said that he was courting the favour of the masses, and that, while he basically wanted to see Pompey destroyed, he was trying to win his friendship in ways by which he could simultaneously please the general populace and increase his own power. As for Cato,* he belonged to the family of the Porcii and modelled himself on the great Cato,* except that he had had more exposure to Greek culture.* [2] He took great care to defend the interests of the common people and was supremely devoted to the public good,* rather than admiring any one man in particular. His suspicion of sole power was such that he hated everything that raised a man above his fellows, and he felt for every member of the commons out of pity for their weakness. [3] More than anyone else, he became the people's friend,* and he used to speak with frankness against injustice even when it was dangerous to do so. What is more, in all this he was motivated not by any desire for power or glory or political office, but only because he wanted to live a life that was free, without there being a tyrant set over him. [4] This was the man who now put himself forward for the first time to argue against the proposal, not out of any hostility towards Pompey, but because there was no precedent.*

23. So the people awarded Pompey these privileges while he was still abroad, but no further honours on his return, even though they would have added more if he had wished it. At any rate, they often voted extravagant honours for men whose power was inferior to his, though it is clear that they did so unwillingly. [2] Pompey was well aware that, in regimes based on personal power,* every honour voted by the people for those who are strong carries with it the implication—even if the vote is freely undertaken—that it is being granted under compulsion, at the instigation of the powerful. He knew that such honours bring no glory to those who accept them, since they are awarded by reluctant people acting under compulsion, and are due to their desire to flatter him rather than their thinking well of him. And so he absolutely forbade anyone from making any such proposals at all, [3] declaring that this was a far better way of going about it than refusing honours that had already been voted on. After all, he used to

say, the latter arouses hatred for the power which prompted the proposal in the first place, and it smacks of overweening arrogance to refuse an offer from people who are certainly your superiors or at least your equals. The other option, however, shows that a man is truly democratic* in action as well as in words—genuinely and not merely for show. [4] In other words, after having been given almost every magistracy and command contrary to precedent,* he was unwilling to accept others, since they would benefit neither him nor anyone else, and would just bring him jealousy and hatred, even from those who were awarding them.*

24. These events took place later, but then,* for the remainder of the year the Romans enjoyed a respite from war, and even held the *augurium salutis* for the first time after many years.* This is a divinatory procedure which involves asking whether the god will allow them to pray for the safety of the people, as though it were wrong to ask for such a thing without the god's permission. [2] The rite was performed every year on a day when no legion marched out to war, or was deployed against an enemy, or fought a battle. Hence, at a time of continuous fighting, and especially during civil wars, the rite was not performed, because of the virtual impossibility of finding a day that was free of all such troubles. [3] Besides, it would have been utterly ridiculous for them deliberately to harm one another in countless ways in the course of their disputes—after all, win or lose, they would be worse off—and then to ask divinity for safety.

25. Anyway, it was possible for the augury to be carried out at this time, but the outcome was faulty, because some birds flew overhead from an inauspicious direction, which meant that the augury had to be taken again. There were other unlucky portents too. [2] Many thunderbolts fell from a clear sky, there was a powerful earthquake, ghosts were seen in a number of places, lights* blazed up into the sky from the west. The significance of these portents was clear to everyone, even a layman. [3] For the tribunes* had enlisted the help of the consul Antonius,* whose character was very like theirs, and one of them was giving access to office to the sons of those who had been exiled by Sulla,* while another was trying to give the right to be members of the Senate and to hold office to Publius Paetus and to Cornelius Sulla,* who had been convicted along with him. [4] Yet another was proposing the cancellation of debts,* and another the distribution of land in Italy and in subject territory abroad.*

These proposals were thwarted before they came to anything by Cicero and others who were of the same persuasion as him, **26.** but Titus Labienus* threw the city into considerable chaos by indicting Gaius Rabirius for the murder of Saturninus.* Saturninus had died some thirty-six years earlier, and the consuls of the time had been authorized by the Senate to deal with him by force of arms. The trial would thus deprive the Senate's decrees of their validity, [2] and as a result the whole political order was threatened with collapse.* Rabirius denied that he was the murderer and said that he had nothing to do with it. However, the tribunes' object was to destroy completely the power and the prestige of the Senate, and they were trying to gain for themselves the ability to do whatever they wanted. [3] Scrutinizing the Senate's decrees and the actions that had been carried out so many years earlier would effectively make it permissible for anyone who wanted to imitate Saturninus to go ahead, and virtually impossible for anyone who did so to be punished. The Senate thought it outrageous in any case that a man of senatorial rank should be put to death when he had done nothing wrong and was now elderly, but they were far more incensed by the fact that the dignity of the constitution was under attack and because the state was being put into the hands of the worst kind of men.

27. The case provoked turbulent outbursts of fervour and altercations between the two sides, the one arguing that the trial should not take place, the other that the jurors should be convened. When, thanks to Caesar* and some others, the latter position won, there was further conflict over what kind of trial it should be. [2] Caesar judged the case in person, along with Lucius Caesar,* because the charge against Rabirius was an unusual one, which is called *perduellio.** They found him guilty, even though they had been chosen not by the people, as was traditional, but by the praetor, who did not have the right to do so. [3] Rabirius appealed,* and would certainly have been found guilty by the people as well, if Metellus Celer,* who was an augur and a praetor, had not stopped them. What happened was that, since he could not get them to listen to his advice in any other way, and they refused to take into account the illegal nature of the trial, he ran up to the Janiculum* before they could vote and pulled down the military flag, which meant that it was no longer lawful for them to give judgement.

28. This matter of the flag is as follows. Long ago, the Romans had many enemies living nearby, and they were afraid that, while they held an assembly by centuries,* some of their enemies might occupy the Janiculum and attack the city. They therefore decided that they should not all vote at once, but that there should always be some men under arms guarding the Janiculum in relays. [2] So they used to mount a guard there whenever an assembly was going on, and when it was time for the assembly to be dissolved, the flag was pulled down and the guards were dismissed, the point being that it was not lawful for any further business to be conducted unless the Janiculum was guarded. [3] This practice was observed only for centuriate assemblies, because they were held outside the city wall and because everyone who bore arms was obliged to attend them. Even today, the practice is still observed as a formality. [4] So, on the occasion in question, when the flag was lowered, the assembly was dissolved and Rabirius was saved. It is true that Labienus could have taken him to court again, but he chose not to.

29. Catiline's downfall* came about as follows and for the following reasons. Since he was standing again for the consulship this year, and doing everything he could to ensure that he got elected, the Senate decided, at the instigation of Cicero above all, that a law should be passed adding ten years of exile to the penalties for bribery.* [2] Realizing the truth, that this decree had been passed on his account, Catiline equipped himself with a body of men and determined to murder Cicero and some of the other leading men during the actual elections.* The idea was that he would then immediately be elected consul, but he was unable to bring it off. [3] Cicero got wind of the plot, informed the Senate about it, and roundly accused Catiline. But the senators found what Cicero was telling them unbelievable and thought that he was lying because of his hostility towards the men, so they did not follow his advice and vote for any of the measures he requested. This made Cicero afraid, seeing that he had given Catiline even more reason to be angry with him, [4] and he did not dare to enter the popular assembly in his habitual fashion, just as he was. Instead, he took with him some of his friends, who were ready to defend him in case of danger, and he wore a breastplate, partly for his own safety and partly to arouse prejudice against the conspirators, because he wore it under his clothes but deliberately let it be seen. [5] This, combined with the fact that there was in any case a rumour going around about his plotting against Cicero, made the people furious, and Catiline's fellow conspirators were too afraid of Cicero to do anything.

30. So others were chosen as consuls.* Catiline's plot was no longer a secret, and his target was now not just Cicero and his associates, but the whole community.* [2] By assuring them of the cancellation of debts and the redistribution of land,* and by making other promises of the kind that would be especially attractive to them, he gathered from Rome itself men of the worst sort, the kind who are always ready for revolution, and he also collected as large a force as he could from the allies.* [3] He prevailed upon the leading and most powerful men among the conspirators (who included Antonius, the consul*) to swear an obscene oath. He sacrificed a slave, and after having the oath sworn over the entrails, he and his fellow conspirators ate them. [4] His main collaborators were, in Rome, the consul and Publius Lentulus,* who had been thrown out of the Senate after his consulship and was currently serving as a praetor in order to regain his seat there; and, in Faesulae,* where his supporters were mustering, [5] Gaius Manlius, who had wide experience of warfare, since he had been a centurion under Sulla. He was also a thorough wastrel. At any rate, he had spent all the substantial wealth he had acquired then on immoral practices, and now he wanted more.

31. They were still making their preparations when information reached Cicero.* The first report he received was about what was happening in the city. This information was contained in certain anonymously written letters, which were given to Crassus and some of the other leading men. In view of this information, a decree was passed declaring a state of emergency* and authorizing the tracking-down of those responsible. [2] Next he received news from Etruria, and the Senate further voted to entrust the consuls with the protection of the city and all its affairs, in the customary form of an instruction to ensure that no harm came to the city.* [3] After these measures had been passed and guard forces had been stationed at many points, signs of revolution in the city died down to nothing, and in fact Cicero was even accused of making an unwarranted allegation, but further information from Etruria* confirmed the allegations and led to Catiline's being indicted for violence.

32. At first, Catiline made a big show of how welcome the indictment was to him, as though his conscience were clear. He made it seem as though he were preparing for the trial, and offered to put himself in Cicero's hands, so that Cicero could keep an eye on him and prevent him from escaping; [2] and when Cicero refused to be his gaoler, he voluntarily took up residence in the house of the praetor Metellus.* This was a ploy to make it less likely that people would think him subversive, while he waited for his fellow conspirators in Rome to strengthen his position. [3] But things did not go according to plan: Antonius hung back in fear, and Lentulus was the last person to do anything on his own initiative. So Catiline told the conspirators to gather at night in a certain house* and, escaping Metellus' vigilance, he went there and told them off for their cowardice and weakness. [4] Then he went through all the various ways in which they would suffer if they were found out, and all they would gain if they were successful. This not only raised their morale, but stirred them up to such an extent that two of them promised to break into Cicero's house at daybreak and murder him.

33. But information leaked out about this too, because Cicero was a man of great influence; his speeches had won him many friends, and made many others fear him, so there were plenty of people to pass this kind of information on to him,* and the Senate voted that Catiline should depart from Rome.* [2] He was delighted to have an excuse to leave, and he went to Faesulae and engaged openly in the war. He assumed the title and insignia of the consuls, and proceeded to organize the men who had previously been collected by Manlius, as well as recruiting others in the meantime—free men first, but then also slaves.* [3] The Romans consequently found him guilty of violence,* and they entrusted the war to Antonius, since they did not know that he was a member of the conspiracy. Meanwhile, they changed their dress.*

These developments meant that Cicero too stayed where he was. [4] He had been assigned the governorship of Macedonia by lot, but he did not go either to that province, from which he had stepped down in favour of his colleague, because he wanted to focus on the courts,* or to Cisalpine Gaul, which he had accepted in its place because of the current crisis. Instead, he made himself personally responsible for the protection of the city, and sent Metellus to Gaul to make sure that Catiline did not take it over.*

34. It was extremely fortunate for Rome that Cicero stayed behind, because Lentulus was getting ready to set fires and commit murder,* with the help not just of his fellow conspirators, but also the Allobroges, who were there on an embassy and were persuaded to join him.* [2] [. . .]* and after arresting those who had been sent for this purpose,

he brought them into the senate-house with the letters, and by offering them immunity exposed the whole conspiracy.* Lentulus was
consequently forced by the Senate to resign from his praetorship, and
was kept under guard along with the others arrested, while a search
was conducted for the rest.* [3] The people were just as pleased about
this* as the senators, and they were especially delighted by the fact
that, during Cicero's speech about the conspiracy,* the statue of
Jupiter was being set up on the Capitol—at the exact same time that
the assembly was taking place!—and, moreover, on the advice of the
haruspices, it was set up facing east, towards the Forum. [4] The *haruspices* had said that a conspiracy would be exposed as a result of this
placement of the statue, and when its erection coincided with the discovery of the conspirators, the people sang the praises of divinity and
expressed even more anger with those who were implicated.

35. Word went around that Crassus too was one of the conspirators, and one of the men who had been arrested gave this information as well, but it was not widely believed.* Some did not think
he deserved to be an object of suspicion in the slightest; [2] others
thought that the story had been made up by the accused as a way of
getting Crassus to use his great power to help them. And if some
people did find the rumour believable, they still did not think it right
to ruin one of the foremost men of Rome and throw the city into further chaos. [3] In the end, then, the allegation had no consequences
whatsoever.

Now, a large number of men, both slaves and free, motivated by
either fear of or pity for Lentulus and the others, were planning to
steal them away and save them from death, but Cicero got wind of the
scheme and had an armed guard occupy both the Capitol and the
Forum at night. [4] At dawn, divinity gave him cause for optimism,
when, in the course of the rites carried out in his house* on behalf of
the Roman people by the Vestal Virgins, the flames leapt up to an
unusually great height. He therefore told the praetors to administer
the oath of enrolment to the people, in case there was any need for
soldiers, while he convened the Senate.* And by stirring them up and
making them afraid, he persuaded the senators to condemn to death
those who had been arrested.*

36. They were not entirely wholehearted, however, and they came
close to releasing the conspirators. It was Caesar's doing.* Everyone
before him had voted that they should be put to death, but he argued

that they should be imprisoned and their property confiscated, [2] and that then they should be placed for safekeeping, some here and some there in towns throughout Italy, on the understanding that there should never be any discussion in the future about pardoning them, and that if any of them escaped, the city from which he absconded should be considered an enemy. Everyone who expressed an opinion after this voted for Caesar's proposal,* and in fact even some of those who had already voted for death changed their minds. But then it was Cato's turn,* [3] and his pronouncing for their execution caused all the rest to do the same.

Not only were the conspirators punished,* then, as a result of this majority vote, but it was also decreed that a sacrifice and a festival* should be held for this, which had never happened before under such circumstances. Others who had been named by informants were being tracked down, and some people were called to account just because they were suspected of being potential conspirators. [4] In the other cases, it was the consuls who carried this out, but a senator called Aulus Fulvius* was killed by his own father. But he was not the only one to do so as a private citizen, as some suppose: many others, private citizens as well as consuls, killed their own sons.*

37. That was the situation then, and on the proposal of Labienus, supported by Caesar, the people once again transferred the election of priests to the popular assembly, which contravened the law of Sulla but was a renewal of the law of Domitius.* Caesar supported Labienus because Metellus Pius* had died and Caesar wanted his priesthood, even though he was young and had not yet held the praetorship. [2] His best hope of gaining the priesthood lay with the masses, especially because he had supported Labienus against Rabirius and had not voted for Lentulus' death,* and he did indeed succeed at this: he was elected Pontifex Maximus, even though many others, not least Catulus, were also candidates for the position.* [3] Caesar proved very ready to flatter and pay court to anyone and everyone, even a person of no distinction; there was nothing he would not say or do in order to get what he wanted. He had no qualms about abasing himself in the short term if it would lead to power in the long term, and the very men he was trying to surpass he treated as his superiors by fawning on them.*

38. Caesar was therefore very popular with the commons, but they were angry with Cicero over the deaths of their fellow citizens.* They

showed their hostility towards him in a number of ways, and finally, on the last day of his term of office, when he was ready to justify and enumerate all the things he had done as consul [2]—he enjoyed singing his own praises almost as much as he enjoyed being praised by others—they made him keep quiet and, with the help of the tribune Metellus Nepos,* forbade him from saying anything apart from the oath. Nevertheless, Cicero managed to retaliate at least to the extent of adding to his oath the claim that he had saved the city, but this only served to make him far more unpopular.*

39. Catiline met his death early in the year in which Junius Silanus   62 BCE
and Lucius Licinius held office.* Although he had a substantial force, he waited for a while to see how Lentulus got on; in other words, he held back in the hope that Cicero and his supporters might be slaughtered first, in which case he would easily see all his other projects to fruition. [2] But then he found out that Lentulus was dead and realized that this was causing many of his fellow conspirators to desert. Since, moreover, Antonius and Metellus Celer were in position near Faesulae and were preventing him from moving,* he had no choice but to risk a battle. Seeing that the two consuls had made separate camps, he launched a strike against Antonius, despite the fact that he was of a higher rank than Metellus and had been assigned a larger force. [3] He chose Antonius because he hoped that, because of his involvement in the conspiracy, he would not put up a fight. But Antonius suspected that this might be the case, and no longer felt any loyalty towards Catiline now that he was weak; after all, friendships and enmities are usually formed with an eye on the others' strengths and one's own advantage. [4] Antonius was afraid, however, that when Catiline saw them fighting with determination, he would curse him and give him away, so, claiming to be ill, he entrusted the battle to Marcus Petreius.*

40. When Petreius joined battle with the insurgents, he cut down Catiline and three thousand others. The terrible loss of life was due to the fact that the rebels fought with great determination. None of them turned tail, all of them fell where they had taken their stand, and in the end even the victors mourned for the nation, because they had taken the lives of so many men of calibre, who may have deserved their fate, but were still fellow citizens and allies. [2] Antonius sent Catiline's head to Rome, so that people could stop being afraid once they knew for sure that he was dead, and was acclaimed *imperator* for his victory, even though the number of dead was less than the officially required total.* Sacrifices* were ordained by decree and everyone changed back into their ordinary clothes* to mark their final deliverance from danger.

41. However, the allies* who had shared in Catiline's undertaking and were still alive were not at peace; their fear of retribution was making them restive. But the praetors who were sent to deal with them caught them off guard while they were still rather scattered and punished them.* [2] Lucius Vettius,* an *eques* who had been a member of the conspiracy but had turned informant in exchange for immunity, had disclosed the names of further conspirators who had remained undetected, and they were being interrogated and punished. At one point, however, after he had accused certain men and had written their names on a tablet, he subsequently wanted to add many more. [3] The senators suspected that he was up to no good and refused to give him back the document in case he erased some of the names. They ordered him to tell them the names of those he was claiming to have left out, without writing them down, and then in shame and fear he denounced no more than a few people. [4] Even so, there was unrest in the city and among the allies because they had no idea who was being denounced. With some needlessly troubled about themselves and others harbouring incorrect suspicions of their neighbours, the Senate decided to publish the list of names. This brought relief to the innocent, while those who were incriminated were put on trial and condemned,* whether they appeared for the hearing or chose not to defend it.

42. So that is what Catiline did and how he fell. He is better known than his accomplishments deserved, owing to Cicero's fame and the speeches he delivered against him. Cicero, however, came close to being taken straight to court for the killing of Lentulus and the other prisoners. [2] In actual fact, although the charge was apparently being levelled against him, its real target was the Senate. Since the senators did not have the right to condemn any citizen to death without the consent of the people,* they were excoriated in the popular assembly, especially by Metellus Nepos.* [3] But Cicero got off scot-free on this occasion, because the Senate granted immunity to everyone who had been in charge at the time, and also declared that anyone who in the future scrutinized their behaviour would be treated as a traitor and an enemy.* This frightened Nepos and he made no further trouble.

43. The Senate prevailed, then, in this case, and also when Nepos proposed that Pompey, who was still in Asia, should be asked to come with his army.* His ostensible reason for making the proposal was for Pompey to stabilize the situation, but in fact Nepos hoped that with Pompey's support, because Pompey favoured the plebs, he would gain in power during the unrest he was stirring up. In any case, the senators blocked the proposal. [2] First, Cato and Quintus Minucius, who were tribunes, spoke against the proposal and told the scribe who was reading it out to desist;* then, when Nepos took up the document to read it himself, they snatched it out of his hands; and finally, when he persisted in trying to recite it from memory, they stopped his mouth. [3] At this, they and others who joined in on either side fell to brawling, with sticks, stones, and even swords as weapons, and the senators convened for a meeting that very day, changed out of their usual clothes,* and instructed the consuls to protect the city and see that it came to no harm.* [4] Nepos, afraid once more, immediately put an end to his public appearances and subsequently, after he had published a pamphlet denouncing the Senate,* he took himself off to Pompey, even though it was illegal for him to be out of the city for a single night.*

44. After all this, even Caesar, who was a praetor this year, stopped trying to challenge the status quo. He had been pushing for Catulus' name to be removed from the temple of Jupiter Capitolinus, since he was accusing him of embezzlement and demanding to see the accounts, and for Pompey to be entrusted with the completion of the work.* [2] Given the size and nature of the structure, it was in certain respects unfinished—or so Caesar was making out, anyway, so that Pompey would gain the glory of completing it and inscribe his own name in place of Catulus'. However, Caesar was not so keen on gratifying Pompey that he was prepared to have the same kind of decree voted against him as against Nepos.* After all, he had not really been acting on Pompey's behalf at all; he wanted to use this proposal to win the allegiance of the plebs for himself.* [3] But everyone was so afraid of Pompey (who had not yet made it clear whether or not he would disband his legions) that when he sent one of his legates, Marcus Piso,* to Rome as a candidate for the consulship, they postponed the voting so that he could be there for it* and elected him unanimously when he arrived—unanimously, because Pompey had recommended Piso to his enemies as well as his friends.

45. Meanwhile, Caesar brought no charge against Publius Clodius when he besmirched the honour of his wife in Caesar's own home, during the performance of the rites which by tradition the Vestal Virgins carry out in the homes of the consuls and praetors, segregated from any male presence.* Caesar acted in this way because he was sure that Clodius' friends would secure his acquittal, [2] but he divorced his wife, explaining that although he did not really believe the rumour, he still could not live with her any more, as long as there was the slightest suspicion that she had committed adultery. A modest wife, he argued, should not only not do wrong, but should not even attract any suspicion of dishonourable conduct.* [3] And another event occurring then was the construction over to the small island in the Tiber of the stone bridge called the Fabrician.*

61 BCE   **46.** The next year, when Piso and Marcus Messalla* were consuls, the leading men brought Clodius to trial.* They did this not just because of their fundamental loathing of him, but also because they wanted to expiate the pollution caused by his act, given that the pontiffs had ruled that as a result the rites had not been properly performed and should be repeated.* [2] He was charged both with the adultery, despite Caesar's silence, and with the mutiny at Nisibis—and, in addition, with having sexual relations with his sister.* Even though the jurors asked the Senate for an armed guard to make sure that they came to no harm at his hands, and were given it, he was acquitted. [3] This provoked Catulus to quip that they had asked for the guard not so that they could safely condemn Clodius, but so that they could keep safe the money that they had accepted as bribes.* Catulus died not long after this; there had never been a man who more transparently made the common good his absolute and unwavering priority.*

[4] In this year, the censors* enrolled everyone who had held office into the Senate, making it exceed the maximum number,* and the people, who up until then had watched gladiatorial contests without a break, went outside in the course of the show to take lunch. This practice, which began then, is still in use whenever the emperor puts on the show.*

47. So much for what was happening in Rome. Meanwhile, the Allobroges* were wreaking havoc in Narbonese Gaul. The governor of the province, Gaius Pomptinus,* sent his legates to confront the enemy, while he took up a position that made it possible for him to keep an eye on what was happening so that he could provide them with whatever help they needed in the way of timely advice and reinforcements. [2] Manlius Lentinus marched against the town of Ventia and terrified the inhabitants so thoroughly that most of them ran away and the rest sent a delegation to sue for peace—but just then the country population arrived to help the townspeople. They took Lentinus by surprise, and he was driven back from the fortress, but he continued to plunder the farmland [3] until Catugnatus, the commander in chief of the Allobroges, came with more troops, including men from other tribes that lived on the banks of the Isère. At first, Lentinus did not dare to prevent their passage across the river; there were too many of their boats, and he did not want them to concentrate their forces at the sight of the Romans drawn up for battle against them. [4] But since the place was wooded right down to the riverside, he laid ambushes among the trees, and intercepted and killed the men as they landed. While chasing down some fugitives, however, he encountered Catugnatus himself, and he and all the men with him would have been killed if a violent storm had not suddenly arisen and prevented the barbarians from pursuing them.

48. Later, after Catugnatus had pulled back some considerable distance, Lentinus again overran the countryside, and he succeeded in taking the fortress where he had earlier been repulsed. Lucius Marius and Servius Galba crossed the Rhône, and after ravaging Allobrogian territory they ended up at the town of Solonium [2] and occupied a strongpoint overlooking the town. They inflicted a defeat on the enemy and set fire to some areas of the town, which was made partly of wood, but they failed to take it because Catugnatus arrived and stopped them. When Pomptinus found out about this, he brought his entire army against the town, took it by siege, and made prisoners of the inhabitants, although Catugnatus escaped. After that, it was relatively easy for Pomptinus to subdue the rest of the territory.

49. During this time, Pompey arrived in Italy* and got Lucius 60 BCE Afranius and Metellus Celer elected consuls,* because he vainly hoped to use them to gain all his objectives. [2] In particular, he wanted his veterans to be given land, and all the arrangements he had made to be ratified. But his hopes in this regard came to nothing at this time because the leading men, who were already displeased with him, prevented the motions from being put to the vote. [3] As for the consuls, Afranius, a better dancer than dealmaker, was no help to him at all, and Metellus was angry with him for having divorced his sister, even though she had borne him children, and worked hard to thwart all his designs. [4] Moreover, Lucius Lucullus, whom Pompey had treated disdainfully once when they met in Galatia,* was a determined adversary, and insisted that he give a separate, detailed account of every single thing he had done, and not ask for the simultaneous acceptance of them all. [5] In any case, he said, it was not right for all his measures—which no one in Rome had had a chance to assess—to be confirmed just like that, as though they were the acts of a despot.* And since Pompey had cancelled some of Lucullus' own measures, Lucullus demanded that his own measures should be examined in the Senate as well as Pompey's, and that they should ratify whichever of them they preferred.

50. Lucullus was strongly supported by Cato, Metellus, and everyone else who held the same views.* At any rate, when the tribune who proposed that land be assigned to those who had served with Pompey added a rider to the effect that allotments should be given to all Roman citizens as well*—an addition that was designed to make them more likely to vote for the proposal and confirm all Pompey's measures—Metellus did all he could to resist and attack him. Eventually, the tribune had him thrown in the prison,* and Metellus wanted the Senate to meet there. [2] When the tribune (Lucius Flavius was his name) placed the tribunes' bench* at the very entrance of the prison and sat there, making it impossible for anyone to enter, Metellus ordered the prison wall to be breached so that the Senate could gain access that way, and he got ready to spend the night where he was. [3] When Pompey found out, he was ashamed—as well as afraid that the people might disapprove—and he ordered Flavius to move. He claimed that the request came from Metellus, but this struck people as unlikely because Metellus' stubborn pride was well known by everyone. [4] And, indeed, when the other tribunes offered to set him free, he refused. Nor did he give in later, when Flavius threatened to prevent his departure for the province which he had been assigned unless he agreed to allow the law to be passed. In fact, staying in Rome was exactly what he wanted to do.*

[5] Metellus and his allies had successfully frustrated Pompey's plans, and Pompey responded by declaring that they were jealous of him and that he would prove this to the plebs. But since he was afraid of incurring still greater shame if he failed at this too, he dropped his demands. [6] So he was brought to the realization that he did not have

real power, but only the title and jealousy that his former power had earned him, which did him no good at all, and he regretted having dismissed his legions so soon* and having delivered himself into the hands of his enemies.

51. Following his trial, Clodius conceived a desire to become a tribune on account of the leading men,* and he urged some of the current tribunes to propose that the office should be opened to patricians as well as plebeians. When they did not do as he wanted,* he forswore his patrician birth and, entering the assembly of the plebs, transferred to plebeian status.* [2] He immediately put himself forward as a candidate for the tribunate, but Metellus, who was related to him and disapproved of what he was doing, made sure that he was not elected.* He used as his pretext that Clodius' change of status had not taken place in the traditional manner, because the only permitted method was the introduction of a *lex curiata*.* [3] That was how this episode ended.

Since Rome and the rest of Italy were bitterly resenting the customs duties,* the law which brought them to an end was universally welcomed, but the senators were annoyed with the praetor who introduced the proposal—it was Metellus Nepos*—and wanted to erase his name from the law and replace it with someone else's. [4] This did not happen, but everyone came to understand that the senators found even benefactions unwelcome when they came from worthless men. Also at the same time* Faustus, Sulla's son, held gladiatorial contests in honour of his father,* put on a magnificent banquet for the people, and provided them with bathing facilities and oil for free.

52. While these things were going on in Rome, Caesar had taken up the governorship of Lusitania after his praetorship.* He could without much effort have cleared the country of brigands—brigandage being a constant menace there—and then stayed quiet, but that was not to his liking. His goal was glory, in rivalry with Pompey and all the others before him who had ever wielded great power, and he had ambitious plans for the future. [2] He was hoping, in fact, to gain some significant achievement there, on the strength of which he would immediately be elected consul and do extraordinary things.* He was motivated especially by the fact that when he was in Gades (he had been a quaestor at the time),* he had dreamt that he was having sex with his mother, and the diviners had given him to understand that he would hold great power.* That was why the sight of a statue of

Alexander the Great in the temple of Hercules there moved him
to groan out loud and bemoan the fact that as yet he had no great
achievement to his name.*

[3] Hence, although, as I have said, he could have lived a life of
peace, he went to the Herminian Mountains* and ordered the inhabitants to move down to the plain. His pretext was to stop them using
these heights as a base from which to conduct plundering raids, but
in fact he knew perfectly well that they would never obey his command, and then he would have an excuse to make war on them.*
[4] That is exactly what happened, and once they had taken up arms,
he conquered them. And when some of their neighbours, frightened
that he would next turn against them, moved their families and their
other valuables to a place of safety on the far side of the Douro, he
stole a march on them while they were busy making these arrangements, occupied their cities, and then joined battle with them. [5] The
barbarians protected their front with their herds, with the intention
of attacking the Romans when they had lost formation and turned
to stealing the cattle; but Caesar ignored the animals, targeted the
soldiers, and defeated them.

53. At this point, Caesar learnt that the inhabitants of the Herminian
Mountains had rebelled and were planning to ambush him as he was
returning. He therefore took another way back and then marched
against them later; he defeated them and harried the fugitives all
the way to the Ocean. [2] When they abandoned the mainland and
crossed over to an island, shortage of vessels forced him to stay
where he was, but he built rafts and used them to send some of his
forces to the island—an action which cost him a lot of men. What
happened was that the commander of this detachment moored at
some land† near the island and had his men disembark, so as to
cross over by foot, but then he was forced off by the rising tide and
he had to put to sea, abandoning his men. [3] They put up a brave
fight, but all of them were killed except for Publius Scaevius, the only
survivor. After losing his shield and taking many wounds, he leapt
into the water and swam to safety.* [4] That was the outcome of
this phase of the operation, but later Caesar crossed over to the
island with his entire army on ships which he had sent for from
Gades, and overcame them without having to fight, because shortage of food had left them in a bad way. Then he sailed to Brigantium,
a town in Callaecia, where the inhabitants, who had never seen a fleet

before, were terrified by the roar of its approach and were easily subjugated.*

54. After these successes, Caesar thought that he had enough of a foundation for the consulship, and he hurried off to the elections even though his successor had not yet arrived in the province. He sought permission to stand for the office even before he had celebrated his triumph, since it was impossible to hold the ceremony beforehand.* [2] And when this was refused, thanks largely to Cato's opposition,* he abandoned the triumph, because, if he were elected consul, he was expecting that to lead to far more and far greater achievements, and far more glorious triumphs. In addition to the omen I have already mentioned, which led him constantly to entertain great ambitions, a horse was born in his stables with clefts in both front hoofs, and while it bore him with its head held high, it refused any other rider.* [3] This too gave him high hopes for the future, so that he did not hesitate to let the triumph go, and he entered the city and canvassed for election. He courted a number of men, not least Pompey and Crassus, so successfully that although they were still at odds with one another at the time, although they had their rival factions, and although each of them opposed everything he saw the other wanting to do, he won them over to his cause and was elected consul by them all unanimously.* [4] And it tells us a great deal about how clever Caesar was that he recognized and managed both the timing and the amount of attention that he paid them, in such a way that he attached them both to himself even though they were at odds with each other.

55. In fact, even this was not enough for him, and he reconciled them with each other as well, not because he particularly needed them to be in accord, but because he could see that they were the most influential men in Rome.* He was certain that he would never become truly powerful without assistance from both or at least one of them, and also that if he got on good terms with just one of them, he would thereby have the other man as his adversary, and would fail thanks to him more than he would succeed thanks to the help of the other. [2] For it was his opinion, in the first place, that everyone puts more energy into opposing his enemies than he does into helping his friends, not just because anger and hatred are more powerful drives than friendship, but also because a man who is acting on his own behalf finds success more pleasing and failure more distressing than a man who is acting for someone else. [3] In the second place, he was also of the opinion that people are more ready to hinder others and prevent them from becoming powerful than they are willing to help them to greatness, not least because a man who stops someone else from gaining power pleases others as well as himself, whereas a man who raises someone up makes him unacceptable to both camps.

56. These, then, were Caesar's reasons for paying court to Pompey and Crassus at that time, and subsequently for reconciling them with each other. In his opinion, he would never become strong without them, nor could he avoid falling out with one or the other of them at some point; but at the same time he knew that they would never cooperate with each other enough to be in a position to overpower him. In other words, he understood perfectly that, in the short term, their friendship would help him gain dominance over others, and, in the long term, they would help him gain dominance over themselves. [2] And so it turned out. They had their own reasons, but as soon as they had made up their minds to do so, Pompey and Crassus were reconciled with each other and made Caesar a partner in their affairs. [3] Pompey had not proved as strong as he had hoped,* and he could see that Crassus was strong and Caesar was getting stronger. He was afraid of being completely ruined by them, and he also hoped to regain his former power with their help if he made them his partners. [4] And since Crassus,* who thought himself superior to everyone else because of his family and his wealth, was far weaker than Pompey and thought that Caesar was headed for greatness, he wanted to make them rivals of each other, with neither of them outstripping the other. He looked forward to a time when, as rivals, they would be equally matched, and when he could therefore profit from the friendship of both of them, while gaining greater honour than either of them. [5] He did not strictly espouse the cause of either the plebs or the Senate, but made increasing his personal power the point of whatever he did. Hence he paid court to them both equally and avoided arousing the hostility of either of them; he advocated measures that would please first one and then the other, while making sure that he would gain credit for everything that was congenial to either of them and had nothing to do with anything they found disagreeable.

57. These, then, were the reasons the three of them found for entering into a pact of friendship; they confirmed the pact with oaths, and managed public business among themselves. From then on, they gave one another and received back from one another whatever they wanted and whatever it suited them to get done under the current circumstances.* [2] Their coalition meant that their factions cooperated as well, and these too did whatever they wanted with impunity, following their leadership in everything. The upshot was that moderation became a rare quality, found only in Cato and anyone else who was willing to appear to share his views. [3] At this period of Rome's history, no politician apart from Cato did anything from pure motives, without any consideration of private gain.* There were men who were ashamed of what was going on, and others who aspired to resemble Cato, and these men played a part in politics from time to time, producing results similar to his; but they did not stay the course, because they were not acting from innate goodness, but from an assumed attitude.

58. This, then, was the state into which these men brought political affairs in Rome at that time, though they kept their pact a secret for as long as they could. They decided among themselves what to do and then did it, but they dissembled and pretended that the opposite was the case, to delay their discovery for as long as possible, until they were adequately prepared. [2] Divinity, however, was not unaware of their actions, and in fact before very long it made perfectly clear to anyone capable of understanding such matters everything that would subsequently happen because of these men.* The city and all the surrounding countryside were suddenly struck by a storm of such ferocity [3] that huge numbers of trees were uprooted, many houses were damaged beyond repair, boats moored in the Tiber sank, whether they were by the city or at the river mouth, the wooden bridge was destroyed,* [4] and a theatre* collapsed which had been built out of timbers for some games. And in the midst of these disasters a great many people lost their lives. These signs were vouchsafed, then, as a kind of image of what the future held for them, on land and on water.

BOOK THIRTY-EIGHT

1. The following year Caesar set out to gain the favour of the plebs as a whole, to win them over to himself even more,* but he also wanted to make it seem as though he was taking care of business for the leading men as well, so that he did not alienate them either, and he often told them that he would propose no measures that went against their interests. [2] And, indeed, he found a way to word a proposal to distribute land to the entire commons so that it earned him not the slightest criticism, and in the case of this proposal too, he made out that he would of course withdraw it if it was not to their liking. So no one was able to find any fault with him for the law.* The swollen mass of the citizens, [3] the chief cause of all the political disturbance, were being diverted to labour and farming, and the extensive regions of Italy that had been abandoned would be inhabited once more, so that there would be enough food not only for those who had been worn out by military service, but also for everyone else—and, what is more, the city would incur no expenses from its own resources, and as for the leading men, so far from being penalized, many of them would gain both honour and power.*

[4] He was planning to distribute all the public land except the Campanian land,* which was so fertile that his advice was that it should be kept as public property, and he stipulated that the rest was not to be bought from people who were reluctant to sell, nor at a price set by the land commissioners, but, first, from people who were happy to sell, and, second, at the price at which the land had been assessed in the census lists. [5] The point, he claimed, was that the state was very well off as a result of all the booty Pompey had seized, as well as from the additional tribute and imposts,* and, seeing that this wealth had been won by Roman citizens risking their lives in battle, the citizenry was exactly what it ought to be spent on. [6] He also wanted the land commission not to have just a few members, because its power would then seem despotic, and no one to be a member if he had a court case pending, because he would not be universally welcome. So he proposed, first, that the commission should have twenty members, to spread the honour among more people, and second, that the

best qualified men should be appointed. He ruled himself out of consideration, however, [7] making this commitment in advance, to ensure that people would not think that he had himself in mind when he made the proposal. It was enough for him, or so he said, to come up with the idea and to make the proposal, but it was obvious that he was trying to please Pompey, Crassus, and the rest.*

2. He incurred no blame, then, for this proposal, and in fact no one even dared to open his mouth in opposition to him. He took the precaution of reading it out in the Senate, and he called on each individual senator by name, asking whether anyone found anything objectionable in the proposal, and promising to emend or erase altogether anything that anyone did not like. [2] By and large, however, all the leading men, or at any rate those who were not in the pact, took it very badly. In fact, the aspect of it that most disturbed them was precisely that he had drafted it in a way that both made it invulnerable to criticism and yet hard on all of them. [3] They suspected—and this was indeed his purpose—that it would enable him to gain the loyalty of the plebs, and thereby prestige and power over all men. Hence, even if no one voiced any objections,* they still withheld their assent. Most of them were satisfied with that posture; they kept assuring him that they would pass a decree but did nothing, and the proposal became subject to petty delays and procrastination.

3. Marcus Cato, however, went further. He was a fair-minded man and opposed to all change, but he lacked authority (and neither nature nor nurture had helped him in this respect),* and although he fell equally short of actually criticizing the measure, he did argue at a general level that they should stick with the status quo and not discard it in any respect. [2] At this, Caesar was ready to have Cato dragged out of the senate-house itself and thrown in the prison.* However, Cato unhesitatingly handed himself over to be taken away, and he was accompanied by quite a few others. One of them was Marcus Petreius,* and when Caesar told him off for leaving before the Senate had been dismissed, he said, 'I'd rather be in prison with Cato than here with you.' [3] This made Caesar feel ashamed, and he released Cato and brought the meeting of the Senate to an end, saying only: 'I offered you the chance to be judges and masters of the law, so that any clause in it that you didn't like would not be put to the people; but since you're refusing to pass a decree, it will be they who decide.'

4. After this incident, for the rest of his consulship Caesar brought no further projects to the Senate, but took all his proposals directly to the people. [2] But since he still wanted some of the leading men to support him in the popular assembly*—he was hoping that they had changed their minds and would now feel some fear of the plebs—he began with his colleague in the consulship and asked him if he found anything to criticize in the bill. [3] But all he said in reply was that he would not tolerate the introduction of any changes during his year of office, so Caesar began to plead with him, and persuaded the people to back him up as well, telling them: 'You'll have your law, if he wishes it.' But Bibulus* cried out in a loud voice: 'Not even if all of you wish it will you have this law this year.' [4] And with these words he left.

Caesar therefore dropped the idea of asking other magistrates the same question, in case he encountered further opposition, but he brought in Pompey and Crassus, even though they were private citizens, and told them to say what they thought of the bill. [5] Not that he was ignorant of their thinking—after all, they were partners in everything—but, first, he wanted to honour them by using them as his advisers for the law even though they were not in office, and, second, he also wanted to intimidate everyone else by having as his supporters the men who were acknowledged to be pre-eminent in the city at the time and had the greatest and widest influence. [6] And at the same time he would please the plebs by demonstrating that their objectives were not misplaced or unjust, but the kind to which even these men gave their assent and approval.

5. Pompey was very glad to speak. 'I am not the only one who approves of this proposal, Quirites,' he said. 'All the rest of the Senate does as well, as one can tell by the fact that they once voted that land should be given to those who served as soldiers not only with me but also with Metellus.* [2] At that time, when the state wasn't well off, it made sense for the grant to be postponed, but now that it has been massively enriched by me, it's only right that the soldiers should be given what they were promised and that everyone else too should profit from the communal effort.' [3] After this introduction, he went through the proposal in detail, arguing in favour of every clause, to the delight of the crowd. In view of this, Caesar asked whether he would be ready and willing to help him defeat their opponents, and he urged the plebs to join him in making this request of Pompey. [4] They did so, and it made Pompey proud that both the consul and

the people were asking for his help, even though he did not currently hold a command. He spoke at length, exalting and glorifying
himself, and ended by saying: 'If anyone dares to draw a sword, I too
will take up my shield.'* [5] Crassus expressed approval of what
Pompey had said as well. As a result, even those who disagreed became
eager for the bill to be passed into law, since it had the support of
these two, who were regarded as good men and were political
opponents of Caesar—or so it was generally supposed, since their
reconciliation was not yet public knowledge.*

6. Bibulus refused to give way, however. He won the support of
three tribunes* and blocked the passage of the law,* and in the end,
when he had run out of reasons for postponement, he declared all the
remaining days of the year, without distinction, to be festal days,
when the people were legally barred from meeting in assembly.*
[2] When Caesar, more or less ignoring him, announced a definite
date for the assembly to meet and pass the law, and the plebs occupied
the Forum the night before, Bibulus arrived with a band of supporters
he had organized. He pushed his way through to the temple of the
Dioscuri,* from which Caesar was delivering his speech, and people
let him through partly out of shame [3] and partly because they could
not believe that he was still going to oppose them. He climbed up and
attempted to speak against the bill, but he was forced off the steps, his
fasces were broken, and various people, including the three tribunes,
were beaten up and injured.*

[4] These were the circumstances under which the bill was passed
into law.* For the time being, Bibulus was content to have escaped
with his life, but the next day he tried to have the law annulled in the
Senate.* He got nowhere, however, because everyone was in thrall to
the fervour of the plebs and no one was prepared to take any action.
[5] Bibulus retired to his house, therefore, and was never again seen
in public at all until the last day of the year; he stayed at home,* and
every time Caesar tried to introduce some reform, he sent ser-
vants to notify him that this was a festal period and that, by law, he
could not properly conduct business at such a time.* [6] One of the
tribunes, Publius Vatinius,* attempted to have Bibulus imprisoned
for this, but he was prevented by his fellow tribunes' opposition.
Bibulus himself, however, withdrew from political life, as I have
said, and the tribunes who had supported him undertook no further
public business.

7. For a while, Metellus Celer, Cato, and thanks to Cato a man called Marcus Favonius, for whom Cato was a role model in everything, refused to take the oath of obedience to the law—a practice that had been introduced earlier, as I said,* and was also used for other bad measures—and insisted that they would never give it their approval, with Metellus, especially, referring to Numidicus.* [2] But when the day came on which they would become liable to the ordained penalties, they did swear the oath. We can attribute this, perhaps, to human nature, in that it is often easier for people to make promises or threats than it is for them actually to carry them out, or to the realization that there was no point in their being punished, because their stubbornness was not going to do the state any good.* [3] So these were the circumstances under which the bill was passed into law, and furthermore the Campanian land was given to fathers with three or more children.* This, then, was the time when Capua was first regarded as a Roman colony.*

[4] By these means, Caesar gained the allegiance of the plebs, and he did the same for the *equites* when he let them off a third of the taxes for which they had contracted. All tax-farming was their responsibility, and although they had often asked the Senate for a rebate, they had always been refused, thanks to opposition from, especially, Cato.* [5] Once Caesar had won over the *equites* without meeting any dissent, he first ratified all of Pompey's measures*—and no one protested, not even Lucullus—and then he had many other proposals passed into law without meeting any opposition. [6] Even Cato did not object, although a few years later, when he was praetor, he never referred to the laws by their title, each of them being a *lex Julia.** It was completely ludicrous, but even though he followed the provisions of these laws in conducting the ballot for jurors, he suppressed their titles. Anyway, there are very many of these laws,* and since they would add nothing to this history, I shall omit them.

8. Quintus Fufius Calenus, however, realized that since everyone's votes were counted together in contentious cases, each of the orders could claim that they had voted for the better side themselves and the others for the worse. So, in his capacity as praetor, he got a law passed to the effect that each of the orders should vote separately. In that way, even if each individual's opinions would remain unknown, because the ballot was secret, it would at least become clear how the order as a whole felt.*

[2] By and large, Caesar introduced proposals, spoke on political matters, and organized absolutely everything in the city as though he were its sole ruler. This led some wags to suppress Bibulus' name altogether; in both speaking and writing, they used Caesar's name twice, saying that the consuls were Gaius Caesar and Julius Caesar. [3] But measures that bore on himself he handled through intermediaries, because he was especially scrupulous about not awarding himself anything. In fact, even this made it even easier for him to get everything he wanted. He would say that he needed nothing and insist that he was content with what he had, [4] but others, claiming that current circumstances made him both necessary and invaluable, proposed all the measures he wanted and had them ratified not only by the plebs, but even by the Senate. [5] For instance, the people awarded him the governorship of both Illyricum and Cisalpine Gaul with the command of three legions for five years,* and the Senate additionally entrusted him with Transalpine Gaul and another legion.*

9. However, Caesar was still afraid that Pompey might make some changes in his absence, since Aulus Gabinius* was going to be consul, so he used ties of kinship to attach both Pompey and the other consul, Lucius Piso, to his circle. He gave his daughter to be Pompey's wife, even though she was already betrothed to someone else, while he himself married Piso's daughter.* [2] So Caesar's strength was buttressed on all sides, but this displeased Cicero and Lucullus so much that they undertook to kill both Caesar and Pompey, using a certain Lucius Vettius as their agent. They failed, however, and in fact came very close to losing their own lives as well. What happened was that Vettius was informed against and arrested before doing anything. He denounced Cicero and Lucullus, [3] and if he had not also accused Bibulus of being their accomplice, it would certainly have gone badly for them. But in fact, because in his defence he was accusing Bibulus, who was the person who had revealed the plan to Pompey, he was suspected of lying about the others too; it was thought that he had been put up to it as part of a campaign purposely designed to bring false charges against Caesar's and Pompey's political opponents. [4] There being no definite proof, various stories circulated about the affair. Vettius was brought before the people and after naming as conspirators only the men I have mentioned, he was thrown into the prison, where, a little later, he was assassinated.*

10. This of course made Cicero suspect to Caesar and Pompey, and he confirmed their suspicion by his defence speech for Antonius. During his governorship of Macedonia, Antonius had done a great deal of harm both to the subject territory there and to allied territory, but he had also been emphatically paid back.* [2] After ravaging the territory of the Dardani and their neighbours, he did not dare to meet their attack, but pulled back and fled with his cavalry, pretending that they were needed elsewhere, and then the enemy surrounded his infantry, drove them forcefully out of the country, and recovered the booty they had collected. [3] When he also raided the allies in Moesia in the same way, he suffered a defeat near the Istrians' city at the hands of the Bastarnae, a Scythian people, who had come to help them,* and he turned tail and fled. Now, that was not what he was taken to court for; he was charged with having been an accomplice of Catiline. Nevertheless, it was his conduct as governor of Macedonia which got him convicted, so that in the end he was not found guilty of the crime with which he was being charged, and was punished for wrongdoing that was not named in the charge.* [4] That was how Antonius' trial turned out. Cicero, who spoke in his defence on this occasion because Antonius and he had been colleagues in the consulship, delivered a lengthy tirade against Caesar, accusing him of having instigated the trial, and he even went so far as to insult him.*

11. This offended Caesar, naturally, but, although he was a consul, he did not respond abusively to Cicero in any of his speeches or in anything he did.* In fact, he used to argue that it was common for ordinary people to deliberately insult their betters; it was an attempt to enmesh them in quarrels, because then, if their betters responded in similar terms, they were effectively treating them as their equals and peers. But Caesar refused to make anyone his rival in this way, [2] and that was why quiescence was his invariable response towards anyone who insulted him. On the occasion in question too, seeing that Cicero was not wanting to slander him so much as he wanted to be slandered back in similar terms, so that he would be his equal, he took little notice of him and no account of anything he said, but let him go on and on insulting him, just as if he were speaking words of praise.

[3] He did not completely disregard him, however. Even though Caesar was genuinely endowed with a forgiving nature and was slow to anger, he still punished plenty of men when the circumstances were important enough to warrant it; but he absolutely never did so

under the influence of passion or in haste. [4] He never succumbed to
anger, but waited for the right moment. In fact, most of the people he
pursued never knew he was after them, because he never acted in
a way that would give the impression that he was retaliating against
people; his constant objective was to manage everything with an eye
on what was good for him personally, while attracting the least jealousy possible. That is why, when he punished anyone, he went about
it unobtrusively and it always took people completely by surprise.
[5] In this way he not only preserved his reputation for equanimity,
but also made sure that no one would suspect anything and make
a pre-emptive strike against him before being punished. What had
already happened in the past was less important to him than making
sure that everything would be fine in the future, [6] and so, when he
was sure that they would do him no further harm, he often forgave
even men who had hurt him badly, or pursued them only to a limited
extent. On the other hand, he also often inflicted disproportionate
punishments on people if his own safety was at stake, saying that what
was done could never be undone, but that at least excessive punishment guaranteed that he would not come to any harm in the future.†

12. For these reasons he did nothing himself on this occasion
either, but realizing that Clodius was willing to help him, as a way of
thanking him for not having accused him of adultery, he secretly
recruited him to deal with Cicero.* [2] First, so that the change of
station should be carried out legally, he transferred Clodius to plebeian status again,* with Pompey's help, and then immediately made
sure that he was elected tribune.* [3] Clodius silenced Bibulus* when
the consul came down to the Forum on the last day of the year and
was intending to accompany his swearing of the oath with a speech
about the political situation, and he also attacked Cicero. [4] Now, it
was not going to be easy, in his opinion, to bring down a man who had
become a highly influential politician thanks to his skill at speaking,
so he decided to win over not just the plebs, but the *equites* and the
Senate as well, even though Cicero stood very high in their estimation.*
He anticipated little trouble in seeing to his downfall if he won them
over to his side, since Cicero's strength depended more on fear than
goodwill.*

[5] There were a great many men who were aggrieved at Cicero's
speeches, and the loyalty of those he had benefited was less steadfast
than the hostility of those he had injured. It was not just that in general

people are more inclined to be angry when people treat them badly than to be grateful when people treat them well, and to think that when they have paid their advocates their fee they have discharged their debt,* while in fact their overriding concern is to find some way to defend themselves against their opponents in court, [6] but Cicero was also arousing the most bitter hostility against himself by constantly trying to prove himself superior to the most powerful of his fellow citizens, and by choosing to speak with intemperate and immoderate frankness* to everyone without distinction. His goal was to gain a reputation for greater intelligence and eloquence than anyone else, and he chose this over being thought a decent man. [7] Because of this, and also because he was the greatest boaster around and regarded no one else as his equal, making it clear in his speeches, as well as by the way he lived,† that he despised everyone and thought no one worthy to live with him on equal terms, he became obnoxious and repugnant,* and as a result even those who approved of him regarded him with jealousy and loathing.

13. Under these circumstances, then, Clodius expected that it would take him little time to deal with Cicero if he could win over the

58 BCE Senate, the *equites*, and the people. He therefore distributed grain free again (when Gabinius and Piso became consuls he carried a measure providing for it to be doled out to the poor),* [2] and he revived the associations known as *collegia* in Latin, which were an ancient institution, but had been suppressed some years previously.* He also prohibited the censors from removing anyone from an order or disgracing anyone, unless he was tried and found guilty by them both.*

[3] After using these measures to seduce them,* he proposed another new law, which requires discussion at some length if it is to be generally comprehensible. Observing the heavens was, as I have said, just one of the methods used for public divination,* but it had the greatest authority—so much so that whereas the auspices were taken in other ways repeatedly and before each individual action, this method was valid once for a whole day. [4] That was its most distinctive feature, but there was also the fact that whereas, for all other kinds of action, observing the heavens either allowed the action to go ahead (with no need to observe them again in each case), or barred and blocked it from happening, it halted the taking of a popular vote either way; it was always taken to be an omen against vote-taking whether it was auspicious or inauspicious.*

[5] I am just writing down what is said about this practice; I am not in a position to explain it.

Now, it was common for men who wanted to block either proposals of laws or appointments of magistrates which were being brought before the people to announce early on that they would be using that day to look for signs from the heavens, so that the people would not be able to ratify any measure that day.* [6] So Clodius, who was afraid that, if he indicted Cicero, some people would use this device to delay and postpone the trial, proposed that no magistrate should observe heavenly phenomena on days when the people had to cast a vote.*

14. These were the proposals he drafted at the time in order to attack Cicero, but Cicero realized what was going on and persuaded one of the tribunes, Lucius Ninnius Quadratus, to oppose them all. This kind of disruption and delay was the last thing Clodius wanted, and he used guile to get the better of Cicero. [2] He first entered into a pact with him, the terms of which were that he would not bring forward any measure against Cicero as long as Cicero did nothing to obstruct any of his proposals, and then, with Cicero and Ninnius immobilized, he secured the passage into law of all his proposals*— and the next thing he did was launch his attack on Cicero. [3] So, for all his vaunted intelligence, Cicero was tricked on this occasion by Clodius, if it is right to say that responsibility lay with Clodius, rather than with Caesar and the others who were his and Clodius' allies.

[4] The next law that Clodius introduced did not appear, on the face of it, to have Cicero as its target. It did not mention Cicero by name, at any rate, but was simply aimed at everyone who might or even had put a fellow citizen to death without his having been found guilty by the people.* In fact, however, Cicero was its primary target. [5] It is true that it applied to the Senate as a whole,* because it was the Senate which had ordered the consuls to see to the protection of the city and it was this order which had permitted the consuls to act as they did, and also because it was the Senate which subsequently condemned Lentulus and the others who were put to death at that time with him.* [6] Nevertheless, since it was Cicero who had denounced the conspirators, who had introduced each proposal and put it to the vote, and who, finally, had had the sentence carried out by the appropriate officials, the blame landed wholly or almost wholly on him. [7] He therefore energetically opposed Clodius in various ways,* and not least by discarding his senatorial robes and going around

dressed as an *eques*,* working day and night to ingratiate himself, as he did the rounds, with everyone who had any influence, whether they were friends or enemies, especially Pompey and Caesar, who was concealing his hostility towards him.

15. Now, Pompey and Caesar did not want it known that they were Clodius' backers, nor did they want to give the impression that his proposals were to their liking, so they next came up with the following scheme to deceive Cicero, one that would maintain their specious front and be impenetrable by him.* [2] Caesar advised him to leave the city, because if he stayed where he was he might lose his life; and, wanting it to be more readily believable that he was offering this advice out of solicitude for Cicero, he promised to use him as one of his legates, so that he could get out of Clodius' way not in disgrace, as someone who was under investigation, but with his head held high in order to take up a position of command. [3] Meanwhile, Pompey tried to dissuade him from this course, which he bluntly called dereliction of duty, and he intimated that Caesar was motivated by hostility and was giving him bad advice; his suggestion, by contrast, was that Cicero should stay in Rome, speak out in his own defence and in defence of the Senate, and retaliate without delay against Clodius. [4] He argued that Clodius would not be able to get anything done with Cicero in town and opposing him, and he added that Clodius would receive his just deserts and that he himself would help achieve that goal.

Faced with these suggestions by Caesar and Pompey—suggestions they offered not because they had contrasting views on the subject, but in order to deceive him without arousing his suspicion—Cicero attached himself to Pompey. [5] He had never had any reason in the past to doubt him, and he felt absolutely confident of being saved by him. After all, he was so widely respected and esteemed that he was often able to protect people on trial from the jurors or even from their prosecutors. [6] And since Clodius had once had a family connection with Pompey* and had served with him in the army for a long time,* it was generally held that he would never act in a way that did not meet with Pompey's approval. As for Gabinius, Cicero fully expected him to take his part since he was a close friend of Pompey, and the same went for Piso, because of his integrity and his kinship with Caesar.*

16. These assumptions led him to anticipate victory, and in fact he was now unreasonably confident,* as before he had been unthinkingly

afraid. And since he was concerned that people would think his leaving the city a sign of a guilty conscience, he expressed his gratitude to
Caesar, but did as Pompey had suggested. [2] So Cicero, thoroughly
duped, was getting himself ready for what he thought would be an
easy victory over his enemies. He had further grounds for optimism
in addition to those already stated, because the *equites* met on the
Capitol* and sent a delegation to the consuls and the Senate to plead
for Cicero; the delegates were some of their own number, but also two
senators, Quintus Hortensius and Gaius Curio.* [3] Ninnius too
helped him in various ways, not least by advising the general populace
to change their clothes as though for a national catastrophe. Even
many senators did likewise,* and refused to change back until the
consuls had rebuked them in an edict.

[4] The opposition was too strong, however. Clodius stopped
Ninnius intervening on Cicero's behalf, and Gabinius refused to allow
the *equites* access to the Senate. In fact, he expelled one of them, who
was being particularly insistent, from the city,* and told Hortensius
and Curio off for attending the meeting of the *equites* and joining the
delegation. [5] Clodius also had these two appear before the popular
assembly and arranged for some men there to thrash them soundly
for their part in the delegation. Next, it was Piso's turn. Although he
was supposed to be on Cicero's side, and although he advised him to
slip quietly away when he saw that it was impossible for him to be
saved by any other means, nevertheless, when Cicero lost his temper
at the suggestion, [6] Piso went to the popular assembly at the earliest
possible opportunity (he was chronically ill), and when Clodius asked
where he stood on the proposed measure, he said only: 'No savage
or grim deed is to my liking.' And when Gabinius was asked the
same question, he did not just fail to speak well of Cicero, but even
denounced the *equites* and the Senate.

17. Caesar—for Clodius sought his opinion on the proposal too,
convening the popular assembly outside the city walls for his sake,†
since he had already set out for his command*—condemned the
illegality of what had happened to Lentulus, [2] but stopped short of
approving the punishment that was being proposed for its perpetrators. He said that his views about what had happened then were
known to everyone, because he had cast his vote for keeping the
conspirators alive,* but that he still did not think it appropriate for
past actions to become subject to newly drafted laws such as the one

currently under consideration. [3] That was what Caesar said, while
Crassus showed a modicum of support for Cicero through his son,
but sided with the plebs himself, and Pompey promised him help, but
ultimately failed to defend him, by coming up with various excuses
and making sure that he was frequently away from Rome.*

[4] When Cicero realized what was happening, he became afraid
and was again tempted to resort to arms; apart from anything else, he
began publicly abusing Pompey. But Cato and Hortensius stopped
him, because they were worried that it might end in civil war, and
then at last, albeit reluctantly, Cicero left Rome, shamed and dis-
honoured because he had gone into exile on his own initiative, as
though he had a guilty conscience. [5] Before setting out, however, he
went up to the Capitol and dedicated a statuette of Minerva, calling
her the Guardian.* Then he slunk off to Sicily, because he had been
their protector* and had high hopes of getting an honourable reception from the communities and individuals, and from the governor.*

[6] After his flight, Clodius' proposal was passed into law,* and so
far from meeting with any opposition, as soon as Cicero was out of the
way it was even supported by, among others, the very men who were
thought to be his most staunch supporters. His property was confiscated, his house was demolished as though it had belonged to a public
enemy, and the plot was consecrated as a temple to Liberty.* [7] He
himself was punished with exile;* he was forbidden to stay in Sicily
because he was banished to a distance of 3,750 stades from Rome;*
and it was also proclaimed that if he ever showed his face within that
exclusion zone, he and anyone offering him shelter could be killed
with impunity.

18. Cicero therefore moved to Macedonia instead and spent his
time there lamenting.* But he fell in with Philiscus, an old acquaintance from Athens,* whom he happened to meet again then, and
Philiscus said,* 'Cicero, doesn't it embarrass you to spend your time
weeping and carrying on like a woman? I'm astonished to see such
weakness in a man like yourself—a man who has enjoyed a long and
varied education, and a well-known speaker in defence of others.'

[2] 'But, Philiscus,' Cicero replied, 'speaking for others and telling oneself what to do are completely different things. What is said on
behalf of others comes from a mind that is firm and sound, and therefore is apposite, on the whole. But when the mind is preoccupied by
personal suffering, it becomes troubled and dark, and cannot work

out what's appropriate. That's why the saying that it's easier to offer advice to others than it is to endure one's own misfortune is right on the mark.'

[3] 'That's just what it is to be human,' Philiscus said. 'But I didn't think that you, who have shown so much good sense and are so practised in wisdom,* would have failed to prepare yourself for all life's contingencies. I thought that you'd be the last person to be caught off guard by some unexpected occurrence. [4] But since that is the state you find yourself in, it might perhaps help if I talk some useful points over with you. That way I might ease your suffering, just as it's a relief when people give one a helping hand with some load—though in fact it will be easier for me than for them, because I shan't be taking on even the smallest part of your load! [5] I'm sure you won't spurn words of consolation from someone else. After all, if you were entirely self-sufficient, we wouldn't be having this conversation. As things are, however, your situation is the one an eminent doctor such as Hippocrates or Democedes* would find himself in if he were to fall ill with a stubborn disease and needed someone else's help to cure it.'

19. 'Well,' said Cicero, 'if you know an argument designed to dispel this mist from my mind* and restore me to the light I once enjoyed, I am very ready to listen. There are many different kinds of drugs, with various powers, and the same goes for words, so it wouldn't be surprising if you were able to dose even me with a little wisdom, for all my brilliance in the Senate, the popular assemblies, and the law courts.'

[2] 'All right, then,' said Philiscus. 'Since you're willing to listen, let's consider first whether your current circumstances are truly bad, and second how we can make them better. First of all, then, it's clear that you're physically healthy and fit, which is of course the greatest blessing nature can give a man. But it is also clear that you are sufficiently endowed with the means [3] of avoiding hunger, thirst, cold, and other vexations which are the result of poverty, and this ability, one might reasonably claim, is the second greatest blessing nature can give a man. In other words, if one has one's health and is assured of a sufficiency without having to worry, one has all the ingredients of a happy life.'

20. 'But none of these things is the slightest use,' Cicero replied, 'when something is disturbing and tormenting a man's mind. An uneasy mind makes a man far more miserable than a sound body

makes him happy. That's where I am now. I see no particular value in
bodily health, at any rate while I have an unhealthy mind, nor, after all
I've lost, do I value being well off in material terms.'

[2] 'Is that what's bothering you?' asked Philiscus. 'Now, if you were
going to be left without enough to live on, it would make sense to be
upset at your losses. But since you have plenty of everything that's
necessary for life, why does it upset you not to have more? Everything
that one has beyond what's necessary to satisfy one's needs is super-
fluous, and it comes to the same thing whether or not one has it.
[3] I mean, I'm sure that unnecessary things played no part in your
past life, and that should lead you to consider either that in those days
you didn't have what you didn't need, or that nowadays you have
things you don't need. After all, most of what you had came to you not
by inheritance, in which case it would make sense if it was especially
important to you, but was won by your eloquence and speeches, and
these are the very things which have also caused you to lose them.*
[4] But there's no point in getting cross if what caused your loss is the
same as what caused your gain in the first place. Consider ship-
captains, for instance: they don't go to pieces when they suffer great
losses, and in my opinion that's because they have enough sense to be
able to work out that the sea gives, but it also takes away.

21. 'But enough about that. What I'm saying is that, in my opinion, all a man needs for happiness is a sufficiency, enough to satisfy
his bodily needs, and I maintain that anything over that causes a man
anxiety and stress, and makes him liable to be envied. [2] Now, you
said that it's impossible to enjoy physical well-being unless the mind
is well too, which is undeniable. If the mind is in a bad way, the body
is bound to be unhealthy too. But still, it seems to me that it is much
easier to secure mental health than physical health. [3] This is because
the body, being made of flesh, has many inherent flaws and needs
plenty of help from divinity, whereas the mind, with its more divine
nature, can easily be regulated and corrected. So let's see whether any
of the things which are good for the mind have been lost to you, and
whether any of the troubles currently afflicting you are such that we
can't break their hold on you.

22. 'First, then, it's clear to me that you are a man of the utmost
good sense.* This is proved by the very large number of times you've
succeeded in convincing both the Senate and the people of your views,
when you had some advice to offer, and the equally large number of

times you've been of assistance to private citizens, when speaking on their behalf. And, second, you're clearly extremely just. [2] At any rate, whatever the situation, you've proved a staunch defender of your country and your friends against schemes designed to do them down. In fact, your current misfortune is precisely a consequence of your constancy in serving the law and the constitution in all you say and do.

[3] 'Then again, the way you spend your time shows that you've attained the highest degree of self-control, since it's impossible for anyone who's a slave to bodily pleasure to be constantly in the public gaze and to make the Forum the centre of his life, where his behaviour by day reveals what he got up to by night. [4] And under these circumstances, given your great intellect and your power as a speaker, I was led to suppose that you were also very brave, but it looks as though you've lost some of your great courage as a result of having been shaken by your unexpected and undeserved setback. [5] Still, your courage will return very soon, and since you have both bodily and mental vigour as a result of these qualities of yours, I fail to see what it is that's upsetting you.'

23. Once he had finished speaking, Cicero said, 'Is it your opinion, then, that there's nothing especially bad about disgrace* and exile? About being unable to spend time at home or with friends? About having been humiliatingly expelled from one's country and forced to live in unfamiliar lands, wandering and called an exile, a source of laughter for one's enemies and of shame for one's family and friends?'

[2] 'No, there's nothing bad about this at all, in my opinion,' Philiscus replied. 'We humans are a compound of two parts, mind and body, each of which, thanks to its very nature, has things that are specifically good and bad for it, and it's reasonable to regard any flaw in them as harmful and shameful, [3] and to consider it beneficial for all to be well with them, as is the case with you today. It's only a matter of convention and personal opinion to regard those other things you mentioned—exile, disenfranchisement, and so on—as shameful and bad. They aren't agents of the slightest harm for either the body or the mind. I mean, can you point to anyone whose body has contracted an illness or even died, or whose mind has been made less just or less knowledgeable, as a result of disgrace, exile, and so on? I know of no such case myself. [4] And the reason is that none of these things is bad in itself, just as neither enjoyment of honour nor living in the country

of one's birth is good in itself. The attributes they have are only those that each of us assigns to them.

'Take disgrace, for example. Conventions for its application differ widely from place to place. [5] There are actions which are considered reprehensible in some societies but praiseworthy in others, and there are actions which are valued in some societies but punished in others. In fact, there are some places where disgrace is completely unknown as both name and practice. All this makes perfect sense [6] as long as one considers anything that has no effect on what is essential to a man's nature to be of no concern to him either. So, just as it would of course be the height of absurdity for whether someone was ill or vicious to be determined by a verdict or a decree, the same goes for disgrace as well.

24. 'The case is no different for exile too, in my opinion. Exile is a departure from home involving disgrace, and this means that if disgrace in itself has no bad consequences, there can be nothing bad about exile either. [2] After all, in the normal course of events plenty of people spend a great deal of time away from home, either voluntarily or involuntarily, and some even spend their whole lives on the move, as if they were constantly being expelled from everywhere, and yet they don't regard themselves as being harmed thereby. [3] What's more, it makes no difference whether a man spends time abroad willingly or unwillingly; a man who gets fit unintentionally is no less strong than one who does so deliberately, and a man who goes to sea reluctantly makes no less money than his counterpart. Besides, I don't see how a man of sense can be said to do things unwillingly.

[4] 'So if the goodness or badness of a situation comes from our doing what we want to do readily and what we don't want to do grudgingly, the solution is easy: all we have to do is willingly put up with everything we are confronted with anyway, never letting anything overpower us, and then all those alleged bad properties of unwillingness are done away with at a stroke. [5] And there's in fact an ancient and excellent saying that, instead of wishing for everything we want to see happen, we should wish for things that are going to happen anyway—the point being that the course of our lives is not subject to our free choice and we are not our own masters. Our actions necessarily depend on the whims of Fortune and on the guardian spirit that has been assigned to each of us for the fulfilment of our appointed destiny.

25. 'That's the way things are, whether we like it or not. Now, if the cause of your distress is not disgrace in itself or exile in itself—if the cause is that you've been disgraced and banished when, so far from having done your country any wrong, you've actually done it a great deal of good—you should bear the following in mind: since you were inevitably destined to have this experience, there is no better or more admirable way for it to have turned out than as it did, with your being treated badly when you have done no wrong. [2] In all your advice and actions, you did your duty by your fellow citizens, serving them not in a private capacity but as consul, and never manipulating affairs for your own personal ends, but acting in obedience to the decrees of the Senate,* motivated as they were not by factional interests but by a concern for the common good. [3] But various people, exploiting their personal power* and driven by a desire to humiliate you, constantly intrigued against you. And this means that it's they who should be troubled and distressed by their wrongdoing, while it's your job—a fine one, as well as necessary—to bear with courage what your guardian spirit has decreed for you.

[4] 'I mean, I'm sure you wouldn't have chosen the alternative, cooperation with Catiline and becoming an accomplice of Lentulus, which would have meant giving your country advice that was the exact opposite of what was in its interests and performing none of the duties it appointed you to carry out; I'm sure you'd have chosen doing right and banishment over doing wrong and staying at home. [5] So, if you're worried about your reputation, it's surely far better to have been sent into exile with no crime on your conscience than it is to have stayed at home a criminal, because—apart from any other considerations—it's those who unjustly banish someone whose reputation becomes tarnished, not the man who has been maliciously expelled.

26. 'Besides, what I hear is that you didn't leave under compulsion or because you'd been convicted in the courts, but of your own free will, because you couldn't stand the prospect of living with men who were deaf to your attempts to improve them, and because you refused to come to grief along with them—in other words, that it wasn't your country you fled from, but those who intrigued against it. One might in fact say that it's they who are disgraced and in exile, [2] because they've banished all that is good from their lives, and you retain your honour and your well-being, because you haven't shamefully enslaved yourself to anyone, and because you have all that befits you, wherever in the world you choose to live, be it Sicily, Macedonia, or anywhere else. I mean, whether we meet with good or bad fortune has nothing to do with where one lives; always and everywhere we make our own homeland, and our own good fortune, by and for ourselves. [3] It was because Camillus understood this that he was happy to live in Ardea;* it was because Scipio thought like this that he was able to live content-edly for the remainder of his life in Liternum.* Do I need to mention Aristides or Themistocles,* whose banishments enhanced their fame? What about Hannibal?* What about Solon,* who voluntarily took himself off abroad for ten years?

[4] 'You too, then, shouldn't regard anything as hard to bear which has no effect on the constitution of either the body or the mind, nor should you resent what has happened to you. As I've already said, we have not the slightest ability to choose to live as we want; instead, we are absolutely required to put up with what divinity has decreed for us. [5] If we do this willingly, it won't cause us distress, but if we do it reluctantly, not only will we not escape our destiny anyway, but we will also upset ourselves to no purpose, and there's nothing worse than that. [6] The proof of this is that people who put up with the most appalling situations with good grace see nothing terrible in their cir-cumstances, whereas those who resent even the slightest of difficulties imagine that all human ills are theirs. Moreover, whether people han-dle a good situation poorly or a bad situation well, the impression of their circumstances which they give to others is the same as the one they have made for themselves.

27. 'All this is what I would have you bear in mind, and then you won't find your current circumstances grievous and you won't be upset if you learn that the men who banished you are prospering. In the normal course of events, worldly success is insubstantial and fleeting, and the greater men become as a result of it, the more readily they fall, as if before a puff of wind. This is especially so at times of civil strife. [2] Driven along, surrounded by turmoil and upheavals, they differ little, if at all, from sailors in a storm. Up and down they're dashed, in this direction or that, and if they make even the slightest mistake they're sure to drown. [3] I could mention Drusus, Scipio, the Gracchi,* and various others, but all you need to do is remember how Camillus, a former exile, subsequently came off better than Capitolinus,* and by how much Aristides later came to eclipse Themistocles.

[4] 'Your chief hope, then, should be that you'll be allowed to return home; after all, you've not been banished because of any crime you committed, and I hear it said that the same men who banished you will miss you, and that everyone will want you back. But even if your circumstances remain the same, you shouldn't let this distress you at all. 28. If you take my advice, you'll be perfectly happy to find an estate on the coast and off the beaten track, where you can combine farming with a bit of history-writing, as Xenophon and Thucydides did.* [2] There's no longer-lasting type of intellectual work, and none that's better suited to every man and every state; and exile provides one with rather productive free time. So if you want to join those historians in true immortality, imitate them. [3] You have enough to live on, and you no longer have any need of honours or distinctions. In so far as these things are worth anything, you've already been consul. There's nothing to be gained from holding office a second, third, or even fourth time, except a string of useless letters, which are no good to anyone, alive or dead. [4] You wouldn't choose to be Corvinus* or Marius, seven times consul,* rather than Cicero. At the same time, you plainly don't want a command, because you turned down the one that was given you,* repudiating the money to be made from it, and repudiating also power that is short-lived and subject to scrutiny by anyone who wants to bring false charges.

[5] 'I mention these things not because any of them is necessary for happiness, but because you've played enough of a part as a politician, when it was required of you, to have learnt from it how the ways of life differ. This puts you in a position to choose the one and reject the other, pursue the one and shun the other. Human life is short, and you shouldn't spend your entire life working for others; now it's time for you to indulge yourself a bit as well. [6] Consider how much preferable tranquillity is to unrest, serenity to turmoil, freedom to slavery, safety to danger, and then you'll want to live as I'm advising you.* If you do so, you'll find happiness, and you'll gain great fame for it—fame that will last for ever, both while you are still alive and after your death.

29. 'However, if you're determined to secure your restoration and your ambition is to shine as a statesman, I don't want to say anything negative, but when I consider the current state of affairs and bear in mind the frankness with which you speak,* and when I see how strong and numerous your adversaries are, I'm afraid that you might suffer

another downfall. [2] If you get sent into exile, you'll suffer no more than remorse, but if something else happens to you, something fatal, you won't even be able to feel regret. But wouldn't it be a terrible thing, a shameful thing, for someone's head to be cut off and set up in the Forum, perhaps, for some man and woman to abuse?* [3] Please don't hate me as a prophet of doom, but pay heed to me as revealing a warning from heaven. You must not be misled by the fact that some of the leading men in Rome are your friends; apparent friends will prove no help to you at all against your enemies, as you already know from experience. [4] Men who lust after personal power value nothing except getting what they want, and it's far from unknown for them to abandon their dearest and closest friends in favour of their bitterest enemies.'*

30. Cicero was somewhat comforted by what Philiscus said, but in fact his exile did not go on for long. His restoration was secured by Pompey, the very man who had been chiefly responsible for his banishment.* This is how it came about. Clodius was bribed to break the younger Tigranes out of the house of Lucius Flavius, where he was still being confined, and set him free,* [2] and when Pompey and Gabinius expressed their disapproval of what he had done, he insulted them in the most outrageous terms, struck and injured some of their retinue, broke the consul's fasces,* and consecrated his property.* [3] This made Pompey furious, particularly because Clodius had used against him the powers which Pompey himself had returned to the tribunes.* He decided to recall Cicero, and he began to negotiate for his restoration straight away, using Ninnius as his proxy. [4] Ninnius waited until Clodius was away, and then he introduced the motion concerning Cicero to the Senate. When one of the other tribunes imposed his veto,* Ninnius not only posted the measure so as to bring it before the plebs,* but also began to oppose all of Clodius' actions. This led to furious disputes, which in their turn led to many injuries on both sides.* [5] But before matters had reached this point,* Clodius decided to get Cato out of the way, to make it easier for him to see all his measures through to a successful conclusion, and at the same time he wanted to punish Ptolemy, who then held Cyprus, for having failed to ransom him from the pirates.* So he annexed the island for the Roman people and sent off Cato, very much against his will, to administer it.*

31. So much for what was happening in the city. Meanwhile, in Gaul Caesar found no one to fight.* Everything was perfectly quiet there, but the peace did not last. First, one war broke out against him that was not of his making, and this was followed by another, so that in the end he got what he most wanted, which was to make victorious war over the whole country.* [2] Here is what happened. The Helvetii, an extremely populous people, had outgrown their land and were no longer self-sufficient.* They were reluctant to send out just some of their people to settle elsewhere, because they were worried that, if they split up, they would become more vulnerable to the schemes of those they had hurt in the past, so they decided to migrate en masse instead, the idea being to find another place to live that was larger and more fertile, and they burnt all their villages and towns to make sure that no one regretted his decision to leave. [3] They added some others who were in the same difficult circumstances as themselves, and set off under the leadership of Orgetorix,* with the plan of crossing the Rhône and settling somewhere close to the Alps.*

But Caesar stopped them from crossing the river, not least by destroying the bridge,* so they sent envoys to him, asking him to let them cross and promising to do no harm to Roman land. [4] Although he was deeply suspicious of them and had no intention of letting them proceed, he was not yet ready for them, so he told them that he would consult with his legates about their request and give them an answer on a given day. In other words, he led them to believe that he was going to let them cross, and meanwhile he dug trenches and built walls in the most critical positions, to make the route impassable by them.

32. So the barbarians waited for a while, and then, when they failed to receive the promised response,* they broke camp. At first, they followed their planned route through the territory of the Allobroges, but after they encountered the obstacles Caesar had placed in their path, they turned aside into the territory of the Sequani. [2] They passed through their land, and then that of the Aedui, who gave them free passage on the condition that they would cause no damage, but they broke their promise and plundered the farmland. The Sequani and the Aedui therefore got in touch with Caesar and asked for his help,* begging him not to let them perish. [3] Even though what they said was at odds with their past behaviour, Caesar still granted their request, because he was afraid that the Helvetii might make for Tolosa,* and he preferred to drive them off with the help of the Sequani and Aedui, rather than fight them when they had joined forces with these

peoples,* which was clearly what was going to happen. [4] He therefore attacked the Helvetii as they were crossing the Saône. The rearguard he destroyed right at the ford, and the forward contingents were so alarmed by the unexpectedness and swiftness of his pursuit, and by the news of their losses, that they decided to come to terms, provided that they were given some land to live in.

33. No agreement was reached, however, because they took it badly when they were asked for hostages, not because of the mistrust it implied, but because they considered it beneath their dignity to give hostages to anyone. So they spurned the truce and continued on their way. Caesar's cavalry rode far ahead of the infantry and began harassing the rearguard, but the barbarians deployed their cavalry to meet the attack and came off best. [2] This victory gave a great boost to their confidence, and they also thought that Caesar was in retreat, partly because of the defeat and partly because of shortage of provisions, which had forced him to turn aside and head for a certain town.* So they advanced no further, and set out after him instead.

[3] When Caesar saw what they were doing, their determination and their numbers worried him. He set out at the double with his infantry for some high ground, while throwing his cavalry forward to bear the brunt of the attack and buy him time to marshal the rest of his forces on suitable terrain. Once again, the enemy routed his troops, and they were making a spirited assault on the hill itself when Caesar suddenly charged down against them—and since his men were attacking from high ground in good order against men who were out of order,* he easily drove them back. [4] After the rout, some of the enemy who had not been involved in the fighting (because there were so many of them, and they were moving at such speed, that they had not all arrived at the same time) suddenly fell on their pursuers in the rear. This created some confusion, but no more than that, [5] because Caesar left the fugitives to his cavalry and turned to face the attackers with his heavy infantry.* He overcame them, and pursued both of the enemy divisions as they raced for their wagons, where they resisted strongly but were finally defeated. [6] After this reverse, the barbarians divided into two contingents. One lot came to terms with Caesar and returned to the homeland they had set out from, where they rebuilt and reoccupied their towns, while the others refused to surrender their weapons. They set out for the Rhine, thinking that they could get back to their ancient land,* but since there were not

many of them and they had already been defeated, the Roman allies through whose territory they passed easily wiped them out.*

34. That was the first war that Caesar fought, and after this beginning he did not remain inactive, but instead found a way simultaneously to satisfy his own desire and please his allies. The Sequani and Aedui saw what he wanted, and that its achievement would match their hopes, so they decided to do him a good turn and at the same time avenge themselves on the Celts* who were their neighbours. [2] These Celts had crossed the Rhine long before, taken some of their territory for themselves, and made them their tributaries, holding some of their people hostage.* And given that the action they were asking for was exactly what Caesar wanted to do, it was not difficult for them to win his help.

[3] The ruler of these Celts was Ariovistus, and he had been confirmed as their king by the Romans. In fact Caesar himself, while he was consul, had seen to his enrolment among the Romans' friends and allies.* This did not bother Caesar in the slightest, however, compared with the glory to be won from the war and the power that such glory would bring him, but he did want the barbarian to provide him with some excuse for falling out with him, so that he would not be regarded as the aggressor.* [4] He therefore sent for him,* making it seem as though he wanted to discuss some matters with him, but Ariovistus refused the invitation. 'If Caesar has anything to say to me,' he said, 'let him come to me himself. I am in no way his inferior, and when one man wants something from another, it is he who should do the travelling.'* [5] Incensed by this, and making out that Ariovistus had insulted the Roman people collectively, Caesar immediately demanded the return of his allies' hostages, and also warned him not to set foot on their land, and not to add to his forces by bringing over further troops from home. [6] He did this not to cow him into submission, but hoping to provoke him to anger and thereby gain a good and plausible excuse for war. And so it turned out. The barbarian was infuriated by Caesar's orders and delivered a long, savage reply. Caesar therefore broke off communications and, before anyone was aware, promptly and pre-emptively established himself in the main town of the Sequani, Vesontio.*

35. Meanwhile, morale plummeted among Caesar's soldiers.* Word had reached them that Ariovistus had a mighty army, and that many more Celts had either already crossed the Rhine to reinforce him, or had gathered right by the river, ready to attack them at short notice. [2] They were terrified by the huge bodies of their opponents, their numbers, their courage, and the boastful threats that their courage empowered them to make; they felt they would be going up against wild beasts, impossible to master, rather than men like themselves. Among themselves, they muttered that the war they were venturing upon was none of their business and had not been voted—that it was a product of Caesar's personal ambition—and they talked of abandoning him if he did not change his mind.* [3] When Caesar found out about this, he chose not to address the bulk of the army; he did not think it advisable to talk about such matters before a crowd, given that a report of what he said was sure to be leaked to the enemy, and he was afraid that, in their mutinous state, the soldiers might cause a breakdown of discipline and damage his enterprise. Instead, he convened his senior and junior officers* and spoke to them along the following lines.*

36. 'My friends, in my opinion different kinds of deliberation are called for depending on whether one is thinking about private matters or public affairs, and the reason, I think, is that an individual's personal objectives are different from those of the community collectively. The course that should be chosen and followed by us as individuals is the one that is the fairest and the most safe, but for a people as a whole it's the one that's the strongest. [2] Even in private matters energy is required, because otherwise fairness won't be preserved, but whereas, at an individual level, the man who most avoids involvement appears to be the safest, a state which followed such a course, especially if that state has an empire, would very quickly be overthrown.* [3] The laws I'm talking about here were not enacted by men, but constituted by nature itself; they have always been in force, they are now, and they will continue to be as long as mortal creatures exist.*

'Since this is so, none of you should be thinking at the moment of what will secure present contentment and safety for him personally, but of what is proper and advantageous for all Romans collectively. [4] There are a number of considerations that would probably occur to you, but bear in mind above all the reasons why we came here, so many of us and of such distinction, senators and *equites*, with a large army and abundant financial resources. [5] We didn't come here for a holiday or a break from our duties, but to manage the affairs of our subjects correctly, protect our allies' property, defend them from those who would do them harm, and increase our own possessions.

[6] 'If this was not what we had in mind when we came here, why on earth did we set out on campaign in the first place, rather than finding some way to stay at home and look after our personal affairs? Surely it would be better not to undertake the expedition at all than to forsake it once assigned to it. [7] Some of us are here because we are legally obliged to carry out the orders given to us by our homeland; others, the majority, came of their own accord, attracted by the honours and profits that warfare brings. In either case, how could it be honourable or right to betray not only the hopes of those who assigned us to the expedition, but our own too? [8] I mean, it's not just that it's impossible for anyone to do so well as an individual that he can avoid being involved in the ruin if the state falls, but also that a successful state relieves the burden of individual misfortunes.

37. 'I'm not thinking of you who are here when I say these things, my comrades and friends, because you're aware of the points I'm making anyway, so you don't need to have them explained to you, and moreover you already take them seriously, so you don't need encouragement to do so. No, I'm saying all this because it has come to my attention that some of the troops are muttering among themselves that the war we've ventured upon is none of our business, and are trying to foment mutiny in the rest of the army as well. [2] I'd therefore like what I'm saying not just to strengthen your loyalty to our homeland, but also to help you explain to the men where their duty lies, because it will be better for them to hear it individually from you over and over again than from me just once. [3] Tell them, then, that it was not by staying at home, nor by evading military service, nor by avoiding warfare, nor by seeking a life of ease that our ancestors made our city great, but by having the mental courage readily to do whatever they were called on to do, [4] and the physical ability to undertake with a will the hard work needed to see their decisions through to fulfilment; by always treating their own possessions as though they belonged to someone else, so that they were expendable, and by treating others' possessions as though they were their own, so that they were attainable; and by equating happiness with doing their duty, and misfortune with passive inactivity.*

[5] 'Thanks to these principles, then, our ancestors, though at first they were very few and the city they lived in was originally as small as

could be, overcame the Latins, conquered the Sabines, and subdued the Etruscans, Volsci, Opici, Lucani, and Samnites—which is to say, in a word, that they subjugated all the territory south of the Alps and repulsed all the foreign peoples who came against them.* 38. The Romans who followed them and our own fathers modelled themselves after them. They did not rest content with what they had, nor was what they inherited enough for them. It was their opinion that indolence would absolutely guarantee their destruction, and hard work their safety. They worried that if their inheritance stayed as it was, it would age and be whittled away, and they were ashamed to receive so much and add nothing to it, so their conquests were far more numerous and far more important. [2] Need I list them—Sardinia, Sicily, Macedonia, Illyricum, Greece, Ionian Asia, Bithynia, Spain, Africa?* The Carthaginians would have given them a fortune to keep them from sailing to Africa; Philip and Perseus would have done likewise to stop them campaigning against them; Antiochus would have given plenty and so would his children and grandchildren to get them to stay in Europe. [3] But the Romans of those days chose the enhancement of the glory and size of their empire over inglorious indolence and wealth enjoyed without fear.

'So did the older men of our generation, who are still alive. They knew that what it takes to gain good things is the same as what it takes to keep them safe, so they not only strengthened their hold on much of what they already had, but added many new possessions. [4] Again, need I list them at this point—Crete, Pontus, Cyprus, Asian Iberia, Asian Albania, both Syrias, both Armenias, Arabia, Palestine?* Previously, we hardly even knew the names of these places, and now we rule over some of them ourselves and have granted the rest to others, which means that they supply us with revenues, troops, honours, and alliances.

39. 'With these examples before you, don't bring shame on your fathers' achievements; don't abandon the empire which is now so great. Our thinking is bound to differ from those who have no possessions like ours. [2] They can be content to take their ease and live in safety as subjects of others, but we have to work, serve as soldiers, and face danger in order to protect our current prosperity. There are many who are plotting against it, since anything that makes men superior to others arouses both jealousy and odium, and consequently there is a state of unending war between those who are worse off and those who are superior to them in any respect.* [3] Perhaps we

shouldn't have grown so exceptionally powerful compared to others in the first place, but since we have become so strong and possess such a vast empire, we are fated either to rule our subjects with an iron hand or to perish utterly ourselves.*

'What I'm saying is that it's impossible for those who have raised themselves so high and gained such great power to live without danger as ordinary men. Let us therefore follow Fortune's lead; of her own accord, without being called on, she supported our fathers and now she attends us. We should not rebuff her. [4] But we won't be following her lead if we throw away our arms, desert our posts, sit uselessly at home, or roam aimlessly in allied territory. No, we must always be armed and ready, which is the only way to preserve peace; we must train ourselves in war-making on the actual field of battle, or there will be no end to the wars we have to fight; [5] we must not hesitate to help any of our allies when they call on us, because that will gain us many more allies; and we must not tolerate any occasion when our enemies stir up trouble, because then no one will choose to wrong us in the future.

40. 'Now, if some god had guaranteed us that, even if we failed to follow the course I've outlined, no one would plot against us and we would always safely reap the benefits of all our possessions, it would still be shameful to suggest that we should do nothing, but at least those who flatly refuse to do their duty would have a plausible reason for doing so.* [2] But if, on the other hand, the possessors of an empire are bound to be liable to many intrigues, and it's right for them to anticipate the attempts of their enemies, and if those who adopt a passive attitude towards their possessions run the risk of losing them, while those who use their prosperity to acquire others' possessions by war are at the same time protecting their own—after all, no one covets his neighbours' property if he's fearful for his own, [3] because fear for what one already has acts as a powerful deterrent against meddling in what does not belong to one—if this is so, how can anyone say that we shouldn't always be acquiring more?*

[4] 'Don't you remember, either from hearsay or from what you've seen yourselves, that none of the Italian peoples refrained from intriguing against our country until our ancestors made their territory the theatre of war, and that the Epirotes* too were only stopped when our ancestors crossed over to Greece? [5] That Philip was going to invade Italy,* until they beat him to it and laid waste his land? That

Perseus, Antiochus, and Mithridates were plotting Rome's destruction, until they did the same to them? There are more instances, but
what would be the point in mentioning them?

[6] 'But what about the Carthaginians?* As long as they came to
no harm from us in Africa, they used to sail over to Italy, where they
overran the land, sacked towns, and even came close to taking Rome
itself; but as soon as the war was carried to them instead, they took to
their heels and every last trace of them disappeared from our land.
[7] The same could be said about the Gauls and Celts as well. As long
as we stayed on our side of the Alps, they often crossed the mountains
and ravaged much of Italy, but once we finally dared to campaign
beyond our borders and beleaguer them with war, and once we took
some of their land for ourselves, we never again saw them make war
in Italy, except once.* [8] Given these facts, to say that we shouldn't
make war is to say that we shouldn't be prosperous, shouldn't have an
empire, shouldn't be free, shouldn't be Romans. [9] You'd find it
completely unacceptable for anyone to say anything like that, and
you'd strike dead a man who did so on the spot. The same goes for the
present situation, my friends. You should treat people who say the
kinds of things I was talking about before in the same way, judging
their meaning not by what they say, but by what they do.

'Anyway, I'm sure that none of you would want to argue that this
was not the right way to think. **41.** But if anyone thinks that our commitment to the war should be less firm because it has not been the
subject of debate in the Senate and no vote has been taken in the
popular assembly, he should consider that, of all the wars we have
ever fought, only some have been prepared and declared in advance,
while the rest have been responses to emerging situations.* [2] Hence,
when it's a matter of wars which started up while we were at home
doing nothing, or where the grievances originally arose through some
embassy, it's important and necessary for an enquiry to take place, for
a vote to be taken, and then for consuls or praetors to be assigned to
them and forces dispatched. [3] But wars which emerge after our
forces have already left and are out in the field shouldn't be subject to
approval, but should be tackled pre-emptively, before they get out of
hand; it's as though the decision to go to war and the ratification of
that decision were taken by the crisis itself.

[4] 'If this weren't the case, why did the people send you here?* Why
did they send me here immediately after my consulship, entrusting

me, unprecedentedly, with a single command lasting five years and equipping me with four legions,* unless they thought that we were bound to have to fight? [5] I'm sure the point was not for us to be maintained while doing nothing, or for us to tour the allied cities and the subject territory* proving even more oppressive than their enemies. No one would agree with that. No, the point was for us to protect our own land, ravage enemy land, and accomplish something that justified our numbers and our costs. [6] That was why we were entrusted and assigned not just this war, but any other war that might arise. It was very sensible of them to have left it up to us to decide whom to fight, instead of voting for the war themselves. From so far away, they wouldn't have been able to get a clear picture of the situation of our allies, and, given that our enemies are well informed and prepared, they wouldn't have attacked them with the same degree of effectiveness. [7] So since we're responsible for both deciding on and conducting this war, and since we're simply responding rapidly to enemies who are openly hostile, we won't be embarking on it in an ill-considered, unjust, or reckless fashion.

42. 'Now, one of you might respond by saying: "What has Ariovistus done that's serious enough to turn him into an enemy instead of a friend and ally?" In reply, I'd ask him to consider that defence against those who want to do one harm entails responding not just to their actions but to their intentions. Their growth needs to be checked early, before one comes to any harm; one should not wait until wrong has actually been committed before retaliating. [2] Well, what more convincing proof could there be of his hostility towards us—his extreme hostility—than his own actions?* I sent him a friendly message, asking him to come and deliberate along with us about how to deal with the present situation, but he didn't come and didn't undertake to come later either. [3] But how was it wrong of me, or unfair or rude, to invite him, as a friend and ally, to a meeting? And, on the other hand, hasn't he taken discourtesy and offensiveness to the limit in refusing my invitation? There are only two reasons he could have had for doing this: either he suspected that he'd come to some harm, or he despised us. [4] If he was suspicious, that's the clearest possible proof that he was intriguing against us. I mean, what reason could he have for being suspicious of us when he has suffered no wrong at our hands? Suspicion is not the product of a sincere and guileless mind; no, suspicion comes easily only to those who have already decided to wrong others, because of their guilty consciences. [5] But if, on the other hand, there was nothing like that going on, and it was a case of his insulting us with arrogant words because he despises us, what must we expect him to do when he moves from words to action? Doesn't such a display of arrogance in a situation where it's going to gain him nothing convict a man of a long history of unjust thinking and action?

'But he went further and told me to go to him, if there was anything I wanted from him. 43. Now, this isn't the insignificant addition you might take it to be, but a clear indication of his thinking. His refusal to come to us might be attributed, in his defence, to caution, illness, or fear, [2] but there's no possible such explanation for his sending for me. It proves that what underlies everything he's done is a refusal to do anything we ask, and moreover that he's ready to issue orders back to us every time. [3] But how insolent and abusive is this behaviour of his! The Roman proconsul sends for a man and he refuses to come, and then he, an Allobrogian,* sends for the Roman proconsul! Don't think that just because it was I, Caesar, whom he snubbed, and I, Caesar, whom he summoned, that this is an insignificant and trivial matter. [4] It was not I who sent for him, nor was it I who was sent for by him; in both cases it was a Roman, a proconsul, and his fasces, dignity, and legions. It's not I as an individual who have dealings with him, but it was all of us collectively who spoke and acted, and it was all of us collectively who were spoken back to and were affected by his behaviour.

44. 'It follows that the more one points out that Ariovistus has been enrolled among the friends and allies of Rome, the more one shows that he deserves our hatred. Why? Because in the name of friendship and alliance he has committed heinous crimes, the like of which not even one of our acknowledged bitterest enemies would ever have dared to commit; it's almost as though he had procured friendship and alliance with us for the sole purpose of being able to wrong us with impunity. [2] At the time when we concluded the treaty with him, the point was not for us to become the targets of his insolence and intrigues, and it won't be we who break the treaty now. We sent envoys to him, taking him still to be a friend and ally, but he . . . well, you see how he's treated us. [3] When he wanted to do us good and expected to be well treated in return, he got what he wanted and it was right that he did so; but by the same token, since he's now

totally committed to the opposite course, it would be perfectly right for him to be considered an enemy. You shouldn't be surprised to hear me say this, even though in the past I occasionally acted on his behalf in the Senate and in the popular assembly. [4] It's not that I've changed my mind between then and now; my views are still the same.* And what are they? To honour men who are good and loyal, and to repay them in the same coin, but to strip men who are bad and disloyal of their honours and to retaliate against them. It's he who's changing, since he's making dishonourable and improper use of the privileges he received from us.

45. 'So I don't think anyone will deny that we'd be perfectly justified in making war on him. He isn't invincible and won't prove a troublesome adversary, as you can tell from all those many others of his race we've defeated in the past,* and especially easily in the recent past, and as you can also deduce from what we know about his position. [2] It's not just that his army is disunited and untrained anyway, but also that at the moment he's completely unprepared, because he's not expecting anything serious to happen. Not one of his neighbours is likely to want to come to help him, then, however much he tempts them with promises. [3] I mean, is there anyone who, lacking any grievance against us, would choose to side with him against us? Isn't it more likely that they'll all support us rather than him, in their desire to overthrow him as a neighbouring tyrant and gain some of his land for themselves?

[4] 'Even if some of them were to join forces with him, we'd still have the advantage. Leaving aside our numbers, our age, our experience, and our successes, everyone knows that while we're covered evenly in armour from head to toe, they are mostly naked, and that while we have a rational and disciplined approach to battle, they always rush furiously forward in no kind of order.* [5] You needn't be alarmed by the force of their charge, or by their great size and the loudness of their cries. Yelling never killed anyone, and physically they can't be any more effective than us: they have the same number of hands as we do, and in fact their size and nakedness make them far more vulnerable. As for their charge, although it's unrestrained and breakneck at first, it rapidly exhausts itself. It's only briefly effective.

46. 'You, of course, know what I'm talking about from experience, having defeated men like them in the past, but I'm addressing you to make sure that, where words are concerned, you don't feel you're being misled by me, and that, where facts are concerned, the expectation you have of victory, based on what you've achieved in the past, is as strong as it might be. [2] But we'll have many Gauls fighting on our side as well, so that even if there is something especially terrifying about these peoples, it will work for us just as much as for them.

'I would ask you, then, not just to take on board what I've been saying, but also to explain it to the rest of the men. [3] Even if some of you dissent, I shall still fight, and I shall never leave the post assigned to me by my country. The Tenth legion will be enough for me,* because I know well that they would readily pass naked even through flames if they were required to do so. [4] As for the rest of you, I would ask you to leave as soon as possible. Please don't linger here doing nothing, using up public money to no effect, claiming for yourselves the results of other men's efforts, and appropriating the booty acquired by others.'

47. After Caesar had finished speaking, not only did no one raise any objections, even if there were people there who held quite the opposite view, but they all, and not least those whose loyalty he doubted, agreed to spread his message. In fact they had no difficulty in persuading the troops to end their mutiny, some because being singled out had aroused their enthusiasm and the rest out of rivalry with the first group. [2] He singled out the Tenth legion because he had always been well disposed towards them. (The citizen legions were named in this way, according to the order in which they were enrolled, and even today the legions currently in existence are named on the same principle.*)

[3] Given the army's determination, Caesar decided to make a move, in case as time went by their enthusiasm waned again, and he immediately broke camp and marched against Ariovistus. His sudden advance so alarmed Ariovistus that he was obliged to engage in talks about peace, [4] but no agreement was reached because Caesar wanted to dictate all the terms and Ariovistus refused to accept any of them.* War therefore broke out, leaving not only the two enemy armies themselves in suspense, but also all the nearby allies and enemies of both sides, because they expected the decisive battle to take place very soon and were sure that the whole region would become subject to the victors. [5] The barbarians had the advantage in terms of numbers and the stature of their men, but the Romans were more experienced and better equipped. And Caesar's sound judgement

turned out to counterbalance the fervour of the Celts, with their reck-less and headlong approach to battle, so that ultimately they were evenly matched, and their hopes and the determination generated by those hopes were also equal.

48. The two sides were encamped close to each other,* but the barbarians' womenfolk, as a result of their divination, forbade the men from joining battle before the new moon. [2] Now, Ariovistus took it very seriously when the women did something like this, so at first he withheld some of his army, even though the Romans were offering him battle, and sent out only his cavalry to engage them, along with the infantrymen deployed with them.* They inflicted heavy losses on the Romans, and this made him contemptuous of them, so he decided to try to seize a position overlooking their entrenchments. [3] He was successful in this, but the Romans occupied another position close by.* Although Caesar drew up his army in battle order and had them wait outside the camp until noon, Ariovistus refused battle, but in the afternoon, as Caesar was withdrawing, he suddenly attacked and came close to capturing the Roman camp. [4] Since things were going so well for him, he stopped paying much attention to the womenfolk, and the next day, when the Romans followed their usual daily routine and formed up in battle array, he led his forces out against them.

49. Seeing them advancing from their encampment, the Romans fell to.* They rushed forward, giving the barbarians no chance to form up in precise ranks, and by attacking at full pelt, shouting out their war cries, they forestalled their javelineers, who were the chief source of their confidence. [2] In fact, they came to such close quar-ters that the barbarians were unable to wield their pikes or their longer swords. They resorted to shoving, therefore, fighting with their bod-ies more than with their weapons, struggling to trip up their attackers and knock down anyone who stood up to them. [3] Many of them, finding themselves denied the use even of their shorter swords, fought instead with hands and teeth, dragging their opponents down to the ground, biting and gouging, making use of the considerable advan-tage their bodily size gave them. [4] But they did no substantial harm to the Romans in this way, because by closing with them the Romans used their superior equipment and skill to cancel out the barbarians' advantage. Eventually, after prolonged fighting of this kind, the Romans gained the upper hand in the evening. Their swords, which were shorter than the Gallic ones and had steel points, proved more effective, [5] and the men themselves were able to sustain the same level of effort for a longer time and therefore held out better than the barbarians, whose staying power did not match the fury of their attacks.

So they were defeated, but they did not turn to flight—not because they did not want to, but because they were too confused and exhausted. [6] They banded together in groups of three hundred or thereabouts, put up a defensive wall of shields on all sides, and stood up straight in such close order that they proved unassailable, and in such a solid formation that they could not be dislodged. In this way, while they did no harm to the Romans, they also suffered no harm themselves.

50. So the barbarians neither advanced against the Romans nor fled, but stood immobile, as though they were in towers. The Romans, therefore, who had shed their spears* right at the start of the battle as being of no use, [2] and were unable to use their swords to engage the enemy at close quarters or reach their heads (which, given that they were fighting with no protective headgear, were the only parts of the barbarians' bodies that were vulnerable), cast aside their shields and fell on them. Some of the Romans attacked from a run, others from closer in, but they all sprang at the enemy, so to speak, and began cutting them down. [3] Many were felled straight away by a single blow, and many others died even before they fell, because the density of their formation kept them upright even after they had been killed. [4] Most of their infantry died like that, either where they were or by their wagons, inasmuch as some of them were driven back to their camp, where they perished along with their womenfolk and children. Ariovistus, however, lost no time in leaving the region with some of his cavalry and making for the Rhine, and although the Romans gave chase, they could not catch up with him. [5] He managed to escape by boat, but the others who were with him were either killed by the Romans, who advanced into the riverbed, or were snatched away by the river itself.

BOOK THIRTY-NINE

1. That was the outcome of this war. Later, at the end of the winter when Cornelius Spinther and Metellus Nepos* took up their consulships, the Romans became involved in a third war. The Belgae,* made up of many intermingled tribes, lived next to the Rhine, [2] with territory stretching all the way to the Ocean facing Britain. In the past, some of them had been allies of the Romans,* while others took no account of them, but at the time in question they could see that things were going well for Caesar and, fearful that he would move against them, they joined forces. Acting in concert, with the exception of the Remi, they plotted against the Romans and bound themselves with oaths, appointing Galba as their leader.*

[3] When Caesar was informed about this by the Remi,* he stationed watchposts in their territory and then made camp by the river Aisne,* where he gathered his soldiers and drilled them. But he did not dare to engage the enemy,* even though they were overrunning the land of the Remi, [4] until, despising him as afraid, they decided to seize the bridge and interrupt his supply columns, which were being provided by the allies and made use of the bridge. Caesar was given advance warning of the offensive by deserters, and at night* he sent his light-armed troops and cavalry against the Belgae. 2. They launched a surprise attack on the barbarians and inflicted heavy casualties, with the result that, the following night, they all retreated back to their homeland, not least because they received news that the Aedui had invaded it.* Caesar saw what was happening, but because of his ignorance of the region* he did not dare to go after them straight away. [2] At daybreak, however, he took the cavalry, leaving instructions for the infantry to follow on behind, and caught up with them.* They thought he had come with only the cavalry, so they chose to fight, but he kept them busy until the infantry arrived, and then, with his whole army available, he surrounded them. Most of them were killed, but he accepted the surrender of the remainder, and then he won over some of the tribes without resistance and some by war.*

3. The Nervii withdrew of their own accord from the plain, since they did not have the forces to match the Romans,* and retreated into

particularly thickly wooded hills. But then, when [. . .] they charged down unexpectedly from there.* Although in the part of the field where Caesar was the barbarians were routed and ran for their lives, the bulk of the Roman army was overwhelmed and their camp fell to the barbarians' first assault. [2] When Caesar, who had advanced some way off the field in pursuit of the fugitives, found out what had happened, he turned back. Finding the barbarians inside the Roman defences, engaged in looting, he surrounded them and massacred them.* After this, he found it relatively easy to subdue the rest of the Nervii.*

4. Meanwhile, their neighbours, the Atuatuci, who were Cimbri in both descent and spirit,* had set out to help, but were forestalled by the defeat of the Nervii. They retreated and, abandoning all their other strongpoints, took refuge in just one fortress, the strongest they had.* [2] Caesar attacked it, but was beaten back day after day, until he set about constructing siege engines. At first, the barbarians watched the Romans cutting wood and making the machines with scorn, since they had no idea what was going on. [3] But when the devices were ready and were being used to bring heavy infantry up to the walls from all sides at once, they were terrified, having never seen anything like it before. They therefore sued for peace, supplied the Romans with food, and threw some of their weapons from the wall. [4] But when they saw that the machines were once again empty of men, and realized that the Romans had given themselves over to celebration, assuming that they had won, they changed their minds.* Their courage revived, and they made a sortie under cover of darkness, hoping to catch the Romans unawares and slaughter them. However, they encountered the pickets (for Caesar always took all the necessary precautions) and their attack failed. None of the survivors was shown mercy; they were all sold into slavery.*

5. By the time the Atuatuci had been vanquished, and many others had been subdued as well either by Caesar himself or by his legates,* it was the start of winter, and Caesar therefore withdrew to winter quarters.* When the Romans at home heard about his achievements, they were astonished that he had overcome so many peoples—peoples whose very names had been unfamiliar before—and they decreed that fifteen days should be given over to sacrifices for his successes, an unprecedented honour.*

[2] Meanwhile, while the weather still permitted campaigning and his force was still intact, one of Caesar's legates, Servius Galba,* had

won over the Veragri, partly by force and partly by surrender, and had even made plans to spend the winter in their country. The Veragri, neighbours of the Allobroges, lived by Lake Leman and their terri-tory extended up to the Alps.* [3] But when most of Galba's soldiers left, some on furlough since they were not far from Italy, and some elsewhere by themselves,* the local inhabitants seized the moment and launched a surprise attack. Driven to recklessness by desper-ation, [4] Galba suddenly burst out of his winter quarters, startling those who were attacking him with the unexpectedness of this bold action, and escaped through their lines to high ground. Once he had reached safety, he then fought them off and subjugated them.* But rather than spend the winter there, he moved to the territory of the Allobroges.*

6. While these events were taking place in Gaul, Pompey had arranged for Cicero's recall to be voted.* In other words, he now brought back against Clodius the very man whose banishment he had seen to with Clodius' help. This goes to show how rapidly human affairs can change, to the extent that one might anticipate help or harm from certain people, but actually get the exact opposite. [2] Pompey had the cooperation of various praetors and tribunes (especially Titus Annius Milo), and it was they who brought the proposal before the plebs.* For the consul, Spinther, who was a personal enemy of Clodius and, when serving as a juror, had voted to convict him for adultery, acting partly as a favour to Pompey and partly to avenge himself on Clodius [. . .]* [3] However, Clodius had the support of others who were in office that year, including his brother, Appius Claudius, who was a praetor, and the consul Nepos, who had personal reasons for hating Cicero.*

7. These two factions, then, made more trouble than before, now that they had the consuls as their leaders, along with the others in the city who were partisans of one side or the other. Many disturbances followed, [2] the worst of which occurred during the actual taking of the vote. Clodius knew that the majority would take Cicero's part, so he came with the gladiators his brother had collected for the funerary contests he was arranging for Marcius (a relative of his), burst into the meeting, and wounded and killed many people.* [3] The proposal was therefore not passed into law, and Clodius became an object of fear to everyone for various reasons, not least the fact that he went around with these gladiators as his bodyguards. He then stood for election to an aedileship, thinking that, if he was appointed, he would avoid being convicted for violence.* [4] Milo had in fact instituted proceedings against him, but he failed to take him to court, because the quaestors, whose job it was to conduct the ballot assigning jurors to the courts, had not been elected, and Nepos ruled that the praetor could not proceed to any trial until the allotment of jurors had taken place. It seems that the aediles had to be chosen before the quaestors, and this proved to be the chief cause of the delay.*

Despite this failure, Milo continued to fight over this same issue and caused considerable chaos. 8. In the end he too gathered a band of gladiators and other supporters. After that, there was no end to the brawling between him and Clodius, and murders were taking place in almost every quarter of the city. [2] Nepos then had a change of heart,* prompted by fear of his colleague, Pompey, and other leading men. The Senate accordingly passed a preliminary motion, introduced by Spinther, that Cicero should return, and both consuls laid the proposal before the people, who voted their approval.* [3] Clodius spoke out in opposition, but he had Milo as a counterweight to prevent him from doing anything violent. In any case, the supporters of the law were much stronger, especially since Pompey and others spoke in its favour.

9. So Cicero returned, and he expressed his thanks to both the Senate and the popular assembly, once the consuls had given him the opportunity to address both bodies.* He was reconciled with Pompey, relinquishing the hatred he bore him for his exile, and before very long he repaid him for his support. [2] There was a severe famine in the city, and the entire populace rushed to the theatre (the kind of theatre, at any rate, that they were still in those days using for the games)† and then to the Capitol where the senators were in session, threatening either to take up arms and kill them themselves, or to burn them alive along with the temples. [3] But Cicero persuaded them to appoint Pompey commissioner of the grain supply, and to award him for this purpose the power of a proconsul both in Italy and abroad for five years.* Once again, then, Pompey was going to rule the entire world, or as much of it as was then under Roman sway*—this time for grain, whereas before it had been to deal with the pirates.

10. As for Caesar and Crassus, although they were basically hostile to Cicero, they expressed a degree of enthusiasm when they realized that his return was certain, and in fact Caesar indicated from abroad

that he was quite well disposed towards him.* But they received no thanks in return, [2] because Cicero knew that their behaviour was not a reflection of their true feelings and considered them the prime movers of his exile. He did not dare to confront them openly, because recent experience had shown him what the outcome was when he spoke with unrestrained frankness, but he wrote a secret book, the title of which showed that it contained a defence of his policies.* [3] He filled it with dire accusations against them and others, but since he was afraid that word of its contents might get out while he was still alive, he sealed it and handed it over to his son,* telling him not to read or publish what he had written until after his death.

11. So Cicero was flourishing once again, and he recovered his property, including the plot where his house had been, even though it had been dedicated to Liberty,* and even though Clodius called it sacrilege and tried to excite religious scruple as a way of stopping him. [2] For Cicero was challenging the introduction of the *lex curiata* by which Clodius had changed status from patrician to plebeian, on the grounds that notice of it had not been posted in the time stipulated by ancestral usage.* In other words, he was attempting to annul Clodius' entire tribunate, during which the decree about his house had been passed, by claiming that, since his change of status had been illegal, every measure passed during it was necessarily invalid. [3] With this argument he persuaded the pontiffs to return the plot of land to him on the grounds that it was not consecrated or hallowed ground.* And in this way he was given not only the plot, but also money to rebuild his house and repair anything else of his that had been damaged.*

12. After this, there was further unrest, due this time to King Ptolemy.* He had given a lot of money to certain Romans—some of it his own and some of it borrowed*—in order to have his rule confirmed and to be named a friend and ally of Rome, and now he was trying to recover it from the Egyptians. [2] They were angry with him not only for this, but also because when they ordered him to insist on the return of Cyprus from the Romans,* or renounce the treaty of friendship he had with them, he refused. Having failed to quell their restiveness by either persuasion or force (he had no mercenaries at his disposal), [3] he fled from Egypt and went to Rome, where he accused his subjects of having thrown him out of his kingdom.* His petition was successful, and he was to be restored to Egypt by Spinther, who had been appointed to the governorship of Cilicia.*

13. In the meantime, the Alexandrians, who either did not know that Ptolemy had left for Italy or thought him dead, replaced him on the throne with his daughter Berenice.* When they learnt the truth, they sent a hundred men to Rome to defend themselves against his charges and to accuse him in return of all the wrongs he had done them. [2] Ptolemy, who was still in Rome, had early warning of their coming and he sent men out here and there to ambush the envoys before they reached their destination. He succeeded in killing most of them as they were en route, and then he killed some of the survivors actually in the city. The rest—some because they were terrified by what he had done, and others because they were suborned—he persuaded not to meet with the authorities and raise the matters they had been charged to raise, and under no circumstances to mention the murders.

14. The affair became so widely talked about, however, that even the Senate erupted in anger. It was above all Marcus Favonius* who urged them to action, on the grounds that, first, a large number of envoys on a mission from allies of Rome had died violent deaths, and, second, it had proved to be another occasion when bribery of Romans had been widespread. [2] In order to learn the truth, they sent for Dio, the envoy with plenipotentiary powers, who had survived the attacks, but Ptolemy's wealth still proved so overwhelmingly powerful even under these circumstances that not only did Dio fail to appear before the Senate, but no mention was made of the murders as long as Ptolemy was in Rome. [3] Later, even after Dio was assassinated, Ptolemy was not held to account for it, chiefly because Pompey had welcomed him into his house* and was strongly supporting him. [4] Subsequently, many others from there were prosecuted for the crime, but few were convicted,* because bribery was rife, and each of the accused stood shoulder to shoulder with his fellows because of his fear for himself.

15. While mortal men were behaving like this under the influence of money, right at the beginning of the following year divinity struck the statue of Jupiter on the Alban Mount* with a thunderbolt, and this delayed Ptolemy's return to Egypt for some time. [2] The reason it did so is that when they consulted the Sibylline verses* they found the following: 'If the king of Egypt arrives in need of help, do not withhold your friendship, but also do not help him with a multitude, or you risk tribulation and danger.' [3] Impressed by the coincidence between these verses and current events, they were persuaded by the tribune Gaius Cato to rescind all that had been voted about Ptolemy.* Now, it was forbidden to announce any of the Sibylline oracles to the people without a decree of the Senate, but this one was made public by Cato. [4] What happened was that the inevitable rumour mill spread word of the gist of the oracle, and Cato became afraid that it would be suppressed. He therefore quickly brought the priests into the popular assembly, and there and then, before the matter had been raised in the Senate in any form, he forced them to divulge the oracle. The more they protested that they had no right to do so, the more insistent the plebs became.*

16. That was how the matter of the oracle turned out, and a Latin translation was made and proclaimed.* In the course of the discussion that followed in the Senate,* some of the senators wanted to have Spinther reinstate Ptolemy without an army, while others argued that Pompey, attended by two lictors, should see to his restoration. [2] When Ptolemy found out about the oracle, he asked for Pompey to be given the job and one of the tribunes, Aulus Plautius, read out his letter in public. However, the senators were afraid that this would still further increase Pompey's power, so they opposed his appointment, using the grain supply as an excuse. [3] These developments happened* during the consulship of Lucius Philippus and Gnaeus Marcellinus,* and when Ptolemy found out about them he gave up hope of being reinstated. He went to Ephesus instead, and took up residence with the goddess.*

17. The previous year, however, something happened which, 57 BCE though a private matter, has some relevance to this history.* Spinther, the consul, wanted to place his son, Cornelius Spinther, in the college of augurs. But it was expressly forbidden by law for any two people from the same *gens* to hold the same priesthood at the same time,* [2] so since Faustus, the son of Sulla, and therefore a member of the *gens* of the Cornelii, had been enrolled in the college first, Spinther had his son adopted into the Manlii Torquati.* In other words, although the letter of the law was observed, it was effectively broken.

18. Next, as soon as Clodius had taken up the post of aedile* in the 56 BCE year of Philippus' and Marcellinus' consulship (he wanted to avoid being taken to court, so he had made sure of his election by factional means), he instituted proceedings against Milo* for furnishing himself with gladiators. In other words, his response to Milo's attempt to

take him to court was to accuse Milo of doing exactly what he himself was doing and exactly what he himself was guilty of. [2] He did this not so much because he expected to get Milo convicted, since he had powerful supporters including Cicero and Pompey, but because he could use the trial as a pretext for attacking Milo and defaming those supporters of his.

19. One of his schemes, for instance, was as follows.* He primed his political friends to shout out 'Pompey!' in mass meetings whenever he asked them, 'Who is it who behaves (or talks) like this?' So he would often suddenly ask the question about Pompey's physical or other idiosyncracies, going through all of them individually and one by one, while phrasing the question as though he were not really talking about Pompey. [2] Some of his friends acted as leaders of the chorus, while others, as is usual in such cases, echoed their cry of 'Pompey!', and the outcome was that Pompey was often made a laughing stock. He was simultaneously furious and reduced to helplessness, because he was not the kind to put up with it and do nothing, but at the same time he could not bring himself to respond in the same vein. Although in theory it was Milo who was on trial, in fact it was Pompey who was being treated as guilty. Nor did he have the opportunity to defend himself, [3] because, in order to raise the stakes, Clodius would not allow the *lex curiata* to be introduced,* and until a vote had been taken on that no other serious business could be conducted in the state, and no trial could take place either.

20. For a while, then, Milo served as an excuse for their insults and murders. But certain portents occurred at this time: on the Alban Mount a little temple of Juno, which was mounted on a sort of table and faced east, was found turned towards the north; a light flashed across the heavens from south to north; [2] a wolf entered the city; there was an earthquake; some Roman citizens were killed by thunderbolts; and in Latinum subterranean noises were heard.* In their search for a remedy, the *haruspices* claimed that some god was angry with them because certain sanctuaries and places not for profane use were being used as places of residence.* [3] So then Clodius began to target Cicero directly.* He delivered a speech* which included a forceful attack on Cicero for having rebuilt his house when the site was consecrated to Liberty, and he even once attacked the house* with the intention of razing it once more to the ground. But Milo made sure that this did not happen.

21. Cicero, however, was as furious with Clodius as if it had actually happened. He kept denouncing him, and in the end, accompanied by Milo and some of the tribunes, he went up to the Capitol and took down the tablets which had been erected by Clodius for his exile.* [2] On this occasion, Clodius came with his brother Gaius,* who was a praetor, and took them away from him, but Cicero next waited until Clodius was out of town and then went back up to the Capitol, removed the tablets, and took them home with him. [3] After this, no tactic was out of bounds for either of them; they seized every opportunity to abuse and slander each other, without refraining from the most disgusting language. [4] Cicero argued that Clodius' tribunate had come about contrary to the laws and that therefore the measures he had taken as tribune were also invalid, while Clodius claimed that Cicero's exile had been decided in accordance with justice and that his recall had been voted illegally.

22. Clodius was coming off worst by a long way in this contest with Cicero, until the arrival of Marcus Cato restored the balance between them. Cato was annoyed with Cicero and was also afraid that everything he had done in Cyprus would be cancelled because he had been sent out there by Clodius during his tribunate, and so he supported Clodius strongly.* [2] He was very proud of what he had achieved, and there was nothing he wanted more than to see his measures ratified. When Ptolemy, who held Cyprus at the time, had heard about the decisions that had been taken in Rome, he did not dare to rise up against the Romans, but at the same time he could not abide the prospect of living if his realm was taken away from him,* [3] so he committed suicide by drinking poison. After that, the people of Cyprus welcomed Cato, in the expectation that the Romans would be their friends and allies, not their masters. [4] This in itself was no reason for Cato to give himself airs, but his administration had been excellent. In particular, he had amassed slaves and a great deal of money from the royal holdings* without attracting the slightest criticism and while accounting impeccably for everything. He therefore claimed that his achievement was just as meritorious as winning a war, since, given how widespread bribery was, disdaining money was a rarer feat than conquering an enemy.

23. So Cato at this time came to be thought deserving of a triumph for what he had done, and the consuls proposed in the Senate that he should be awarded a praetorship, even though he was not yet legally eligible.* In fact, he was not appointed to the post, because he himself spoke against it, but even this increased his fame. [2] Clodius made an attempt to have the slaves who had been brought from Cyprus named after him, on the grounds that it was he who had sent Cato there, but he failed thanks to Cato's opposition. They were known as the 'Cypriots' instead, although it was mooted in some quarters that they should be called the 'Porcians';* but this was another idea that Cato ruled out. [3] Clodius, enraged by Cato's opposition, began to disparage his administration of Cyprus and insisted on seeing his account books. He did this not because it would enable him to convict Cato of any wrongdoing, but because almost all the written records had been lost at sea,* and he expected this request to gain him some leverage. [4] Moreover, even though he was not in Rome, Caesar was helping Clodius at this time too; some writers even report that he was priming Clodius by letter with the charges to bring against Cato. One way in which Cato's name was being blackened was by the allegation that it was he who had persuaded the consuls to propose the praetorship for himself, and that he had made a big show of voluntarily renouncing it in order to avoid the ignominy of failing to be appointed.

24. So Clodius and Cato kept up the fight, and meanwhile Pompey met with some delay in the distribution of the grain.* Many slaves had been freed because of the hopes he had aroused, and he wanted to take a census of them to enable the dole to go ahead in a methodical and orderly manner. [2] This proved fairly easy to manage, thanks to a combination of his own skill and the abundance of grain, but his bid for the consulship turned out to be troublesome and earned him criticism. [3] Clodius' behaviour irritated him, but the most annoying thing was the disdain with which he was treated by others who were not his equals; his sense of his own worth, and the fact that he expected to receive more honour than all of them, even though he was not in office, made him feel slighted. [4] He was occasionally able to rise above this, however. His immediate response to being disrespected was anger, but after a while, once he had taken into account his own merits and the worthlessness of his enemies, he stopped treating them as important.

25. But Pompey bitterly resented Caesar's increasing strength.* The people were so impressed by Caesar's achievements that they even sent a senatorial delegation to organize what they supposed to be a completely subjugated Gaul, and they were so encouraged by the

hopes he inspired in them that they also voted him large sums of money.* [2] Pompey tried to persuade the consuls not to be in too much of a hurry to read out Caesar's letters, but to conceal the contents as long as possible, until the fame of his exploits prevailed of its own accord, and he also tried to persuade them to send someone to replace him even before the expiration of his command.* [3] So intense was his rivalry that he even disparaged and tried to cancel the measures he himself had helped Caesar put in place. It infuriated him that Caesar was being lavishly garlanded and was putting his own achievements in the shade, and he rebuked the people for belittling him and aggrandizing Caesar. [4] He was particularly annoyed when he saw that their memory of a man's achievements lasted only until something new came along; that they eagerly welcomed every fresh development, even if it was less important than what had preceded it, just because they had had enough of what was familiar* and enjoyed novelty; and that, under the influence of envy, they annulled everything that had seemed good before, while, under the influence of hope, they exaggerated the importance of every newly emerging occurrence.

26. All this was what he found hard to bear, and since he was getting nowhere with the consuls and could see that Caesar was becoming too powerful for him to trust, he was not inclined to take the situation lightly. It was his opinion that there were two things which ruin friendship, fear and envy, and that friendship exists only when there is equivalence of fame and power. [2] The bond of friendship, he believed, is strong as long as people are equal in terms of glory and power, but when one person surpasses another to any degree, then the inferior envies and hates his superior, and the stronger despises and abuses the weaker. And so, given such feelings on both sides—with one person irritated by his inferiority and the other exulting in his superiority—they end up exchanging their former friendship for animosity and antagonism. [3] This was the kind of thinking that led Pompey to arm himself against Caesar, and since he thought that it would not be easy for him to see to his downfall by himself, he attached Crassus even more firmly to himself in order to gain his support.

27. Having decided to work together, Pompey and Crassus realized that they could not hope to achieve anything as private citizens, but they thought that if they became consuls and used the position to take control of affairs, following Caesar's example, the balance would

be corrected and they could reasonably expect to get the better of him
before long, seeing that they were two and he was one. [2] So they
completely dropped the pretence they had affected whereby, if any of
their friends urged them to seek the consulship, they claimed that
they had no longer wanted it. Now they openly sought it, even though
up until then they had been supporting others' bids for the position.
[3] However, they declared their candidacy outside the legally prescribed period,* and a number of people made it clear that they would
not allow them to be appointed, including the consuls themselves
(Marcellinus in particular carried weight*). They accordingly tried to
have the elections cancelled for that year through the agency of Gaius
Cato and others, so that an *interrex** would be appointed, and they
could then legally seek and gain the position.

28. The realization of this plan was ostensibly in the hands of
agents who were deployed on various pretexts,* but in fact Pompey
and Crassus themselves were the prime movers. At any rate, they
made no secret of their resentment of anyone who opposed them. The
senators were furious, so much so that on one occasion they got
up and left the building while the wrangling was going on. But that
put only a temporary halt to the conflict, and when the same thing
happened again, [2] the senators voted to change their clothing* as
though for some national catastrophe, even though Cato dashed out
of the meeting, since he was getting nowhere by arguing, and dragged
people in off the streets* to prevent any decision being taken [3]—the
point being that no vote was supposed to be taken if there were any
non-senators inside the chamber—but some of the other tribunes
intercepted the outsiders and stopped them entering. So this decree
was passed, and it was also proposed that the senators should not
attend the games which were taking place at the time.* [4] When Cato
spoke out against this too, the senators rushed out in a body and
returned after changing their clothing, in the hope that this would
frighten him. He still refused to moderate his stance, however, so they
all trooped together to the Forum, and when a crowd gathered to see
what was going on, they induced in them a state of utter despondency.
[5] In his address to them, Marcellinus lamented the state of affairs,
while the rest of the senators wept and groaned, so that no one had
a word to speak against him. Afterwards, they returned immediately
to the senate-house, intending to deal severely with those who were
responsible.

29. While all this was going on, Clodius had once again leapt over to Pompey's side* and taken up his cause, in the hope that, if he helped him bring any of his current projects to a successful conclusion, Pompey would become his devoted friend. So he presented himself before the people in his usual clothes, without having changed them as the decree required, and delivered a speech in which he denounced Marcellinus and the others. [2] This made the senators furious, so he interrupted his speech to the plebs and rushed to the senate-house. But there he came close to losing his life. The senators confronted him and stopped him from entering the chamber, [3] and then he was surrounded by *equites*. He would have been torn to pieces if there had not been a good response when he cried out and called on people to help him. A lot of men ran up bearing brands and threatening to burn the senators alive along with the senate-house if they harmed a hair on his head. So Clodius was narrowly saved from certain death.

30. But this did not deter Pompey at all, and on one occasion he rushed to a meeting of the Senate to voice his opposition to a vote they were about to take, and succeeded in stopping the measure being passed. Later, when Marcellinus asked him in public if it was true that he wanted the consulship, hoping that he would balk at admitting that he was putting himself forward for it, Pompey replied that, while it was true that honest men gave him no reason to want the position, he was strongly attracted to it so that he could deal with the trouble-makers. [2] So Pompey stopped concealing his intentions, while Crassus, when asked the same question, neither admitted nor denied it, taking the middle road as usual and saying that he would do whatever was in the public interest.*

Marcellinus and many others became frightened by how organized and coordinated Pompey's and Crassus' opposition was, and they stopped coming to the senate-house. [3] Since, then, no meeting of the Senate had the legal minimum number for a vote to be taken about the elections, no election-related business could be conducted at all,* and so the year came to an end. [4] However, the senators refused to change back into their ordinary clothes, or attend the games, or take part in the feast in honour of Jupiter on the Capitol,* or go to the Alban Mount for the Latin Festival,* which was being held there for the second time because of a procedural irregularity. Instead, they spent what was left of the year as though they were as powerless as slaves and did not have the right to choose magistrates or conduct any other public business.

31. Subsequently, then, Pompey and Crassus were appointed consuls after an *interregnum*.* None of the other candidates who had declared earlier stood against them. Lucius Domitius, who had canvassed for election right up until the last moment, set out from his home for the assembly under cover of darkness, but the slave who was lighting his way with a torch was murdered and he was too frightened to carry on.* [2] So, since they met with no opposition at all, and also since Publius Crassus, Marcus' son, who was one of Caesar's legates at the time, brought soldiers to Rome for that very purpose,* it was not difficult for them to get elected.

32. Once they had taken over leadership of the state like this, they arranged for the remaining offices to be given to their friends. They also made sure that Marcus Cato was not elected praetor,* because they suspected that he would not condone the situation, and they did not want him to gain legal authority for his protests. [2] The election of praetors went ahead without any trouble, because Cato eschewed violence, but bloodshed attended the election of the curule aediles,* and even Pompey was thoroughly spattered with blood. [3] Nevertheless, since Pompey and Crassus were in charge of the elections, they made sure that both these and all the other posts that were subject to election by the people were filled in a way that suited themselves, and they got on good terms with the plebeian aediles and most of the tribunes. Two tribunes, however, Gaius Ateius Capito and Publius Aquillius Gallus, refused to compromise with them.

33. Once all the positions had been filled, they turned their attention to attaining their goals. They never brought up what it was they wanted in either the Senate or the popular assembly, and insisted that they had no need of anything. [2] But Gaius Trebonius, one of the tribunes, proposed that one of them should be assigned Syria and the neighbouring territories* as his province, and the other the Spains (where there had been a recent uprising),* in both cases for a term of five years, with as many soldiers at their command as they wanted, whether citizens or auxiliaries, and with the right to make war and peace on whomever they pleased.* [3] This provoked widespread outrage, especially among Caesar's friends,* who thought it likely that, once Pompey and Crassus attained their ends, they would curb Caesar, who was due to give up his command before long. Some of them were therefore prepared to argue against the proposal, but the consuls, wanting to make sure that their plans were not thwarted, won them over by extending Caesar's command as well for (as accurate enquiry shows) a period of three years.* [4] However, they delayed formally presenting any proposal about Caesar to the people until their own provinces had been confirmed. And the confirmation went ahead because Caesar's friends kept quiet, now that they had had the wind taken out of their sails like this, and most other Romans, enslaved by their fear, did nothing and were happy just to remain alive.

34. Cato and Favonius, however, resisted them at every turn.* They had various allies, of whom the most important were the two tribunes, but there were only a few of them and their enemies were many, so their fearless speaking got them nowhere. [2] Favonius was allowed only one hour by Trebonius to argue against the proposal, and he spent it complaining loudly and uselessly about just this restriction of his time. Cato was granted two hours for his speech, [3] but as usual he started by condemning the present situation and the general state of affairs, and used up his time before getting around to any of the particular issues he had in mind. It was not that he did not have the time to do so, but he wanted to be silenced by Trebonius while making it plain that he still had something to say, so that he could censure him for that too, since he knew perfectly well that he would not be able to persuade the people to vote as he wished on any issue even if he had the whole day to speak. [4] So when he was told that his time was up, he did not stop straight away, and then, after he was pushed and dragged from the meeting, he came back. Eventually the order was given for him to be taken off to the prison, but he still did not moderate his behaviour.*

35. So that day passed without the tribunes having the opportunity to speak at all. I should explain that in all the popular assemblies, or at any rate those which involved decision-making, private citizens were allowed to speak before any office-holders.* [2] The reason for this, apparently, was to make sure that any private citizen could speak his mind with complete freedom—that is, to ensure that he would not refrain from expressing his views because those of a more powerful person than himself had been heard first.

[3] Gallus was afraid that the least that might happen to him the next day was his being shut out from the Forum, so he went into the senate-house the evening before and spent the night there. It was not

just that it was a safe place, but also that he could leave there at day-break and join the people. [4] But Trebonius foiled his plan by locking all the doors of the senate-house and forcing him to spend not only the night there but most of the next day as well. Meanwhile, during the night others occupied the place where the meeting was to be held,* and in the morning they tried to bar Ateius, Cato, Favonius, and their allies. [5] Favonius and Ninnius* somehow managed to sneak inside, however, and Cato and Ateius climbed on the shoulders of some of the bystanders and were hoisted up by them. They then declared a celestial omen* in an attempt to get the meeting dissolved, but some of the tribunes' attendants drove them both out, and in the process their companions were injured and a few were even killed.

36. So the proposal was passed into law. As the meeting was break-ing up and people were starting to leave, Ateius took Gallus, who was covered with blood (he had been struck as he was being forcibly evicted from the senate-house) and led him before those who were still there. By letting them see the state he was in, and by delivering a predictable speech, he whipped them up into a fury. [2] When the consuls heard about this, they ran over—they had been keeping an eye on developments from somewhere close by—and frightened the two tribunes into submission, thanks to the sizeable body of men they had with them. They then immediately convened an assembly and put the measure relating to Caesar to the vote.* The same people tried to argue against this as well, but they were unable to achieve anything.

37. After the consuls had seen this measure into law, they enacted harsher penalties for bribery*—as though they themselves were any the less guilty because they had seized power by force rather than bribery.* [2] They also planned to curb personal expenditure,* which had become truly excessive, even though there was no one who lived more luxurious and indulgent lives than themselves. In fact, it was exactly this that stopped them enacting the law. [3] Hortensius, one of the most extravagant men in Rome, got them to drop the proposal by expatiating on the greatness of the city* and praising them for all their domestic opulence and generosity to others—which is to say that he used their lifestyles to support his argument. [4] His oppos-ition shamed them, and they also did not want people to think that, out of jealousy perhaps, they were forbidding others from doing as they themselves did, so they withdrew the motion of their own accord.

38. Meanwhile, in the course of these same days, Pompey dedicated his theatre,* the one which is still a source of pride for us. He used the new theatre as the venue for a musical and gymnastic show, and in the Circus he organized a horse race and the slaughter of all kinds of wild animals, in great numbers.[2] Five hundred lions were finished off in five days, for instance. In one event, eighteen elephants were pitted against heavy-armed foot soldiers. Only some of the elephants were killed on the spot, however, while the rest died a little later, because, contrary to Pompey's expectations, the audience felt sorry for a few of them when they were too injured to carry on fighting, [3] as they walked around, groaning, with their trunks pointing skyward. In fact, this behaviour of theirs gave rise to the idea that it was not random or aimless, but they were crying out the oaths which had given them the confidence to sail from Libya, and were calling on divinity to avenge their deaths. [4] For it is said that they refused to set foot on the ships until they had received a promise under oath from their drivers that they would come to no harm. [5] I have no idea whether or not this is true, but at any rate, according to some authorities, it is not just that elephants understand the language spoken by people in their native country, but they are also aware of heavenly phenomena. In fact, they say, at the time of the new moon, before the moon is visible to the human eye, elephants find their way to running water and perform a kind of purification of their bodies.* [6] That is what I have heard, anyway, and I have also heard that it was not Pompey who built this theatre, but a man called Demetrius,* a freedman of his, who used money he had gained while serving with Pompey on campaigns. If that is so, then it was absolutely right for Demetrius to have attributed the building to Pompey, so that he would not be vulnerable to idle gossip about how his freedman made so much money that he could undertake such a hugely expensive project.

39. Be that as it may, although Pompey delighted the general populace with these entertainments, nothing could have gone down worse with them than the levies of troops* which he and Crassus held for the commands they had been assigned. In fact, most people had a change of heart and began to speak well of Cato and his allies. [2] Pompey and Crassus did not dare to respond to this by resorting to force, and they restrained themselves likewise with regard to proceedings that had been instituted by some of the tribunes who were opposed to what was going on, which were nominally directed against their legates, but in fact against the consuls themselves.* What they did instead, and they were joined by their partisans in the Senate, was change their clothes as though for a catastrophe.* [3] They soon came to regret this, and changed back into ordinary clothes without giving any reason for doing so, but the tribunes were still determined to quash the levies and to have a second vote taken about the consuls' commands. This did not bother Pompey, [4] because he had sent his legates out to his province straight away and was happy to stay in Rome himself.* He claimed that he could not leave even if he wanted to—that he had to be there anyway to take care of the grain situation. In other words, he was in control of the Spains through his legates, and at the same time managing the affairs of Rome and the rest of Italy himself.

[5] But neither of these considerations applied to Crassus and he committed himself to the use of armed force. When the tribunes realized that, as long as they were unsupported by weaponry, their plain speaking was not enough to stop him getting his way, they dropped their demands, and turned instead to uttering dreadful imprecations against him (as though they were not also cursing the state through him). [6] First, on the Capitol, where Crassus was offering the customary vows for the success of his expedition, the tribunes kept proclaiming celestial omens and other portents,* and then, as he was setting out, they called down many terrible curses on him. Ateius even tried to have him thrown into the prison, [7] but when some of the other tribunes opposed this, fighting broke out between them and during the stalemate Crassus left and crossed the *pomerium*.* Whether it was a coincidence or a result of these curses, it was not long before Crassus met disaster.*

56 BCE   **40.** Caesar, however, during the consulship of Marcellinus and Philippus,* had campaigned against the Veneti, who live by the Ocean.* They had seized some Roman soldiers who had been sent to request grain, and then they detained the envoys who came to negotiate for their release. Their plan was to exchange them for their own people who were being held as hostages by the Romans.* [2] So far from returning the hostages, however, Caesar sent bodies of men out in various directions, some to plunder the territory of those who had joined the Veneti in their uprising as a way of preventing them from joining forces, and others to watch over the territory of the Roman allies in case they became restive.

[3] Caesar himself marched against the Veneti.* In the interior, he built the kind of boats that he had been told were suitable for the tidal ebb and flow of the Ocean* and had them sail down the Loire—and wasted almost all the campaigning season to no purpose. [4] For the enemy cities, built as they were on heavily fortified strongpoints, were unapproachable, and with the Ocean surging around almost all of them as well, it was impossible for either the army or fleet to attack, whether at high or low tide. [5] There was absolutely nothing Caesar could do, until Decimus Brutus* arrived with swift ships from the Mediterranean.* Actually, Caesar did not anticipate making any progress with these ships either, but the barbarians' contempt for the slightness and the frailty of the boats brought about their defeat.*

41. These boats were built on the light side for the sake of speed, in conformity with our naval practices, while the barbarians' boats were a great deal larger and sturdier, because, given the constant tidal backflow of the Ocean, they often needed to rest on dry land, and they also had to be capable of withstanding its ebb and flow. [2] The barbarians, therefore, who had never come across a fleet like the Romans' before, judged from the appearance of the ships that they would be ineffective, and as soon as they were lying at anchor they launched their ships against them, thinking that it would not take them long to sink them with just their poles. They were driven along by a sustained and powerful wind, of which their leather sails were capable of absorbing the whole force and more besides.

42. As long as the wind was high, Brutus did not dare to advance against them; the number and size of their ships deterred him, to say nothing of the violence of the wind and the force of their attack. Instead, he took up a position near land, from where he could either repel their assault or abandon the ships altogether. [2] But then the wind suddenly fell, the sea grew calm, and the barbarians' ships, now reliant on oars,* lost much of their forward motion; in fact, their great weight meant that they were almost at a standstill. Emboldened by this, Brutus seized the opportunity to advance against them and attack. He inflicted a great deal of damage on the enemy, while coming off unscathed himself, by outflanking them and breaking through their line, [3] and by sometimes ramming* and sometimes backing off, wherever and as often as he liked. He attacked with impunity whether many of his ships took on a single barbarian vessel, whether numbers were equal, or even whether his ships were outnumbered by the enemy. [4] Wherever he had the upper hand he stuck close to the enemy, smashing their hulls until they sank or boarding them from all directions, with his marines taking many lives in the hand-to-hand fighting; and wherever he was outnumbered, he had no difficulty in withdrawing. In short, the advantage always lay with him.

43. The barbarians had no archers, and they had not equipped themselves with stones either, since they had seen no need for them. Consequently, although they could hope to fight off men who came to close quarters, they were unable to cope with an enemy who stood a little way off. [2] So the men, incapable of mounting any kind of defence, were being wounded and killed, and the boats were either being holed by the Romans' rams, or had been set on fire and were burning, or had been taken in tow and were being hauled away, as though they had been abandoned by their crews. [3] When the surviving marines saw how desperate the situation was, some of them committed suicide rather than be taken alive, while others leapt into the sea, hoping either to swim over to the enemy ships and board them, or at least not die at Roman hands. [4] The barbarians were a match for the Romans in terms of determination and bravery,* but they were thoroughly demoralized at having been let down by the sluggishness of their ships. To guard against the possibility that the wind might pick up again at some point and set the barbarians' ships in motion once more, the Romans employed long-handled scythes from a distance, with which they cut through the ropes and shredded the sails.* [5] Since the barbarians had no choice but to fight a kind of land battle on their ships against an enemy who was fighting a sea battle, they died in large numbers on the spot, and all the survivors were captured. Caesar killed the most eminent of the prisoners and sold the rest.*

44. He next campaigned against the Morini and their neighbours, the Menapii.* He expected an easy victory, thinking that they would be intimidated by what he had already achieved, but he failed to subdue any of them. [2] These barbarians had no towns but lived in huts, and they retreated with the most valuable of their possessions to the most densely wooded area of the mountains. Under these circumstances, in every engagement they inflicted far more casualties on the Romans than they suffered themselves. Caesar tried to advance into the mountains by cutting a path through the woods, but the mountains were too extensive and winter was too close, so he gave up.

45. While Caesar was still in the territory of the Veneti, one of his legates, Quintus Titurius Sabinus, had been sent against the Venelli,* whose leader was Viridovix. At first, Sabinus was dismayed by the enormous numbers of the barbarians, and felt he would have done enough if he just kept his defences from being overrun, [2] but his confidence picked up when he saw that their numerical advantage made them too bold and that there was no real reason to fear them. Most barbarians, in fact, make all kinds of fearsome boasts while taunting and threatening an enemy, which turn out to be vain. However, he still did not dare to engage them openly, their numbers being a serious deterrent, [3] and instead he induced them to launch a reckless assault on his entrenchments, which were on high ground.

One evening he sent one of the allies, who spoke the same language as the Venelli, to their camp. The man, posing as a deserter, managed to convince them that Caesar had been defeated,† [4] and since they believed this information, despite being sated with food and drink* they recklessly set out against the Romans to forestall their escape. Since, to their way of thinking, not even the fire-bearer should survive,* they carried or dragged sticks and logs with them in order to burn the Romans alive.* [5] They attacked up the hill and made rapid progress, because they met with no opposition, since Sabinus made no move until the majority of them were within his reach. Then he charged down at them without warning from all directions at once. He overwhelmed the front ranks and sent them all flying in disarray down the slope, [6] where they stumbled over one another and their logs, and took so many lives that none of them, and none of the other tribes either, offered any further resistance. [7] Gauls are in fact irrationally excessive whatever situation they are faced with; they moderate neither their boldness nor their fear, but careen from the one to desperate cowardice and from the other to reckless boldness.*

46. At about the same time, Publius Crassus,* the son of Marcus Crassus, subjugated almost all of Aquitania.* These people are Gauls as well, with a territory that borders Celtic lands and extends along the Pyrenees to the Ocean. [2] In the course of his campaign there, Crassus won a battle against the Sotiates and then besieged and captured their town.* He lost a few men to a treacherous attack during peace negotiations, but he punished the barbarians severely for this too. [3] When he saw that some of the other tribes* had banded together, that they counted among their number some of Sertorius' former troops* from Spain, and that with the help of these men they were approaching the war in a more strategic and less impulsive manner, assuming that shortage of food would soon drive the Romans out of the country, Crassus pretended to be afraid of them. This earned him their contempt, but he was still not able to tempt them to fight, and so, with them thinking that they were safe for the foreseeable future, he launched a surprise attack. [4] At the point where the two armies clashed, Crassus was unsuccessful, because the barbarians raced out of their camp and repelled him vigorously; but while their army was engaged there, he sent some men around to the far side of their camp. They took it over, since it was undefended, and then passed through it and fell on the enemy from the rear. This tactic enabled Crassus to annihilate these barbarians, and the rest of them, with a few exceptions, came to terms without further fighting.

47. These events took place in the summer. While the Romans were in winter quarters in friendly territory, two Celtic tribes, the Tencteri and the Usipetes, crossed the Rhine and entered the territory of the Treveri.* They came over partly in response to pressure from the Suebi and partly at the invitation of the Gauls. [2] They were alarmed at finding Caesar there* and sent envoys to negotiate with him, with a request either for land or for permission to take some. Caesar was having none of it, however, so then they promised to return to their homeland of their own accord and asked for a truce.* [3] Subsequently, however, their men of military age saw a small cavalry squadron of his* approaching and, regarding them as no threat, changed their minds. They called a halt to their journey, defeated the horsemen (who were not expecting to be attacked), and, elated by this success, committed themselves to war.

48. Their elders, however, condemned this action and, contrary to the wishes of the younger men,* went to Caesar and asked him for forgiveness, laying the blame on a minority. Caesar detained them in his camp, telling them that he would give them a reply before long,* [2] and then set out against the others. They were in camp, and he attacked them while they were taking their siesta and not expecting any hostile action, seeing that their elders were with him. He burst into the camp, denying their foot soldiers time even to pick up their weapons, and slaughtered them in droves by the wagons, where they were hampered by the jumble of women and children.*

[3] Their cavalry was absent at the time, and as soon as they found out what had happened they set out for home and found refuge among the Sugambri. Caesar sent envoys and demanded their surrender—not that he expected them to be handed over to him, because the tribes on the far side of the Rhine were not afraid enough of the Romans to obey this kind of command from them, but he needed a pretext for crossing the river.* [4] For Caesar had a burning desire to do something that his peers had never done in the past, and he expected to be able to keep the Celts far from Gaul by invading their homeland. So when the cavalry were not surrendered to him and he was invited over by the Ubii, who were at odds with the Sugambri, their neighbours, he built a bridge* and crossed the river. [5] But finding that the Sugambri had withdrawn into their strongholds,* and that the Suebi were mustering their forces to come to their aid, he crossed back within twenty days.*

49. The sources of the Rhine are located in the Celtic Alps near Raetia,* and then it flows in a westerly direction, with Gaul and its inhabitants on its left bank and the Celts on the right, before finally issuing into the Ocean. [2] Just as it is now, the Rhine has always been regarded as the border between these peoples, ever since they gained their separate names.* In ancient times, however, both peoples were called Celts, whichever side of the river they lived on.

50. So at that time Caesar became the first Roman to cross the Rhine, and later, in the consulship of Pompey and Crassus,* he also crossed over to Britain. [2] This country is 450 stades* distant from the mainland at its closest point, which is the part of Belgic territory that is occupied by the Morini, and from there it runs parallel to the rest of Gaul and extends out into the sea past almost all Spain as well.* [3] Even its existence was unknown to the earliest Greeks and Romans, while to their descendants it was a matter of dispute whether it was an island or part of a continent. Many people wrote about it, taking one side or the other in the debate, but they wrote from a position of ignorance because they had neither seen the place with their own eyes nor heard about it with their own ears from the inhabitants, but relied instead just on their own capacity for learned disputation. [4] By now, however, it has been proved beyond the shadow of a doubt that it is an island, first under Agricola's propraetorship* and now under the emperor Severus.*

51. Since the rest of Gaul was quiet and he had won over the Morini,* Caesar was eager to invade Britain.* The voyage over with

55 BCE

the infantry went perfectly, but he was unable to make land at the best possible place, because the Britons had advance warning of his approach and occupied all the landing-points on the coastline facing the mainland. [2] Caesar therefore rounded a certain prominent headland* and sailed along the coast on the other side of it. Once he had got the better of the enemy who attacked as he was disembarking his men in the shallows there, he managed to establish a beachhead on dry land before their reinforcements arrived, and then he repelled them too when they attacked. [3] Not many of the barbarians were killed, because they were chariot-drivers and horsemen, so they easily escaped the Romans, whose cavalry had not yet arrived. Nevertheless, the reports they had been receiving from the mainland about the Romans frightened them, and so did the fact that the Romans had braved the crossing in the first place and been able to set foot on their land, so they sent some of the Morini,* who were friends of theirs, to Caesar to sue for peace on their behalf.

When he demanded hostages from them, they agreed at first, 52. but then both the fleet that was there and the one that was on its way were damaged in a storm, and they changed their minds. They did not openly attack the Romans, since the camp was strongly guarded, [2] but when some Romans were out foraging for supplies they let them in, giving them to believe that the country was friendly, but then killed them all, apart from a few* who were saved when Caesar rushed to their rescue. After that, they attacked the Roman camp itself, but that did not go well for them and they achieved nothing. It took a number of defeats,* however, before they were ready to come to terms. [3] Actually, in the normal course of events Caesar would never have chosen to make peace with them, but winter was approaching and he did not have enough troops available there to wage war in winter, since the force that was on its way had come to grief and the Gauls had taken advantage of his absence to revolt. So he reluctantly came to an agreement with them, under which he demanded more hostages, though he received only a few.*

53. So Caesar sailed back to the mainland and quelled the disturbances there.* He had gained nothing from Britain either for himself or for Rome except the glory of having campaigned there. Nevertheless, he was extremely proud of what he had done, and the Romans at home regarded it as an amazing exploit. [2] Seeing that places previously unknown had been opened up and places formerly unheard of

had been made accessible, they decreed a festal period of twenty days,* because they took the future possibilities of these places to be present certainties, and celebrated the successes they expected to follow as though they had already happened.

54. While these events were taking place, there was an uprising in Spain, and so it was assigned to Pompey.* Some peoples had risen up, making the Vaccaei their leaders. They were caught off guard by Metellus Nepos and defeated in battle, [2] but as he was besieging Clunia* they attacked him and won. Although they saved the town, however, they were defeated elsewhere, but not badly enough to make their subjugation imminent. In fact, they had such a numerical advantage over their opponents that Nepos was content to follow the risk-free course of inactivity.

55. At about the same time, Ptolemy was restored to Egypt and recovered his kingdom,* despite the fact that the Romans had rescinded their vote to help him* and were still indignant about all the bribery he had employed. [2] Pompey and Gabinius saw to it. Personal power and abundant wealth carried so much more weight than the decrees of the people and the Senate* [3] that Pompey sent orders to Gabinius, who was the governor of Syria at the time, and Gabinius mobilized his forces, and between them—the one acting from good-will and the other because he had been paid—they restored him against the wishes of the state, taking no account either of it or of the Sibyl's oracles.

[4] Gabinius was in fact later put on trial for this, but Pompey and money ensured his acquittal.* Roman affairs were in such chaos at the time that all Gabinius had to do was disburse to some of the magistrates and jurors a tiny proportion of the money he had received as a bribe, and they completely ignored their duty. Moreover, by showing how easy it was to buy immunity from punishment, they taught others to do wrong for money. [5] So on that occasion Gabinius secured his acquittal by these means, but later he was taken to court for other crimes, including the extortion of more than 100 million denarii from his command, and this time he was found guilty.* This took him completely by surprise, since money had seen to his acquittal in the earlier trial, and now it was largely because of that earlier trial that he was being condemned over money. [6] It was a shock for Pompey as well, because earlier, even though he was far from the city, he had managed to save Gabinius through the agency of his friends in

Rome, but now, despite being on the outskirts of the city and all but present in the courtroom itself, he failed.

56. This was how it happened. Gabinius had mistreated Syria* in many ways, and in fact did far more harm than the raiding,* which was then at its height. But since he regarded all the profit he made from there as negligible, his first thought was to mount an expedition against the Parthians and their wealth, and he began to make his preparations. [2] Phraates had been assassinated by his sons, and Orodes was now on the throne. He expelled his brother, Mithridates,* from his kingdom of Media, and Mithridates took refuge with Gabinius and persuaded him to help with his restoration. [3] But when Ptolemy arrived, bearing a letter from Pompey,* and promised to enrich both him and his men, with a down payment immediately and the rest to be paid once he had recovered his kingdom, Gabinius abandoned the Parthian project and set out at once for Egypt. [4] He did this even though governors of provinces were legally required to stay within their own borders and were not allowed to start wars of their own accord,* and even though the people and the Sibyl* had said that Ptolemy was not to be restored. But as far as Ptolemy was concerned, the more obstacles that were placed in his way, the more money he spent overcoming them. [5] So Gabinius set off, leaving his son Sisenna,* who was little more than a boy, in charge of Syria—with very few men under his command, thus making the province for which he was supposed to be responsible even more vulnerable to raiders.* [6] When he arrived in Palestine, he arrested Aristobulus, who had escaped from Rome and was causing trouble, and sent him to Pompey.* Then, after fixing the level of tribute the Jews were to pay, he invaded Egypt.

57. The ruler of Egypt at the time was Berenice,* and even though she was afraid of the Romans, she took no appropriate steps to meet the emergency. All she did was send for a certain Seleucus,* as a scion of the royal house that had once flourished in Syria, and have him officially registered as her husband, thus making him jointly responsible for her kingdom and the war. [2] But when it became clear that he was a nonentity, she had him killed and came to an identical arrangement with Archelaus (the son of the Archelaus who had deserted to Sulla), a man of action and energy who was living in Syria.*

Gabinius could have nipped this adverse development in the bud, because he had Archelaus under arrest, since he was already suspicious of him, and was therefore in a position to avoid any further trouble from that quarter. [3] But he was afraid that, if there was no trouble, Ptolemy would reduce the amount of money that he had agreed to give him, on the grounds that he had done nothing remarkable, and in fact he hoped that Archelaus' cleverness and formidable reputation would earn him even more. So once Archelaus too had lavishly bribed him, Gabinius was happy to let him go, while making out that he had escaped.*

58. Gabinius thus reached Pelusium* without encountering any opposition. He advanced from there with his army in two divisions, each of which defeated the Egyptians that came out to meet them on a single day, and then he overcame them again in a naval battle fought on the Nile and in a land battle as well. The Alexandrians are very good at putting a bold front on everything and at giving expression to everything that occurs to them, [2] but they are the most useless people in the world when it comes to facing the horrors of war. And this is so despite the fact that very serious riots are very common in Alexandria,* and always involve bloodshed, because even life pales into insignificance for them compared to the quarrels of the moment, and in the course of these riots they make killing their goal as though it were the finest and most important thing in the world. [3] So Gabinius defeated them, taking a great many lives in the process, including that of Archelaus, and before long he was the master of all Egypt. He then handed the kingdom over to Ptolemy,* who killed not only his daughter, but also the most eminent and wealthy men of the land, because he was badly in need of money.

59. So Gabinius recovered Ptolemy's kingdom for him, but he sent no dispatch home about what he had done, because he did not want to be the one to report his own lawbreaking. But, of course, an act of this magnitude could not be kept hidden, [2] and the Roman people soon heard about it. And when the Syrians roundly condemned much of what Gabinius had done, especially because in his absence they had been badly mauled by the raiders, and the tax-farmers,* who had been prevented by the raiding from collecting the taxes, were heavily in debt, they became angry, put forward motions, and were ready to condemn him. [3] Cicero laid into him with particular vehemence, and advised them to consult the Sibylline verses again, since he expected to find that they stipulated how an infringement was to be punished.

60. Pompey and Crassus were still consuls, and Pompey was looking after his own interests, while Crassus had received not only Pompey's favour, but also money that had been sent to him by Gabinius. They openly defended Gabinius' actions, insulted Cicero in various ways, especially by stigmatizing him as an exile,* and refused to put any-
thing to the vote. [2] But when their term came to an end, and Lucius Domitius and Appius Claudius took over from them, a plurality of views was again aired, with most people coming out against Gabinius. [3] Domitius was an enemy of Pompey because they had been rivals for the consulship* and he resented the fact that it was Pompey who had been elected, and, although Claudius was related to Pompey,* he still wanted to be a demagogue and do the people's bidding to a cer-tain extent—and he also expected to get a bribe from Gabinius if he created a little confusion.* So they both worked constantly against Gabinius. [4] Another factor that told heavily against him was that he had refused to accept a legate sent to him by Crassus to succeed him, and clung on to his command as though it were everlasting. So it was decided, over Pompey's objections, that the Sibylline verses should be consulted.*

61. Meanwhile, the Tiber suddenly burst its banks* and flooded all the level ground in the city and some of the higher ground as well. Perhaps there had been exceptionally heavy rain somewhere upstream from the city, or perhaps a strong onshore wind had forced its outflow into reverse, or perhaps, and most probably, as was suspected at the time, it was the work of some god. [2] The houses, which were made of brick, absorbed the water and collapsed, and every beast of burden drowned. As for the people, all those who did not get out in time and escape to the highest ground died in the houses or on the streets. Since the disaster continued for many days, even the houses that stayed standing were weakened, and either immediately or subse-quently caused a great many injuries. [3] In addition to suffering from these misfortunes, the Romans expected even worse to come, since, as they saw it, divinity had become angry with them for the restoration of Ptolemy, and they were eager to put Gabinius to death even before he returned to Rome, since it was believed that the sooner they killed him, the less they would suffer. [4] They were so insistent that, even though nothing to this effect had been found in the Sibylline oracles, the Senate still issued a decree instructing both the magistrates and the people to subject him to the most harsh and cruel treatment.

62. While this was going on, however, money sent ahead by Gabinius ensured that he would avoid punishment, on this ground at any rate, not just before he returned but afterwards as well. Nevertheless, his guilty conscience made him so ashamed and mortified that he delayed his return to Italy, and then entered the city under cover of darkness* and did not dare to show his face outside his house for a great many days. [2] The charges against him were many, and there were many accusers. First, then, he was put on trial for his most serious offence, the restoration of Ptolemy. It is hardly an exaggeration to say that the entire population crowded around the courtroom, and they were frequently moved to tear him limb from limb, especially because Pompey was not there and Cicero accused him with the greatest vehemence.* [3] But despite their mood he was acquitted.* It was not just that he spent enormous sums of money himself, given the seriousness of the offence with which he was charged, but he also had the strong support of Pompey's and Caesar's friends, who argued that the Sibyl's assertion referred to a different time and a different king, and relied above all on the point that her verses stipulated no punishment for what he had done.

63. The people were strongly inclined to kill the jurors as well, but they escaped, so they focused on the remaining charges against Gabinius, and made sure that he was at any rate found guilty of them.* [2] Partly because they were afraid of the people, and partly because they had been given little by Gabinius (whose disbursements were less generous because of the relatively unimportant crimes he was being tried for, and because he was confident of winning again), the jurors who were assigned to his case convicted him, even though Pompey was nearby and Cicero spoke in his defence. [3] Pompey had been away attending to the supply of grain, a large amount of which had been ruined by the floods,* and he rushed back for the first trial—he was in Italy—but arrived too late, so he stayed where he was in the outskirts of the city until the second trial was over.* [4] Pompey was not allowed to enter the city since he now held the post of proconsul, so the people were convened outside the *pomerium*,* where he defended Gabinius at length, read out a letter Caesar had sent him which contained a plea on Gabinius' behalf, and asked the jurors to acquit him. [5] As for Cicero, Pompey not only prevented him from accusing Gabinius again, but actually persuaded him to speak in his defence—as a result of which Cicero came even more to be charged with being a defector* and to be spoken of as such. Still, Cicero did Gabinius no good at all: he was convicted at this trial, as I have said, and went into exile, though he was later brought back by Caesar.*

64. During this same time,* Pompey's wife died after giving birth to a baby girl.* Whether it was arranged by Pompey's and Caesar's friends, or was just the work of people who wanted to please them, her body was snatched away immediately after the funeral oration she received in the Forum and was buried in the Campus Martius.* This happened despite the fact that Domitius argued against it, saying, among other things, that, without a decree being passed, it was sacrilegious for her to be buried in a sacred place.

65. Meanwhile, Gaius Pomptinus celebrated his triumph over the Gauls,* after staying outside the *pomerium* up until then while permission was being refused. [2] And he would have failed to get it even then if Servius Galba, who had served alongside him and was currently a praetor, had not surreptitiously, and before day had quite broken, allowed some people to vote, even though it was illegal for any business to be brought before the people before the first hour.* In response to this, some of the tribunes, who had been unable to attend the assembly, made trouble for him during his triumph,* at any rate, and there was even some loss of life.

BOOK FORTY

1. These were the events that took place in Rome, which was then in 54 BCE the course of its seven hundredth year.* In Gaul in the same year,* the consulship of Lucius Domitius and Appius Claudius, Caesar made his preparations, which included building ships that were a cross between his own fast ships and the local transport vessels. He wanted them to be as light as possible, but at the same time capable of withstanding the buffeting of the waves and of being drawn up on the shore without being damaged. [2] At the start of the sailing season,* he crossed over once again to Britain. He gave as his pretext that they had not sent him all the hostages they had promised,* thinking that he would give up on them, since he had withdrawn the first time without achieving anything. But in actual fact his craving for the island was so strong* that he would have come up with some other pretext if it had not been this one. [3] He landed at the same place as before.* The number of his ships and the fact that they made their approach simultaneously at many points deterred any opposition, and he immediately secured the roadstead.

2. Because they failed for these reasons to prevent his approach, and because the larger army he had come with* frightened them more than the last time, the barbarians carried all their most valuable possessions into the most densely wooded part of the nearby territory. [2] Once they had made them safe by cutting down the surrounding trees and piling more timber on top of these logs, so that they were inside a rough stockade,* they set about harrying the Romans' foraging parties. At one point, after they had lost a battle in open country, they tempted the Romans to pursue them off the battlefield, and then it was their turn to inflict a lot of casualties.* [3] Later, when the Roman ships were once again damaged by bad weather, the barbarians sent for allied forces and launched an attack on the ship enclosure itself,* after putting Cassivellaunus* in command, who was said to be the foremost ruler on the island. [4] In the first clashes, the Romans were discomfited by the assault of the barbarians' chariots, but then they opened up gaps in their ranks and let the chariots pass through, while shooting at them from the sides as they raced past, and this tactic* enabled them to meet the enemy as equals.

3. For the time being, both sides stayed where they were, but later, after the barbarians had got the better of the infantry but had been worsted by the cavalry, they retreated to the Thames. After they had blocked the ford with stakes—some visible, some underwater—they made camp. [2] But Caesar attacked fiercely and forced them to abandon the palisade. He then laid siege to the fortress* and drove them from there as well, and meanwhile another Roman force repelled those who were attacking the roadstead.* Cowed into submission, the barbarians came to terms,* which included the giving of hostages and the paying of an annual tribute.

4. After this, Caesar withdrew altogether from the island.* He left no troops there because he did not think it would be safe for them to spend the winter in a hostile land, or that it was a good idea for him to stay away from Gaul any longer. He contented himself with what he had gained so as not to risk losing even that by seeking for more.* [2] Subsequent events proved this to have been a sound decision. When he set out for Italy to spend the winter there, the Gauls became restive, despite the many troops that were garrisoned on each of the tribes,* and some of them went so far as to rise up in open revolt. If he had been wintering in Britain when this happened, all Gaul would have been in turmoil.

5. It was the Eburones* who initiated the fighting, under their leader Ambiorix. They claimed to have risen up because they resented the presence of the Romans on their land, under the command of Caesar's legates, Sabinus and Lucius Cotta. But the truth was* that they despised Sabinus and Cotta* as not strong enough to resist them, and did not think that Caesar would be able to respond rapidly with an offensive against them. [2] They therefore launched a surprise attack on the Romans. They were expecting to capture the camp at their first assault, but they failed at that and resorted to trickery instead. Ambiorix had his troops occupy the best place for an ambush and then held a meeting with the Romans at his request. He made out that he had not wanted war [3] and that he regretted it himself, while warning them to be on their guard against the rest, who, he said, were not taking orders from him and were going to attack the Romans that night.* He told them that it was too risky to stay in Eburonia* and advised them to leave at the earliest possible opportunity and go to some of their comrades who were wintering nearby.*

6. The Romans were taken in by what Ambiorix said,* especially because he had been treated with considerable generosity by Caesar and he appeared to be repaying this debt. They quickly packed up the camp and set out after nightfall*—and were very badly mauled when they fell into the ambush. [2] Cotta died straight away along with many of his men. Ambiorix got Sabinus to come to him for protection—he had not taken part in the attack* and Sabinus still thought him trustworthy—but instead he seized him, stripped him of both his weapons and his clothes, and killed him with a javelin, saying, among other things: 'How can men like you want to rule over men like us?' [3] That was these men's fate.* Their surviving comrades managed to break through to the entrenchments they had set out from, but when the barbarians attacked them there too and they could neither keep them at bay nor escape, they killed one another.

7. After this, some of the other nearby peoples revolted. They included the Nervii,* even though Quintus Cicero* was wintering among them; he was the brother of Marcus Cicero and one of Caesar's legates. Ambiorix added the Nervii to his army* and attacked Cicero. [2] It was a closely fought struggle, and after taking some prisoners Ambiorix tried to trick Cicero too,* but when that did not work, he put him under siege. Thanks to the large number of men he had available, to the experience he had acquired when he had fought as an ally of the Romans,* and to certain items of information he learnt from various captives, he soon had Cicero surrounded by a palisade* and ditch. [3] There was, predictably, a great deal of fighting, in which barbarian losses far outnumbered those of the Romans, just because there were more of them. But their numerical superiority meant that they did not even notice their losses, while the Romans, who had been few in the first place, became easy to encircle as their numbers daily decreased.

8. There was a good chance that their position would fall. They lacked medical supplies to treat their wounds, and the unexpectedness of the siege meant that they did not have much food.* No one came to relieve them either, although there were plenty of Romans in winter quarters not far off, because the barbarians kept a close watch on the roads, captured everyone sent out to seek help, and killed them right before the eyes of their comrades. [2] However, one of the Nervii, who was well disposed towards Rome as a recipient of Roman benevolence, and was one of the besieged along with Cicero, supplied him with a slave to act as a messenger. Because he dressed and spoke like a native, he was able to mingle with the enemy

as if he were one of them without being caught, and then to continue on his way.

9. The news reached Caesar before he returned to Italy, while he was still on the march,* and he turned back. As he passed the places where his men were in winter quarters, he collected them and hastened on his way.* Meanwhile, he sent a cavalryman on ahead because he was afraid that Cicero might give up hope of being relieved and be defeated before he got there, or even come to terms. [2] He did not trust the Nervian's slave, even though he had solid proof of his loyalty; he was worried that he might be overcome by pity for his compatriots and do the Romans serious harm. So he picked from the ranks of the allies a horseman who knew their language, dressed him in their clothes,* and sent him on his way. [3] To make sure that he would give nothing away, voluntarily or involuntarily, he wrote everything that he wanted to say to Cicero in Greek,* instead of entrusting the man with a verbal message. Thus, even if the letter fell into enemy hands, it would still be incomprehensible to the barbarians and would make them none the wiser. It was also his usual practice, whenever he was sending a confidential message to anyone, to substitute, for any given letter of the alphabet, the one that came fourth after it, so as to make the message indecipherable to most readers. [4] Anyway, the horseman reached the Roman camp, but was unable to approach right up to it, so he tied the letter to a javelin and, pretending that he was trying to kill one of the enemy, deliberately made it lodge in a tower.* Once Cicero had been informed in this fashion that Caesar was on his way, his spirits rose along with his determination to hold out.

10. For a long time, the barbarians were unaware that Caesar was on his way with reinforcements, because he travelled by night and then bivouacked by day in very secluded places, so as to catch them as unprepared as possible, but in the end the rejoicing of the besieged made them suspect that he was coming. They sent out scouts, who came back with the report that Caesar was already close, and they set out against him, hoping to take him by surprise. [2] But Caesar was forewarned. He stayed where he was for the night and just before dawn occupied a strongpoint, where he made the smallest possible camp. He wanted to give the impression that he had only a few men, that he was exhausted from the march, and that he was frightened by their approach, and in this way to tempt them on to the hill he had occupied. [3] And that is exactly what happened: the barbarians fell for it and saw no reason to expect trouble from him. They attacked up the hill and were so badly defeated that they called a halt to their war against him.

11. So they and all the other peoples were subjugated for the time being, but they remained ill disposed towards the Romans. At any rate, when Caesar was sending for the leaders of each tribe and punishing them, the Treveri became afraid that they would be punished as well and renewed war with the Romans, at Indutiomarus' instigation.* [2] They persuaded some other tribes who shared their fears to join the insurrection and marched against Titus Labienus,* who was in the territory of the Remi, but the Romans caught them unprepared with an attack and crushed them.*

So much for events in Gaul; Caesar spent the winter there, thinking that he would be able to pacify them completely.* 12. Meanwhile, Crassus was eager to achieve something that would bring him both glory and profit.* But since he realized that there was no chance of that in Syria, because the people were peaceful and those who had formerly resisted the Romans were too weak to make trouble, he marched against the Parthians. He did so despite the facts that he had no grievance to bring against them* and no vote had been passed authorizing him to undertake the war,* because he kept hearing of their immense wealth, and he also expected that Orodes would easily be overcome since he was only recently established on the throne.* [2] He therefore crossed the Euphrates and advanced far into Mesopotamia, plundering and ravaging as he went, because the barbarians had not been expecting his invasion and did not have the land under close guard. Silaces, who was the satrap* of that region at the time, was therefore soon beaten near Ichniae* (as this stronghold is called), since he had only a few cavalrymen to fight with, and he withdrew, injured, so that he could personally tell the king about Crassus' invasion.

13. It did not take long for Crassus to win over the fortresses and especially the Greek cities, including the one called Nicephorium.* In fact, many of the colonists, Macedonians and other Greeks who had fought alongside them,* resented the oppressive regime they were living under and were happy to go over to the Romans, of whom they had great expectations, since they thought of them as philhellenes. [2] The inhabitants of Zenodotium, however, pretended that they were going to change sides as well and invited some of the Romans to

the city, but when they came inside, they seized them and put them to death, and for this they were expelled.* Otherwise, Crassus did little harm and suffered little as well.

[3] There can be no doubt that all the rest of the country west of the Tigris would have fallen to him if he had fully and consistently taken advantage of his own forward momentum and the barbarians' panic, and also if he had wintered where he was and kept the country under close guard.* [4] But in fact, once he had captured the places he could take straight away, he ignored everywhere else—and turned his back on those places too. He resented having to spend time in Mesopotamia and longed for the leisure he could enjoy in Syria, and in doing so he gave the Parthians time to prepare and to make life very difficult indeed for the soldiers who had been left behind in the region.*

14. This was the start of the war between the Romans and the Parthians. The Parthians live beyond the Tigris, mostly in fortresses and strongholds, but by now they also have cities, especially Ctesiphon, where the king has a palace.* They were one of the ancient barbarian races, [2] and they were already known by this name under the Persian kings.* At that time, however, they occupied only a small portion of the country and had not expanded their sway beyond their borders. It was after the demise of the Persian empire, when the Macedonians' power was at its height and Alexander's successors, in the course of their conflicts with each other, appropriated various parts of the former empire to create their own kingdoms, [3] that the Parthians first attained prominence under a man called Arsaces, which is why the kings who came after him were called the Arsacids.* They prospered, took over all the territory of their neighbours, occupied Mesopotamia with satrapies,* and eventually attained a position of such glory and power that they not only waged war against the Romans at the time in question, but still today are regarded as constant adversaries. [4] They are fearsome fighters, but nevertheless they owe their reputation above all to the fact that, although they have gained no territory at the expense of the Romans and have even lost certain portions of their own empire, they have so far never been subjugated, and even now they still hold their own whenever war breaks out between us.*

15. Many books discuss the origins of the Parthians, and describe their land and their distinctive customs, and I do not propose to cover these topics. But what follows is a description of their weaponry and the way they go about warfare, included because my account has

reached a point where the information will be useful, making an investigation of these matters pertinent. [2] They do not use shields at all, but fight as mounted archers and lancers, mostly armoured.* Their infantry division, which consists entirely of archers, is small and made up of the weaker men.

They practise archery and horse-riding from an early age, and both the climate and the land help them hone these two skills. [3] The country is mostly flat, and is therefore excellent for raising horses and perfect for riding. At any rate, they bring whole herds with them even when they are campaigning, so that they can use different horses for different occasions, and so that they have the ability to charge up suddenly from a considerable distance and then abruptly make themselves scarce. [4] And since the climate in that part of the world is very dry, with hardly any moisture in the air, it keeps their bowstrings at maximum tautness, except in deep winter—which is why they never go out on campaign in that season. For the rest of the year, however, they are almost impossible to defeat in their own country and anywhere else that has similar characteristics. [5] They can endure the sun even when it is at its most scorching because they are used to it, and they have discovered many remedies for the shortage of drinking-water and the difficulty of finding it, which is another reason why they find it easy to repel invaders. If they venture beyond their borders, over the Euphrates, they have in the past prevailed in the occasional battle or in sudden raids, [6] but they are incapable of fighting any enemy relentlessly and continuously, because they find themselves in territory and climatic conditions that are completely alien to them, and because they bring with them supplies of neither food nor money.

16. Such, then, are the Parthians and their ways. After Crassus' invasion of Mesopotamia, described above, Orodes sent envoys to him in Syria, to express his anger at the invasion and ask what his reasons were for making war on him.* He also sent Surenas* with an army to the places that had fallen to the Romans and had changed sides. [2] He himself was intending to march against the Armenia that had formerly belonged to Tigranes,* to prevent its current ruler, Tigranes' son Artabazes,* from sending any help to the Romans out of fear for his own land. [3] Crassus told Orodes that he would tell him his reasons for making war in Seleucia* (a city in Mesopotamia which even now has a very large Greek population). At this one of the

Parthians tapped the palm of his left hand with the fingers of his right hand and said, 'There'll be hair sprouting here before you reach Seleucia.'

53 BCE   17. At the beginning of the winter when Gnaeus Calvinus and Valerius Messalla became consuls,* many portents occurred, even in Rome itself. Eagle owls and wolves were spotted in the city, dogs prowled the streets doing damage wherever they went, some statues dripped sweat and others were struck by lightning,* [2] and, partly because of political rivalry, but largely because of auguries and celestial signs, it was not until the seventh month that the magistrates were finally appointed. But the portents did not make it clear what outcome they indicated; after all, the city was in turmoil, the Gauls had risen up once again in rebellion, and without being aware of it,† they were now at war with the Parthians. [3] But as Crassus was crossing the Euphrates at Zeugma* (the place gained its name at the time of Alexander's expedition, because that was where he crossed the river), he received signs that were unmistakable and easily comprehensible.*

18. First, there was what happened to the 'eagle'. This is a miniature temple with a golden eagle housed inside it. Every enrolled legion has one of these eagles,* and it never leaves winter quarters unless the entire legion takes to the field. [2] It is carried by one man on the end of a long pole, which has a sharp butt-spike so that it can be fixed in the ground. What happened was that one of these eagles refused to join Crassus as he crossed the Euphrates; it stuck in the ground as though it had taken root there, and it took the combined strength of a number of men to pull it out. [3] This eagle was forced to accompany the expedition even though it did not want to, but one of the large standards*—one of those that resemble sails and have the names of the legion and the commanding officer written in purple on them—was upended and fell into the river from the bridge. [4] This was caused by a strong gust of wind, so Crassus cut down all the other poles that were the same length, making them shorter and easier to carry steadily, but he only increased the intensity of the portents. As they were actually crossing the river, such a thick fog enveloped the soldiers that they tripped over one another and could see nothing of the enemy's country until they set foot on it. [5] Moreover, the sacrifices carried out for both the crossing and the landing were highly unfavourable.* As if that were not enough, they were buffeted by

a powerful wind, thunderbolts crashed down, and the bridge broke up before all the men had crossed.

Since these events made it easy enough for anyone, however stupid and ignorant he was, to understand that they were not going to fare well and that they would not be coming back, the men became terrified and morale plummeted in the camp. **19.** In an attempt to restore their spirits, Crassus addressed the troops and said: 'Men, you shouldn't let the destruction of the bridge dismay you or take it as an unfavourable omen, [2] because I hereby give you my solemn assurance that I have decided to return through Armenia.' At these words, the men started to feel better, but then he added a few more in a loud voice: 'Don't worry! None of us will be coming back from here.' [3] When the troops heard this, they regarded it as at least as significant an omen as the others and their spirits fell even more. They took no notice of the rest of his speech, in which he belittled the barbarians, played up Roman strength, and promised them money and rewards for valour. [4] Nevertheless, they still followed him, and no one spoke a word or did anything to oppose him, perhaps just because that was the law, but also because they were already terrified and incapable of planning or doing anything that would secure their safety. At any rate, for the whole of the rest of the expedition they behaved as though they had been condemned to death by some god, and they were crushed both physically and mentally.

20. But it was Abgar of Osrhoene* who did them the most harm. Although he had concluded a treaty with the Romans during Pompey's time in the East, he now took up the barbarians' cause instead. Alchaudonius* the Arab did the same as well, but then he always went over to the stronger side. [2] He openly revolted, making it a straightforward matter to take precautions against him, but Abgar pretended that he was Crassus' friend, when in fact he was backing Orodes. He spent a fortune in support of Crassus, learnt all his plans, and communicated them to the Parthian; and as if that was not enough, he dissuaded Crassus from putting into practice any of his ideas that were sound, while urging him to pursue those that were disadvantageous.

[3] His final act of treachery was as follows. Crassus was planning to set out for Seleucia, and he expected to get there safely with his army and supplies by travelling alongside and then on the Euphrates. It would then be a simple matter for him to cross over to Ctesiphon* with the help of the people of Seleucia, whom he believed he would

win over without difficulty, seeing that they were Greeks. [4] But Abgar
made him drop this plan on the grounds that it would be time-
consuming, and persuaded him to join battle with Surenas, who was
nearby and had only a small force.* **21.** He was constantly in Surenas'
company, pretending to be spying, and once he had made the arrangements that would see to Crassus' death and Surenas' triumph, he led
the unsuspecting Romans out to what he claimed would be an easy
victory—and then, in the midst of the action, he joined in the attack
on them.

[2] The battle went as follows.* The terrain being undulating and
wooded,* the Parthians concealed most of their forces before con-
fronting the Romans. When Crassus saw them—not the elder Crassus,
but the younger,* who had joined his father from Gaul—[3] he thought
he was seeing their entire army and expected to make short work of
them. He advanced against them with the cavalry,* and when they
deliberately turned and fled, he set out after them, thinking that victory was his. In doing so, he opened up a considerable gap between
himself and the infantry, and then he was surrounded and slaughtered.

22. After this, so far from adopting evasive measures, the Roman
infantry resolutely joined battle with the Parthians to avenge the
younger Crassus' death. But the numbers of the enemy and their tactics, and especially Abgar's treachery, made it impossible for them to
achieve anything worthy of themselves. [2] If they chose to adopt
a tight formation, presenting a solid fence of shields against the
enemy's arrows, the lancers charged, killing some and completely
scattering the rest. And if they adopted a looser formation to thwart
the lancers, they became vulnerable to the archers. [3] Many of the
Romans died because they panicked just at the approach of the lancers or when they were surrounded by the enemy cavalry, while others
were knocked dead to the ground by the lances or carried along trans-
fixed on their points. [4] Meanwhile, dense volleys of arrows rained
down on them from all sides at once, killing many outright and making many others unfit for combat. The arrows plagued everyone.
They flew into their eyes and pierced their hands and every other part
of their bodies; they penetrated their shields and deprived them of
the protection they provided, forcing them to expose themselves and
risk being wounded by every incoming missile. [5] So a man might be
wounded again and again while defending himself against a shaft
or while pulling one out from where it had lodged. All this made it

impossible for them to move to another position, but it was also impossible for them to stay put. Neither option would make them safe; both entailed death for them, the first because safety was impossible and the second because it made them easier to wound.

23. That was the situation while they were still fighting only the enemies they knew about, since Abgar did not set about them straight away. When he joined the attack on the Romans,* the Osrhoeni assaulted them in the rear, which was exposed because the Romans were facing the other way. This also made it easier for the Parthians to kill the Romans, because when they wheeled around to confront the Osrhoeni, they put the Parthians in their rear. [2] Again they turned to face the Parthians, then back to the Osrhoeni, then back to the Parthians once more. Their formation was considerably disrupted as a result of these manoeuvres, as they were constantly turning this way and that, forced to face whichever foe was injuring them at the time, and this meant that they fell foul of one another's swords, and many were actually killed by their comrades. [3] In the end, they were pinned in such a confined space that they were no longer able to move, since they were compelled, in the face of the enemy's constant attacks from all directions at once, to protect their exposed parts with the shields of the men standing beside them. There were so many bodies that they could not even find a secure footing but kept tripping over them. [4] It was midsummer and the battle was being fought in the midde of the day, so the heat, the thirst, and the dust (which the barbarians multiplied as much as they could by all riding around the Romans at once) affected the survivors terribly, and these factors alone were responsible for a great number of deaths in which enemy weaponry played no part.

24. The Romans would have been completely wiped out if the barbarians' lances had not become bent or broken, if their bowstrings had not snapped from constant use, if they had not run out of arrows,* if their swords had not all become blunt, and, most importantly, if the men had not become exhausted by all the killing. [2] So the barbarians withdrew, because night was approaching and they had a long ride ahead of them. I should explain that these barbarians never make camp near the enemy, however weak they may be, because they never dig entrenchments and because neither their cavalry nor their archers are any use against a night attack. [3] However, they took no prisoners then, because the sight of the Romans still armed and on their feet,

with none of them discarding his weaponry or turning to flight, made them think that they still had some strength and dissuaded them from laying hands on them.

25. So Crassus, and all those who still could, set out for Carrhae, which had been kept loyal by the Romans who remained inside.* But many of the wounded stayed where they were, since they were unable to walk and had no wagons or even people to support them, because the others had been glad just to get themselves away. [2] Some of these men died from their wounds or put an end to their lives themselves, and others were captured the next day. Of those who escaped,† many died on the road when their strength gave out, and many others died later because they were denied proper care straight away. [3] For in his despondency Crassus did not think it would be safe for him to stay even in the town, and he decided to flee as soon as possible.* Since there was no way he could leave by day without being spotted, he resolved to escape by night, but he was foiled by the moon, which was full, and aborted the plan. [4] So the Romans waited for a night with no moon, but then, since they set out in the dark, in a land that was unfamiliar and hostile, and in a state of abject fear, they became separated. Some of them were captured the next day and killed, but others made it safely to Syria with Cassius Longinus, the quaestor,* [5] or gained the mountains with Crassus himself* and prepared to escape through them to Armenia.

26. When Surenas found out that the Romans were on the loose, he was worried that if they simply went elsewhere they would resume the war, but he was reluctant to attack them in the highlands, where he could not make use of his cavalry. Since the Romans were heavy infantrymen who would be fighting with the advantage of high ground, and since their desperation would make them reckless, they would be difficult opponents. So he sent envoys to them, ostensibly to offer them a peace treaty with the stipulation that they should evacuate the entire country east of the Euphrates. [2] Crassus did not hesitate for a moment, but trusted him completely.* He could not have been more frightened, his mind was clouded by dismay at the disaster which had overtaken him personally and the state as a whole, and he could see how reluctant his men were to undertake the long, hard journey through the mountains, and how afraid they were of Orodes. All this made him quite incapable of seeing what he ought to do, [3] so he was ready to come to terms. Surenas, however, refused to conclude the treaty through proxies, and said that he wanted to meet with Crassus personally, his intention being to get him alone, with just a few men, and seize him. [4] They therefore decided to meet in the space between the two armies with an equal number of men from each side. Crassus came down from the hills, and Surenas sent him a horse as a gift, to hasten his arrival.

27. Now Crassus hesitated, but while he was wondering what to do the barbarians seized him and forced him up on to the horse. The Romans responded by catching hold of him themselves and engaging the enemy. For a while they held their own, but then reinforcements came to help the barbarians and they were overcome. [2] Since the barbarians were on level ground and had been told what to expect, they were able to reinforce their men before the Romans up in the hills could do so. All those accompanying him fell, while Crassus was either killed by one of his own men to prevent him from being taken alive, or died from the serious wounds inflicted on him by the enemy. [3] That was how Crassus met his end. Some report that the Parthians poured molten gold into his mouth to mock him.* He was indeed so obsessed with money, despite his great wealth, that he regarded men as poor and pitied them if they were unable to support an enrolled legion out of their own resources.* [4] Most of his men escaped* through the mountains to friendly territory, but some fell into enemy hands.

28. For the time being, the Parthians did not advance beyond the Euphrates, but recovered all the territory east of it. Later, however, they also invaded Syria,* though not with a large force, because they supposed that the province had no commander or troops. As a result, Cassius easily drove them out, since there were not many of them. [2] At Carrhae, the soldiers had offered Cassius the overall command because of their loathing for Crassus, and moreover, in view of the magnitude of the catastrophe, Crassus himself had freely given Cassius permission to accept, but he had turned it down. On this later occasion, however, he had no choice but to take charge of Syria, not just in the immediate crisis, but for the longer term.* [3] And in fact the barbarians did not keep away from it, but invaded again with a larger army.* This was nominally under the command of Pacorus, Orodes' son, but was actually led by Osaces, since Pacorus was still only a boy. They got as far as Antioch, subduing all the country as they went, [4] and hoped to conquer the rest as well, since there were no

Romans there with a force that could match theirs, and the inhabitants resented Roman rule and favoured the Parthians, as their neighbours and kin.

29. When they failed to take Antioch, where Cassius vigorously beat off their assaults and they were unable to mount a siege, they turned to Antigonia.* Since the outskirts of the city were thickly planted with trees, and they neither dared nor were able to charge through them on horseback, [2] they decided to cut down the trees until the whole place was bare, so that then they could approach the city confidently and safely. But they failed at this; it was extremely laborious work, which was just a waste of time, and any of them who were detached from their units were harassed by Cassius. So they decamped and left, with the intention of marching against another target. [3] Cassius' response was to set an ambush on the road they were going to take. When they reached that point, he confronted them with only a few men. That tempted the barbarians into pursuing him as he fled—and then he surrounded them. Osaces was among those who fell, and after his death Pacorus abandoned Syria and did not return to it again.*

30. Pacorus had only just left when Bibulus arrived to govern Syria,* although, to prevent the resulting factional violence from candidates, it had been voted that no praetor or consul should leave to take up a command abroad immediately after the end of his term of office, or in fact within five years afterwards.* [2] Bibulus kept the subject territory at peace* and managed to turn the Parthians against one another.* He got on good terms with Ornodapates, a satrap who held a grudge against Orodes, and persuaded him, by means of envoys, to crown Pacorus king and launch a joint campaign with Pacorus against Orodes. [3] Thus the war between the Romans and the 51 BCE Parthians came to an end, during the consulship of Marcus Marcellus and Sulpicius Rufus,* in the fourth year after it had begun.

31. In that same period Caesar fought and regained control of Gaul, putting an end to the disturbances there. He achieved a great deal, either himself or through his legates, and I shall describe only those most worthy of mention.* [2] After recruiting the Treveri, who were still angry at the death of Indutiomarus, Ambiorix united almost all the region* and sent for mercenaries from the Celts.* [3] Labienus, who wanted to bring the Gauls to battle before these mercenaries arrived, therefore invaded the territory of the Treveri.* Since they were waiting for the reinforcements, they chose not to fight back, but took up a position with a river between the two armies and did nothing. So Labienus convened his troops and addressed them* with words that were bound to frighten his own men and increase the confidence of the enemy. [4] He said that they should withdraw back to Caesar and safety before the Celtic reinforcements arrived, and he immediately gave the order to pack up camp. He set out not long afterwards, and what happened was exactly what he had expected. [5] When the barbarians found out what was going on—they always took care to be well informed, and in fact that was why Labienus revealed his plans in public—they believed that he was genuinely afraid of them and that his flight was a true flight. So they quickly crossed the river and set out confidently against the Romans, with each man advancing as fast as he could. [6] What Labienus confronted, then, was no coherent body of men. He overwhelmed the first to arrive, and then easily turned the rest to flight as well with the help of these panicked men. Many of the barbarians were killed by the Romans as they fled in disarray, falling over one another as they were pushed back towards the river.

32. Many of them escaped even so, but of these Caesar was interested only in Ambiorix, who fled from one place to another, wreaking havoc wherever he went, and caused Caesar a lot of trouble as he searched and hunted for him. Try as he might, however, Caesar failed to catch him, so he marched instead against the Celts, on the grounds that they had intended to help the Treveri. [2] This time too he achieved nothing, and he soon retreated for fear of the Suebi, but he won the glory of having crossed the Rhine again.* He also destroyed the bridge,* but only the section of it on the barbarians' side, and built a guard-post on it to maintain the constant threat of his crossing.

[3] He was angry that Ambiorix was still at large,* so he next allowed his country to be plundered by all comers, even though it had not been involved in the rebellion.* He published this permit widely, to attract as many people as possible, and many Gauls and Sugambri accordingly came for the booty.* [4] But the Sugambri, not content with pillaging Eburonian territory, attacked the Romans as well.* They waited until they were away foraging for food, assaulted their camp, and killed a lot of the men who returned to put up a fight when they realized what was going on. [5] The Sugambri were worried about how Caesar would respond to this, so they hastily withdrew back home, but because of winter and the troubled political situation

in Rome, he was unable to have his revenge. He dismissed his men to their various winter quarters, while he went off to Italy, ostensibly to attend to Cisalpine Gaul, but in fact so that he could keep an eye on events in the city from close at hand.

33. Meanwhile, the Gauls rose up again.* The Arverni rebelled under the command of Vercingetorix* and killed all the Romans they found in their towns or countryside.* They then proceeded against the Romans' allies, treating fairly those who were willing to join their insurgency, but dealing harshly with the rest. [2] Caesar returned from Italy when he heard the news and found that the Arverni had invaded the territory of the Bituriges. His army was not yet at full strength, however, so rather than coming to the defence of the Bituriges, he launched a retaliatory invasion of Arvernian territory.* This drew them back home, and Caesar retreated before them, since he did not think that he was yet a match for them.

34. The Arverni therefore returned to the attack on the Bituriges. They captured one of their towns, Avaricum,* and held out in it for a very long time. They were soon besieged by the Romans, but it proved difficult to approach the wall, which was surrounded on one side by an almost impassable marsh and on the other by a swiftly flowing river. Moreover, given their great numbers, they easily repelled the Romans' assaults, and when they made sorties out of the town they wreaked havoc. [2] In the end, they burnt everything in the vicinity, not just farmland and villages, but also towns from which they expected that the enemy would receive aid, and they seized all the supplies that were being conveyed to the Romans from their more distant allies, so that the Romans, the town's supposed besiegers, were themselves under siege.* [3] This went on until one day, winter having set in,* torrential rain and a violent wind assailed them as they were attacking a section of the wall. The Romans were the first to be driven away and back to their tents, and then the barbarians were forced to shut themselves inside their houses too—and after they had left the battlements, the Romans suddenly returned to the attack, while the walls were undefended. [4] They captured a tower straight away, before the enemy realized they were there, and then it was little trouble for them to gain control of the whole place. They plundered the entire town, and avenged themselves for all they had suffered during the siege* by slaughtering all the inhabitants.*

35. After this, Caesar launched a campaign against their country. Faced with the prospect of war, the remaining Arverni secured the bridges he was going to have to use, leaving Caesar uncertain how to get across the river.* He marched for miles along the river bank, trying to find a suitable place where he could ford the stream, [2] and eventually he found such a place, a dark and wooded spot. He sent the baggage train and most of the army on ahead, telling them to adopt a long, drawn-out column, so as to make it seem as though they were all there. [3] He kept the strongest men from the army behind with him, however, and they cut down trees, constructed rafts,* and crossed the river on them, while the barbarians' attention was focused on those who were marching on ahead and they assumed that Caesar was with them. [4] Next, Caesar had those he had sent on ahead return under cover of darkness, and he transported them across the river in the same way. Then he took control of the country, while the people fled for safety to Gergovia,* taking all their most valuable possessions with them.

Caesar put them under siege, but it cost him a great deal of wasted effort.* **36.** The fortress was on top of an easily defensible hill, which had been further strengthened by well-built walls. The barbarians had occupied all the surrounding high ground,* so as to have the place under close guard, and this meant that not only were they safe staying where they were, but they also usually came off best when they launched an assault down the slope. [2] Caesar had not been able to find a naturally secure position and was encamped on the plain, so that whereas he never had advance notice of anything, the barbarians, looking down on his camp from on high, could choose the best times for their assaults. [3] And if they accidentally advanced too far and were driven back, it did not take them long to regain the safety of their lines, because there was no way for the Romans to get close enough to the places held by them for their stones and javelins to be effective.

[4] Caesar was wasting his time. It was true that his frequent attacks on the hill where Gergovia itself was situated had gained him control of a part of it,* which he fortified and which acted as a base from which he could more easily attack the rest, but overall he was being beaten. [5] So since he had lost a lot of men, and could see that the enemy was invulnerable, and since in the meantime the Aedui had risen up in rebellion, and since, moreover, when he was away dealing

with the Aedui, the men he left behind suffered badly,* he raised
the siege.*

37. At first, the Aedui had observed the terms of their agreements
and had sent Caesar aid, but later they went to war, though not of
their own free choice: they were tricked into it by Litavicus, among
others. Litavicus had tried in various ways to get them to take up arms
against the Romans, with no success, so he saw to it that he was given
the job of taking a body of men to Caesar, ostensibly as allies, and he
set out as if that was what he was going to do. [2] But instead he sent
horsemen on ahead, having instructed some of them to come back and
say that their companions and the rest of the Aedui who were already
in the Roman camp had been seized by the Romans and killed, and
then he roused their anger even more by delivering a speech which
tallied with what the messengers had said. [3] So the Aedui rose up
in revolt themselves, and persuaded others to join them. But as soon
as Caesar was informed of this, he sent them the Aedui who were in
his camp and he was supposed to have killed, to make it absolutely
clear that they were still alive, and accompanied them himself with
the cavalry.*

So on this occasion the Aedui reconsidered and came to terms.
38. But later, after the Romans had been beaten at Gergovia during
Caesar's absence and had then withdrawn all their forces from there,
those of the Aedui who had been involved in the insurrection and who
persisted in wanting change became afraid that, since the Romans
were now not otherwise occupied, they would punish them,* and they
rose up in rebellion. [2] When the Aedui who were in Caesar's army
heard about this, they asked Caesar for permission to return home,
assuring him that they would completely quell the trouble. They were
allowed to leave, and they came to Noviodunum,* where the Romans
had deposited their money and grain, and a great many hostages as
well. With the help of the inhabitants they caught the unsuspecting
garrison off guard, wiped it out, and took possession of everything
there. [3] They burnt the town to the ground, because it was strategic-
ally located and they did not want the Romans to make it one of their
bases for the war, and roused the rest of the Aedui to insurrection.
Caesar tried to march against them straight away, but was foiled by
the Loire and turned against the Lingones.* [4] He met with no success there either, but Labienus seized the island in the Seine,* once he
had defeated the barbarians' first line of defence on the mainland and

had had his men cross the river at many points at once, both upstream and downstream, because he was afraid that his passage would be blocked if he crossed at just one point.

39. But before this happened, Vercingetorix, expecting no trouble from Caesar because of his setbacks, marched against the Allobroges,* and when Caesar responded by setting out to help them, Vercingetorix intercepted him in the territory of the Sequani* and surrounded him. [2] So far from harming him, however, quite the opposite happened. The Romans had so little hope of survival* that he left them no choice but to fight bravely, while he lost because his numerical advantage made him reckless. His defeat was partly due also to the Celts who were fighting for the Romans.* [3] Insatiable in their charges† and reinforcing their daring with their physical strength,* they broke through the encirclement. After this lucky break, Caesar kept up the pressure, pinned those of the enemy who had escaped inside Alesia, and put them under siege.*

40. Before being entirely surrounded by Caesar's circumvallation, Vercingetorix sent away the cavalry. He did this so that they could feed their horses (there being no fodder in Alesia), but also instructed each contingent to return to their homeland and bring back both supplies and reinforcements. [2] But they were late in getting back and food began to run out in Alesia, so Vercingetorix drove all the most expendable people, including the children and womenfolk, out of the town, in the vain hope that they would be saved by the Romans as booty, or at least that those who remained would survive since their food supplies would last longer. [3] But Caesar was not so well supplied with food himself that he could feed these people. Thinking that they would certainly be taken in and their return would make the enemy's shortage of food more acute, he drove them all back again. [4] So these outcasts died the most miserable of deaths between the town and the camp, shut out by both sides.*

As for the reinforcements*—the cavalry and other troops who were being fetched—the barbarians did not have much longer to wait for their arrival, but when they came they were repulsed in a cavalry battle, as the Romans, with the help of [. . .]* [5] Later, they tried to get through the surrounding siege walls and into the town by night,* but that was a disaster. The Romans had dug concealed trenches in the places where the terrain was suitable for horses, with stakes fixed in them, and then had made everything on the surface look the same as the surrounding ground, [6] so that both men and horses fell unawares into these trenches and came to grief. They still did not give up, however, until they had formed up for battle again right by the siege walls and been defeated, along with the defenders who had come out from the town.*

41. Vercingetorix was free and uninjured, and could have escaped, but on the basis of his past friendship with Caesar he hoped to be pardoned by him.* He came to him unannounced and appeared out of the blue before the dais where Caesar was sitting. Some people were alarmed, because he was very tall anyway and in his armour he cut a fearsomely impressive figure. [2] But when silence fell he said nothing and just fell to his knees, with his hands clasped, and begged for mercy. At this, everyone else felt sorry for him, as they recalled his former good fortune and saw the wretched state he was in now, but Caesar turned against him the very thing that Vercingetorix had been most counting on to save him. [3] That is, by contrasting his friendship with his hostility, Caesar showed his offence to have been that much the worse. That was why he felt no pity for him at the time, and in fact had him bound in chains; and that was why subsequently, after Vercingetorix had been paraded in his triumph, he put him to death.*

42. But that happened later. At the time in question, he won over some of the remaining tribes by agreement, but others he subjugated by victory in battle.* The neighbouring Belgae resisted for a long time under Commius, an Atrebatian, whom they had made their leader.* Two battles took place involving just the cavalry, but they were indecisive, and then in the third engagement the infantry was involved.

The battle was evenly matched at first, but then, when the Roman cavalry fell unexpectedly on the barbarians' rear, they turned to flight. [2] Afterwards, the survivors abandoned their camp by night and set fire to a wood through which they passed; they left behind only their wagons, in the hope that they and the fire would delay the enemy and give them time to get away to safety. [3] But their hopes were dashed. As soon as the Romans found out about their flight, they set out after them, and when they came across the fire they either extinguished it or hacked their way through it—and some men even ran right through the middle of the flames. So they caught up with the enemy, took them by surprise, and slaughtered huge numbers of them.*

43. After this, some of the others surrendered, but the Atrebatian, who had escaped, still remained active, and at one point attempted to

ambush Labienus. [2] After he had lost the battle, he was persuaded
to hold a conference with Labienus, but before any agreement had
been reached he was wounded by one of the Romans,* who doubted
that he was really there to make peace. Commius escaped and resumed
making trouble for the Romans, but eventually he gave up the futile
endeavour. He negotiated for his associates an unconditional amnesty
for all their past deeds and pardon for himself, as some report, on the
condition that he should never come within sight of any Roman.*
[3] So this group of rebels made peace, and the rest were subdued
before long, either willingly or by warfare. And then Caesar employed
garrisons, punishments, levies of money, and payments of tribute*
to humble some of them and tame others.

44. So all this fighting came to an end in the year of the consulship 50 BCE
of Lucius Paullus and Gaius Marcellus.* Because of the situation in
Gaul and the term granted him for his command, Caesar was now
due to leave Gaul and return to Rome. The term was now at an end,*
the war was over, and he no longer had any plausible reason not to
dismiss his legions and resume life as a private citizen. [2] But the city
was racked by political feuding, Crassus was dead, and Pompey was
once more in power, having served as consul for a third time and successfully obtained an extension of his command in Spain for a further
five years.* He was no longer on good terms with Caesar, especially
after the death of the child* [3] who had been the only bond keeping
them friends. Caesar was therefore afraid that, if he were deprived of
his soldiers, he would be at the mercy of Pompey and his other enemies,* and so he did not discharge them.

45. In the course of these same years factional strife had been
a common occurrence in the city, especially over the elections; it was
only in the seventh month, for instance, that Calvinus and Messalla 53 BCE
were appointed consuls.* [2] Even then, in fact, the elections would
not have gone ahead had Quintus Pompeius Rufus not been thrown
into the prison* by the Senate, despite the fact that he was the grandson of Sulla and a tribune.* The same penalty was also decreed for
everyone else who had planned mischief, and responsibility for acting
against them was entrusted to Pompey. [3] Sometimes the auspices
delayed the elections by refusing to favour the *interreges*,* but it was
mainly the tribunes who prevented the other magistrates being elected,
and they managed the city's affairs so that even the games were being
organized by them, not the praetors.* That was also why Rufus was

thrown into the prison. [4] He later saw to the imprisonment of Favonius,* who was one of the aediles; the charge he brought against him was trivial, but he no doubt wanted to have a companion in his disgrace.

All the tribunes came up with various pretexts for obstructing the elections, including the proposal that the consuls should be replaced by military tribunes, so that a larger number of magistrates should be appointed, as in the past.* [5] No one else was convinced by them, however, so the tribunes argued that at least Pompey should be made dictator.* This device enabled them to hold things up for a very long time, since Pompey was out of town, and none of those who were available could bear either to vote for the proposal, because Sulla's savagery had made the institution of dictatorship universally hated, or to refuse Pompey the position, because they were afraid of him.

46. When at last Pompey returned, not only did he turn down the offer of the dictatorship, with apparent sincerity, but he also made arrangements for the consuls to be elected.* But they too did not appoint their successors, because of the turmoil arising from the murders, though they convened the Senate dressed not in their senatorial robes but as *equites*, as though they were mourning a great catastrophe.* [2] They also passed a decree that no former praetor or consul should assume a command abroad before five years had passed.* It was hoped that the introduction of an interval before they held such power would restrain their eagerness for office, because as things were their canvassing took extreme and diseased forms. [3] Candidates vied with one another over how much money they spent, and even more so in their frequent brawls, during one of which even the consul Calvinus was injured. So there was no consul, praetor, or prefect of the city* 52 BCE appointed for the following year, and at the beginning of the year the Romans therefore had no government at all.*

47. Nothing else good followed this, and the market which was traditionally held every ninth day fell on the first day of January.* [2] This caused the Romans some alarm, because it did not seem a mere coincidence but a portent of some kind, and there were other events that were also disturbing: an eagle owl was seen and caught in the city, a statue dripped sweat for three days, a light flashed across the sky from south to east, and not only thunderbolts, but even clods of earth, stones, fragments of pottery, and gouts of blood frequently flew through the air.* [3] But in my opinion, the decree that had been passed right at the end of the previous year about Sarapis and Isis was no less of a portent. What happened was that the Senate decided to demolish their temples,* which had been built by certain individuals at their own expense. [4] For a long time after that they did not pay cult to these gods, and even when it was finally agreed that they should be worshipped publicly, they established their temples outside the *pomerium*.*

48. That was how things stood in the city at the time. With no one in charge, murders were taking place almost every day and the elections could not be held,* even though men wanted to hold the offices and were employing bribery and bloodshed to get them. [2] Milo, for instance, who was seeking a consulship, encountered Clodius on the Appian Way, and though at first he did no more than wound him, he went on to kill him* because he did not want to be prosecuted by him for the wounding. His thinking was that, once he had freed all the slaves who had taken part in the affair, which he did immediately, it was more likely that he would be acquitted of murder if Clodius were dead, than of assault if he were alive. [3] When the news reached Rome towards evening,* it caused a furious uproar. As far as the factions were concerned, it was a reason for them to go to war and make trouble, while even the neutrals were angry, for all their hatred of Clodius, out of natural human feeling, and because they saw an opportunity for getting rid of Milo.

49. Finding the people already in this excitable state, Rufus and Titus Munatius Plancus fanned the flames. In their capacity as tribunes, they brought Clodius' body into the Forum just before daybreak, placed it on the Rostra, and displayed it to everyone. [2] With tears in their eyes, they delivered a predictable harangue, so that the people were inflamed by what they were hearing as well as what they were seeing; they cast aside their religious scruples, disregarded all the funerary norms, and came close to burning down the entire city. They picked up Clodius' body, carried it into the senate-house, and dressed it;* then they made a pyre out of the benches and burnt both the body and the building. [3] This was not prompted by the kind of sudden impulse that typically comes over crowds; it was a premeditated act, as is proved by the fact that later that day, at the ninth hour,* they even held the funeral banquet* right there in the Forum, with the senate-house still smouldering.

They also tried to burn down Milo's house. [4] They failed, because it had many defenders, but Milo was so terrified because of the murder that for a while he went into hiding, with a guard not just of ordinary citizens, but also of *equites* and a few senators. But after this subsequent development, he hoped that the Senate's anger would be diverted to the pollution perpetrated by his opponents—[5] and indeed the Senate did meet in the afternoon on the Palatine,* pushed into an early response by exactly this event, and they voted that an *interrex* should be chosen,* and that he and the tribunes, and Pompey as well, should be responsible for the protection of the city and see that it suffered no harm*—and so he showed himself in public* and pursued his bid for the consulship just as energetically as before, if not more so.

50. There were many further outbreaks of fighting and killing after this, which led the Senate to adopt the measures I have just mentioned and send for Pompey, entrust him with recruiting fresh troops,* and change their dress.* [2] He soon arrived, and they assembled under guard outside the *pomerium*, near his theatre.* They decided to gather up Clodius' bones, and they put Faustus, the son of Sulla, in charge of rebuilding the senate-house. [3] I should explain that the old building, the *Curia Hostilia*, had been remodelled by Sulla; this explains the commission to Faustus and their decree that the building, when reconstructed, should be named after Sulla.*

The city was in suspense while waiting to find out which magistrates would rule it; some argued for Pompey as dictator, others for Caesar as consul. [4] (The people were so determined to honour Caesar for his achievements that they voted sixty days of sacrifices for them.*) But the senators, including Bibulus, who would be the first to be asked to express his opinion, were afraid of both men and checked the popular mood by giving the consulship to Pompey, to avoid his being appointed dictator, and to him alone,* so that he would not have Caesar as his colleague. [5] This was an unprecedented innovation, but it seemed to them to be the right move; since Pompey favoured the plebs less than Caesar, they hoped to sever relations between him and them altogether and make him their man. And that is what happened. He was so delighted by this novel and unusual honour that his policies no longer took the wishes of the people into consideration, and absolutely everything he did was designed to please the Senate.*

51. However, he did not want to hold office alone; he had the glory of the appointment, but he was also anxious to avoid the jealousy it

would entail.* He was also afraid that, since the position was vacant, Caesar would be foisted upon him as his colleague* by the zealous support of his troops and the plebs. [2] So, in order to avoid giving Caesar the impression that he was being altogether overlooked (which would give him a good reason to be angry), with the help of the tribunes he arranged for him to be allowed to seek election to the consulship when the laws permitted,* even if he was absent from Rome.* Then he chose as his colleague Quintus Scipio, his father-in-law,* who had a charge of bribery pending. [3] Quintus Scipio was by birth the son of Nasica, but he had been adopted into the family of Metellus Pius in order to inherit the estate, and therefore bore the name of Metellus as well.* He had married his daughter to Pompey,* and in return received the consulship and was spared prosecution.*

52. Very many men were called to account on this charge, especially because under Pompey's laws* the courts were conducted more strictly. He himself drew up the list of men from which the final selection of jurors by lot was going to be made,* and he limited the number of advocates to speak on either side, so that jurors would not be baffled and confused by a plethora of speeches. [2] He ruled that the prosecution was to be allowed two hours to speak and the defence three. And he corrected the most detrimental practice of all, which was that people on trial called character witnesses*—a detrimental practice because a great many men escaped justice just because trustworthy witnesses sang their praises—by ruling that from then on defendants should be allowed no character witnesses at all. [3] This was just one of a number of measures that were instituted for all the courts alike. As for those charged with electoral bribery, he induced men who had already been convicted on such a charge to prosecute them, by offering them a not inconsiderable reward: if anyone secured the conviction of two men for offences similar or less serious than those for which he had been convicted, or one man for a more serious offence, he would be granted a pardon.*

53. Many men were convicted as a result of these measures. One of them was Plautius Hypsaeus, who had been a rival of Milo and Scipio for the consulship.* All three had dispensed bribes, but Plautius was the only one to be brought to justice for it. [2] Scipio was indicted by two prosecutors, but thanks to Pompey the case never came to court.* Milo was not charged with bribery, because he had to face the more serious charge of murder, but when he was tried on that

charge, he was found guilty* since he was not able to employ violence. This was because Pompey had the rest of the city under guard and came into the court with armed soldiers. [3] When some people made an uproar at this, Pompey told his men to drive them out of the Forum by striking them with the flat sides of their swords, and when that did not make them stop, and they just taunted him as though they were being struck for fun, a few of them were wounded and killed.*

54. After this, the courts met without further disruption. A lot of guilty verdicts were handed down for other crimes, and those convicted of Clodius' murder included Milo,* even though he had Cicero to defend him. [2] What happened was that, when the orator saw Pompey and his soldiers in court contrary to custom,* he became frightened out of his wits, and the upshot was that he delivered none of his prepared speech, but just muttered a few faint and awkward words,* and was then glad to retire. The speech which is in circulation today* and which purports to be the one that was delivered at the time in Milo's defence was written by Cicero some time later, at leisure and when his confidence had returned. [3] In fact, the following story* has been handed down about it. When Milo read the speech (which Cicero had sent him, since he was in exile), he wrote back, saying that it was lucky that this version of the speech had not been delivered in court, because if he had been defended so effectively he would not now be eating such splendid mullets in Massilia* (which is where he was staying during his exile). [4] He wrote this not because he was happy with his lot—in fact he pushed hard and often for his return*—but to tease Cicero for having worked up and sent him a futile speech, as though it could do him some good, when he had said nothing helpful at the time of his trial.

55. So Milo was convicted, and so were Rufus and Plancus (as soon as they stepped down from their offices) and many others along with them, for the burning of the senate-house.* Plancus was convicted despite the fact that he had the support of Pompey, who even sent the court a document that was simultaneously a eulogy of Plancus and a plea for mercy in his case. [2] But Marcus Cato, who was going to be a juror, said that he would not admit Pompey's character evidence in contravention of his own laws.* But Cato never had an opportunity to vote, because Plancus rejected him, as one who would be sure to vote for his condemnation. (By the Pompeian laws, the defendant and the prosecutor each had the right to eliminate five jurors from those who were going to serve.*) [3] But the other jurors found Plancus guilty, because they thought it wrong to acquit him when he was on trial for the same crimes for which they had already condemned Rufus. And when they saw that Pompey was on Plancus' side, they took the opposite position because they wanted to prove themselves to be jurors and not his mere slaves. [4] But on this occasion too, in prosecuting Plancus, Cicero performed just as poorly as he had when defending Milo.* The same sight greeted his eyes in the courtroom, and in both cases Pompey opposed him by his advice and his actions. This was the main factor which set them against each other again.*

56. While seeing to all this, Pompey also revived the election law, which had somehow fallen into disuse, that all candidates had to present themselves without fail before the assembly,* to make sure that no absentee could be elected. He also ratified the decree which had been passed a short while before that those who had held office in the city were not to draw lots for a command abroad until five years had passed.* [2] And yet, even though he drew up these measures at this time, a little later he was not ashamed to take Spain for a further five years,* and to allow Caesar, whose friends had been kicking up a terrible fuss, to seek election to the consulship even in his absence, as had been voted.* [3] He achieved this by adding a rider to the law,* saying that men would be allowed to seek election in their absence only if official permission were granted to them by name and unequivocally. But this amounted to not banning the practice at all, because anyone with any influence would certainly manage to get an exemption from the law voted for him.

57. These were the measures taken by Pompey. Meanwhile, Scipio proposed no new laws, but repealed Clodius' law about the censors.* Although on the face of it he did this as a favour to the censors, since he gave them back the powers they had formerly enjoyed, it did not turn out like that at all. [2] There were many unworthy men in both the equestrian and the senatorial orders, but while the censors had not been allowed to remove from the lists anyone unless they had been accused and convicted, they could not be criticized for failing to erase any names. [3] But once their old powers were restored, which permitted them to scrutinize the lives of individuals and erase names on their own authority, they found themselves in a quandary: they did not dare to offend so many people, but neither did they want to be

reproached for not removing unsuitable people, and this meant that no one, if he had any sense, wanted to be a censor any more.*

58. So much for the vote that was passed with regard to the censors. Cato did not otherwise want to hold office,* but he saw that Caesar and Pompey were growing too great for the constitution, and suspected that either they would share power between themselves, or they would fall out with each other and the winner of the ensuing civil war, which would be no slight affair, would rule by himself. [2] So, wanting to see to their downfall before they became adversaries, he put himself forward as a candidate for the consulship so that he could resist them, since as a private citizen he would have no authority. However, Caesar's and Pompey's sympathizers guessed what he was up to and made sure that he was not elected. Instead, Marcus Marcellus and Sulpicius Rufus were elected,* [3] the one because of his legal expertise and the other because of his skill as an orator. But they were chosen above all because, while avoiding the use of bribery or violence, they managed to flatter and appeal to everyone across the board, whereas Cato courted no one's favour.* [4] This was the last time Cato ever sought the consulship. He used to say that an honest man should neither avoid the leadership of the state, if there were people who wanted to employ him, nor seek it too eagerly.

51 BCE   59. Marcellus immediately set to work, and since he was a partisan of Pompey,* everything he did was designed to bring about Caesar's downfall. He proposed numerous measures against him,* including that a successor should be sent out to him now before the due time.* Opposition to the proposal came from Sulpicius and some of the tribunes—the tribunes because they wanted to please Caesar, and Sulpicius made common cause with them and the people because† he thought it wrong to terminate a man's command when he had done nothing to deserve it. [2] Now, Pompey had already left the city as though he were going to campaign in Spain, but at the time in question he was still in Italy, and, having delegated responsibility for Spain to his legates, he kept watch on the city.* So when he heard about this, [3] he pretended that he too did not approve of Caesar's being deprived of his command, but he set about arranging matters so that when Caesar's time was up—which was no distant prospect, but due to happen the very next year—he would lay down his arms and return to Rome as a private citizen.* [4] He accordingly arranged* for Gaius Marcellus to become consul and for Gaius Curio to become

a tribune; Marcellus,* who was Marcus' cousin (or perhaps his brother, as an alternative version has it), was an enemy of Caesar despite being related to him by marriage, and Curio* had long been hostile towards Caesar.

60. Caesar could not face becoming a private citizen after such an important and lengthy command, and he was afraid of falling into the clutches of his enemies,* so he made plans to hold on to his position in spite of them. He enrolled additional soldiers,* collected money, manufactured arms and armour, and made sure that his leadership pleased all his men. [2] Meanwhile, because he wanted to arrange things in Rome as well, prior to his return, and to do so in a way that would make people see that he could get things done by persuasion and did not always resort to violence, he decided to effect a reconciliation with Curio, because he was a member of the Curiones family, because he was sharp-witted and a talented orator with a great deal of influence over the plebs, and because he spent lavishly on absolutely any project which he expected either to raise him above others or help someone else. [3] Caesar aroused Curio's expectations with numerous promises, paid off all his debts* (which were many because of his extravagance), and bound him to himself. In view of the importance of his present projects, he disbursed large amounts of money, knowing that he would recover it if those projects came to fruition, and he also promised certain people extraordinary wealth, when he had no intention of giving them even the minutest fraction of what he promised. [4] He ingratiated himself not only with free men but even with slaves, if they had any kind of influence with their masters.* As a result, many *equites* and senators put themselves at his service.

61. So Curio joined Caesar's side, but he did not immediately begin to work for him openly. He was looking for a plausible excuse so that it would seem that he had changed his position because he was compelled to, not because he wanted to. And he also thought that the more time he spent with Caesar's enemies, pretending to be their friend, the more secrets of theirs he would learn and the more important they would be. [2] So he dissembled for as long as he could, and to deflect all suspicion that he had changed his position and was not still a leading opponent of Caesar in all his thoughts and words, he even delivered speeches against him from the start of his tribunate and introduced many outrageous proposals.* [3] Some of the measures he

50 BCE

proposed were hostile to the Senate and its leading members, who were particularly loyal supporters of Pompey, not because he wanted or expected any of them to be passed, but because, while these proposals were in the process of being rejected, in the first place, none of the many proposals being made by Caesar's opponents could be put to the vote, and, secondly, it would give him an excuse for changing his position.

62. Once he had wasted a great deal of time by means of this tactic, camouflaging his intentions differently each time, so that none of his proposals even came close to being ratified, he pretended to be annoyed, and asked for an extra month to be inserted for the proposals to be passed into law. This was a practice that was adopted when it was appropriate,* but not for this reason, as Curio knew, since he was a pontiff. [2] But he kept insisting that it was necessary and made a big show of putting pressure on his fellow priests. In the end, when he was unable to win their compliance (which he did not want to do anyway), he gave this as a reason for refusing to allow any other business to be put to the vote. Claiming that he was unable to get anything done by working against Caesar, he now began openly to argue that Caesar was in the right [3] and to put forward all sorts of proposals which were unlikely to be accepted.* The most important of these was that either everyone in arms should disarm straight away and dismiss their legions,* or they should not deprive Caesar of his forces and hand him over to those of his adversaries. [4] He made this proposal not because he wanted Caesar to disband his army, but because he was certain that Pompey would not go along with it, and thus Caesar too was given a plausible reason for not dismissing his troops.

63. Since Pompey was unable to get anything done by other means, he shed all pretence, adopted a harsh approach, and openly worked against Caesar in all he said and did. He was thwarted at every turn, however. [2] Caesar's many supporters included Lucius Paullus,* who was consul along with Marcellus, and Lucius Piso, his father-in-law, who was a censor. I should explain that Appius Claudius and Piso were made censors then,* albeit unwillingly in Piso's case. [3] Piso was an ally of Caesar's because of their kinship, while Claudius was on Pompey's side and was therefore an opponent of Caesar. Nevertheless, not the least help Caesar received came from Claudius, even if it was unintentional. What happened was that he overcame his colleague's objections and expelled a great many *equites* and senators*—and thus made all of them sympathetic to Caesar's cause. [4] Piso, who was basically reluctant to make trouble and was busy ingratiating himself with people, trying to keep them on good terms with his son-in-law, did nothing of the kind himself, but he did not oppose Claudius when he removed from the Senate all the sons of freedmen* and many of the well-born as well, including Sallustius Crispus, the historian.* [5] However, when Curio was threatened with expulsion,* Piso (with the help of Paullus, to whom he was related) persuaded his colleague to reconsider.

64. Claudius may have failed for this reason to have Curio's name deleted, but he did not conceal his opinion of him when he spoke in the Senate, and Curio became so enraged that he ripped Claudius' clothes. Marcellus therefore had him restrained and, thinking that the Senate would agree to stern measures against him—and because of him, against Caesar as well—he brought forward proposals about him. [2] At first, Curio argued against any such proposal being put to the vote, but when he realized that the majority of the senators who were present on that occasion were either on Caesar's side or were terrified of him, he allowed the vote to go ahead, [3] adding only: 'I know that I always try to do what is best and most expedient for my country, but I hereby entrust myself, body and soul, to you. Deal with me as you see fit.' Marcellus therefore accused him, certain that he would be convicted, [4] and when the majority voted to let him off,* he was furious. He dashed out of the meeting and went to Pompey, who was in the outskirts of the city,* and on his own initiative, although there had been no official vote on the matter, he put the protection of the city in his hands and gave him two citizen legions.*

I shall now explain the reasons why these legions had been brought together and were present at that time. **65.** On an earlier occasion, while he and Caesar were still on good terms, Pompey had given him one of the enrolled legions for use in his campaign,* because he was not involved in any war at the time and Caesar was in need of troops. [2] After they had fallen out with each other, Pompey wanted not just to get that legion back from Caesar, but to take another one from him as well, so he made up a story to the effect that Bibulus needed soldiers for his war against the Parthians, and to make sure that no new troops would be enrolled—he was claiming that the matter was urgent and that they had more than enough legions anyway—he arranged for it to be decreed that both of them, both he and Caesar, should send Bibulus one legion. [3] But then Pompey sent Bibulus none of his own men, but ordered those who were responsible for making the arrangements to request that legion, the one which he had earlier given to Caesar. So, although in theory both of them were involved, in fact both legions were contributed by Caesar alone. [4] He knew what was going on, but he went along with it because he did not want to be accused of disobedience, and especially because he was planning to use this as an excuse for recruiting far more troops than those he had lost.

66. So these legions were assembled as though for use against the Parthians,* but since they were not needed there, seeing that there was nothing for them to do, Marcellus, fearing that they would be restored to Caesar, had declared that they should stay in Italy, and now handed them over to Pompey, as I have said. [2] This happened towards the end of the year and would not remain valid for long, since it had been approved by neither the Senate nor the people, so Marcellus won over to Pompey's side Cornelius Lentulus and Gaius Claudius, who were the next year's consuls,* and got them to issue the same order. [3] Since those who had been elected as magistrates were at the time still allowed to issue edicts and do other things which fell within their responsibilities even before they took up office,* they considered this too to be within their powers. And although Pompey was invariably scrupulous in all that he did, nevertheless his need of soldiers was such that he did not look closely into where these troops came from or how he came by them, but merely accepted them with pleasure. [4] However, the outcome was not at all what one might have expected from such a bold move; they were content with having displayed their hostility towards Caesar. They took no further steps to strengthen their position, and their action provided him with a good excuse for hanging on to the legions he had. Curio bitterly condemned the consuls and Pompey before the plebs for what they had done, and as soon as his term of office came to an end, he set out to join Caesar.*

APPENDIX
ROMAN NAMES; MONEY AND MEASURES OF DISTANCE; CALENDAR

Roman Names

THE names of Roman male citizens normally had three elements: a *praenomen* or first name, which was the individual's personal name; a *nomen*, which was the name of their *gens* (see Glossary, p. 284); and a *cognomen* or added name. There were very few male *praenomina*, and these were regularly abbreviated as shown in the list below. *Cognomina* originated as personal names, often alluding to some characteristic of the bearer, but many were inherited and so came to designate a family branch of a larger *gens* (e.g. the Cornelii Lentuli). Some holders of a hereditary *cognomen* acquired an additional personal *cognomen* (e.g. P. Cornelius Lentulus Spinther). Women were regularly called just by the feminine form of their father's *nomen* (e.g. Julia). Dio follows Roman practice in using men's names either on their own or in various combinations. In the Index, individuals are listed by their *nomen*, with cross-references from their *cognomen*. Following usual anglophone practice, the name Pompey has been used throughout this work for Cn. Pompeius Magnus, Catiline for L. Sergius Catilina, and Octavian for the dictator Caesar's heir between his adoptive father's death in 44 BCE and his assumption of the name Augustus in 27.

ABBREVIATIONS OF COMMON PRAENOMINA

A.	Aulus	P.	Publius
Ap.	Appius	Q.	Quintus
C.	Gaius	Ser.	Servius
Cn.	Gnaeus	Sp.	Spurius
D.	Decimus	Sex.	Sextus
L.	Lucius	T.	Titus
M.	Marcus	Ti.	Tiberius
M.'	Manius		

Roman Money and Measures of Distance

4 sesterces = 1 denarius. Greek writers consider 1 denarius = 1 drachma, and 6,000 denarii or 24,000 sesterces = 1 talent.

1 Roman mile = 1.48 km/0.92 mile.

The Roman Calendar

The Republican Roman calendar used a 355-day year in which March, May, Quintilis (July), and October had thirty-one days each, February twenty-eight, and the rest twenty-nine. To bring the calendar in line with the solar year, February was shortened to twenty-three or twenty-four days and followed by an intercalary month of twenty-seven days. Intercalation was the responsibility of the College of Pontiffs and only erratically carried out (see 40.62.1), so that the calendar was often significantly ahead of the solar year. In 46 BCE Julius Caesar introduced the system still in general use today, with modifications introduced by Pope Gregory XIII in 1582.

Calendar dates in the Explanatory Notes are those of the calendar then in force, except where otherwise specified. The Romans stated dates as before the kalends (the first of the month), nones (fifth or seventh), or ides (thirteenth or fifteenth), but dates are here given just as days of the month.

EXPLANATORY NOTES

THE references in the left-hand column are to chapter and section numbers (chapter numbers are set in bold type and section numbers in square brackets in the translation). For recurring terms, see the Glossary, pp. 283–8; for abbreviations of Roman *praenomina*, see Appendix, p. 161.

The following abbreviations of ancient works are used:

App.	*BC*	Appian,	*Bella Civilia* (*Civil Wars*)
	Celt.		*The Celtic Book*
	Mithr.		*The Mithridatic Book*
	Syr.		*The Syrian Book*
Caes.	*BG*	Caesar,	*Bellum Gallicum* (*Gallic War*)
Cic.	*Att.*	Cicero,	*Letters to Atticus*
	Cat.		*Catilinarians*
	Fam.		*Ad Familiares* (*Letters to His Friends*)
	Har. resp.		*De Haruspicum responso*
	Imp. Pomp.		*De Imperio Cn. Pompeii* (*On the Command of Gnaeus Pompeius*)
	QF		*Ad Quintum Fratrem* (*Letters to His Brother Quintus*)
	Sest.		*For Sestius*
Plut.	*Caes.*	Plutarch,	*Caesar*
	Cato		*Cato the Younger*
	Cic.		*Cicero*
	Crass.		*Crassus*
	Luc.		*Lucullus*
	Pomp.		*Pompey*
Sall.	*Cat.*	Sallust,	*Catiline's Conspiracy*
Suet.	*Jul.*	Suetonius,	*The Deified Julius*

Asconius is cited by the page numbers of the edition of A. C. Clark, reprinted in Asconius, *Commentaries on Speeches by Cicero*, trans. and comm. R. G. Lewis, Clarendon Ancient History Series (Oxford, 2006). The fragments of Sallust's *Histories* are cited by the numeration of Sallust, *Fragments of the Histories*, ed. and trans. J. T. Ramsey, Loeb Classical Library (Cambridge, MA, 2015).

BOOK THIRTY-SIX

1a *[From Xiphilinus' epitome]*: Book 36 began with events of the year 69 BCE, but a small initial section is missing in our manuscripts. Passages from Xiphilinus' epitome, which itself started with Dio's Book 36, partially preserve the lost material, covering events at Rome, Metellus' departure for Crete, and the start of Dio's account of Lucullus' campaign in this year, and are printed here in italics to distinguish them from Dio's surviving text. See Introduction, p. x.

Hortensius: Q. Hortensius Hortalus, recognized as the leading advocate of the day until outdone by Cicero's successful prosecution of Verres in 70. At this period, the Senate decreed the incoming consuls' provinces before their election, in accordance with a law passed by C. Gracchus in 123 BCE. They drew lots for them on entry into office, and declining a province was not uncommon.

the war against the Cretans: the Cretan cities' links with pirates brought them into conflict with M. Antonius during his command against the pirates *c*.74–71. Antonius agreed terms following a defeat, but a stern ultimatum was subsequently issued by the Senate, and its rejection led to the war.

Metellus therefore set out for Crete . . .: Q. Caecilius Metellus, consul in 69 along with Hortensius. Xiphilinus gave a summary of the whole of Metellus' Cretan war now, before passing to Lucullus' campaign. However, surviving manuscripts show that Dio narrated the closing phase of the war under the year 67 (36.18–19), and he may have covered all the hostilities (which probably did not get under way until 68) at that point. Dio's editors accordingly insert Xiphilinus' summary of the war there (see 36.17a).

1b.1 *Mithridates and Tigranes of Armenia*: Xiphilinus here inaccurately summarizes events which will have been narrated at length in Dio's preceding books. Mithridates VI Eupator had from 120 been king of Pontus, comprising the Black Sea coast of Asia Minor and its hinterland, and had fought wars with the Romans in 89–85 and *c*.83–81. Their final war began in 74 or 73 with Mithridates' invasion of Bithynia, following its bequest to Rome by its last king. L. Licinius Lucullus, consul in 74, was assigned and annually renewed in the command against Mithridates and campaigned successfully against him, driving him out of his kingdom and forcing him to take refuge with his son-in-law Tigranes II, king of Armenia from *c*.95. Following Tigranes' refusal of his demand for the surrender of Mithridates, Lucullus invaded his territory in 69. Dio's account in 36.1–17 of Lucullus' campaigns in 69–67 forms the first extended episode of the book. Plutarch (*Luc.* 25–36) and Appian (*Mithr.* 84–90) provide parallel narratives. All three writers drew on Sallust's account in books 4 and 5 of his *Histories*, from which fragments survive. Cicero in 66 gave a tendentious outline of the Romans' difficulties (*Imp. Pomp.* 4–5, 22–26).

Tigranocerta: Tigranes' ancestral kingdom of Armenia was a mountainous region to the east of the upper Euphrates and north of the eastern Taurus range (see note to 36.16.1), but he had expanded his rule far to the west and south, in Mesopotamia and Syria, at the expense of the Parthians, Seleucids, and others (see note to 36.53.2), and had founded Tigranocerta as the capital of his new empire, peopling it with Greeks and non-Greeks deported from the regions to its west. Its precise location remains disputed, but is best placed in the upper valley of the Tigris, between that river and the Taurus range, perhaps at modern Arzan.

1b.2 *naphtha*: a flammable mineral oil for which ancient Mesopotamia was noted.

he advanced: by laying siege to Tigranocerta, Lucullus achieved his aim of bringing Tigranes to battle, inflicting a crushing defeat despite his greatly inferior numbers. The battle took place on 6 October 69 (Plut. *Luc.* 27).

1b.3 *his tiara and the diadem*: the tiara was a tall rounded headdress worn by the Parthian kings and other rulers in the region, and the diadem, a band worn round this hat or the hair, was generally recognized as the mark of monarchy in this period (see 36.52.3).

1.1 *Arsaces of Parthia*: Arsaces was the name of the founder of the Parthian royal dynasty (see note to 40.14.3), and the name was also borne by all his successors. Tigranes and Mithridates made their appeal to Phraates III, who had recently succeeded his father Sinatruces. Dio (36.45.3) wrongly dated his accession later.

some disputed territory: in northern Mesopotamia, including Adiabene and Gordyene, acquired by Tigranes from Parthia early in his reign. The region remained in dispute after Tigranes' defeat: 37.5.3.

1.2 *the very next campaign . . . would be against him*: Sallust in his *Histories* (4.60) composed a letter purporting to be sent by Mithridates to Arsaces warning that, if he did not support them, he would be the next victim of the Romans' 'deep-seated desire for empire and riches'. Sallust was surely Dio's source here, but he has generalized the argument into a characteristic reflection on the compulsions of human nature, with echoes of Thucydides' Mytilenean Debate (Thucydides 3.39.4, 45.4). Insatiable success and unlimited greed for more (*pleonexia*) are favourite themes for Dio (e.g. frgs. 26.3, 36.25, 39.3, 40.36–38, 52.1, 55.7; 37.6.1; 44.29.2).

2.1 *did not pursue Tigranes*: after the defeat Tigranes had withdrawn to Armenia. As Dio's further indications show, Lucullus spent the remainder of 69 in establishing control over Tigranes' southern empire.

accuse him of being unwilling to conclude the war: for this agitation at Rome, see also Plut. *Luc.* 24, 33. Plutarch represents it as starting earlier, when Lucullus extended the war into Tigranes' territory.

2.2 *returned the province of Asia to the praetors then*: Lucullus had been granted the province of Cilicia along with the command against Mithridates in 74, to which were added Asia then or later and Bithynia in *c.*70. Asia was assigned a praetor as governor (as had earlier been normal) in 69. A contributory factor in that case may have been Lucullus' defence of the provincials of Asia against Roman tax-farmers (*publicani*) and moneylenders, which had led to agitation at Rome (Plut. *Luc.* 20). However, his absence beyond the Euphrates now prevented him from direct involvement in the government of the province, so, despite Dio, the replacement may not have been hostile to Lucullus. The same may also have been true of the decision to make Cilicia a province for the consuls of 68 and its allotment to Q. Marcius Rex, mentioned by Dio only at 36.15.1. Both decisions may have been made by the Senate as part of its normal allocation of provinces.

they sent the consul of that year to succeed him: in 67 the consul M.' Acilius Glabrio was assigned Lucullus' remaining province Bithynia–Pontus and the command against Mithridates by a law carried through the popular assembly by the tribune A. Gabinius (36.14.4; Sallust, *Histories* 5.11). Gabinius aroused hostility to Lucullus by displaying a picture of his rich villa during his speeches (Cic. *Sest.* 93).

2.5 *Alchaudonius*: ruler of the nomad Rhambaeans in northern Mesopotamia (Strabo 16.2.10). For his treachery in 53, see 40.20.1.

3.1 *Lucullus . . . sent . . . to Arsaces*: so also Appian (*Mithr.* 87), whereas Plutarch (*Luc.* 30) has the Parthian king taking the initiative.

3.2 *Sextilius*: one of Lucullus' legates, who had played a prominent part in the operations at Tigranocerta. Dio's manuscripts give his name as 'Secilius', clearly in error.

3.3 *winning over much of Armenia*: the reference is in fact to Tigranes' southern empire. Lucullus' gains included Sophene and Gordyene.

4.1 *Quintus Marcius*: Q. Marcius Rex. Dio's parenthesis on the consulship appears to have been his only reference to domestic events of this year.

Lucius Metellus: L. Caecilius Metellus, brother of the consul of 69.

the man chosen to replace Metellus: perhaps an otherwise unknown Servilius Vatia (Vatia is given as the name of one of the consuls of the year in a late and often unreliable consular list).

4.2 *he advanced against them*: in summer 68, Lucullus crossed the eastern Taurus mountains (see note to 36.16.1) and campaigned in Armenia. According to Plutarch (*Luc.* 31–32), Lucullus won a victory at the crossing of the river Arsanias, in which Tigranes and his forces fled with heavy losses, but he was prevented from continuing his advance to the capital, Artaxata, by wintry weather and his troops' reluctance.

6.1 *marched against Nisibis*: after withdrawing back across the Taurus, Lucullus resumed his assault on Tigranes' southern holdings. Nisibis is modern Nusaybin, in north-east Mesopotamia.

6.2 *now one of our possessions and . . . a colony of ours*: the Romans acquired Nisibis from Parthia in 165 CE, and in 198 Septimius Severus made it the capital of his new province of Mesopotamia and granted it the privileged status of a *colonia* (see Glossary, p. 283).

his brother: Gouras (Plut. *Luc.* 32).

8.1 *much of Armenia and the Pontus region*: the losses in 'Armenia' are detailed at 8.1–2 and 'around Pontus' in 36.9.1–5. Here, as at 36.3.3, Dio uses the term 'Armenia' as including Tigranes' extended empire south of the Taurus mountains, and it will have been there that Tigranes now recovered some of his losses.

8.2 *Lucius Fannius*: Fannius and his associate L. Magius had been officers of the Valerian legions (see note to 36.14.3), but had deserted first to Mithridates and then to Lucullus.

9.1 *the other Armenia and the rest of his former territory*: chapters 9–10 record Mithridates' reoccupation of much of his former kingdom in autumn 68. By the 'other Armenia' Dio means Lesser Armenia, a mountainous region south-east of his ancestral kingdom of Pontus which Mithridates had acquired early in his reign.

9.2 *Marcus Fabius*: M. Fabius Hadrianus, legate of Lucullus from at least 72, had been left in command of the force garrisoning Pontus.

9.5 *over seventy years old*: Mithridates was in fact only 65. The error appeared already in Sallust's *Histories* (5.5), no doubt Dio's source.

10.1 *Cabira*: modern Niksar, in the Lycus valley under the Paryadres mountains. Mithridates had built a palace there. The Lycus and Iris valleys formed the heartland of his Pontic kingdom.

Triarius . . . on his way from Asia to Lucullus: C. Valerius Triarius, a legate of Lucullus from the start of the war. Triarius' departure from the province of Asia may have been prompted by the arrival of the praetorian governor (36.2.2).

as large a force as he could in the circumstances: presumably the combined garrison forces of Pontus and Bithynia, perhaps totalling four legions.

10.2 *Comana*: in the Iris valley, about 30 km (19 miles) south of Cabira. Its site is a hill in the modern Gümenek district, 9 km (6 miles) north-east of Tokat.

11.2 *two cities in Cappadocia . . . to the same traditions*: Pontus and Cappadocia each had a sanctuary-city called Comana for the worship of the Anatolian goddess Ma. At each the goddess was identified with the Greek Artemis and her cult-statue was held to have been brought there by Iphigenia and her brother Orestes. In Greek legend Agamemnon was required to sacrifice his daughter Iphigenia to Artemis before the Trojan War. In one version she was saved by Artemis and taken to be her priestess in the Tauric Chersonese (modern Crimea), and different accounts were then given of her subsequent fate: many held that she had escaped with her brother and Artemis' statue, and various cities claimed to have been her refuge. Dio's origin in neighbouring Bithynia may account for this digression. He speaks of both cities as in Cappadocia because in his day Pontus was part of that province, to which it had been assigned by Trajan, but his description of them as 'not very far from each other' is odd.

12.1 *Manius Acilius and Gaius Piso were consuls*: M.' Acilius Glabrio and C. Calpurnius Piso.

Gaziura: a royal fortress dominating the Iris valley, near modern Turhal, about 20 km (12 miles) west of Comana.

12.2 *Dadasa*: not otherwise known.

12.3 *Triarius reluctantly set out*: since Triarius had summoned Lucullus, Dio's view that he was seeking to delay battle until his arrival is more plausible than the claim of Plutarch (*Luc.* 35) and Appian (*Mithr.* 89) that he was eager to win a victory before Lucullus arrived. The Romans sustained heavy losses at Triarius' defeat: Plutarch states that over 7,000 were killed, and both he and Appian say that these included 150 centurions and twenty-four military tribunes. As ancient sources for the later battle confirm, Triarius' defeat took place near Zela (modern Zile), on a tributary of the Iris, where Caesar won a great victory over Mithridates' son Pharnaces in 47.

13.1 *as I have already said*: in a lost passage before the start of our manuscripts.

14.2 *Talaura*: this city's location is disputed. Dio's account suggests that it was not far from Zela, but, according to Appian (*Mithr.* 90), Mithridates moved to Lesser Armenia, where Lucullus found him.

Mithridates, from Media: Media here means Media Atropatene, off the south-west coast of the Caspian Sea. Previously united with the rest of Media to its south, its governor Atropates had established it as an independent kingdom in 321 BCE. See note to 39.56.2 for the possible identity of this Mithridates with the Parthian prince mentioned there.

14.3 *The Valerians*: these two legions were originally enlisted in 86 and were brought to Asia by the consul L. Valerius Flaccus, who had been sent there by Cinna's government to replace their enemy Sulla in the command against Mithridates. Valerius was killed in a mutiny led by his legate C. Flavius Fimbria, who took over his army, but in 85 it deserted to Sulla and Fimbria committed suicide. On his return to Italy in 84, Sulla left these legions behind as the garrison for the province of Asia, and Lucullus took them over on his arrival in the East in 74. Lucullus probably had two other legions with him, which he had taken over in Cilicia on his arrival in 74. He had brought one legion out then, but had probably left this behind in Pontus when he advanced to Armenia, and it had thus become part of Triarius' force.

had enlisted again after being discharged from service: Dio is confused here. The Valerian legions were in continuous service from 86 until their discharge by Lucullus in late 67 (see note to 36.15.3).

restive in Nisibis: in winter 68/7, after its capture.

14.4 *Publius Clodius*: Dio's first mention of P. Clodius Pulcher, born *c*.92 and later to play a leading part as a popular leader in Roman politics until his death in 52. The Claudii Pulchri were a leading branch of the patrician *gens Claudia*, which had been prominent at Rome since the fifth century and had a reputation for (usually anti-popular) arrogance. Clodius' elder brother Ap. Claudius Pulcher was serving as a legate with Lucullus, who had sent him in 71 to demand Mithridates' surrender from Tigranes. As Dio notes, one of their three sisters (all called Clodia) was married to Lucullus and one to Q. Marcius Rex (36.17.2). On his return home Lucullus divorced his wife, alleging incest between her and Clodius.

Claudius by some: most members of his *gens* preferred the *au* form of the name, but Clodius and his sisters appear to have preferred the *ō* form, in his case perhaps as a marker of his *popularis* sympathies.

Lucullus' replacement: see 36.2.2 and note.

15.1 *the refusal of Marcius . . . to send the help he asked for*: for the appointment
of Q. Marcius Rex, consul 68, to replace Lucullus as governor of Cilicia,
see notes to 36.2.2, 17.2. Two fragments of Sallust (*Histories* 5.12–13)
relate to Lucullus' appeal to Marcius as he was approaching Cilicia and
show that he was bringing three legions.

15.3 *turned off in that direction*: By winter 67/66 Lucullus with what was left of
his army seems to have withdrawn westwards to Galatia, where he met
Pompey in 66 (see 36.46).

discharged . . . withdrew altogether: Gabinius' law providing for the replacement of Lucullus by Acilius Glabrio also ordered the discharge of the
Valerian legions. According to Plutarch (*Luc.* 35), they agreed to remain
with Lucullus' stationary army until the end of the summer, but insisted
on their discharge then.

16.1 *the first Roman to cross the Taurus*: the Taurus range divides SE Asia Minor,
Syria, and Mesopotamia from the lands to the north. The reference here
is to Lucullus' initial traverse of the western part of the Taurus range
before crossing the Euphrates and invading Tigranes' southern territories
in 69. In 68 he had crossed its eastern part to invade the Armenian heartland, returning south later in the year.

if he had been willing to bring the war to a rapid end: here Dio unfairly
accepts the claim of Lucullus' critics (see notes to 36.2.1–2).

unable to control his men: for Lucullus' inability to win their loyalty, see also
Plut. *Luc.* 33.

16.3 *Pompey . . . enrolled the Valerians again*: after he had taken over the Mithridatic
command in 66 (36.46.1).

17.1 *wreaked havoc on Cappadocia*: not Mithridates (as Dio claims), but Tigranes,
who had expelled its king Ariobarzanes several times before and now did
so again.

17.2 *his soldiers refused to follow him*: asserted as Marcius' pretext also by Sallust,
Histories 5.13, no doubt Dio's source.

went to Cilicia instead: Cilicia had been assigned as Marcius Rex's province, no doubt primarily for him to act against its pirates. Nothing further
is known about his activity there, but he achieved enough to be decreed
a triumph, never celebrated.

Menemachus: perhaps the same man as the Menemachus who was one of
Mithridates' commanders at the start of the war.

17.3 *Clodius was captured by pirates*: while serving as Marcius' naval prefect.
See 38.30.5.

out of fear of Pompey: now arrived on his command against the pirates (see
note to 36.17a).

went to Antioch in Syria: his activity there is not otherwise known, but he
must have been acting for Marcius rather than independently, as Dio's
hostile account suggests. Antioch and its environs were all that was left of

the Seleucid kingdom. Tigranes had taken it over in 83, but had lost control in 69 through Lucullus' assault on his southern empire. The Seleucid claimant Antiochus XIII had then taken over and been recognized as king by Lucullus. However, by 67 he had been ousted by his cousin Philip II. Philip was supported by the Arab dynast Aziz and Antiochus by Sampsiceramus, ruler of Emesa, but both these rulers were also pursuing their own ambitions. See further note to 37.7a.

17a *[From Xiphilinus' epitome]*: the surviving portion of the manuscript L, from which the other surviving manuscripts derive, begins at 36.18.1; 36.1.1–17.3 are preserved in the manuscripts V and P, but two leaves are missing between 36.17.3 and 18.1. This lost passage will have covered the end of Dio's account of Asian events in this year and the opening of his account of at least the final stage of Metellus' war in Crete (see note to 36.1a). Dio's editors accordingly print Xiphilinus' summary of the Cretan war at this point.

Pompey the Great: Cn. Pompeius Magnus. Pompey (his usual name in English) became recognized as the Republic's leading general through his part in successive civil wars, first in support of Sulla (from whom he received the *cognomen* Magnus, 'the Great') and subsequently against Lepidus and Sertorius. Following his consulship in 70, he declined a province, but he was appointed to the command against the pirates under a law passed by the tribune A. Gabinius in 67. Dio narrates this at length at 36.20–37, but his decision to narrate the end of the Cretan war first obliged him to anticipate Pompey's role here.

command of the entire sea and of land up to three days' march from the sea: under Gabinius' law. For its scope, see 36.23.4, 36a, 37.1. The law defined Pompey's land command as extending up to 50 Roman miles from the sea (see note to 36.36a). This provision meant that his authority overlapped with that of other proconsuls, including Metellus (all of Crete fell within the 50-mile limit). Most scholars hold that the law defined his power (*imperium*) in these overlapping areas as equal to theirs, as Velleius states (2.31.2), rather than greater, as Tacitus (*Annals* 15.2.3) may imply.

Metellus brought the Cretan war to an end: other sources show that Metellus began in the west of the island, capturing first Cydonia and then Cnossus after sieges. After Pompey's arrival in Cilicia in 67, the Cretan cities which were still resisting made an approach to him, offering to surrender to him rather than to Metellus. Pompey responded favourably, but Metellus disregarded his intervention and completed the conquest of the island.

triumph: after completing the war in 67, Metellus stayed on to settle Crete as a province, returning to Rome in 65. However, political opposition prevented him from celebrating his triumph until 62.

additional name 'Creticus': victorious commanders were often granted a *cognomen* taken from the name of the people they had conquered.

18.1 *his lust for power*: dynasteia, the term used here, is employed regularly by Dio for informal political power (see Introduction, p. xxii). Dio, like other sources, emphasizes Metellus' harshness. The contrast with Pompey's mild treatment of the pirates may have prompted the Cretan appeal to him.

Octavius: L. Octavius, an officer of Pompey, sent to receive Cretan cities' surrender.

Cornelius Sisenna: L. Cornelius Sisenna, one of the legates assisting Pompey in operations against the pirates and based in Greece. Sisenna wrote a history of the Italian allies' rebellion against Rome (91–88 BCE) and the ensuing civil wars, of which numerous fragments survive.

19.1 *Aristion*: an otherwise unknown Cretan leader.

Lucius Bassus: a legate of Metellus, otherwise unknown.

19.3 *the Cretans lost their liberty*: Dio's word *katedoulōthēsan* literally means 'were enslaved'. Crete now became a taxpaying Roman province. Unlike other Greek writers about Rome, Dio commonly speaks of Roman rule as enslavement: see further M. Lavan, *Slaves to Rome* (Cambridge, 2013), 106–11.

Panares and Lasthenes: leaders of the Cretan resistance to both Antonius and Metellus. Metellus' resentment at their removal from his triumph led him to take part in the opposition to the ratification of Pompey's eastern settlement (Velleius 2.40.5; cf. Dio 37.49).

20.1 *how things stood with Pompey*: Pompey had been mentioned in the accounts of Lucullus' and Metellus' campaigns to which the opening sections of the book were devoted (36.16.3, 17.3–19.3), but with this link Dio brings him centre stage for the next major episode, his command against the pirates (36.20–37). Most of this section is devoted to Pompey's appointment (36.23.4–37.1), but this is framed by briefer surveys of the pirate crisis and of his rapid campaign. The weakness of the Seleucid monarchy and the rough terrain of western Cilicia led to its becoming a hotbed of piracy from the later second century, and the chaotic conditions of the Mithridatic wars and the accompanying civil wars exacerbated the problem, so that by the later 70s piracy had become a serious menace across the Mediterranean. Similar, but more vividly detailed, accounts of the problem are given by Cicero (*Imp. Pomp.* 31–33, 53–55), Plutarch (*Pomp.* 24), Appian (*Mithr.* 92–93), and Florus (1.41).

as long as human nature remains the same: Dio's words are directly borrowed from Thucydides' famous reflections on civil strife (3.82.2). On Dio's views on human nature, see Introduction, pp. x, xxiii.

21.1 *achieved in league with others*: referring back to the lost part of Dio's work. For Cretan involvement with pirates, see note to 36.1a. Complicity with pirates was also alleged against Mithridates and Sertorius.

22.2 *Ostia*: at the mouth of the Tiber, not yet a port, but a way station for ships sailing to Rome.

23.2 *when they were disturbed by some news*: campaigns against the Cilician pirates were conducted by M. Antonius in 102 and P. Servilius Vatia in

78–74, and a Mediterranean-wide command against pirates was held, with little success, by M. Antonius in 74–72.

23.4 *Aulus Gabinius . . . made a proposal*: for the terms of Gabinius' law, see also 36.17a, 36a, 37.1. This law and Manilius' law conferring the command against Mithridates on Pompey the following year were the first of the laws granting extraordinary provincial commands which played a crucial part in the downfall of the Republic. This, and the bitter opposition it faced, led Dio to give Gabinius' law extended treatment, exploring its implications through speeches: see further Introduction (pp. xviii–xix). Gabinius and his colleagues in 67 were the first to make significant use of the tribunes' power to propose legislation after its abolition by Sulla *c.*81 and restoration by Pompey and Crassus as consuls in 70. For Gabinius' law terminating Lucullus' command, see note to 36.2.2.

a man of the worst sort: Gabinius may have served with Pompey in his earlier commands and subsequently owed him much, including appointment as his legate against Mithridates and the consulship of 58. Dio's hostility to Gabinius may have been influenced by Cicero's bitter attacks, but he is regularly critical of radical tribunes. His cynicism about the motives both of Gabinius and of the senatorial opposition reflects his overall view that, with few exceptions, the political class of the Late Republic pursued selfish motives rather than the common good: see Introduction, p. xxiii.

23.5 *did not actually name Pompey*: Dio's language here has often been taken to imply that Gabinius carried two laws, a first establishing the command and a second appointing Pompey. However, both Dio and our other sources envisage only a single law. Dio's implication is that Gabinius first proposed the law at a public meeting (*contio*) without naming the appointee, deliberately leaving it to his audience to propose Pompey. Subsequently the law will have been formally promulgated (see Glossary, pp. 285–6) with him as the named commander.

24.1 *while the Senate was in session*: Gabinius may have brought his bill to the Senate for consideration, or the consul Piso may have put it for discussion.

24.3 *Piso . . . was seized*: he had compared Pompey with Rome's first king, Romulus (Plut. *Pomp.* 25). Dio had been narrating events of the year 67 since 36.12.1, but, following the excursus on the long-running pirate crisis, he takes this opportunity to remind readers of the year.

leading men: the *dynatoi* (literally, 'the powerful men'). Dio frequently uses this word as a designation for the most influential senators, particularly when they were in opposition to the plebs or those who claimed to be its champions. Roman writers sympathetic to them sometimes spoke of this group as the *optimates* (literally, the 'best men').

24.4 *Lucius Trebellius and Lucius Roscius*: for their actions, see 36.30. Trebellius is known only from this episode. For L. Roscius Otho's law on theatre seating, see 36.42.1.

as they had promised: Trebellius had promised the Senate that he would die rather than allow the law to be passed (Asconius 72).

day . . . for voting . . . this . . . happened: from here until 36.36a, Dio narrates the events on the day Gabinius' bill was voted into law. On the voting day or earlier, the magistrate proposing a bill was required to hold an informal meeting (*contio*), at which private citizens (in practice normally senators) were given the opportunity to speak for or against the bill, before proceeding to the *comitia*, in which the citizens voted on the law in their voting-groups (tribes) (see Glossary, p. 283). Both procedures were held in the Forum.

24.5 *against his will*: Pompey was notorious for dissembling his ambitions. Dio, always keen to expose pretensions, highlights this trait here and at 36.45.1 and 39.33.1.

24.6 *jealousy*: the jealousy (*phthonos*) to which those who achieve exceptional prominence are liable is a recurrent theme for Dio, and he repeatedly presents Pompey as seeking but failing to avoid it (36.26.1–2, 43.4; 37.23.3–4, 50.6; 40.51.1; Introduction, pp. xxiii, xxvi).

25.1 *spoke as follows*: Pompey's speech and Gabinius' response were perhaps made at an earlier assembly convened by Gabinius rather than on the voting day, when Pompey was absent from Rome according to Plutarch (*Pomp.* 26). Fragments (5.16–18) show that Sallust's *Histories* included speeches for both Pompey (in indirect speech) and Gabinius (in direct speech). Dio may have made use of these (and possibly of versions in other historians), and some close similarities suggest that he also drew on the speech which Cicero made the following year supporting Manilius' law giving Pompey the Mithridatic command (*Imp. Pomp.*, esp. 27–28 and 61–62; C. Burden-Strevens, *Cassius Dio's Speeches and the Collapse of the Roman Republic* (Leiden, 2020), 70–9). Dio's introductory remarks (36.23.4, 24.5–6) indicate that he intended both speeches to be read as insincere. See further Introduction, p. xix.

Quirites: a name given to the citizens of Rome in their peacetime activities, commonly used by speakers addressing their assemblies.

25.2 *in the war against Cinna . . . very young*: born on 29 September 106, Pompey served under his father, Cn. Pompeius Strabo, who commanded an army against the Italian rebels in 89–88 and against Cinna and his associates in the civil war in 87.

in Sicily and Africa . . . did not yet fully count as a youth: when Sulla returned to Italy in 83, Pompey joined him in the ensuing civil war with an army he had raised himself. In 82–81 Pompey, appointed to the command by Sulla, wiped out the opposition forces in the provinces of Sicily and Africa. Dio exaggerates his youth, but he was far below the usual age for army command, normally first held following the praetorship, so around 40.

in Spain . . . not yet a senator: Pompey held the command against Sertorius and his associates in Spain from 77 to 71, while still an *eques* (see Glossary, p. 284). Uniquely, he did not enter the Senate until his consulship in 70.

25.3 *no one else . . . willing or able to take it on*: the Senate agreed to the appointment of Pompey to the command against Sertorius in 77 after both the
consuls of the year had refused it.

triumph . . . contrary to custom: Pompey was the first to hold a triumph
while holding command as a private citizen rather than in or following
a magistracy. However, his triumph over Sertorius in 71 was his second:
despite Sulla's opposition, he had triumphed in 81 or 80 following his
return from Africa.

27.4 *no one else . . . suitable . . . except him*: see note to 36.25.3.

28.1 *increasing your possessions . . . and acquiring those of your enemies*: alleged as
Roman war aims also at 38.36.5 ff. (Caesar speaking). It was not in fact
until his Mithridatic command that Pompey acquired new territory for
the empire.

28.2 *still only an eques*: see note to 36.25.2.

30.1 *Trebellius . . . failed to gain permission to speak*: the magistrate who had
summoned a *contio* (in this case Gabinius) controlled who spoke.

opposed the taking of the vote: tribunes' powers included the right to veto
a wide range of public business, including the passing of laws.

30.2 *fresh motion about Trebellius himself*: Tiberius Gracchus, as tribune in 133,
overrode a fellow tribune's veto by carrying a law deposing him from
office. Gabinius set about following this precedent, until Trebellius withdrew his veto. In the tribal assembly, the votes of the thirty-five tribes were
taken, counted, and announced successively, and once a majority of the
tribes had voted in favour of a law, it was declared passed. Asconius (72)
reports the incident in more detail.

30.3 *power*: *dynasteia* (see note to 36.18.1). Roscius' two-finger gesture and the
crowd's reaction is also reported by Plutarch (*Pomp.* 25).

30.4 *Catulus . . . urged . . . to speak*: Q. Lutatius Catulus had been consul in 78
and a loyal supporter of Sulla and his political settlement, and is spoken
of by Cicero and others as a conservative leader in the Senate in the years
up to his death in or soon after 61. Other evidence confirms that Catulus
spoke against Gabinius' law. Dio seems to have placed his speech at such
a late point for dramatic effect: Catulus is more likely to have spoken earlier,
before Trebellius' veto, and may in fact have spoken at an earlier meeting,
as Plutarch suggests. Convention obliged Gabinius, as proposer, to allow
some opponents of his law to address the people. Dio's claim that he
expected Catulus to speak in its favour must be his own implausible speculation. Cicero (*Imp. Pomp.* 52) shows that Hortensius too spoke against
Gabinius' law in both the Senate and the assembly. (This passage does not
imply that Catulus did not speak against it, as some scholars claim.)

30.5 *everyone . . . honoured him as one who always said and did what was in their
best interests*: Cicero praised Catulus in similar terms, and Dio himself later
says that he always put the common good first (37.46.3). However, here he
is more ambivalent: he merely reports the general esteem for Catulus and

has earlier asserted that the senatorial opponents of Gabinius' law would have preferred inaction against the pirates to giving the command to Pompey (36.24.1).

addressed them somewhat as follows: on this speech and its significance, see Introduction, p. xix. For its echoes from Demosthenes, see B. S. Rodgers, 'Catulus' Speech in Cassius Dio 36.31–36', *Greek, Roman and Byzantine Studies* 48 (2008), 295-318, at pp. 313–17.

31.3 *illegal*: the long series of commands which Pompey held as a private citizen did not in fact contravene any law. The reference is to the *leges annales*, laws which specified minimum intervals between the tenure of various magistracies.

Marius . . . consul six times in rapid succession: C. Marius was consul in 107 and every year from 104 to 100, and commanded against the Numidian king Jugurtha in 107 and the northern invaders the Cimbri and Teutones in 104–101. In 88 a tribune's transfer of the command against Mithridates from the consul Sulla to Marius led to civil wars, during which Marius became consul again in 86, dying shortly afterwards.

31.4 *Sulla too*: on his return from the First Mithridatic War, Sulla was victorious in civil war in 83–82 and then brutally purged his opponents, holding the dictatorship and (in 80) a second consulship. Dio later represents Pompey as deliberately avoiding the example of Marius and Sulla (37.20.6).

32.1 *not . . . motivated . . . by a desire to denigrate Pompey*: other sources tell us that Catulus praised Pompey in his speech (Velleius 2.32.1; Plut. *Pomp.* 25).

democracy . . . equality: for similar association of ideas, see 44.2.1 and 52.4.3–4. By 'democracy' Dio means simply republican government, and he later makes explicit his belief that by this time it had ceased to be viable (see Introduction, p. xxii).

32.3 *Sertorius*: see notes to 36.25.2–3.

33.2 *purple-bordered togas*: the *toga praetexta*, worn by consuls, praetors, and other high-ranking magistrates (and also by high-born boys).

34.1 *the dictatorship*: a dictator had been appointed when required from the fifth to the third century, either for military command or for some other purpose such as conducting the election of magistrates or resolving civil strife. When appointed, the dictator held office without a colleague and with greater power (*imperium*) than the other magistrates, but was required to abdicate when his task had been completed and within six months from his appointment. No dictators were appointed after 202 until the office was revived in 82 as a means of giving constitutional form to Sulla's supremacy after his civil-war victory and again for Caesar from 49 until his death in 44. After Caesar's assassination, the dictatorship was abolished. Dio had devoted an excursus to the dictatorship, partially preserved in the epitome of Zonaras (7.13.12–14), when reporting its establishment, and awkwardly drags it in here, although effectively admitting its irrelevance.

A dictatorship was proposed for Pompey in 53 and 52 (see notes to 40.45.5–46.1, 50.3–4).

34.2 *sent to Sicily and achieved nothing*: A. Atilius Calatinus, in 249, during the First Punic War.

34.4 *disaster . . . on their own heads*: the speaker's reference is to the civil wars of the 80s, but Dio points ahead too to the later civil wars.

36.3 *for his assistance*: a novel feature of Pompey's pirate command was that his legates (who held *imperium* delegated from him, with the title *legatus pro praetore*) operated in separate regions, each with their own force, and his ability to coordinate their operations across the Mediterranean was a key element in his rapid success. Dio makes Catulus offer misguided criticisms of this aspect of the appointment, proposing an evidently unworkable alternative of independent commands.

36.4 *other magistracies to be abolished*: wild exaggeration. For the relationship of Pompey's pirate command to that of other proconsuls, see note to 36.17a.

at that time [. . .]: one leaf is missing from the manuscript L at this point, which will have covered the end of Catulus' speech and the passing of Gabinius' law. The two fragments which follow are among the numerous short quotations from Dio's history in a Byzantine grammatical work entitled *On Syntax* and are cited as from Book 36. This work's cited book numbers are often wrong, but, if these fragments are from Book 36, they must have stood in the missing final section of Catulus' speech. For the risk of jealousy for Pompey, see note to 36.24.6.

36a *shouted out 'You!'*: Xiphilinus' epitome passes over Catulus' speech except for this incident, also reported by several other sources.

four hundred stades from the sea: unlike Dio himself (see note to 38.17.7), Xiphilinus reckons the Greek stade as equating to one-eighth of a Roman mile. The law probably defined Pompey's power as extending 'up to the fiftieth milestone from the sea' (so Velleius 2.31.2), i.e. 74 km (46 miles).

37.1 *fifteen legates . . . as much money and manpower as he might want*: varying details on the resources granted to Pompey are given by Appian (*Mithr.* 94) and Plutarch (*Pomp.* 25–26). Probably the law specified upper limits and substantially smaller forces were actually needed for Pompey's short campaign. Pompey deployed thirteen legates to various zones across the Mediterranean, each with their own squadron, and these may be all the legates he appointed.

37.2 *Piso*: C. Calpurnius Piso, as consul in 67, had received as his province both Cisalpine Gaul (i.e. northern Italy) and Transalpine Gaul (i.e. southern France, referred to here by Dio, following his usual practice, by its later title Gallia Narbonensis, which it held from Augustus' reign on). Although Piso remained at Rome for most of his consulship, he appears to have already assumed command of this province, governing it through legates.

removed him from office: the consulship. Plutarch (*Pomp.* 27) tells us that Gabinius had a law drafted to depose Piso from the consulship and that Pompey's intervention came when he visited Rome after clearing the pirates from the western Mediterranean.

37.3 *pacified most of it within a single year*: an understatement—Pompey completed his campaign against the pirates in three months, by midsummer 67. Dio's very brief and vague account of the campaign makes a deliberate contrast with his extended treatment of the law granting his appointment. Other sources show that in the first phase Pompey and his legates swept the Mediterranean clear of pirates, and he then advanced on Cilicia, rapidly secured the surrender of the pirate strongholds, and resettled many of the pirates in Cilicia and elsewhere.

37.6 *sacked by Tigranes*: for Tigranes' deportation of Cilicians to Tigranocerta, see 36.2.3.

38.1 *in the year of the consulship of Acilius and Piso*: Dio here passes to his next major narrative section, treating further events at Rome in 67 (36.38.1–42.2) and 66 (36.42.3–44.5). He had been narrating events occurring in various theatres in the year 67 since 36.12.1, but for clarity reminds his readers of the date here, as earlier at 36.24.3.

law . . . electoral bribery . . . fine: numerous laws had been passed on electoral corruption (*ambitus*), and a permanent court (*quaestio*) had been established for this offence, perhaps in 122. A *lex Cornelia*, probably passed by Sulla, imposed a ten-year ban on standing for office on candidates convicted of *ambitus*. The consuls' law now increased this to a lifetime exclusion from office and membership of the Senate, plus a fine, but permitted those convicted to remain at Rome. The law (*lex Calpurnia Acilia*) stood in the name of both consuls, but Piso had the lead responsibility, and it is accordingly attributed to him alone by other sources.

38.2 *the tribunate had regained its ancient power*: in 70 (see note to 36.23.4). But this cannot have directly increased competition for the other offices.

struck off by the censors: one of the functions of the censors was to revise the membership of the Senate, expelling those they deemed guilty of misconduct. Censors (traditionally elected every five years) had been appointed in 70 for the first time since 86, and had expelled an unparalleled sixty-four senators. The attempts of those expelled to regain office and with it membership of the Senate were a major factor in the intensified electoral competition of the following years.

38.3 *did not come to court*: two (perhaps rival) prosecutors apparently initiated proceedings, but were then bribed to desist. For a similar allegation see next note. A fragment of Sallust's *Histories* (4.71) reporting Piso's agreeing to pay an unknown person the huge sum of 3 million sesterces must relate either to this incident or to bribery before his election.

38.4 *Gaius Cornelius*: Cornelius had served as Pompey's quaestor, probably in Spain, and his activity as tribune in 67 may be seen as continuing the reform programme which Pompey had initiated as consul in 70. In 66 an attempted prosecution of Cornelius for *maiestas* (treason) over his conduct as tribune was disrupted by gang violence, and was then dropped, allegedly because of bribery. The case was brought to trial in 65 (with Catulus, Hortensius, and others acting as prosecution witnesses), but Cicero appeared for the defence and Cornelius was acquitted. Further information on Cornelius' tribunate and trials is provided by Asconius (57–81), citing and commenting on fragments from Cicero's two published speeches *For Cornelius*. See M. Griffin, 'The Tribunate of C. Cornelius', *Journal of Roman Studies* 63 (1973), 196–213.

39.1 *illegal . . . before they had taken place*: one of the provisions of the second-century laws Aelia and Fufia, which regulated legislative procedure, prohibited the carrying of a law between the announcement of an election and the vote. Cornelius' and the consuls' *ambitus* laws will have been proposed in July, the normal time for elections, and so after Cornelius' other measures, discussed below.

armed guard: according to Asconius (74–5), Piso was driven from the Forum by rioting *divisores*, and then ensured the passage of the consular law by proclaiming that all those who desired the safety of the Republic should come to vote for it and proceeding to the assembly with a body-guard. The *divisores* were officials of the voting tribes, whose role was to distribute legitimate gifts from the tribes' patrons, but were also much involved in electoral bribery.

39.2 *Cornelius . . . brought forward a proposal*: according to the more plausible account of Asconius (57–9), Cornelius began his tribunate by proposing a motion in the Senate prohibiting individuals from lending to ambassadors (which had proved a lucrative method of extortion from Rome's subjects), and, when this was rejected by the Senate as unnecessary, retaliated by promulgating a law that 'no one should be dispensed from the laws except by vote of the people'. Dio was primarily interested in Cornelius' action against electoral corruption, and this may have led to confusion in his notes about its relation to his law on dispensations, which will in fact have been brought forward earlier in the year.

39.4 *without holding a vote*: the violence against Piso and Cornelius' dismissal of the assembly is also reported by Asconius 58, with details of the preceding developments: Cornelius' dispensations law was obstructed by a fellow tribune, P. Servilius Globulus, who forbade the public scribe to pass the text to the herald and the herald to read it (required procedure before the vote on a law). Cornelius himself then began to read out the text, prompting Piso's intervention.

added a rider to the law: Asconius (59) tells us that the revised law provided that 'no one should be dispensed from the laws in the Senate unless at least two hundred were present' and that 'no one should exercise a veto when referral on these matters was made to the people'. The inclusion of these compromise provisions, following a Senate meeting, enabled the law to be passed without opposition.

40.1 *Cornelius got this law passed*: i.e. the dispensations law. Dio does not here clearly distinguish it from the (in fact later) *ambitus* law.

principles . . . to judge court cases: the urban and peregrine praetors (see Glossary, p. 286), who had chief responsibility at Rome for private law cases, issued an edict at the start of their term setting out the principles they would follow, and this practice had played an important part in the development of the civil law. Praetors mainly took over their predecessors' edicts, but were free to make modifications. Cornelius' law prohibited praetors from departing from their own edicts. Provincial governors issued similar edicts, and it is possible that Cornelius' law also applied to them.

finalized: the praetorian edict was codified under Hadrian (emperor 117–38 CE), and thereafter only the emperor could make changes.

40.3 *concerned at that time to stamp out corruption*: Dio passes from corruption in Roman elections to corruption in the government of the provinces, using this theme to link the trial of Cotta and the praetorship of 'Lucullus' (see note to 36.41.1), of which the latter certainly and the former probably occurred in 67, the year Dio is currently narrating.

Marcus Cotta: M. Aurelius Cotta. As consul in 74, he had been assigned the province of Bithynia, and he retained it until *c.*70. In 71 he sacked Heraclea Pontica after a two-year siege.

Publius Oppius: Cotta sent Oppius home and subsequently had him put on trial at Rome. Cicero appeared for the defence, and surviving fragments of Cicero's speech and Sallust's *Histories* (3.80–81) show that the allegations against Oppius included trying to corrupt the troops with largesse, embezzling their supplies, and drawing a dagger when dismissed.

profited from Bithynia: it is uncertain whether Cotta was convicted for extortion (*repetundae*) from the provincials, or for embezzlement (*peculatus*), for misappropriation of the booty from Heraclea. On Cotta's trial see J. Linderski, *Roman Questions II* (Stuttgart, 2007), 115–29.

40.4 *elevated . . . to consular rank*: the laws under which some, and perhaps all, the criminal courts (*quaestiones*) operated prescribed that those convicted should lose their membership of the Senate and their prosecutor be rewarded by promotion to their senatorial rank.

Carbo . . . found guilty: C. Papirius Carbo, praetor in 62 and governor of Bithynia from 61 to 58. His conviction will have been for extortion (*repetundae*).

41.1 *Lucius Lucullus*: this name is certainly an error, probably by a scribe rather than by Dio himself, since Lucullus is known to have gone out to govern Africa after his praetorship in 78 and Dio's mention of Acilius shows that he is referring here to one of the praetors of 67. The individual in question is probably the historian L. Lucceius, who prosecuted Catiline in 64 and stood for the consulship of 59.

refused to take it up: praetors went out to govern a province after their year of office, having drawn lots for the available provinces, but it was quite common at this period for them to decline a governorship.

41.2 *Acilius*: M.' Acilius Glabrio, consul in 67.

chair: the curule chair (*sella curulis*), an ivory folding stool which was used by consuls, praetors, and other high-ranking magistrates and was one of the insignia of their office. Acilius was within his rights in having the chair broken: a consul of 115 had done this and also torn the clothes of a praetor who had failed to stand for him.

42.1 *Roscius . . . Manilius when he was tribune*: L. Roscius Otho was tribune in 67 (for his opposition to the Gabinian law, see 36.24.4, 30.3), C. Manilius in 66. In this period tribunes entered office on 10 December and consuls on 1 January, and so Manilius was able to pass his freedmen law before the new consuls entered office. Dio erroneously calls him 'Mallius' throughout, using the form normally used by Greek writers for the Roman name Manlius.

Roscius was praised for his law: not by everyone according to Plutarch (*Cic.* 13), who tells us that at a theatrical performance in 63 Roscius was applauded by the *equites*, but hissed by the common people because of their being placed behind them. (An alternative explanation of the demonstration is proposed by J. T. Ramsey, 'Asconius on Cicero's Son-in-law Lentulus, His Apprenticeship under Pupius Piso, and the De Othone', *Ciceroniana On Line* 5 (2021), 19–28.) Roscius' law reserved the first fourteen rows of the ramped seating for the *equites* (still behind the senators, who sat on the flat, immediately beside the stage).

42.2 *gave . . . freedmen the right to vote alongside the men who had freed them*: further details on this law are given by Asconius 45, 64–6. The voting rights of freedmen had been contentious since the fourth century. They were generally restricted to the four urban tribes, but repeated attempts had been made to permit them to vote in the thirty-one rural tribes as well, which would have given their votes much more weight. A law to this effect, carried with violence by the tribune P. Sulpicius Rufus in 88, was later cancelled by Sulla, and now revived by Manilius and passed on 29 December (the last day of the year on the pre-Julian calendar). Asconius (45) asserts that the law was carried with the help of 'a gang of freedmen and slaves' who were blocking the way to the assembly, but counter-violence was organized by the young L. Domitius.

42.3 *Lucius Tullus and Aemilius Lepidus took up their consulships*: L. Volcacius Tullus and M.' Aemilius Lepidus. Dio's manuscripts write 'Tullius' for 'Tullus'.

the Senate rejected his law: the Senate now again exercised its power, previously used several times in the early first century, to decree that 'the Roman people was not bound' by a law. Such declarations could be made if a law was considered to have been passed 'against the auspices' and perhaps also by violence. Besides the violence, Manilius' law may have been annulled on the ground that it was passed when the Compitalia were being celebrated (festival days were not available for legislation).

Crassus and some others: no other source reports this allegation.

42.4 *so he curried favour with Pompey instead*: Dio's insinuation that it was only the failure of his freedmen law which prompted Manilius to propose Pompey's command is implausible and probably his own speculation.

assign Pompey the command of the war . . . and . . . the governorship of both Bithynia and Cilicia: by promulgating a law to this effect. Fuller details of the law's terms are given by Plutarch (*Pomp.* 30) and Appian (*Mithr.* 97). It granted Pompey the command and provinces formerly held by Lucullus (except for the province of Asia) and assigned him all the armies currently in those provinces as well as the force already under his command. Additional provisions included the power to make war and peace and form alliances at his discretion.

43.1 *against the proposal*: opinion among senior senators was in fact more divided. Catulus and Hortensius spoke against the law, arguing (as earlier against Gabinius' law) that the command would be a dangerous innovation, giving one man too much power, but four ex-consuls spoke in its favour (Cic. *Imp. Pomp.* 51–63, 68).

Marcius and Acilius: for the supersession of Lucullus by Marcius and Acilius, see 36.2.2, 14.4–15.1, 17.1–2.

43.2 *commissioners to set the captured territories in order*: it was standard Roman practice after a major war for a commission of ten envoys (*decem legati*) to be sent out to set conquered territory in order in conjunction with the victorious commander. Dio is inconsistent on whether the commission was appointed by the people (as here) or the Senate (36.46.1); he may be in error here, or alternatively the Senate's appointment may have been confirmed by a law.

Caesar and Marcus Cicero: the published version of Cicero's speech is extant (*Imp. Pomp.*)—it was his first in the assembly rather than a court. Dio is our only source for Caesar's support for Manilius' law. Plutarch (*Pomp.* 25) claims that Caesar was the only senator to speak in support of Gabinius' law conferring the pirate command on Pompey, and that he did so not for Pompey's sake, but because he had throughout sought the people's favour. C. Julius Caesar (b. 100) was only a junior senator (he had been quaestor in 69), while Cicero (b. 106) was now praetor: as rising stars, it was natural for them both to seek Pompey's favour and a share in his huge popularity. This appears to be Dio's first mention of Caesar: his alleged desire to oust Pompey in the people's favour becomes a recurrent theme (37.22.1, 44.2; 38.1.1). On Cicero, Dio is often negative, drawing on earlier writers' attacks. See further Introduction, pp. xxiv–xxvi.

43.4 *passed in his favour at some point*: Dio points ahead to the grant of Caesar's great command in 59 (38.8.5).

43.5 *win support from both*: Dio says nothing of Cicero's primary target at this time, the consular elections in 64 (the first year in which he was eligible). To secure election as consul for 63, particularly as a 'new man' (the first member of his family in the Senate), Cicero needed to build as wide a support base as possible. Although this was mainly a matter of maximizing his personal connections, it also included striking a careful balance between avoiding giving offence to influential conservative senators like Catulus and winning popular support by assisting Pompey and his supporters such as Manilius and Cornelius (whom he defended in 65: see note to 36.38.4). However, Dio exaggerates Cicero's inconsistency, and the specific instances of double-dealing he provides here are misinterpretations.

better sort . . . riff-raff: Dio more often uses neutral words like 'leading men' (*dynatoi*) and 'people' (*plethos, homilos*), as earlier in this passage, but here switches to the value-laden terminology often used by conservative Roman writers like Cicero himself. His Greek word *beltious* corresponds to the Latin *boni* or *optimates* ('good men', 'best men').

44.2 *speak in support of Manilius*: Plutarch (*Cic.* 9) gives a clearer account. Manilius' term as tribune ended on 9 December 66. He was then indicted for *repetundae* before Cicero, who as praetor in 66 had been allotted the presidency of this court. The *nominis delatio*, the laying of the formal charge, took place on 28 December, and Cicero, disregarding the normal interval for gathering evidence, set the first hearing for 29 December, the last day of the year. At an assembly (*contio*) summoned by tribunes, probably on the same day, Cicero justified his choice of this date as in Manilius' interest and promised to undertake his defence. It remains unclear why the prosecution brought the case so late in the year, when it would be bound to run on to the next year, and why the charge was *repetundae* (normally used for extortion by provincial governors). Cicero's reason for setting the first hearing so soon is also obscure, but it cannot have been as hostile to Manilius as Dio claims. See further J. T. Ramsey, 'The Prosecution of C. Manilius in 66 BC and Cicero's Pro Manilio', *Phoenix* 34 (1980), 323–36.

defector: Dio drew this charge against Cicero from the anti-Ciceronian tradition, but may have been the first to apply it in this context. The charge occurs in the *Invective against Cicero* falsely attributed to Sallust, and Dio repeats it at 39.63.5 and in the anti-Ciceronian speech which he composed for Fufius Calenus (46.3.4).

prevented the court from being convened: further proceedings in fact followed against Manilius in 65, probably on a charge of *maiestas* for his violent conduct as tribune. Manilius initially used gang violence to disrupt the trial, but, when it resumed under the consuls' protection, he was convicted, perhaps in his absence (Asconius 60, 66). These developments probably enabled Cicero to avoid going through with his promise to defend him.

44.3 *found guilty of corruption*: P. Autronius Paetus and P. Cornelius Sulla were elected consuls for 65, but were prosecuted for electoral corruption (*ambitus*) under the law passed in 67 (36.38), and, despite attempts to disrupt the trial by violence, found guilty. Autronius was involved in Catiline's conspiracy in 63 and exiled for it in 62. Sulla too was prosecuted in 62, but acquitted, with Cicero and Hortensius as his defenders.

chosen to replace them: L. Aurelius Cotta and L. Manlius Torquatus had been defeated by Autronius and Sulla, but successfully prosecuted them and were then elected in their place.

44.4 *Gnaeus Piso*: Cn. Calpurnius Piso, a still junior member of his noble family. He was quaestor this year (see below).

Lucius Catilina . . . was therefore resentful: L. Sergius Catilina (referred to hereafter by his usual name in English, Catiline). Charismatic and ambitious, he came of a patrician but recently undistinguished family. Hostile sources allege outrages in his early career—cruelty under Sulla, sexual misdemeanours later. After his praetorship (in or before 68), he had governed the province of Africa, and on his return in 66 was indicted for extortion (*repetundae*). He then stood for the consulship of 65 (probably at the second election, after the conviction of Autronius and Sulla), but his candidacy was disallowed by Volcacius Tullus, the presiding consul, on the ground that 'he had not been able to give notice of his candidature within the legally required period' (Sall. *Cat.* 18.3; cf. Asconius 89). Catiline's *repetundae* trial was held in the later part of 65, with Clodius as prosecutor. His distinguished character witnesses included the consul Torquatus, and he was acquitted, allegedly through corruption.

the plot was discovered: a conspiracy by some or all of Autronius, Sulla, Catiline, and Piso is reported by various sources, and some versions also allege involvement by Crassus and Caesar. Abortive plots are reported as planned for 1 January against the lives of the new consuls and for 5 February for a wider massacre of senators. The first plot may originally have been attributed just to Autronius and Sulla, whereas the second plot seems to be associated particularly with Catiline and Piso. Dio mentions only the first plot. Although our sources report the conspiracy as fact, there was probably no truth in any of the allegations, which will have resulted from the tense conditions of endemic violence and corruption. Piso's death and Catiline's later conspiracy will have fuelled the allegations against them. On the growth of the tradition, see esp. R. Seager, 'The First Catilinarian Conspiracy', *Historia* 13 (1964), 338–47.

granted a bodyguard by the Senate: reliable information, attested only by Dio. The bodyguard was probably for the new consuls' entry into office on 1 January.

44.5 *vetoed by one of the tribunes*: another reliable detail mentioned only by Dio. The vetoed decree was probably proposed in the Senate on or soon after 1 January 65 and provided for investigation of the plot allegations.

some command: as governor of Nearer Spain, with the rank of *quaestor pro praetore*, an exceptional appointment for a quaestor. Sallust (*Cat.* 19.1–2) says that he was appointed at the urging of Crassus, who favoured him as an enemy of Pompey.

the inhabitants . . . suffering under his abuses: Sallust (*Cat.* 19.3–5) and Asconius (92) give both this explanation and an alternative, that he was killed by Spanish cavalry who were clients of Pompey. Pompey retained much influence in Spain from his command there in the 70s against Sertorius.

45.1 *to Crete against Metellus*: for Pompey's dispute with Metellus, see 36.17a–19. In 36.44.5 Dio slipped ahead to later events without making it explicit. He now reverts to the year 66, and begins his next major section covering Pompey's eastern campaigns down to his return to Rome and triumph. This extends to 37.23, interrupted only by a short section (37.8–10) on events at Rome in 65 and 64. Plutarch (*Pomp.* 31–45) and Appian (*Mithr.* 97–118) provide parallel narratives.

pretending to be annoyed: as before Gabinius' law conferring his pirate command (36.24.5–26.4). The same pretence is attributed to Pompey now by Plutarch (*Pomp.* 30).

45.2 *sent Metrophanes . . . with words of friendship*: only Dio mentions Pompey's diplomatic initiative. Some scholars doubt its authenticity, arguing that Pompey needed military success against Mithridates. Metrophanes is previously known only as an officer of Mithridates.

45.3 *friendship with Phraates on the same terms*: i.e. a renewal of the treaty concluded by Lucullus (36.3.2). That treaty had in fact been with Phraates himself, who had succeeded his father in 70/69 (see note to 36.1.1).

Tigranes' Armenia: i.e. Tigranes' ancestral kingdom (see note to 36.1b.1). Dio gives further details on Phraates' invasion at 36.51.1–2.

46.1 *re-enlisting the Valerians*: see notes to 36.14.3, 15.3, 16.3.

Lucullus met him: at Danala (Strabo 12.5.2). The encounter only took place because Lucullus' designated successor, Acilius Glabrio, had not advanced into central Anatolia to take over Lucullus' army and confront Mithridates (36.17.1).

commissioners . . . to arrange a settlement for the region: see note to 36.43.2.

47.1 *fled . . . since his forces were smaller*: Mithridates now withdrew from eastern Pontus towards the upper Euphrates (which formed the boundary with Tigranes' kingdom), with, according to Plutarch (*Pomp.* 32) and Appian (*Mithr.* 97), 30,000 infantry and 2,000 or 3,000 cavalry. In the first years of the war his forces had greatly outnumbered those of the Romans.

Armenia: i.e. Lesser Armenia (see note to 36.9.1).

48.1 *region . . . called Anaïtis*: on the upper Euphrates, also known as Acilisene. The Iranian goddess Anaïtis had numerous sanctuaries in eastern Anatolia. See further note to 36.53.5.

48.2 *reinforced by Marcius' troops*: the three legions which had been commanded by Q. Marcius Rex in Cilicia, from where they were now brought up (see note to 36.15.1). It has been estimated that these reinforcements brought the total size of Pompey's army to around 50,000 men (P. A. Brunt, *Italian Manpower 225 BC–AD 14* (Oxford, 1971), 457–60).

Mithridates . . . decided to move: Dio does not make it clear that Pompey
had maintained a lengthy siege of Mithridates' hillfort camp, for forty-
five days according to Plutarch (*Pomp.* 32; cf. App. *Mithr.* 99).

49.8 *died in large numbers*: more than 10,000 according to Plutarch (*Pomp.* 32)
and Appian (*Mithr.* 100). Dio's is the fullest and most vivid account of
the battle.

50.1 *join Tigranes*: for Tigranes' earlier support of Mithridates, see 36.1b–8.

the younger Tigranes' grandfather: King Tigranes had married Mithridates'
daughter Cleopatra.

why he refused to give him shelter: an additional reason for Tigranes'
repudiation of Mithridates was no doubt that he now judged it safer to
make his peace with Pompey.

headed for Colchis instead: Colchis was a region on the east coast of the Black
Sea, now western Georgia. Mithridates had acquired control of the eastern
Black Sea coast from Pontus round to the Bosporan region early in his reign.
After evading Pompey in 66, he fled with some 3,000 men across the moun-
tains from the Euphrates headwaters to Colchis, and, after wintering at
the Greek city of Dioscurias, at the northern edge of the Colchis plain, he
continued across the western edge of the Caucasus mountains to the
Bosporus. Appian (*Mithr.* 101–2) gives a fuller account of his movements.

50.2 *the Maeotis and the Bosporus*: the Maeotis is the Sea of Azov. The Bosporus
is the strait connecting the Black Sea to the Sea of Azov (the modern
Kerch Strait). The strait was often known as the Cimmerian Bosporus, to
distinguish it from the southern exit of the Black Sea, which still retains
the ancient name Bosporus. The term Bosporus was also applied to the
region on either side of the Kerch Strait, comprising the Taman peninsula on the east and the Crimea (the ancient Tauric Chersonnese) on the
west. This region, which included a number of Greek cities, had formerly
been an independent kingdom, but had become part of Mithridates'
empire early in his reign.

Machares . . . gone over to the Roman side: Mithridates had installed
Machares as ruler of the Bosporan region *c.*80, but, when Lucullus drove
Mithridates out of his kingdom, Machares switched sides, securing
Roman friendship.

killed . . . by courtiers: according to Appian (*Mithr.* 103), Machares committed suicide to avoid falling into Mithridates' hands.

50.3 *Phasis*: the modern Rioni, the principal river of Colchis, rising in the
mountain ridge to its east.

Nicopolis: in Lesser Armenia, near the upper Lycus river (at the modern
Yesilyayla). The city was founded near the hill where Pompey had besieged
Mithridates (Strabo 12.3.28; see note to 36.48.2), not, as Dio claims (so
also App. *Mithr.* 105), at the site of his final victory, which was further east.
It was the first of Pompey's city foundations in Mithridates' former king-
dom (cf. note to 37.20.2). The foundation of a city with this name ('Victory

City') was one of the many ways in which Pompey imitated Alexander, who had founded a Nicopolis at Issus to commemorate his victory there over Darius. Augustus and Trajan were to follow suit.

Cappadocia: see note to 36.11.2.

51.1 *Tigranes, the son . . . fled to Phraates*: the younger Tigranes had married Phraates' daughter (37.6.4).

51.2 *Artaxata*: the capital of the ancestral kingdom of Armenia, said to have been founded on the advice of Hannibal. Its site, on the river Araxes, is about 20 km (12 miles) south-west of Yerevan, the capital of modern Armenia.

52.2 *voluntarily came to his camp*: the probably stage-managed scene of Tigranes' self-abasement before Pompey and reinstatement in his ancestral kingdom is described in similar terms by several other sources. Given its remoteness, allowing Tigranes to retain the kingdom was the only realistic solution, and Pompey gained the maximum political capital from the manner in which it was conducted.

52.3 *tunic . . . candys . . . tiara . . . diadem*: the royal dress and insignia, derived from that of the Persian kings (see note to 36.1b.3). The candys was a type of coat.

prostrate himself: prostration (in Greek, *proskynēsis*) was required by eastern kings of their subjects, but despised by Greeks and Romans as appropriate only before gods.

53.2 *his more recent acquisitions*: for Tigranes' ancestral kingdom and his own extensive acquisitions, see note to 36.1b.1. Lucullus had deprived him of most of these territories, but he had been able to recover some after Lucullus' withdrawal in 67.

Sophanene: earlier writers, including Strabo, Plutarch, and Appian, use the name Sophene (in late antiquity Sophene and Sophanene were distinct regions). Sophene was a territory between the Euphrates and the Tigris, south of Acilisene (Anaïtis) and south-west of Armenia, which controlled the major route from central Anatolia to Mesopotamia. It had originally been part of Armenia, but had been an independent kingdom during the second century and was acquired by Tigranes early in his reign.

money: other sources tell us that Pompey obliged Tigranes to pay an indemnity of 6,000 talents, and he then voluntarily paid a donative to the troops as well (50 drachmae to ordinary soldiers and substantially more to officers).

53.5 *Anaïtis*: both here and at 36.48.1 the name 'Anaïtis' has been restored by editors for corrupt manuscript readings. The reference here cannot be to the same region as at 36.48.1. If the name is correct here, it may designate another territory named after the goddess Anaïtis.

Cyrnus: this river (called Cyrus by some ancient writers) is the modern Kura (Georgian Mtkvari), which rises in north-east Turkey and flows through eastern Georgia and Azerbaijan to the Caspian Sea, with the

Caucasus range to its north. In antiquity its middle course (now in Georgia) was occupied by the Iberians and its lower course by the Albanians. Pompey's camps will have been in the border region between them. He probably reached it from Armenia past Lake Lychnitis (now Sevan), descending by the river Aghstafa. On Pompey's reason for wintering in this location see note to 37.1.1.

53.6 *enrolled Tigranes among the friends and allies*: of the Roman people. Pompey secured this formal recognition for Tigranes after his return to Rome.

brought his son to Rome under guard: the younger Tigranes was paraded in Pompey's triumph, and subsequently detained under house arrest (see note to 38.30.1).

54.1 *Saturnalia*: celebrated for several days starting on 17 December.

54.2 *Metellus Celer ... Lucius Flaccus*: Q. Caecilius Metellus Celer and L. Valerius Flaccus, both legates of Pompey who returned to hold praetorships in 63. Pompey was at this time married to Metellus' half-sister Mucia.

BOOK THIRTY-SEVEN

1.1 *both the Albanians and the Iberians*: these campaigns brought Pompey further military glory, but he may have diverted to the lower Cyrnus valley primarily in order to forestall Mithridates from taking refuge with these peoples.

1.2 *Albania on one side and Armenia on the other*: in fact Albania was south-east and Armenia south of Iberia.

1.3 *Acropolis*: often, probably wrongly, identified with Harmozica (near modern Mtskheta).

2.2 *Pelorus*: an unidentified tributary of the Cyrnus.

3.1 *the Phasis was quite close*: Pompey had followed the Cyrnus up to western Iberia, and from there he crossed the Surami range into the Colchis plain.

set out according to this plan: other ancient sources claim, like Dio, that its inaccessibility prevented Pompey from pursuing Mithridates to the Bosporus. Some modern scholars doubt the difficulty and Pompey's intentions.

3.3 *via Armenia*: Pompey probably followed the mountain route which runs from modern Kutais in the Colchis plain to Akhaltsikhe on the upper Cyrnus, and then, after crossing the Armenian plateau, reached the lower Cyrnus as before by the Aghstafa valley. By choosing this route, he avoided returning through the Iberian heartland.

3.5 *Cambyses*: modern Iori, a tributary joining the Cyrnus from the north.

3.6 *Abas*: also known as the Alazonius, modern Alazani, another northern tributary of the Cyrnus, which formed the boundary between the Iberians and Albanians.

4.4 *festival*: see note to 36.54.1. *Io Saturnalia* was the traditional cry made at the festival.

5.2 *Phraates . . . wanted to renew their treaty*: originally made with Lucullus in 69 (36.3.2) and renewed by Pompey when he took over the command in 66 (36.45.3). The Parthian embassy reached Pompey while he was still in Albania in 65, but Dio makes this the starting point for a continuous narrative of Pompey's dealings with the Parthians over 65 and 64 (37.5.2–7.4). Dio is our fullest source for these events, but his account is hostile to Pompey, giving a satirical interpretation of his motives. On Pompey's own movements in this period, see notes to 37.7.5–7a.

Gabinius: see note to 36.23.4. Gabinius was now serving as one of Pompey's legates (having been ineligible for such an appointment in 66 against the pirates, since he had carried the law creating that command as tribune in 67).

5.3 *Gordyene . . . disputing with Tigranes*: early in his reign Tigranes had acquired much territory in northern Mesopotamia and the upper Tigris valley which had formerly been under Parthian control, including Adiabene and to its north Gordyene (see note to 36.1.1). When Pompey stripped Tigranes of his territorial gains in 66 (36.53.2), Phraates had evidently occupied all this territory, at least some of which Pompey may have promised him under their treaty. By his request for treaty renewal, Phraates was seeking Pompey's approval for these gains, but Pompey instead insisted that Gordyene should be restored to Tigranes.

5.4 *Afranius*: L. Afranius had already served as Pompey's legate against Sertorius and was now doing so again. Pompey had left him in charge of Armenia when he advanced against the Albanians and Iberians. After expelling Tigranes from Gordyene, Afranius pursued him as far as Arbela, in Adiabene (Plut. *Pomp.* 34, 36).

5.5 *Carrhaeans*: Carrhae (modern Harran), in northern Mesopotamia, on the river Balikh, a tributary of the Euphrates, had been refounded as a Macedonian military colony under the Seleucid kings. Its inhabitants also helped Crassus after his disastrous nearby defeat in 53 (40.25).

6.1 *greedy for more*: on this theme in Dio, see note to 36.1.2. Dio portrays Pompey here as behaving as Mithridates and Tigranes had warned Phraates that he would (36.1.2), an unfair claim, since at this point he was not seeking expansion, just the recovery of territory for Tigranes. Here, as elsewhere (frgs. 5.4, 36.21; 49.36.1), Dio insists that the outcome of war is determined by might, not right.

6.2 *address him only as 'King'*: in the letter sent by Pompey (now back in Pontus: Plut. *Pomp.* 38) in response to Phraates' embassy (37.5.4). Some of the Parthian king's subordinate rulers were styled kings. The title 'King of Kings' had first been adopted by the Achaemenid kings of Persia, whom the Parthian Arsacids had supplanted. Lucullus had insulted Tigranes in the same way (Plut. *Luc.* 21).

triumph over him in Rome: Dio's wording here is confused. Tigranes' son was paraded in Pompey's triumph. Also displayed were a picture showing the elder Tigranes in flight and a placard listing him among the defeated kings, no doubt with his title of 'King of Kings'.

6.3 *forbidding him from crossing the Euphrates*: according to Plutarch (*Pomp.* 33), Phraates asked that the Euphrates should be used as his boundary with the Romans, but Pompey replied that the just boundary would be used. The Euphrates cannot have been fixed as the boundary in Lucullus' and Pompey's treaties with Parthia, as some scholars have supposed: such a provision would have made no sense before Pompey's decision to annex Syria as a province.

6.4 *supported by Tigranes' son*: a confusion by Dio, since Tigranes' son was now Pompey's prisoner (36.53.4). Phraates' embassy had unsuccessfully asked for the young man to be handed over to him as his father-in-law (Plut. *Pomp.* 33).

Lucius Caesar and Gaius Figulus were consuls: L. Julius Caesar and C. Marcius Figulus. L. Caesar was a remote cousin of the future dictator.

7.1 *Mithridates . . . still in arms*: Appian (*Mithr.* 106) confirms that Pompey used such arguments to decline Tigranes' request for military help against Phraates. Pompey can never have intended to be dragged into a war with Parthia, and achieved a successful outcome by inducing the kings to accept Roman arbitration to resolve their conflict. Dio presents an ironic but implausible picture of Pompey as desiring an expansionist war against Parthia, but taking fright and then pretending noble sentiments to justify his change of plan.

as Lucullus had: Lucullus' advance against Armenia had eventually led to his losing control of Pontus (36.12–17). Dio himself approved of giving up 'aiming for more' for fear of endangering what one has, and later interprets actions of both Caesar and Augustus in this way (40.4.1; 54.9.1; 56.33.5).

7.3 *complaints . . . against each other*: the details of the arbitrated settlement are unknown. Tigranes appears to have retained Gordyene.

7.4 *the winner . . . easier for the Romans to subdue*: as Phraates had earlier been warned (36.1.2). The anti-Roman explanations Dio gives for the kings' reconciliation are probably his own (implausible) conjectures.

7.5 *also wintered then in Aspis*: i.e. the winter of 65/64. Having taken his Parthian narrative (37.5.2–7.4) down to late 64, Dio now doubles back to resume his account of Pompey's other activities. In late 65, Pompey returned from Albania through Armenia to Lesser Armenia, the location of Aspis (otherwise unknown) and Symphorium (also known as Sinoria).

her son: Xiphares, put to death by Mithridates on hearing of Stratonice's treachery.

7a *[From Xiphilinus' epitome]*: one leaf is missing from the manuscript L at this point. The lost passage covered Pompey's activity in 64, followed by the start of Dio's account of events at Rome in 65. Pompey spent the first part of 64 in Mithridates' former kingdom of Pontus, organizing it as a province jointly with Bithynia. He then advanced through south-east Anatolia to Syria, where his legates were already active. The summary at the start of the book (see p. xxx) describes this part of the book as covering 'How Pompey added Pontus to Bithynia' and 'How Pompey subjugated Syria and Phoenicia'.

kings and dynasts who approached him: during the year Pompey settled the organization of the central and eastern parts of Anatolia which were outside the Roman provinces by confirming in power the kings of Cappadocia and Commagene and appointing minor rulers in Galatia and elsewhere.

settled Coele Syria and Phoenicia: Pompey brought under Roman control both northern Syria, which was all that was left of the Seleucid kingdom, and the former Seleucid territories to its south. Various local rulers were left in place, but the remainder became the new Roman province of Syria. Here (as at 36.11.1–2, 50.3; 37.15.2, 52.1) Dio used the provincial nomenclature of his own day (reproduced by Xiphilinus): shortly before Dio wrote, Septimius Severus had divided Syria into two provinces: Syria Coele in the north and Syria Phoenice in the south. This departed from earlier usage, in which the name Coele Syria was applied to various regions in southern Syria.

Antiochus: Antiochus XIII, who had recovered northern Syria and been recognized as king by Lucullus after Tigranes' withdrawal in 69. However, since he had been unable to maintain control (see note to 36.17.3), Pompey reasonably decided that making Syria a Roman province was the only way to ensure its stability. He justified his decision on the ground that the Romans' expulsion of Tigranes from Syria made them its rightful rulers (App. *Syr.* 49; *Mithr.* 106).

governed in the Roman fashion: here, as in Bithynia–Pontus, Pompey made detailed regulations for the province's administration (cf. 37.20.2).

8.1   *praise . . . not only for this*: Dio has interrupted his narrative of events in the East to double back to recount events at Rome in the years 65 and 64 (37.8.1–10.3). He had already narrated events there at the start of the year 65 at 36.44.3–5. This section probably opened with Caesar's aedileship. The exceptionally ambitious Caesar made the most of the opportunities of the office: Suetonius (*Jul.* 10–11) and Plutarch (*Caes.* 5–6) supply further details. Besides his games, Caesar honoured the memory of Marius (whose wife had been his aunt) by restoring on the Capitol the trophies of his victories which had been removed by Marius' opponent Sulla, and it was probably this that Dio reported immediately before our text resumes.

the Roman and the Megalensian Games: the games for which Caesar and his colleague were responsible as curule aediles. The *ludi Megalenses* (honouring Cybele) were held over seven days in April, and the *ludi Romani* (honouring Jupiter) over fifteen days in September.

gladiatorial contests to commemorate his father: under the Republic gladiatorial shows were only held to honour a deceased relative, but were often given long after their death. Caesar's father had died in 85, but he held the show now to maximize the impact of his aedileship: 320 pairs of gladiators fought, the Senate having banned more as a security measure.

Marcus Bibulus: M. Calpurnius Bibulus served as Caesar's colleague again as praetor in 62 and consul in 59, becoming his bitter enemy as a result.

8.2 *named after Castor alone*: see note to 38.6.2.

9.1 *she-wolf . . . Remus and Romulus*: a statue of the infant Remus and Romulus suckled by the she-wolf had been erected at Rome as early as 296. The famous she-wolf statue in the Capitoline Museum has recently been shown to be medieval.

tablets on which the laws were inscribed: the texts of new laws were posted in bronze in a public place, often the Capitol.

haruspices: see Glossary, p. 284.

conspiracies . . . might be exposed: for the apparent fulfilment of this prophecy on 3 December 63, see 37.34.3–4.

9.3 *censors*: see Glossary, p. 283. Plutarch (*Crass.* 13) identifies these censors as Crassus and Catulus, but explains their disagreement as over Crassus' wish to make Egypt a province (see note to 39.12.1). The censors of 70 were the last to complete their tasks. Censors were appointed in 65, 64, 61, 55, and 50, but all resigned with their work uncompleted: see A. E. Astin, 'Censorships in the Late Republic', *Historia* 34 (1985), 175–90.

lived north of the Po: those south of the Po received full Roman citizenship after the Social War, but the Transpadani received just Latin rights, under which their magistrates became citizens, by a law passed by Pompey's father in 89. The censor who wanted to give them full citizenship now was probably Crassus. Caesar had already taken up their cause, and eventually granted them citizenship as dictator in 49.

9.4 *successors*: L. Aurelius Cotta (consul in 65) was censor in 64, but his colleague is unknown.

tribunes . . . afraid of being expelled from the Senate themselves: probably especially Q. Mucius Orestinus, who had offended the Senate by vetoing a law on electoral corruption (Asconius 83).

9.5 *at that time*: in 65.

not suitable co-inhabitants: other sources show that Papius' law expelled non-citizens from Rome and established a special tribunal against those illegally enrolled as citizens. Dio's statement implies that inhabitants of Italy up to the Alps were exempt from the expulsion. His reference to 'what is now Italy' must have this meaning (cf. 41.61.4 and 48.12.5), and the expulsion cannot therefore have been directed against the Transpadani, as often supposed.

10.2 *efforts of Julius Caesar*: as the appointed president for the year of the murder court (*quaestio inter sicarios*), in which these trials were held (Suet. *Jul.* 11). Further details on the trials are supplied by Asconius 90–1: only relatively unimportant individuals were convicted.

who had killed Lucretius on Sulla's orders: L. Bellienus, an uncle of Catiline. Q. Lucretius Ofella (or Afella), although a henchman of Sulla's, had persisted in standing for the consulship in 82 against his wishes.

who had killed many . . . proscribed by Sulla: L. Luscius. As dictator Sulla had posted lists of those whose lives were forfeit (proscriptions).

10.3 *acquittal of Catiline*: after his defeat at the consular elections for 63, oddly unmentioned by Dio. Catiline's prosecutor was L. Lucceius (see note to 36.41.1), but ex-consuls testified in his defence. On his earlier career, see note to 36.44.4.

10.4 *Cicero . . . with Gaius Antonius as his colleague*: Antonius had campaigned in alliance with Catiline in a bitterly fought election, but the reputation and connections which he had won through his oratory enabled the 'new man' Cicero to top the poll. C. Antonius Hybrida, of a distinguished family, managed to reach the consulship despite having been expelled from the senate by the censors of 70.

Mithridates and Catiline: this linkage provides Dio with a neat transition to the major events of 63 and also back to his interrupted account of eastern events. He now narrates first the death of Mithridates (37.11–14) and then the rest of Pompey's eastern command, continuing down to his return in 62 and triumph in 61 (37.15–23), before returning to narrate the events of 63 in Rome and Italy (37.24–38).

11.1 *invade Italy*: other sources report Mithridates' final plans and his end, diverging on some details and with Appian (*Mithr.* 107–112) providing the fullest account. The grand design for an invasion of Italy is probably an invented rumour: more likely, Mithridates merely aimed to hold out in the Bosporan region.

11.4 *cities*: in the Bosporan region, where Mithridates had been established since 65 (see note to 36.50.2).

12.3 *Panticapaeum*: modern Kerch, on the western side of the straits. Founded from Miletus *c*.600, it was the principal city of the Crimean part of the Bosporan region.

13.2 *antidotes, taken as a precautionary measure*: numerous ancient sources record this and other aspects of Mithridates' expertise in poisons.

13.3 *their swords and spears*: other accounts report Mithridates as killed at his own request by his Celtic troop commander Bituitus.

14.1 *among the tombs of his ancestors*: at Sinope.

14.2 *enrolled him among the friends and allies*: of the Roman people, as for Tigranes (see note to 36.53.6). Pharnaces continued as ruler of the Bosporan kingdom until 47, when, having attempted to use the Roman civil war to recover his father's kingdom, he was defeated by Caesar at Zela and killed soon after.

15.1 *Once these regions were under control*: Dio now backtracks to cover Pompey's own activity in 63 (37.15–16). Pompey in fact only learnt of the death of Mithridates when approaching Jerusalem. A fuller and more accurate account of his dealings with the Jews and Nabataeans is provided by the Jewish writer Josephus (*Jewish Antiquities* 14.29–81; *Jewish War* 1.127–59). Pompey's primary aim in this campaign will have been to ensure the security of his new province of Syria by making a satisfactory settlement of the territories to its south.

to the Red Sea: the kingdom of the Nabataean Arabs (ruled since *c*.84 by Aretas III) centred on Petra, but extended to the Red Sea. It subsequently continued as a Roman client kingdom until 106 CE, when Trajan annexed it as the Roman province of Arabia.

still at war: Josephus does not support this account of aggression by Aretas in Syria, mentioning only his involvement in the Jewish civil war.

15.2 *under a garrison*: in fact Pompey was diverted from his planned Nabataean campaign by events in Judaea and then set out on his return home, leaving M. Aemilius Scaurus, who had been his quaestor, as acting governor of Syria. Scaurus marched against Petra, but accepted Aretas' submission, imposing a 300-talent payment, but no garrison.

Syria Palaestina: the name of the territory in Dio's own day. Judaea, annexed as a Roman province after the exiling of its last king in 6 CE, was renamed Syria Palaestina by Hadrian, after crushing the Bar Kokhba revolt in 135.

Hyrcanus and Aristobulus: of the Hasmonean dynasty. Successive Hasmonean rulers had secured Jewish independence from Seleucid rule in the mid-second century BCE, and then greatly increased their territory. Each ruler held the post of High Priest, and the later Hasmoneans also took the title of king. Alexander Jannaeus (104/3–76) left the rulership to his widow Salome Alexandra, with his elder son Hyrcanus becoming High Priest. After Salome's death in 67, Hyrcanus and Aristobulus disputed both the rulership and the priesthood. According to Josephus, Pompey sought to resolve the dispute on his arrival in Damascus in 63, but Aristobulus' resistance obliged Pompey to move against him with his army.

15.3 *put him in chains*: Dio conflates the abortive negotiations conducted by Aristobulus from the fortress of Alexandrion and his later submission as Pompey approached Jerusalem. Aristobulus then promised Pompey money and admission to Jerusalem, but his troops there refused to comply and Pompey then put him under arrest.

16.3 *attacked with maximum force*: Dio oversimplifies. The Law permitted the Jews to fight in self-defence on the Sabbath, but not to take any other military action, and so the Romans used those days to complete their siege-works uninterrupted.

16.4 *captured one Saturn-day*: Josephus' statement that the Temple was captured on the 'day of fasting', which must mean the Day of Atonement (around October), is often doubted.

   wealth was plundered: both Cicero (*For Flaccus* 67) and Josephus insist that Pompey left the Temple treasures untouched. The siege had lasted three months.

   Aristobulus . . . to captivity: Aristobulus was taken to Rome with his family and was paraded in Pompey's triumph. For the subsequent activity of Aristobulus and his son Alexander, see notes to 39.56.1, 6. Pompey confirmed Hyrcanus as High Priest and as ruler of a much-reduced territory, now tributary to Rome, but forbade him to wear a diadem, the recognized mark of kingship. Hyrcanus held on as ruler until overthrown by the Parthians in 40.

16.5 *Jews*: ethnographic accounts of the Jews were common in histories (e.g. Tacitus, *Histories* 5.2–10) and other Graeco-Roman literature. Dio, sparing with such digressions, gives only a brief and selective account (37.16.5–17.4) before passing to the more esoteric topic of the planetary week (37.18–19). His treatment is unusual for its lack of overt hostility to the Jews and their practices.

17.1 *living among the Romans*: Jewish communities were widespread across the Roman empire, and successive emperors confirmed their right to observe their customary practices, but Dio's reference is probably particularly to the community at Rome, which flourished despite occasional expulsions and other repressive measures.

17.3 *open and roofless*: a mistaken claim. The reference is to the temple rebuilt under Herod the Great (king of Judaea 37–4 BCE) and destroyed by Titus when he captured Jerusalem in 70 CE.

18.1 *assigning days . . . to the planets*: Dio's reference to the Jewish practice of honouring Saturday as their Sabbath provides the peg for an excursus explaining the planetary week. Seven-day weeks had long been established in Babylonia and among the Jews, but such a week with the days named after the planetary gods is first attested in the later first century BCE (in Italy). The week is based on a geocentric system in which the planets (including the Sun and Moon) are ordered according to their supposed distance from the Earth (Saturn, Jupiter, Mars, the Sun, Venus, Mercury, the Moon). Dio reports two explanations of how this sequence generates that of the planetary week (Saturn, Sun, Moon, Mars, Mercury, Jupiter, Venus). The first, for which Dio supplies a musical interpretation (36.18.3–4), is based on the fact that the successive planetary days are each fourth in order from their predecessor in a recurring Saturn–Moon sequence (thus Sun is fourth from Saturn, Moon from Sun, Mars from Moon, etc). Dio's second explanation (36.19), which must provide the correct account of the planetary week's origin, treats the seven planets as ruling the hours as well as the days, with the allocation of days to planets thus generated by the twenty-four-hour cycle in each day.

Egyptians: supposed founders of astrology. Both the Saturn–Moon planetary sequence and the planetary week were probably devised by Greek specialists in astronomy and astrology in second-century BCE Alexandria. See further I. Bultrighini and S. Stern, 'The Seven-day Week in the Roman Empire: Origins, Standardization, and Diffusion', in S. Stern (ed.), *Calendars in the Making: The Origins of Calendars from the Roman Empire to the Later Middle Ages* (Leiden, 2021), 10–79.

18.3 *tetrachord*: a group of four notes spanning the interval of a fourth, fundamental in Greek musical theory.

18.4 *musical to the structure of the heavens*: philosophers had long claimed to discern a relationship between musical intervals and the structure of the cosmos, and particularly, from Plato on, the planetary orbits (the 'harmony of the spheres').

20.1 *achievements narrated above*: after the excursuses of 37.16.5–19.3, Dio now returns to his narrative of Pompey's activity, continuing it down to his return to Rome in 61 (37.20–23), without indicating that he has run ahead of the year 63 until 37.24.1 (for his purpose, see Introduction, p. xvi).

fortresses: cf. 37.14.3.

20.2 *founded eight cities*: this number perhaps relates just to Pontus and Cappadocia (cf. App. *Mithr.* 117). Pompey also founded cities in Cilicia for former pirates, and in the other conquered territories: according to Plutarch (*Pomp.* 45), a placard at Pompey's triumph proclaimed that he had founded thirty-nine cities overall. Dio has already mentioned two: 36.37.6, 50.3.

land: unless otherwise disposed of, the former royal estates became the property of the Roman people. However, Pompey granted much of this land to kings, minor rulers, or cities.

revenue: Plutarch reports another triumphal placard as claiming that Pompey had added 85 million denarii to the annual Roman tax revenue, previously 50 million.

regulations . . . established by him: Pliny's letters to Trajan show that detailed regulations made by Pompey for the governance of the cities of Bithynia–Pontus (known as the *lex Pompeia*) were still in force when he was governor of the province (*c.*110–12 CE).

20.3 *account of it*: Velleius (2.40.2) and Plutarch (*Pomp.* 43) report contemporaries' fears that the returning Pompey would use his army to seize power at Rome and praise for his discharging the troops at Brundisium. Only Dio claims that Pompey could easily have succeeded in such a coup, and that he later came to regret dismissing his troops early (37.50.6). Seizing and retaining power in this way would not have been as straightforward as Dio claims, and Pompey is unlikely to have contemplated doing so.

20.4 *goodwill of almost all . . . where he held sway*: the solid support which Pompey enjoyed among Rome's eastern allies and subjects was shown in the civil war of 49–48.

20.6 *as soon as he reached Brundisium*: in December 62 Brundisium (modern Brindisi) was the normal port for Adriatic crossings from Greece to Italy. Pompey probably left four legions in Cilicia and Syria and brought eight legions home (about 30,000 men) (Brunt, *Italian Manpower*, 460).

hatred that Marius and Sulla had aroused in people: for their cruelty after their civil-war victories in respectively 87 and 82. Dio had made Catulus use the example of Marius and Sulla to warn against giving Pompey a great command (36.31.3–4).

21.1 *entitled by his achievements*: for victors taking *cognomina* from the nations they had conquered, see note to 36.17a.

triumph: over two days, on 28–9 September 61. Fuller descriptions are provided by Plutarch (*Pomp.* 45) and Appian (*Mithr.* 116–17); for an excellent discussion, see M. Beard, *The Roman Triumph* (Cambridge, MA, 2007), 7–41. Dio focuses instead on Pompey's supposed restraint over honours.

regarded as greater: i.e. a full or curule triumph, rather than an ovation, in which the commander processed on foot or on horseback rather than on a chariot. The Senate awarded ovations for victories it deemed not to have qualified for a full triumph (in this period, only for slave wars).

not sanctioned . . . without the troops who had shared in his victory: Dio's claim is outdated. From 200 BCE some commanders who had passed their troops on to their successors had been permitted to triumph. Plutarch (*Pomp.* 43) says that Pompey ordered his troops to reassemble at Rome for his triumph, but no source mentions their presence there.

21.2 *all his wars at once*: i.e. the wars fought from 67 to 63, from the pirate campaign on.

the inhabited world: no doubt represented by a globe, common on contemporary coinage as a symbol of Roman world domination. Other sources speak of Pompey as having extended the frontiers of the empire to the ends of the earth, and as having won his three triumphs from each of the three continents.

21.3 *'Magnus' . . . before these successes*: see note to 36.17a. The *cognomen* 'the Great', although acquired long before, was eminently appropriate now, as Pompey sought to associate himself with Alexander, wearing what was claimed as Alexander's cloak in his triumph.

21.4 *triumphal toga at the chariot-races*: Velleius (2.40.2) tells us that the privilege was conferred on Pompey by a law passed in 63 by the tribunes T. Ampius and T. Labienus, and confirms that he only exercised it once. The chief entertainments at the games (*ludi*) were chariot-racing (in the Circus Maximus) and theatrical performances. At the games, former holders of higher magistracies were entitled to wear the *toga praetexta* (see note to 36.33.2), and those who had triumphed also wore a laurel wreath, as at their triumph. Thus, of those mentioned by Dio, the only exceptional distinction conferred on Pompey was the right to wear at the Circus the embroidered purple toga (*toga picta*) worn by a triumphing commander.

support of Caesar . . . objections of Marcus Cato: mentioned only by Dio. They may have spoken on the law both in the Senate and at a *contio*.

22.1 *already introduced Caesar*: in 36.43.2–4 and 37.8.

Cato: M. Porcius Cato (95–46 BCE). Cato first came to prominence for his contribution as tribune elect to the debate on the Catilinarians in December 63 (37.36.2), and thereafter, despite his junior status, rapidly emerged as a leader of the conservative element in the Senate. As earlier with Caesar, Dio opts to introduce him in the context of his stance towards Pompey.

the great Cato: the Younger Cato's great-grandfather, also M. Porcius Cato. The first member of his family to enter the Senate, he was consul in 195 and censor in 184. An outstanding orator, Cato was noted for his feuds and for his championship of traditional values. He also wrote the first prose works in Latin.

exposure to Greek culture: although scathing about some aspects of Greek culture, the Elder Cato in fact had a good knowledge of Greek literature. The Younger Cato was a convinced Stoic, and sought to apply its rigorous principles in his public life.

22.2 *supremely devoted to the public good*: at 37.57.3 Dio praises Cato as the only one of his contemporaries solely concerned for the public good (but at 37.46.3 he gives Catulus comparable praise). Cato's uprightness was lauded by both contemporaries and later writers.

22.3 *the people's friend*: *dēmerastēs*, literally 'lover of the people', a rare word Dio later applies to Brutus and Cassius (47.38.3). By this Dio means a champion of the Republic and opponent of those aiming at personal power, using *dēmos* as usual for the whole Roman people. Similarly, at 43.11.6, he describes Cato at his death as *dēmotikōtatos* ('most demo-cratic'). However, Dio also slips here into misidentifying Cato, in reality an arch-conservative, as a supporter of the 'common people' (*plēthos*).

22.4 *no precedent*: untrue. The right to wear the *toga picta* at the Circus had been conferred on Aemilius Paullus in 167, after his victory over the last king of Macedon.

23.2 *regimes based on personal power*: *dynasteiai* (see Introduction, p. xxii).

23.3 *democratic*: i.e. republican (see Introduction, p. xxii).

23.4 *contrary to precedent*: by getting his early commands, his first two triumphs, and his first consulship while still an *eques* (see 36.25.2–3).

jealousy and hatred . . . awarding them: in this chapter, as at the time of the piracy command, Dio portrays Pompey as trying to avoid the jealousy and hatred necessarily accompanying success (see note to 36.24.6). The elab-orate reflections on avoiding honours which he attributes to Pompey are echoed in the advice he makes Maecenas give Augustus (52.35.1–2). Dio envisages the situation in terms more appropriate to later times: further honours or offices were not considered for Pompey immediately after his return from the East; Caesar after his civil-war victory was the first to accumulate excessive honours, criticized by Dio in terms similar to those used here (44.3.2–3).

24.1 *then*: i.e. in 63, the consulship of Cicero and Antonius. Dio here returns to his narrative of the year to deal with events at Rome. Only now does he acknowledge that, in continuing Pompey's story down to his return and triumph (37.20–23), he had looked ahead to later developments (which he leaves undated).

augurium salutis . . . after many years: Dio gives the clearest extant account of this ritual. It may have been last performed in 160, and was revived now probably when news of Mithridates' death reached the Senate (so around May 63). It was next performed in 29, following the defeat of Antony and Cleopatra.

25.2 *lights*: probably meteors.

25.3 *tribunes*: Dio's portrayal of the tribunes as presenting a coordinated extremist programme is misleading, as shown by A. Drummond, 'Tribunes and Tribunician Programmes in 63 BC', *Athenaeum* 87 (1999), 121–67. Only the proposals relating to Autronius and Sulla and to land were promulgated when the new tribunes entered office on 10 December (see note to 36.42.1); the agitation over the sons of the proscribed came later, and the debt proposal is Dio's error.

consul Antonius: although Antonius had campaigned for the consulship with Catiline (see note to 37.10.4), Dio is wrong to portray him as a revolutionary in office. Cicero secured his collaboration by an exchange of provinces before the start of their term. See notes to 37.30.3, 33.4.

sons of those . . . exiled by Sulla: 'exiled' is Dio's slip for 'proscribed'. Sulla had banned the sons of those he proscribed from holding office. By a speech made probably in July 63, Cicero induced them to abandon their attempt to stand (only Dio says that it was backed by a tribune). The ban was lifted by Caesar in 49.

Paetus and . . . Sulla: P. Autronius Paetus and P. Cornelius Sulla, banned for life from office and the Senate following their conviction for electoral corruption in 66 (see notes to 36.38.1, 44.3). On entry into office, the tribune L. Caecilius Rufus, Sulla's half-brother, promulgated a law which would have replaced the lifelong ban imposed under the *ambitus* law of 67 by the ten-year exclusion prescribed by the earlier law. At Sulla's request, Caecilius withdrew the proposal on 1 January, and he subsequently offered to veto the land law (Cicero, *For Sulla* 62–66).

25.4 *cancellation of debts*: debt remission was mooted by Catiline in summer 63 (see note to 37.30.2), but the silence of our other sources shows that it cannot have been raised earlier in the year.

distribution of land in Italy and . . . abroad: on entry into office, P. Servilius Rufus, with support from some other tribunes, promulgated an agrarian law. The published versions of three of Cicero's four speeches against the law survive, providing detailed but heavily biased information. The law proposed a ten-man commission to make land allotments in Italy (not also the provinces, as Dio claims), using existing public land and land acquired by purchase, to be funded from various sources including the sale of public land overseas. Cicero claims that the law was hostile to Pompey and hints at powerful backers, including Crassus, but these allegations may be groundless. The proposal was soon withdrawn, but allotments were eventually provided by Caesar's legislation in 59.

26.1 *Titus Labienus*: as tribune he also procured honours for Pompey and elections for priesthoods, both in association with Caesar (37.21.4, 37.1). He served as Caesar's chief legate in Gaul in 58–51, but sided with Pompey in the civil war. Labienus came from Picenum, in eastern Italy, where Pompey had long had great influence.

Rabirius for the murder of Saturninus: L. Appuleius Saturninus was a radical and violent tribune in 103 and 100. At the elections of 100 he and his associate C. Servilius Glaucia murdered an opponent and then seized the Capitol. The Senate reacted by passing its 'last decree' (see note to 37.31.2) and the consul Marius then suppressed them by force. Saturninus, Glaucia, and their supporters surrendered to Marius, who pledged their safety, but were lynched by a mob. Rabirius is said to have displayed Saturninus' head at parties. Labienus' uncle had been among those killed. Rabirius' trial is also known through the partially preserved speech made by Cicero in his defence and a brief reference by Suetonius (*Jul.* 12). It probably took place in July/August 63.

26.2 *political order was threatened with collapse*: Cicero in his speech portrayed the prosecution as an attack on the right of the consuls and Senate to defend the Republic against sedition, and Dio follows suit. However, Cicero conceded that Labienus' case was directed particularly at the violation of Marius' pledge (*For Rabirius* 28).

27.1 *thanks to Caesar*: Suetonius (followed by many modern scholars) claims that Caesar was the instigator of the prosecution.

27.2 *Lucius Caesar*: see note to 37.6.4.

perduellio: treason. The prosecution employed (doubtless for spectacular effect) a rare procedure under which the case was initially heard by a board of two (*duumviri*) and the sentence was public scourging. This procedure is otherwise attested only in some accounts of two very early trials, and was either archaic or an antiquarian invention.

27.3 *Rabirius appealed*: so also Suetonius. However, Cicero got the duumviral process quashed (*For Rabirius* 10–11), and Rabirius' subsequent trial before the assembly was thus a separate process. In this period criminal trials were normally held in jury courts rather than before the assembly.

Metellus Celer: see note to 36.54.3.

Janiculum: the ridge on the west bank of the Tiber.

28.1 *assembly by centuries*: comitia centuriata (see Glossary, pp. 283–4). This assembly, before which *perduellio* trials were held, had originally been military in character, and so took place outside the city, in the Campus Martius. Dio's excursus on the flag is our only reference to this practice.

29.1 *Catiline's downfall*: having pointed ahead to it at 37.10.4, Dio now starts his narrative of Catiline's uprising and its defeat in 63 (37.29–36) and 62 (37.39–42). Our other sources include Cicero's *Catilinarians* and other speeches, Sallust's monograph, and the later accounts of Plutarch, Appian, and Suetonius. Dio's account differs in various respects from other versions.

law . . . for bribery: for the existing law on electoral corruption (*ambitus*), passed in 67, see note to 36.38.1. A new law had been proposed in 64, but vetoed by a tribune. The present law (*lex Tullia Antonia*), which stiffened both the scope of the offence and the penalty, was carried on the Senate's authority by both consuls, with Cicero taking the lead, in response to pressure from one of the candidates, Ser. Sulpicius Rufus, who threatened to prosecute his rivals Catiline and Murena. Only Dio explains Catiline's conduct as a reaction to the law.

29.2 *murder Cicero . . . elections*: Cicero gives his own account of the events described at 29.2–4 at *For Murena* 50–52, according to which news spread of a private meeting at which Catiline had declared himself the leader of the 'wretched'; Cicero then had the election (scheduled for the next day) postponed to permit a Senate meeting, at which Catiline, challenged by him, was defiant and the Senate failed to pass a strong enough decree; Cicero then, knowing that Catiline was accompanied by armed conspirators, presided over the election guarded by friendly strongmen and wearing a conspicuous breastplate. Elsewhere Cicero explicitly claims that Catiline was planning to kill him and others there (*Cat.* 1.11; *For Sulla* 51).

30.1 *chosen as consuls*: D. Junius Silanus and L. Licinius Murena. Probably the elections, originally scheduled for July as usual, had been postponed to 23 September to allow time for the *ambitus* law, and then, after the second postponement, were held a day or two later: see J. T. Ramsey, 'The Date of the Consular Elections in 63 and the Inception of Catiline's Conspiracy', *Harvard Studies in Classical Philology* 110 (2019), 213–69. In late November Sulpicius and Cato carried out their threat to prosecute Murena for corruption, but he was defended by Cicero and acquitted.

not just Cicero . . . but the whole community: Cicero (*Cat.* 1.12), Sallust (*Cat.* 26.5), and others make similar statements. Catiline cannot have decided on a general uprising until after his electoral defeat, but, if the elections took place as late as September, preparations must have begun earlier. Sallust misdates the formation of the conspiracy to the previous year (*Cat.* 17, 20–23).

30.2 *redistribution of land*: debt is said to have been a major factor in the conspiracy's support, but only Dio reports Catiline as promising land redistribution.

allies: the allied communities south of the Po had all been made Roman citizens after the Social War, but here (as at 37.10.4, 40.1–41.4) Dio anachronistically uses 'allies' for Catiline's supporters in rural Italy.

30.3 *Antonius, the consul*: other sources report doubts about Antonius' loyalty, but only Dio includes him in the conspiracy here and below (37.32.3, 33.3, 39.3–4; 38.10.3), surely in error (see note to 37.25.3).

30.4 *Publius Lentulus*: P. Cornelius Lentulus Sura, consul in 71, but expelled from the Senate by the censors of 70. Of an outstanding family, he was fond of identifying himself as the third Cornelius (after Cinna and Sulla) fated by an oracle to rule Rome. Sallust (*Cat.* 17.3–4) names ten further senators and four *equites* as in the conspiracy.

Faesulae: an ancient city in northern Etruria (modern Fiesole). Sulla had founded a veteran colony on confiscated land there and elsewhere in Etruria, and the force Manlius raised there included both the dispossessed and discontented Sullan settlers like Manlius himself.

31.1 *information reached Cicero*: further details on the information and the resulting decrees are provided by Plutarch (*Cic.* 15; *Crass.* 13, citing Cicero's memoir on his consulship) and Sallust (*Cat.* 29). Dio may imply two Senate meetings, but a single meeting is more likely, probably to be identified with the meeting on 21 October, at which Cicero predicted (accurately) that Manlius would rise in arms on 27 October and claimed that Catiline was planning a massacre of senators for 28 October (Cic. *Cat.* 1.7).

state of emergency: a *tumultus*. This declaration (reported only by Dio) permitted the raising of emergency levies. It must have been a response to the situation in Etruria rather than Rome, and so Dio has placed it too soon.

31.2 *instruction to ensure that no harm came to the city*: the so-called 'last decree of the Senate' (*senatus consultum ultimum*), giving such an instruction to the consuls and/or other magistrates. The passing of this decree required them to take all necessary steps to restore order, but the magistrates themselves remained fully answerable for their actions. The decree had been passed first in 121 against Gaius Gracchus and in 100 against Saturninus, and most recently in 77 against Lepidus' uprising.

31.3 *further information from Etruria*: L. Saenius read a letter in the Senate reporting that Manlius had mobilized on 27 October and trouble was also reported elsewhere in Italy. Measures taken in response included the setting of watches in Rome and despatch of forces to Faesulae, Capua, Apulia, and Picenum (Sall. *Cat.* 30). It was probably at this meeting that the *tumultus* decree was passed.

32.2 *the praetor Metellus*: in fact M. Metellus, confused by Dio with the praetor Q. Metellus Celer (see note to 36.27.3), who, like M.' Lepidus and Cicero himself, had refused to receive Catiline (Cic. *Cat.* 1.19).

32.3 *gather at night in a certain house*: belonging to M. Porcius Laeca, on the night of 6–7 November.

33.1 *pass . . . information on to him*: Cicero learnt of the meeting from his regular informant, the conspirator Q. Curius, through Curius' lover Fulvia. Instead of reporting this, Dio opts to stress Cicero's influence, as at 38.12.4.

depart from Rome: the Senate did not vote for Catiline to leave Rome, as Dio claims. At the meeting, on 7 or 8 November, Cicero challenged him to leave without putting it to a vote. Cicero later published his speech as his *First Catilinarian*.

33.2 *organize the men . . . also slaves*: according to Sallust (*Cat.* 44.6 and 56.1–5), new recruits enabled Catiline to form his forces into two full legions, but he rejected slaves.

33.3 *guilty of violence*: it is unlikely that Catiline's trial for violence (37.31.3) was concluded in his absence, as Dio appears to think. Dio may have confused it with the declaration of Catiline as an enemy of the Roman people (Sall. *Cat.* 36.2).

changed their dress: assumed military cloaks (*saga*), commonly adopted during a *tumultus* (see note to 37.31.1), and retained now until the final victory over Catiline (37.40.2).

33.4 *to focus on the courts*: As usual (see note to 36.1a), the consuls' provinces will have been decreed by the Senate before their election, and they had then drawn lots. Shortly before entering office, they agreed to swap. Dio misunderstands Cicero's motive. Macedonia offered the greater opportunity for military success and enrichment, and yielding it to Antonius helped Cicero to ensure his compliance against radical tribunes and Catiline (Sall. *Cat.* 26.4).

to Gaul . . . Catiline did not take it over: Cisalpine Gaul, comprising the Po plain and its mountain fringes, was at this period administered as a province and so separately from the rest of Italy. When Cicero resigned it, it became one of the praetors' provinces, and Cicero and Antonius ensured that Metellus Celer was assigned it in the ballot. However, he was sent first to Picenum and the Ager Gallicus to deal with the uprising there (see note to 37.31.2). In January 62 he blocked Catiline's escape across the Apennines (see note to 37.39.2), and then assumed command of Cisalpine Gaul. Dio thus conflates Celer's two commands.

34.1 *set fires and commit murder*: planned for 17 December. Dio gives a very brief account of Lentulus' plot and its exposure (37.34.1–2), resuming ampler treatment thereafter. Fuller reports are provided by Cicero (*Cat.* 3.3–15) and Sallust (*Cat.* 39.6–47.4).

persuaded to join him: false—the embassy in fact informed Cicero of Lentulus' overture and collaborated in the conspirators' entrapment. The Allobroges, from Transalpine Gaul, had sent the embassy to protest at Roman misgovernment; for their subsequent rebellion, see 37.47–8.

34.2 *[. . .]*: a short passage has been omitted from our manuscript, in which Dio reported Cicero's discovery of the plot and the ambush on the night of 2–3 December through which he obtained letters incriminating the main conspirators. Cicero is the subject of the following sentence.

exposed the whole conspiracy: this Senate meeting was held on 3 December in the temple of Concord. Conclusive proof of the guilt of Lentulus and his chief associates was provided by the letters and the evidence given by the Allobroges and by T. Volturcius, the conspirator who was escorting them to visit Catiline on their way home. Volturcius was granted immunity rather than the ambassadors: since they had collaborated with Cicero, they did not need the grant.

the rest: four others were arrested along with Lentulus and executed on 5 December. Four others implicated were to be sought, but their fate is unknown.

34.3 *The people . . . pleased about this*: Sallust (*Cat.* 48.1) says that the plebs had previously favoured Catiline's revolutionary design, but were now alienated by the planned arson.

Cicero's speech about the conspiracy: the *Third Catilinarian*, delivered to the assembly on 3 December, directly after the Senate meeting. Cicero dilates there (18–22) on the coincidence that the statue had been erected that morning as a proof of divine support. Dio embellishes further, having the statue erected as Cicero spoke. For the issuing of the *haruspices*' advice in 65, see 37.9.2.

35.1 *not widely believed*: Crassus was implicated in evidence given to the Senate by L. Tarquinius on 4 December (Sall. *Cat.* 48.3–9). The striking similarity between Sallust's and Dio's accounts of the senators' reactions shows that Sallust must be his source for this incident.

35.4 *rites carried out in his house*: for the Bona Dea ('Good Goddess'), held annually, as this passage shows, on the night of 4–5 December, at the house of one of the consuls or praetors (see note to 37.45.1).

convened the Senate: on 5 December, again in the temple of Concord.

condemn to death those . . . arrested: the Senate could not yet function as a law court, as it did under the emperors. The vote gave Cicero its backing, but the responsibility for executing the prisoners without trial remained his alone. Cicero indicated his preference for the death penalty in an intervention in the debate, later written up as his *Fourth Catilinarian*, but Dio here exaggerates his role in achieving this outcome.

36.1 *Caesar's doing*: as praetor designate, Caesar spoke after the ex-consuls. Cicero (*Cat.* 4.8, 10) and Sallust (*Cat.* 51.43) confirm that, as Dio implies, Caesar's proposal was for permanent imprisonment, misrepresented as temporary by Plutarch (*Cic.* 21; *Caes.* 7) and Appian (*BC* 2.6).

36.2 *Everyone . . . voted for Caesar's proposal*: an oversimplification. Tiberius Claudius Nero, an ex-praetor, proposed that the guards should be strengthened and the decision postponed, and this got some support.

Cato's turn: as tribune designate, he spoke after the ex-aediles. Sallust provides his own versions of Caesar's and Cato's speeches (*Cat.* 51–52).

36.3 *punished*: Cicero had the prisoners executed immediately after the Senate meeting.

a sacrifice and a festival: a *supplicatio*, a rite in which the whole Roman
people made offerings and prayers to gods displayed on couches outside
their temples. *Supplicationes* were commonly voted in thanksgiving for
military victories, and Cicero made much of being the first to be so
honoured for a different achievement. Dio's dating is incorrect: the *supplicatio* was decreed at the Senate's earlier meeting on 3 December.

36.4 *senator called Aulus Fulvius*: it was actually his father who was the senator
(Sall. *Cat.* 39.5).

many . . . killed their own sons: exemplary tales were told of consuls executing their sons for a public offence, notably the first consul Brutus and
T. Manlius Torquatus in 340. Roman fathers were deemed to have the
power of life and death over their sons, and Dio, contradicting a source,
insists that many private citizens had killed their offending sons, but few
other instances are known. See further W. V. Harris, 'The Roman Father's
Power of Life and Death', in R. S. Bagnall and W. V. Harris, *Studies in
Roman Law in Memory of A. Arthur Schiller* (Leiden, 1986), 81–95.

37.1 *renewal of the law of Domitius*: Cn. Domitius Ahenobarbus, as tribune in
104, passed a law by which the members of the major priestly colleges,
previously co-opted, were to be elected by seventeen of the thirty-five
voting tribes from candidates nominated by the priests. As only Dio tells
us, co-optation was restored by Sulla as dictator in 82/81, and Labienus'
law now restored Domitius' arrangement. These laws did not affect the
selection of the Pontifex Maximus, the head of the College of Pontiffs,
which had from earlier times been conducted by the same electoral
procedure: Dio is thus wrong to suppose that Labienus' law directly
helped Caesar's election. For Caesar's collaboration with Labienus, see
37.21.4, 27.1.

Metellus Pius: Q. Caecilius Metellus Pius, consul in 80 and a leading supporter of Sulla and his regime, had been Pontifex Maximus from 81.

37.2 *not voted for Lentulus' death*: Caesar was in fact elected Pontifex Maximus
earlier, perhaps in late September or October. Postponing his mention of
Labienus' bill and Caesar's election till the end of the year enables Dio
both to avoid interrupting his Catiline narrative and to draw a contrast
between the relative popularity of Caesar and Cicero (37.37–38), as earlier
at 36.43.3–44.2.

candidates for the position: only pontiffs were eligible. The other candidates, Catulus (see notes to 36.30.4–5) and P. Servilius Vatia Isauricus,
were both ex-consuls. Caesar was not the first junior candidate to succeed
against senior rivals (R. Morstein-Marx, *Julius Caesar and the Roman
People* (Cambridge, 2021), 65–6). Dio does not mention Caesar's heavy
expenditure on the election, and the subsequent attempt of Catulus and
others to implicate him in Lentulus' plot (Sall. *Cat.* 49; Plut. *Caes.* 7–8).

37.3 *fawning on them*: cf. the similar judgements on Caesar's motivation at
36.43.2–4; 37.22.1, 56.1.

38.1 *deaths of their fellow citizens*: although the conspirators' arson plans lost them popular support (see note to 37.34.3), there was widespread disapproval of the executions. However, Dio goes too far in portraying the hostility as general and the tribunes' silencing of Cicero as the people's initiative.

38.2 *Metellus Nepos*: Q. Caecilius Metellus Nepos, younger brother of Metellus Celer. Like Celer, he had served as a legate to their brother-in-law Pompey in 67–63. He was active against Cicero from his entry into office as tribune on 10 December 63. On 29 December, the last day of Cicero's term as consul, Nepos and a fellow tribune, L. Calpurnius Bestia (allegedly one of the conspirators), prevented him from making a speech from the Rostra and permitted him only to swear the consuls' customary oath that they had observed the laws.

far more unpopular: not according to Cicero himself, who claimed that the people responded to his oath to have saved the Republic and the city by unanimously shouting their agreement (*Fam.* 5.2.7; *Against Piso* 7).

39.1 *Catiline met his death . . . Junius Silanus and Lucius Licinius held office*: see note to 37.30.1. Sallust (*Cat.* 56–61) provides a fuller account of Catiline's defeat and death, which occurred in January 62.

39.2 *Antonius and Metellus Celer . . . preventing him from moving*: the battle in fact took place west of Faesulae, near Pistoria (modern Pistoia) (Sall. *Cat.* 57.1–4). Catiline was aiming to flee across the Apennines en route for Transalpine Gaul, but Metellus Celer (see note to 37.33.4) deployed in the Po valley, probably near Bononia (modern Bologna), to block his descent.

39.4 *Marcus Petreius*: Antonius' legate, with over thirty years' military experience. Sallust does not doubt that it was lameness (presumably gout) which prevented Antonius from taking part.

40.2 *officially required total*: a commander who won a significant victory was customarily hailed *imperator* by his troops, and then sought the Senate's recognition of the title and vote of a *supplicatio*. A minimum number killed for an acclamation (variously reported as 6,000 or 10,000) was in practice not enforced. Antonius was the first commander to be acclaimed for a civil-war victory.

Sacrifices: a *supplicatio* (see note to 37.36.3)

back into their ordinary clothes: instead of *saga* (see note to 37.33.3).

41.1 *allies*: supporters in rural Italy (see note to 37.30.2).

praetors . . . punished them: uprisings among the Paeligni (in central Italy) and in Bruttium (in the southern tip) were suppressed by respectively M. Calpurnius Bibulus and Cicero's brother Quintus, both praetors in 62.

41.2 *Lucius Vettius*: Vettius gave information both about the Paelignian uprising and alleged conspirators at Rome. Caesar counter-attacked successfully when Vettius attempted to incriminate him. Vettius turned informer again in 59 (38.9.2–4).

41.4 *put on trial and condemned*: in early 62 Autronius and five others were convicted under the Plautian law on violence (*vis*) for their involvement with Catiline and went into exile.

42.2 *the consent of the people*: required for capital trials by a law passed by Gaius Gracchus in 123 (see note to 38.14.4).

especially by Metellus Nepos: tetchy letters between Nepos' brother Celer and Cicero (*Fam.* 5.1–2) show that Nepos followed up his attack on 29 December (37.38.2) with an assembly speech on 3 January, to which Cicero responded in the Senate with a speech which he later published. In fragments of this speech Cicero insists that 'it is your act which is under attack, senators', a view which Dio follows here (cf. note to 37.26.2).

42.3 *treated as . . . an enemy*: Dio is our only source for this immunity decree.

43.1 *Pompey . . . with his army*: Nepos' proposal was a law which he attempted to pass through the assembly. A fuller account of the resistance is provided by Plutarch (*Cato* 26–29). Pompey had been summoned back from Spain in 71 to help with suppressing Spartacus' revolt, and Nepos' bill sought to repeat this against Catiline. Nepos had ties with Pompey (see note to 37.38.2) and was seeking to advance his interests, but probably without Pompey's knowledge.

43.2 *told the scribe . . . to desist*: laws were in fact read out by a herald (*praeco*). A similar conflict had occurred over Cornelius' dispensations law in 67 (see note to 36.39.4).

43.3 *changed out of their usual clothes*: adopting mourning dress. Mourners wore a dark toga (*toga pulla*) and sometimes adopted the same dishevelled appearance as a suppliant (cf. 38.14.7, 16.3; 40.46.1). On the use of mourning dress as a political ploy at this period, see A. Dighton, '*Mutatio Vestis*: Clothing and Political Protest in the Late Roman Republic', *Phoenix* 71 (2017), 345–69.

see that it came to no harm: the Senate's 'last decree' (see note to 37.31.2). Only Dio reports its passing now.

43.4 *pamphlet denouncing the Senate*: an assembly speech according to Plutarch (*Cato* 29).

for a single night: such absences were banned for tribunes so that they would be always available to assist members of the plebs. Other sources report a move to deprive Nepos of his office.

44.1 *the completion of the work*: the great temple of Jupiter on the Capitol had been destroyed by fire in 83. The rebuilding had been begun by Sulla, and, after his death, had been entrusted by the Senate to Catulus, who dedicated the rebuilt structure in 69. Caesar had been in bitter conflict with Catulus the previous year (see note to 37.37.2) and started this agitation against him on 1 January 62, the first day of his praetorship (Suet. *Jul.* 15).

44.2 *decree . . . as against Nepos*: the 'last decree' (37.43.3). Caesar in fact gave strong support to Nepos' bill and shared in the Senate's sanctions (so Suetonius and Plutarch, omitted by Dio).

allegiance of the plebs for himself: once again Dio insists that Caesar only supported Pompey for his own advancement, as at 36.43.3–4 and 37.22.1.

44.3 *Marcus Piso*: M. Pupius Piso Frugi. Piso had served continuously as Pompey's legate from 67 to 62.

postponed . . . there for it: Plutarch (*Cato* 30; *Pomp.* 45) says that Cato induced the Senate to reject a request from Pompey for the elections to be postponed to enable him to canvass for Piso in person. This can be reconciled with Dio's statement by supposing that the Senate granted a short postponement to allow Piso to stand, but refused a longer postponement until Pompey's return. However, Piso could easily have returned by July 62, the normal time for the election, and Dio may have misinterpreted Pompey's request.

45.1 *rites . . . segregated from any male presence*: for the Bona Dea, held annually on the night of 4/5 December (see note to 37.35.4). The ceremony was held in Caesar's house as one of the praetors; the location was the Domus Publica, his official residence as Pontifex Maximus. Clodius (see note to 36.14.4) entered office as quaestor the following day. During the rites a male intruder was discovered, disguised as a female lute-player, was identified by women present as Clodius, and then escaped. The allegations that Caesar's wife Pompeia was Clodius' lover and complicit in the intrusion may not have been true. Sources for the incident and Clodius' trial include contemporary letters of Cicero (*Att.* 1.12–16) and Plutarch's accounts (*Caes.* 9–10; *Cic.* 28–29). For discussion, see W. J. Tatum, *The Patrician Tribune: Publius Clodius Pulcher* (Chapel Hill, NC, 1999), 62–86.

45.2 *any suspicion of dishonourable conduct*: Suetonius (*Jul.* 74.2) and Plutarch report Caesar's statement more pithily and show that he made it as a witness at Clodius' trial. Caesar evidently wished to avoid quarrelling with the well-connected Clodius, and (contrary to Dio's implication) did not divorce Pompeia until January 61, after the Senate voted for a trial.

45.3 *called the Fabrician*: the Pons Fabricius, linking the Campus Martius to the Tiber Island. It is the best preserved ancient bridge in Rome, with inscriptions recording its construction by L. Fabricius as commissioner of roads (*curator viarum*). Dio is following traditional practice in Roman annalistic historiography in including minor urban events here and at 37.46.4, 51.4: see Introduction, p. xiv.

46.1 *Marcus Messalla*: M. Valerius Messalla Niger.

brought Clodius to trial: the ex-praetor Q. Cornificius raised the matter in the Senate, probably on 1 January; the Senate referred it to the Vestals and pontiffs who ruled that a religious offence (*nefas*) had been committed; the Senate then attempted to get a tribunal established with specially selected jurors, but Clodius' trial eventually went ahead under a law carried by his supporter, the tribune Q. Fufius Calenus, under which the jurors were selected in the normal way by the lot.

should be repeated: Dio may be wrong here. The Vestals had repeated the rite immediately after Clodius' escape, and this may have been deemed sufficient.

46.2 *sexual relations with his sister*: the three offences listed by Dio were all used against Clodius by the prosecution, but the formal charge was the sacrilege, which was assimilated to *incestum*, the religious offence of violating a Vestal. Lucullus, as a prosecution witness, brought up the mutiny (reported by Dio at 36.14.4) and the alleged incest with his then wife. Allegations of incest were also made against Clodius with his other two sisters, the wives of Marcius Rex and Metellus Celer, but these appear not to have come up at the trial. Here and later (see note to 38.12.1), Dio omits Cicero's appearance as a prosecution witness, exploding Clodius' alibi: this and his associated attacks on Clodius initiated the feud which led in 58 to Cicero's exile.

46.3 *accepted as bribes*: Catulus' jest is reported by Cicero (*Att.* 1.16.5), who had no doubt that bribery determined the outcome. Thirty-one jurors voted for acquittal, twenty-five for conviction.

made the common good his . . . priority: Dio here adopts as his own the view of Catulus' public-spiritedness which he had earlier reported as contemporaries' consensus (36.30.5). Elsewhere he regards Cato as the only man of his time solely devoted to the public interest (37.22.2, 57.3).

46.4 *censors*: an inscribed law enables them to be identified as L. Julius Caesar (consul 64) and C. Scribonius Curio (consul 76)—see C. Nicolet, *Insula Sacra, la loi Gabinia-Calpurnia de Délos (58 av. J.-C.)* (Rome, 1980), 111–25. Unlike their predecessors in 65 and 64 (37.9.3–4), they carried out most of their duties, holding a census and letting tax contracts, and were still in office in June 60. However, for unknown reasons they resigned without completing the census or holding a *lustrum*, the closing ceremony.

exceed the maximum number: often thought to have been 600 after Sulla, but in fact unknown. From Sulla's time, all magistracies from the quaestorship upwards conferred membership of the Senate for life, except for those expelled by censors for moral failings. Fear of expulsion had led to the failure of the censorship of 64, but the present censors avoided trouble by making no expulsions.

whenever the emperor puts on the show: the gladiatorial show in 61 will have been given in honour of a deceased relative (see note to 37.8.1). The lunch-break became standard in the imperial period, when gladiatorial shows were no longer funerary and mainly given by the emperors. It was then common to hold a wild beast hunt (*venatio*) in the morning, followed by the gladiators in the afternoon.

47.1 *Allobroges*: this Gallic people, living between the Rhône and the Isère, had been conquered in 122–121 and formed the most northerly community in the province of Transalpine Gaul, referred to here by Dio, as before (see note to 36.37.2), by its later title of Gallia Narbonensis. They had been restive under earlier governors, and had brought grievances to the Senate in 63 (see note to 37.34.1). Dio appears not to have realized that they were Roman subjects.

Gaius Pomptinus: praetor in 63, and proconsul of Transalpine Gaul 62–59. Dio's is our only detailed account of his campaigns there, which may have extended over more than one year. The places named are not otherwise known.

49.1 *During this time, Pompey arrived in Italy*: a loose synchronism—Pompey reached the vicinity of Rome by late December 62. Dio now continues Pompey's story from where he had left it at 37.23.4.

got Lucius Afranius and Metellus Celer elected consuls: they were elected in or after late July 61 (Cic. *Att.* 1.16.13), taking office on 1 January 60. Both Afranius and Celer had been Pompey's legates (see notes to 36.54.2 and 37.5.4). Pompey is said to have used lavish bribery to get the 'new man' Afranius elected. As a member of the noble Metelli, with many past consulships, Celer did not need Pompey's electoral help and had broken with him before the elections: Pompey had divorced his half-sister Mucia on arrival at Rome (without stating a reason, but allegedly for adultery with Caesar).

49.4 *when they met in Galatia*: 36.46.1–2.

49.5 *as though . . . the acts of a despot*: unlike Lucullus (see note to 36.43.2), Pompey had made his eastern settlement alone, rather than with the customary ten-man senatorial commission.

50.1 *who held the same views*: other opponents of the ratification were Celer's second cousin Metellus Creticus (36.17a–18; Velleius 2.40.5) and perhaps Crassus (App. *BC* 2.9).

given to all Roman citizens as well: i.e. all should be eligible to apply for allotments. Dio is our only source for Flavius amending his law (for the procedure, see note to 40.57.3).

thrown in the prison: the Carcer, at the foot of the Capitoline hill. Tribunes were entitled to take this action in opposition to a magistrate (most recently in 91).

50.2 *tribunes' bench*: the *subsellium*, their distinctive seating.

50.4 *what he wanted to do*: a war scare led to Transalpine Gaul being assigned as a consular province and probably allotted to Celer in March 60, but was over by May. Celer never reached the province, and may have resigned the command in order to remain at Rome, where he died at the end of March 59.

50.6 *regretted having dismissed his legions so soon*: implausible speculation by Dio (see note to 37.20.3). Dio again emphasizes Pompey's failure to avoid 'jealousy' (see note to 36.24.6).

51.1 *on account of the leading men*: a phrase like 'his hatred of' may be missing from our text before 'the leading men'. Dio had attributed Clodius' prosecution to the 'leading men' (37.46.1). Clodius returned to Rome this year after serving as quaestor in Sicily.

did not do as he wanted: Clodius was in fact supported by the tribune C. Herennius, whose attempts to get a law passed transferring him to the plebs were frustrated by vetoes (Cic. *Att.* 1.18.4–5, 19.5). The law cannot have been intended to make patricians eligible for the tribunate, as Dio claims.

transferred to plebeian status: probably by having himself adopted by a plebeian.

51.2 *made sure that he was not elected*: by declaring (with the Senate's support) that Clodius was still a patrician and so ineligible for the tribunate. Metellus Celer may have been Clodius' half-brother and married to his half-sister (cf. Tatum, *Patrician Tribune*, 34–6).

lex curiata: a law passed by the *comitia curiata* (see Glossary, p. 283), a requirement for *adrogatio*, the adoption procedure for an adult who, like Clodius, had no surviving direct male ancestors. Clodius' adoption was approved by this method in 59 (see note to 38.12.2).

51.3 *customs duties*: *portoria*, charged on imports and exports at Italian harbours, and collected by contractors (*publicani*). Cicero claimed that it was the oppressive conduct of the collectors which made the duties unpopular (*QF* 1.1.33). Pompey's new revenues made their abolition possible.

senators . . . annoyed with . . . Metellus Nepos: because of his conduct as tribune in 62 (37.42–44), and perhaps also over his introduction of this law, which the Senate may have intended for another magistrate.

51.4 *at the same time*: i.e. in the same year.

gladiatorial contests in honour of his father: cf. note to 37.8.1. Faustus Cornelius Sulla inherited the dictator's wealth and served under Pompey in the East, but his career was to be cut short by the civil war.

52.1 *Lusitania after his praetorship*: Caesar arrived in his province of Hispania Ulterior (Further Spain) in spring 61 and immediately embarked on his campaign; he returned to Rome in early summer 60. Dio has delayed his account until this point in order to lead straight on from it to Caesar's election to the consulship and alliance with Pompey and Crassus. The province extended north from the settled region of the Guadalquivir Valley to the still not fully pacified Lusitani between the rivers Tagus and Douro. Beyond the Douro lay the Callaeci, so far attacked only by D. Junius Brutus *c.*135. Augustus later divided Ulterior into Lusitania and Baetica, and, as usual, Dio uses the provincial name current in his own day.

52.2 *do extraordinary things*: Dio had previously stressed Caesar's ambition and desire for the people's favour (36.43.3–4; 37.22.1, 37.3, 44.3), and now introduces his wider aspirations, anachronistically reporting the Gades incidents from Caesar's quaestorship and the horse portent (see note to 37.54.2) to build the case. Dio focuses exclusively on Caesar's military activity in Spain, of which he gives the only detailed account. Other sources report his creditors' attempt to delay his departure for the province and his civil administration there. See further J. Osgood, 'Caesar and Spanish Triumph-Hunting', in C. H. Lange and F. J. Vervaet (eds.), *The Roman Republican Triumph beyond the Spectacle* (Rome, 2014), 149–62.

Gades . . . quaestor at the time: Gades (modern Cadiz), founded by the Phoenicians, had been a favoured ally of Rome since 206. Caesar had served as quaestor in Hispania Ulterior in 69–68.

hold great power: according to Suetonius (*Jul.* 7), the diviners interpreted the dream to mean that Caesar would rule the world, since the earth was parent of all. Dio later (41.24.2) explains Caesar's grant of citizenship to Gades in 49 as in return for the dream 'from which he drew hope of monarchy'.

no great achievement to his name: 'at the age by which Alexander had already conquered the world' (Suetonius). Suetonius gives the same date and context as Dio for Caesar's regretful comparison with Alexander, but Plutarch (*Caes.* 11) says that it occurred during Caesar's governorship in Spain and was a response to reading a history of Alexander.

52.3 *Herminian Mountains*: usually identified with the Serra da Estrela, Portugal's highest mountain range, rising to 1,993 m.

excuse to make war on them: cf. 38.34, interpreting the campaign against Ariovistus as driven just by Caesar's personal ambition. Here, however, Dio is unfair: as he admits, raiding was an endemic problem in the region, and moving mountain-dwellers to plains was an established Roman practice. Caesar's campaign appears to have had lasting effect: no later warfare is recorded against Lusitani.

53.3 *Scaevius . . . swam to safety*: Valerius Maximus (3.2.23) and Plutarch (*Caes.* 16), mislocate Scaevius' feat to Britain. Dio misses out the punchline: after escaping, Scaevius asked Caesar's pardon for losing his shield.

53.4 *Brigantium . . . subjugated*: Brigantium was on the north coast of modern Galicia, at either A Coruña or nearby Betanzos. Caesar's long and risky voyage there from south of the Douro, rounding Cape Finisterre, was a grandiose demonstration, the first Atlantic expedition by a Roman force.

54.1 *impossible . . . beforehand*: Caesar arrived near Rome in June 60, after the election date had been announced. As a proconsul, he would lose his *imperium* (see Glossary, pp. 284–5) and so his right to triumph if he crossed the *pomerium*, the sacred boundary of the city, before holding his triumph. He therefore asked the Senate for a dispensation from the legal requirement that those standing for election had to present their candidacy within the city. (This requirement may have been introduced only in 63 or 62, but personal candidature within the city had been normal practice long before.) The Senate may already have approved Caesar's request for a triumph (44.41.3; App. *BC* 2.8), but there would not have been time before the candidacy deadline for the necessary law to extend his *imperium* for the day of the triumph.

54.2 *Cato's opposition*: Cato used a filibuster to prevent the Senate reaching a decision (Plut. *Caes.* 13; *Cato* 31), the first attested of his many resorts to this tactic.

refused any other rider: Suetonius (*Jul.* 61) tells us that the *haruspices* interpreted the human appearance of the horse's feet as portending world rule for Caesar and that Caesar set up a statue of the horse in front of the temple of Venus Genetrix, which he dedicated in 46. The horse was probably born later, but transferred here by Dio as part of his cumulative portrayal of Caesar's grand ambitions.

54.3 *elected consul . . . unanimously*: senatorial conservatives got M. Calpurnius Bibulus, Cato's son-in-law and Caesar's enemy (see note to 37.8.1), elected as his colleague, with L. Lucceius, who had combined with Caesar, being defeated. Both Caesar's and Bibulus' campaigns are said to have used heavy bribery (Suet. *Jul.* 19.1).

55.1 *reconciled . . . the most influential men in Rome*: the common modern description of this grouping as the 'First Triumvirate' is misleading, since the triumvirate assumed by Antony, Octavian, and Lepidus in 43 was a formal magistracy, whereas Caesar, Pompey, and Crassus formed just an informal alliance, primarily to support Caesar in his consulship. According to Plutarch (*Caes.* 13; *Crass.* 14; *Pomp.* 47) and Appian (*BC* 2.9), the alliance was initially formed to support Caesar's election, but more probably Pompey and Crassus supported his candidacy independently and Caesar reconciled them as allies after his election, as Suetonius (*Jul.* 19) and Dio imply. Velleius (2.44.2–3) and Plutarch give similar accounts of the allies' motives, elaborated by Dio at much greater length, further developing his portrayal of Caesar's cunning and ambition (cf. 36.43.3; 37.22.1, 37.3, 44.2, 52.1).

56.3 *not . . . as strong as he had hoped*: cf. 37.50.6.

56.4 *Crassus*: M. Licinius Crassus, of a prominent noble family and hugely wealthy, had supported Sulla in his civil war, crushed Spartacus' slave revolt in 72–71, and shared the consulship with Pompey in 70. He had been on poor terms with Pompey since 71, when Pompey, by dealing with stragglers on his way back from Spain, had taken some of the glory of Spartacus' defeat. Dio will have covered Crassus' activity in 72–70 in the lost part of his history, but since then has mentioned him only in connection with Catiline's conspiracy (37.31.1, 35.1–2), and now offers a highly schematic analysis of his motivation. (Crassus is not named in Dio's reference to his censorship in 65: see note to 37.9.3.) Crassus had been close to Caesar, allegedly standing surety for his debts in 62 (Plut. *Caes.* 11; *Crass.* 7).

57.1 *get done under the current circumstances*: according to Suetonius (*Jul.* 19.2), the agreement was that 'nothing should be done in the state which displeased any of the three'.

57.3 *without any consideration of private gain*: cf. 37.22.2.

58.2 *because of these men*: contemporaries came to regard Caesar's compact with Pompey and Crassus as the cause of the ensuing civil war. Dio, a keen believer in portents (see Introduction, p. xv), interprets the storm damage as pointing to this outcome, and so uses it for a fitting conclusion to the book.

58.3 *wooden bridge . . . destroyed*: the Pons Sublicius, Rome's oldest bridge, reputedly constructed by King Ancus Marcius. It was frequently destroyed by floods, but always repaired.

58.4 *theatre*: until the construction of Pompey's theatre (see note to 39.38.1), plays were put on at the games in temporary wooden theatres.

BOOK THIRTY-EIGHT

1.1 *win them over to him even more*: Dio has portrayed Caesar as consistently seeking to win the devotion of the common people for himself (36.43.3; 37.22.1, 37.2–38.1, 44.2), and now represents Caesar's agrarian laws as completing the process (38.2.3, 7.4). He accordingly gives the first law extended coverage (38.1.2–7.2), including both reported speech and brief direct speech. Dio's more selective treatment of the rest of Caesar's consulship (38.7.3–12.7) is organized thematically with some chronological dislocation, especially at 38.9–10, where the focus switches to Cicero, initiating the account of his fall which continues up to 38.30. The inferior accounts of Plutarch and Appian have much more chronological confusion. Vivid political information is provided by surviving letters from Cicero to Atticus, written between April and September 59. For recent discussions, see S. Chrissanthos, *The Year of Julius and Caesar: 59 BC and the Transformation of the Roman Republic* (Baltimore, 2019); Morstein-Marx, *Julius Caesar*, 116–91; D. Rafferty, 'Caesar's First Consulship and Rome's Democratic Decay', *Klio* 104 (2022), 619–55.

1.2 *fault . . . the law*: previous agrarian laws had all been proposed by tribunes, and unsuccessful attempts had been made by Rullus in 63 and (with Pompey's support) Flavius in 60 (see notes to 37.25.4 and 50.1–4). Consuls normally legislated only on the authority of the Senate, and Caesar now began by seeking its approval. The law was on the same broad lines as Rullus' and Flavius' bills, but omitted some of their most contentious features. Existing public land was to be distributed except in Campania, and additional land for distribution was to be obtained by voluntary purchase using Pompey's profits. The allotments were envisaged as not only settling Pompey's veterans, but also meeting the generally agreed need to reduce the city population. Dio reports Caesar's arguments at length and sympathetically.

1.3 *gain both honour and power*: as land commissioners.

1.4 *the Campanian land*: the *ager Campanus*, the former territory of the city of Capua, confiscated after the crushing of its revolt to Hannibal in 211, and subsequently worked by tenant farmers. Caesar's second agrarian law provided for its distribution (38.7.3).

1.5 *additional tribute and imposts*: the direct and indirect taxes from Pompey's new provinces.

1.7 *please Pompey, Crassus and the rest*: Pompey and Crassus were both elected to the land commission. Caesar's stipulations about the commission countered criticisms such as Cicero had made about the commission to be created under Rullus' bill (*On the Agrarian Law* 2.15–24).

2.3 *no one voiced any objections*: unlikely. Objections were surely raised, e.g. to the distribution of existing public land. Caesar's backers must have supported the law in the Senate debate.

3.1 *lacked authority . . . in this respect*: an oddly negative assessment of Cato (contrast 37.22.1–3, 57.2–3).

3.2 *the prison*: the Carcer (see note to 37.50.1). Other sources show that Caesar's action was provoked by Cato's filibustering to prevent a vote (cf. note to 37.54.2). The occasion is variously reported, but Dio must be right to locate it in the Senate's debate over the first agrarian law.

Marcus Petreius: see note to 37.39.4. He governed Further Spain as Pompey's legate from 55 and fought on the Pompeian side in the civil war. His objection now may have been to Cato's imprisonment rather than the law itself.

4.2 *the popular assembly*: a magistrate holding a public meeting (*contio*) could summon anyone he wished for interrogation. Caesar must have summoned Bibulus now for intimidatory effect rather than, as Dio supposes, in the hope that he would concede (cf. 36.30.4–5).

4.3 *Bibulus*: Dio normally gives the names of both consuls when mentioning their election and/or entry into office, but he emphasizes Caesar's dominance by not naming Bibulus as his colleague in the consulship until this point.

5.1 *also with Metellus*: a law, probably passed by a tribune Plotius in 70, had provided for land to be purchased and distributed to the veterans of the war waged in Spain against Sertorius by Pompey and Metellus Pius, but had not been implemented on the ground of shortage of funds.

5.4 *will take up my shield*: 'sword and shield' according to Plutarch (*Caes.* 14; *Pomp.* 47).

5.5 *not yet public knowledge*: the passage is oddly worded, since the reconciliation was just between Pompey and Crassus, and Caesar had throughout been on good terms with them both. By now, the agreement between the three may have been common knowledge.

6.1 *three tribunes*: Q. Ancharius, Cn. Domitius Calvinus, and C. Fannius.

blocked the passage of the law: Suetonius (*Jul.* 20.1) says that Bibulus attempted to block the law by obnuntiating. Any magistrate was entitled to 'watch the sky' for unfavourable auspices before an assembly vote. *Obnuntiatio* is usually held to be an announcement that an unfavourable auspice had been observed, but it may have been enough to announce that the sky was being watched. See further 38.13.3–6; L. G. Driediger-Murphy, *Roman Republican Augury* (Oxford, 2019), 127–60.

festal days . . . meeting in assembly: assemblies could only be held on days specified in the calendar as *comitiales*, and not on these if they coincided with *feriae*. *Feriae* were holidays held for various religious observances, and, although many were on fixed dates, some were moveable and scheduled each year by magistrates' proclamations. Some scholars dismiss Dio's report as a misunderstanding of obnuntiation, but Bibulus may have used both blocking devices.

6.2 *the Dioscuri*: the brothers Castor and Pollux. Their temple, in the southeast corner of the Forum, was usually known as the temple of Castor (37.8.2). The front of the temple podium, with stairs on each side, was regularly used as a speakers' platform and for voting on laws.

6.3 *beaten up and injured*: the violence prevented the tribunes from vetoing the law. Bibulus was also accompanied by Cato and Lucullus. On arrival he had excrement poured over him.

6.4 *the bill was passed into law*: by late January or February 59.

annulled in the Senate: as for Manilius' freedmen law in 66 (see note to 36.42.3).

6.5 *Bibulus . . . stayed at home*: for eight months according to Plutarch (*Pomp.* 48), but this is too short, unless Bibulus only withdrew after the passage of the Campanian land law (38.7.3), as some scholars suppose (e.g. Morstein-Marx, *Julius Caesar*, 142–3).

business at such a time: Bibulus may have continued to announce *feriae*, but he mainly relied on sky-watching. Caesar's opponents claimed that all his later laws were invalid because Bibulus had been watching the sky when they were passed. However, against this it could be argued that obnuntiations could only take effect if delivered in person.

6.6 *Publius Vatinius*: Caesar's most active supporter among the tribunes of 59, and a loyal adherent thereafter.

7.1 *introduced earlier, as I said*: in a lost passage, probably in Dio's account of the agrarian law of Saturninus (see note to 37.26.1), passed with violence in 100, which (like Caesar's) had included a clause requiring all senators to swear to observe the law. Similar oath-clauses are found in some late second-century laws known from inscriptions.

Numidicus: Q. Caecilius Metellus Numidicus (consul 109), not a direct ancestor of Metellus Celer, but from the same distinguished family, had been exiled for refusing to swear to Saturninus' agrarian law.

7.2 *not going to do the state any good*: Plutarch (*Cato* 32) claims that Cicero used this argument to persuade Cato to swear to the law. Dio will have found this explanation for the recalcitrants' yielding in his sources, but offers the weakness of human nature as an alternative.

7.3 *three or more children*: the *ager Campanus* (see note to 38.1.4) and the nearby *ager Stellas* were distributed by a second law passed in May 59. The three-child requirement shows that this distribution was not targeted at veterans. Other secondary sources confirm this requirement and assert that 20,000 allotments were made under the law, perhaps too high a figure.

Roman colony: those receiving allotments under the first law were mostly settled individually, but under the second law Capua was refounded as a colony, as had been abortively attempted in 83 and under Rullus' law in 63.

7.4 *tax-farming . . . Cato*: tax-collection methods varied between provinces. Contracts for collecting the taxes of the province of Asia were auctioned at Rome to public contractors (*publicani*), who were leading *equites*. In November 61 the successful company, which had overbid, asked the Senate to cancel their contract, with support from Crassus and Cicero, but over the following months Cato prevented this being approved. Caesar's law remitting a third of the contracted payment, passed by April 59, rewarded Crassus for his support and won him equestrian favour, but in July *equites* showed hostility at the theatre.

7.5 *ratified . . . Pompey's measures*: his eastern settlement. For the earlier opposition, see 37.49.2–50.1.

7.6 *lex Julia*: Roman laws were known by the proposer's *nomen* (the name of his *gens*, see Glossary, p. 284).

very many of these laws: only two laws not mentioned by Dio are known to have been passed by Caesar as consul, one recognizing Ptolemy XII as king of Egypt (see note to 39.12.1), and the other reforming the procedure of the court for *repetundae* (extortion). As praetor in 54, Cato was president of that court and so acting under Caesar's law, although refusing to cite it by name.

8.1 *order as a whole felt*: under the *lex Aurelia* of 70 BCE, criminal juries were composed equally of senators, *equites*, and *tribuni aerarii* (see Glossary, p. 287). Calenus' law prescribed that each division should cast their ballots in a separate urn with the totals for conviction and acquittal put on public record. Calenus was a supporter of Caesar in 59 and subsequently. As tribune in 61, Calenus had been responsible for the composition of Clodius' jury (see notes to 37.46.1–3), and the scandal over Clodius' acquittal may have prompted him to this legislation.

8.5 *Illyricum and Cisalpine Gaul . . . for five years*: by a law passed by Vatinius (see note to 38.6.6), which created an extraordinary command like those Pompey had been given in 67 and 66. Illyricum at this date denoted the north-east coast of the Adriatic. Caesar may originally have planned to campaign in Illyricum, to which the Dacian king Burebista posed a potential threat.

Transalpine Gaul and another legion: if the *lex Vatinia* was passed in March, this additional assignment (proposed by Pompey in the Senate) may have followed the death at the end of the month of Metellus Celer, who had probably been assigned the province, but had not yet set out. However, Celer may have resigned the province in 60 (see note to 37.50.4), and some scholars date the *lex Vatinia* to May or early June.

9.1 *Aulus Gabinius*: for Gabinius' close ties with Pompey, see note to 36.23.4.

married Piso's daughter: Cicero learnt of Pompey's marriage to Julia around the beginning of May (*Att.* 2.17.1), and Caesar's marriage to Calpurnia, daughter of L. Calpurnius Piso, probably followed soon after. Julia had previously been betrothed to a Servilius Caepio. Dio wrongly implies that the marriages followed the consular elections: the latter in fact took place on or after 18 October (*Att.* 2.20.6).

9.4 *Vettius . . . was assassinated*: the Vettius affair took place around August 59. Cicero gave Atticus the following account at the time (*Att.* 2.24.2–3). Vettius, earlier an informer against Catilinarians (37.41.2), tried to get the young C. Scribonius Curio, who had been agitating against Caesar and his associates, to conspire to kill Pompey. Curio told his same-named father (consul in 76), who told Pompey. Vettius was called before the Senate, where he denounced Curio, other young nobles, and Bibulus as complicit in the plot, although Bibulus had warned Pompey of an earlier threat. Vettius was then put in chains, but the next day Caesar and Vatinius called him before a public meeting, at which he made different denunciations, including against Lucullus and (without naming him) Cicero. Subsequently Vettius was murdered in prison. Whether, as Cicero believed, Caesar was behind Vettius' initial attempt to frame Curio and his associates, or who else (if anyone) was behind him, remains unknown. Other sources give varying versions, but only Dio holds that the murder plot was genuine. His claim that Cicero and Lucullus were behind it is absurd, and he is also wrong in dating the episode before the events leading up to Clodius' election to the tribunate.

10.1 *Antonius . . . paid back*: Roman governors had been intermittently active beyond the northern frontiers of Macedonia since its establishment as a province in 146, and major advances were made in 76–72, when both C. Scribonius Curio and his successor M. Terentius Varro Lucullus reached the Danube. Curio operated in the north-west, defeating the Dardani, who dwelt in and beyond the upper valley of the river Axius (modern Vardar). Lucullus' successes in the north-east included securing the submission of the Greek cities on the west coast of the Black Sea, from Apollonia up to Istria, just south of the Danube delta. As governor from 62 to 60, Antonius campaigned unsuccessfully in both these regions: Dio provides our fullest account. By 'subject' and 'allied' Dio refers respectively to taxpaying provincials and nominally independent allied states, but the terms are misapplied here: the Dardani had not yet been brought under secure Roman control, and Antonius' eastern campaign was probably not against Istria and other Greek cities, but against the inhabitants of their hinterland (the modern Dobrudja). Moesia was the name of the region south of the lower Danube in Dio's day, organized as a province in the early empire and split into two provinces under Domitian.

10.3 *Bastarnae . . . had come to help them*: from their home north of the lower Danube.

not named in the charge: Antonius' trial took place in March or early April 59. The formal charge was probably *repetundae* (extortion), but other evidence shows that the chief prosecutor, M. Caelius Rufus, also exploited both Antonius' military incompetence and his connections with Catiline. Dio, wrongly believing in Antonius' complicity in the conspiracy (see note to 37.30.3), errs now in making it the formal charge.

10.4 *insult him*: Cicero's relations with Antonius had become strained, but he felt obliged to defend him as his consular colleague and for his part in suppressing Catiline. Cicero later claimed that in his speech he had merely made some complaints about the political situation which seemed relevant to the case, but these had been misreported (*On His House* 41).

11.1 *did not respond abusively . . . in anything he did*: at 11.1–6 Dio digresses to credit Caesar with what he appears to regard as wise policy for a leader against his opponents. Dio later, like others, applauds Caesar's clemency as a civil-war victor (e.g. 41.63 and 44.45–47), but he repeats the present passage's description of his patient and covert punishment of his enemies at 43.13.2.

12.1 *recruited him to deal with Cicero*: Dio's overlooking of Cicero's role at Clodius' trial (see note to 37.46.2) leads him to misinterpret Clodius as acting merely as the agent of Caesar and his allies (so also 38.14.3, 15.1). Clodius sought the tribunate both to avenge himself on Cicero and to further his own ambitions, and acted independently both before and during his tribunate. By enabling Clodius to become a plebeian, Caesar and Pompey probably intended no more than to keep Cicero in check.

12.2 *transferred Clodius to plebeian status again*: by adoption by a (much younger) plebeian, P. Fonteius, enacted by a law passed by the *comitia curiata* (see notes to 37.51.2 and 39.11.2). Caesar convened the meeting as consul and gave his approval as Pontifex Maximus, while Pompey assisted as augur. According to Cicero (*On His House* 41), the law was passed just three hours after his critical remarks at Antonius' trial.

elected tribune: in July or August. Clodius would not have needed Caesar's help to get elected.

12.3 *silenced Bibulus*: Clodius, having entered office on 10 December 59, restricted Bibulus to the customary oath to have observed the laws, as tribunes had done to Cicero in 63 (see note to 37.38.2).

12.4 *stood very high in their estimation*: Cicero (himself of equestrian origin) had strong support from the *equites* and always promoted their interests, but, although he had close connections with many individual senators, his relationship with the great noble families was uneasy.

more on fear than on goodwill: Dio's assessment here (38.12.4–7) is one of the most negative passages in his portrait of Cicero, drawing on the anti-Ciceronian tradition and with some similarities with Plutarch's criticisms (see Introduction, p. xxv). Some of its themes have been touched on earlier (37.33.1, 35.4, 38.2).

12.5 *advocates . . . debt*: Dio overlooks that advocates were prohibited from taking a fee by the *lex Cincia* of 204 BCE. Cicero sometimes profited indirectly from his advocacy, e.g. through loans or inheritances.

12.6 *intemperate and immoderate frankness*: Dio regards 'frankness' (*parrhesia*) in other contexts as admirable (e.g. 37.22.3), but in this excessive form as one of Cicero's chief weaknesses (cf. 38.10.4, 20.3, 29.1; 46.9.4, 29.1). See further C. Mallan, 'Parrhēsia in Cassius Dio', in C. H. Lange and J. M. Madsen (eds), *Cassius Dio: Greek Intellectual and Roman Politician* (Leiden, 2016), 258–75.

12.7 *obnoxious and repugnant*: the same Greek words are used in criticism of Cicero by Plutarch (*Cic.* 24), on whom Dio may be drawing (F. Millar, *A Study of Cassius Dio* (Oxford, 1964), 49).

13.1 *grain . . . doled out to the poor*: the four laws reported at 38.13.1–6 were all promulgated by Clodius when he entered office and were passed at an assembly on 4 January 58. The laws established Clodius as a champion of the plebs, and should not be interpreted (as by Dio) merely as preparation for his attack on Cicero. For discussion, see Tatum, *Patrician Tribune*, 114–38. A monthly sale of grain at a cheap price to Roman citizens resident in Rome had been instituted by Gaius Gracchus in 123, suspended by Sulla in 81, and gradually reinstated in 73 and by Cato as tribune in 62. Clodius' law made the distribution free for the first time (Dio's 'again' is an error, unless the word is corrupt).

13.2 *collegia . . . suppressed some years previously*: *collegia* were urban religious and social associations, mostly based on trades and/or localities. In response to their involvement in political violence from 67 on, the Senate in 64 had banned some *collegia* in the city of Rome (not all, as Dio implies). Clodius' law lifted this ban and permitted the formation of new *collegia*. Cicero claimed that Clodius organized the new *collegia* for political gang violence.

found guilty by them both: censors could impose various status penalties on those they deemed to have committed moral offences, including exclusion from the Senate or the *equites*. Under Clodius' law they could only impose such sanctions after holding a judicial hearing and perhaps after others had launched accusations. Clodius probably justified the law as protection against arbitrary penalization, particularly for radical tribunes and their supporters. Hearings under the law were held by the censors of 55, but it was repealed in 52 (40.57.1–3).

13.3 *to seduce them*: i.e. the Senate, *equites*, and people (38.12.4, 13.1). Dio interprets Clodius, like Caesar (38.1.1–7.4), as using legislation to win over the various orders of Roman society to support his further aims. The grain and *collegia* laws won Clodius the devotion of the urban plebs, but the measure on the censorship is unlikely to have brought him significant elite support.

Observing the heavens . . . public divination: Dio here expands on an account of the auspices in a lost passage from his early books. Through the auspices Jupiter was deemed to show whether a course of action would have a favourable outcome. Magistrates took auspices before many public acts, in Rome by watching the sky for thunder and lightning and observing the flight of birds and on campaign by observing whether kept chickens fed. Besides these specially sought ('impetrative') auspices, both these and other signs could be casually met with ('oblative' auspices).

13.4 *auspicious or inauspicious*: thunder or lightning on the observer's left was a favourable auspice for other actions, but any thunder or lightning prevented the holding of a voting assembly.

13.5 *any measure that day*: for such obstructing announcements (*obnuntiationes*), see note to 38.6.1. Here, as there, Dio overlooks Bibulus' use of this device in 59.

13.6 *when the people had to cast a vote*: by this law Clodius made modifications to assembly procedures, previously regulated by two second-century laws (*lex Aelia*, *lex Fufia*), in order to restrict the use of the delaying tactics deployed by Bibulus in 59. The precise terms of the law are disputed. Both obnuntiation and the declaration of additional *feriae* continued to be used to block assembly votes.

14.2 *secured . . . all his proposals*: Clodius' pact with Cicero is mentioned only by Dio and may not be historical. Cicero later regretted not opposing at least the *collegia* law (*Att.* 3.15.4), but at the time he may have judged that opposition would be futile.

14.4 *found guilty by the people*: other sources describe the law as directed against anyone who had put a Roman citizen to death without trial, and Velleius (2.45.1) specifies the penalty as interdiction from fire and water. The law reaffirmed and strengthened Gaius Gracchus' law of 123 prohibiting a Roman citizen being tried for a capital penalty unless by order of the people.

14.5 *applied to the Senate as a whole*: cf. Dio's similar interpretation of Rabirius' trial and Metellus Nepos' action against Cicero in 63 (37.26.1–2, 42.2).

put to death . . . with him: for the Senate's 'last decree' against Catiline and vote for the execution of Lentulus and his associates, see 37.31.2, 35.4–36.3. Dio is our only source to link the 'last decree' to the executions.

14.7 *opposed Clodius in various ways*: further details are given by Cicero himself in speeches after his return from exile (esp. *For Sestius* 15–54) and by Plutarch (*Cic.* 30–31). Cicero later regretted opposing the law (*Att.* 3.15.5).

dressed as an eques: a defendant in a trial and his close connections customarily appealed for the jury's pity by appearing dishevelled and with dirtied clothes (*sordidatus*), and, although not on trial, Cicero now did the same. Dio mentions only one aspect of his dress change, his switch from the broad-striped senatorial tunic to the narrow-striped tunic of an *eques* (cf. 40.46.1 and 56.31.2).

15.1 *scheme . . . impenetrable by him*: the alleged trick practised on Cicero by Caesar and Pompey is implausible and perhaps Dio's own invention. Cicero's letters show that Caesar's offer of a legateship was in fact made in summer 59, when Pompey also gave him his guarantee that Clodius would not attack him (*Att.* 2.19–24). Although Clodius in 58 claimed to have their backing for his attack on Cicero, their failure to support him was more probably due to reluctance to resist Clodius on the issue.

15.6 *once had a family connection with Pompey*: through Mucia, divorced by Pompey in 62 (see note to 37.41.1).

served with him . . . for a long time: probably in the pirate campaign.

Gabinius . . . Piso . . . with Caesar: for Gabinius' ties with Pompey and Piso's with Caesar, see notes to 36.23.4 and 38.9.1. Dio fails to mention that Clodius secured their compliance against Cicero with a law assigning their provinces (Macedonia for Piso; Cilicia, later changed to Syria, for Gabinius).

16.1 *confident*: writing to his brother in December 59, Cicero was still confident that he could defeat any attack by Clodius (*QF* 1.2.16).

16.2 *the equites met on the Capitol*: accompanied by many others, all having changed to dirtied clothes in solidarity with Cicero.

Hortensius and . . . Curio: only Dio mentions their role in the delegation. The orator Hortensius had long been a conservative leader in the senate. C. Scribonius Curio (consul 76) had taken a less consistent stance, but had been opposed to Caesar and his associates since 59.

16.3 *many senators did likewise*: according to Cicero (*Sest.* 26–27, etc.), a packed Senate passed a decree that they should change to dirtied clothes.

16.4 *expelled one . . . from the city*: L. Aelius Lamia. Gabinius 'relegated' Lamia 200 miles from the city, a sanction rarely used against citizens under the Republic.

17.1 *outside the city walls . . . for his command*: Cicero's evidence (*Sest.* 33, etc.) shows that Gabinius, Piso, and Caesar all spoke at the same meeting (*contio*), held in the Circus Flaminius, a large open space west of the city, just outside the *pomerium*, the city boundary. Once a proconsul had left the city for his command, he could not re-enter it without losing his *imperium* (see note to 36.54.1).

17.2 *vote for keeping the conspirators alive*: 37.36.1–2.

17.3 *away from Rome*: Cicero's supporters appealed unsuccessfully to Pompey at his villa in the Alban Hills (near modern Albano Laziale). Plutarch implausibly claims that Cicero went there himself, but Pompey slipped out by another door.

17.5 *Minerva . . . the Guardian*: Jupiter shared his great temple on the Capitol with Juno and Minerva. Cicero dedicated this statuette, which had previously stood in his house, there with the title *custos urbis* ('Guardian of the City'). It was shattered in a storm in 43, in Dio's view a portent of his death later that year (45.17.3).

their protector: having earlier served in Sicily as quaestor, Cicero had successfully prosecuted its corrupt governor Verres in 70, so establishing himself as the Sicilians' patron.

> *reception . . . the governor*: Cicero did not reach Sicily, as Dio implies. The governor, his former friend C. Vergilius, forbade him entry, and Cicero accordingly went straight from southern Italy to Macedonia.

17.6 *passed into law*: in mid-March, on the same day as Cicero's departure from Rome.

> *demolished . . . temple to Liberty*: the prestigious house, next door to Clodius', on the northern slopes of the Palatine, which Cicero had borrowed heavily to buy in 62, was plundered and burned immediately after his withdrawal. Clodius later dedicated a shrine to Libertas on part of the site. For Cicero's later recovery of his house, see 39.11.

17.7 *punished with exile*: after Cicero's withdrawal, Clodius promulgated and (in late April) carried a second law explicitly directed against Cicero, exiling him and confiscating his property. Dio here summarizes some of its terms.

> *3,750 stades from Rome*: i.e. 500 Roman miles (= 740 km/460 miles). Dio reckoned a Roman mile as equivalent to 7.5 Greek stades. Cicero (*Att.* 3.7.1) and Plutarch show that the exclusion zone was to be reckoned as from Italy, not Rome.

18.1 *lamenting*: Cicero crossed the Adriatic to Dyrrachium and then moved on to Thessalonica, returning to Dyrrachium in November. Numerous letters, especially to Atticus, express his resentment and despair.

> *Philiscus . . . acquaintance from Athens*: Cicero spent six months in Athens in 79 BCE, studying philosophy and rhetoric. Dio's casual reference here suggests that he had mentioned the visit earlier, in his lost books. Philiscus is otherwise unknown and must be Dio's invention. Dio may have chosen the name in compliment to a contemporary Philiscus, who was professor of rhetoric at Athens and visited Rome *c*.213 CE, where he may have met Dio.

> *Philiscus said*: Philiscus' dialogue with Cicero (38.18–29) is Dio's free invention. Consolations for exile were an established literary genre (e.g. Plutarch, *On Exile*; Seneca, *Consolation to Helvia* 1–14), and Philiscus' proofs that exile is no evil are commonplaces from this tradition, deriving from Stoic and Cynic philosophy. On the dialogue's relationship to its narrative context, see Introduction, p. xx.

18.3 *good sense . . . wisdom*: Plato defined four cardinal virtues, which Stoic philosophers later made canonical (see note to 38.22.1). Plato made *sophia* (wisdom) the first virtue, but the Stoics usually substituted *phronesis* (good sense, prudence, sometimes defined as knowledge of what should and should not be done). 'Practised in wisdom' may allude to Cicero's philosophical interests: he studied philosophy intensively in his youth and wrote numerous philosophical treatises in his final years.

18.5 *Hippocrates or Democedes*: Hippocrates of Cos, the most famous of ancient physicians, lived in the later fifth century BCE, but little is certainly known of him. Democedes of Croton practised as a physician in the later sixth

century in various Greek cities and at the Persian court, from which he
escaped back to Croton.

19.1 *dispel this mist from my mind*: the wording echoes Plato's *Alcibiades II*
(150e). This work is now regarded as spurious, but was accepted as Plato's
in Dio's time.

20.3 *eloquence and speeches . . . also caused you to lose them*: alluding not only to
Cicero's stand against sedition (as at 38.22.2), but also to the damage done
by his unrestrained frankness (38.10.4, 12.5–7, 29.1).

22.1 *utmost good sense*: at 38.22.1–5 Philiscus praises Cicero as an exemplar of
the cardinal virtues of good sense (see note to 38.18.3), justice (*dikaio-
syne*), self-control (*sophrosyne*), and (but for a temporary lapse) courage
(*andreia*). Rhetorical handbooks recommended their use as a template in
speeches of praise. On their use by Dio, see K. Welch, 'Cassius Dio and
the Virtuous Roman', in J. Osgood and C. Baron (eds.), *Cassius Dio and
the Late Roman Republic* (Leiden, 2019), 97–128.

23.1 *disgrace*: atimia. Dio sometimes uses this word for 'loss of rights' (Latin
infamia), a lesser penalty than exile or death, imposed for various offences
incurring disrepute (so e.g. 52.7.1 and 56.25.7), but here it refers more
broadly to disgrace (as e.g. 40.45.4).

25.2 *in obedience to the decrees of the Senate*: the 'last decree' and the execution
vote (cf. note to 38.14.5).

25.3 *personal power*: dynasteia (see note to 36.18.1). The reference is to Caesar,
Pompey, and Crassus, held by Dio to be behind Clodius' actions against
Cicero (see note to 38.12.1).

26.3 *Camillus . . . in Ardea*: M. Furius Camillus was reputedly the Roman commander at the capture of Veii in 396, but exiled in 391. He is said to have
spent his exile in the Latin city of Ardea, but then been recalled to save
Rome from the Gauls in 390, followed by many later achievements. Apart
from Solon, all those mentioned in this passage were noted instances of
men obliged to leave their city despite great services.

Scipio . . . in Liternum: P. Cornelius Scipio Africanus defeated Hannibal to
win Rome's second war with Carthage, and in 190 served as legate to his
brother in the war against King Antiochus III. Following their victory,
corruption charges were brought against both brothers. Africanus avoided
trial by withdrawing to his villa in Liternum, on the Campanian coast,
dying there in 183.

Aristides or Themistocles: both were Athenian politicians who suffered
ostracism, by which a citizen against whom sufficient votes were cast had
to leave the city for ten years. Aristides, who was famed for justice, was
ostracized in 482, allegedly through the intriguing of Themistocles, but
recalled against the Persian invasion in 480. Themistocles was ostracized
around 470, and later fled into exile when accused of treason.

Hannibal: accused of intriguing against Rome, Hannibal fled Carthage in
195, taking refuge first with Antiochus, later with King Prusias of Bithynia.

The manuscripts give the name as 'Annius', which must be a corruption for Hannibal.

Solon: introduced reforms and a new law code at Athens, probably in 594, and is said to have then left Athens voluntarily for ten years.

27.3 *Drusus, Scipio, the Gracchi*: M. Livius Drusus was assassinated in 91 when, as tribune, he was attempting to carry a law granting Roman citizenship to the Italian allies. P. Cornelius Scipio Aemilianus destroyed Carthage in 146 and Numantia in 133, but his sudden death in 129, when he was opposing the Gracchan land commission, was widely regarded as an assassination. Tiberius and Gaius Sempronius Gracchus were reforming tribunes who died in the resulting upheavals in respectively 133 and 121.

Capitolinus: M. Manlius Capitolinus was said to have prevented the Gauls from capturing the Capitol in 390, but to have been executed in 385/4 for aspiring to tyranny.

28.1 *Xenophon and Thucydides did*: Thucydides, the historian of the Peloponnesian War, and his continuator Xenophon were both exiled from Athens and had estates elsewhere (Thucydides in Thrace and Xenophon at Scillus in Elis), and later writers assumed that they had written their histories there. Dio may have had in mind his own use of his Campanian villa for writing his history (76.2.1), but is also alluding to Cicero's aspirations to write history, later mocked by his anti-Ciceronian speaker Calenus (46.21.4).

28.4 *Corvinus*: M. Valerius Corvus, or Corvinus, was reputed to have held six consulships between 348 and 299.

Marius, seven times consul: see note to 36.31.3.

turned down the one that was given you: for Cicero's first exchanging and later declining his consular province, see notes to 37.33.4. He served reluctantly as proconsul of Cilicia in 51–50.

28.6 *live as I'm advising you*: Philiscus advises Cicero to switch to cultured leisure, a lifestyle recommended particularly by Epicurean philosophy, and always rejected by Cicero, in his writings (e.g. *Republic* 1.1–12) as in his career, in favour of active political involvement.

29.1 *frankness with which you speak*: *parrhesia*, already identified as a key weakness of Cicero at 38.12.6.

29.2 *for some man and woman to abuse*: here Philiscus prophesies Cicero's eventual fate. In late 43 Octavian allied with Antony (against whom he had previously fought in alliance with Cicero and the Senate) and Lepidus, and the three seized power as triumvirs and proscribed their enemies. Cicero was killed on 7 December, and his head and hands were displayed on the Rostra (the speakers' platform) in the Forum. Antony is said to have abused the head, and Dio alone adds that his wife Fulvia did so too, stabbing the tongue with her hairpins (47.8.4).

29.4 *abandon ... friends in favour of ... enemies*: alluding both to Pompey before Cicero's exile and Octavian in 43.

30.1 *responsible for his banishment*: Pompey's change of heart played a key part in Cicero's recall, but Dio exaggerates his responsibility as for the exile. At 30.1–4 Dio summarizes events at Rome down to the end of 58; more details are given in Cicero's speeches and letters and by Asconius (46–7).

Tigranes . . . free: Clodius disrupted Pompey's eastern arrangements by a law relating to Galatia and (in May) by the release of the younger Tigranes (on Clodius' possible motives, see Tatum, *Patrician Tribune*, 168–70). Detained since 66 (36.53), Tigranes was paraded in Pompey's triumph and then kept under house arrest. Flavius, who had acted for Pompey as tribune in 60 (37.50.1–4) and was now a praetor, unsuccessfully tried to recapture Tigranes in a scuffle outside Rome, reported in detail by Asconius 47. Tigranes' subsequent fate is unknown.

30.2 *the consul's fasces*: broken in rioting, as in 67 and 59 (36.39.3 and 38.6.3).

consecrated his property: to Ceres, the goddess of the *plebs*. This ritual act had been deployed by several tribunes against magistrates with whom they were in dispute. Ninnius retaliated by consecrating Clodius' property, but neither consecration took practical effect.

30.3 *powers . . . returned to the tribunes*: see note to 36.23.4.

30.4 *imposed his veto*: on 1 June, on Ninnius' motion, the Senate voted unanimously for Cicero's recall, but the decree was vetoed by Aelius Ligus. For Ninnius' earlier support for Cicero, see 38.14.1–2, 16.3–4.

bring it before the plebs: only Dio says that Ninnius promulgated a law recalling Cicero, perhaps in error.

disputes . . . injuries on both sides: Dio passes over developments later in the year. On 11 August a slave, found with a dagger in the Senate, said that Clodius had sent him to kill Pompey. Pompey then withdrew to his house for the rest of the year, where Clodius' gangs put him under siege. On 29 October eight tribunes promulgated a law recalling Cicero, but nothing came of it. For Cicero's recall in 57, see 39.6–8.

30.5 *before matters had reached this point*: here, at the end of his domestic section, Dio inserts one earlier event. Cato left on his mission in late March or April, shortly after Cicero's departure for exile.

failed to ransom him from the pirates: in 67 (36.17.3). Ptolemy is said to have offered two talents, deemed so paltry by the pirates that they released Clodius for free. Since 80, Cyprus had been ruled by this Ptolemy and Egypt by his brother Ptolemy XII Auletes (see note to 39.12.1).

Cato . . . to administer it: Clodius carried a first law annexing Cyprus and confiscating the royal property, and a second appointing Cato to the task, probably as *pro quaestore pro praetore*. His mission also included restoring exiles in Byzantium. The justification used for the annexation may have been the will of an earlier Ptolemy who had bequeathed his kingdom (Egypt and Cyprus) to the Roman people. After Cato's departure, Cyprus formed a province with Cilicia until 47, when Caesar restored it to Ptolemaic rule. For Cato's mission, see further 39.22; F. K. Drogula, *Cato the Younger* (New York, 2019), 158–69; L. Calvelli, *Il tesoro di Cipro: Clodio, Catone e la Conquista romana dell'isola* (Venice, 2020).

31.1 *in Gaul . . . no one to fight*: Dio devotes the rest of Book 38 to the warfare in Gaul in 58, recounted by Caesar himself in the first book of his *Gallic War*. Caesar's much more detailed account is Dio's main source for the campaigns in Gaul, and, although he makes some use of other sources, many of the divergences are Dio's own: see further Introduction, pp. xii–xiii.

victorious war over the whole country: for Dio's portrayal of Caesar as driven to war by his desire for military glory, see 37.52.1–3; 38.34; Introduction, p. xiii.

31.2 *Helvetii . . . no longer self-sufficient*: the Helvetii were separated from the Germans by the Rhine, from the Sequani by the Jura mountains, and from the Allobroges (see note to 37.47.1) in the Roman province by Lake Leman and the Rhône.

31.3 *set off under . . . Orgetorix*: according to Caesar (*BG* 1.2–4), the ambitious Orgetorix was the original promoter of the migration, but died before it set out.

close to the Alps: Dio's error. The Helvetii aimed to settle in the territory of the Santoni, on the Atlantic coast north of the Gironde estuary. The Allobroges' territory provided an easier route than the Jura crossing for the start of the journey.

bridge: at Geneva. Caesar hastened there from Rome on hearing of the Helvetii's plan.

32.1 *promised response*: Caesar says that he gave the envoys a negative response on the agreed day, 13 April.

32.2 *Sequani and . . . Aedui . . . asked for his help*: according to Caesar, the Sequani gave the Helvetii passage and the Aedui appealed to him. The Aedui occupied most of modern Burgundy and were long-standing allies of Rome.

32.3 *Tolosa*: modern Toulouse, chief settlement of the Tolosates and in the Roman province. Caesar claims (*BG* 1.10.2) that the Helvetii's planned settlement in the territory of the Santoni would have threatened this region, in fact some 200 km (124 miles) south.

when they had joined forces with these peoples: Dio's own conjecture. Caesar does not mention such concerns.

33.2 *a certain town*: Bibracte, chief settlement of the Aedui. Its site has been excavated at Mont-Beuvray, 22 km (14 miles) west of Autun.

33.3 *out of order*: disrupted by the hurling of the Roman throwing spears (*pila*) (*BG* 1.25.2; cf. note to 38.50.1).

33.5 *face the attackers with his heavy infantry*: in fact, just with the rear line of the infantry, while the first two lines continued the pursuit.

33.6 *to their ancient land*: probably referring not to the land they had just left, but to what is now south-west Germany, identified as the original homeland

of the Helvetii by Tacitus (*Germania* 28.2). If so, Dio owes this detail to
a source other than Caesar.

allies . . . wiped them out: according to Caesar, these recalcitrants were
brought back to him and then 'treated as enemies', i.e. executed or enslaved.
The Helvetii surrendered in early July 58. Caesar (*BG* 1.29) cites records
as showing that 368,000 persons took part in the migration, but only
110,000 returned home.

34.1   *Celts*: i.e. Germans. Before Caesar the inhabitants of both modern France
and central Europe were collectively known as Celts by Greek and Gauls
by Roman writers. In Caesar's account the Rhine is treated as a boundary
between Gauls to its west (whom Caesar conquered) and Germans to its
east. The distinction was artificial (there was little ethnic or cultural difference between the peoples on the two banks), but it subsequently
became standard. Dio observes the distinction, calling the peoples on the
west bank Gauls (*Galatai*), but those on the east bank Celts (*Keltoi*) rather
than Germans. This was probably a literary preference, retaining the term
used by classical Greek writers, rather than a political choice marking disapproval of expansion beyond the Rhine (so A. C. Johnston, 'Rewriting
Caesar: Cassius Dio and an Alternative Ethnography of the North', *Histos*
13 (2019), 53–77).

34.2   *holding some of their people hostage*: as Caesar explains (*BG* 1.31–2),
Germans under Ariovistus had crossed the Rhine some years earlier at the
request of the Arverni and Sequani to help them against the Aedui. Many
more Germans had subsequently settled west of the Rhine; the Aedui had
suffered successive defeats, most recently at Magetobriga (probably in
61), and both they and the Sequani had been obliged to give hostages and
pay tribute. After Caesar's victory over the Helvetii, Gallic delegations
begged him to help them against Ariovistus.

34.3   *among the Romans' friends and allies*: as consul in 59, Caesar had secured
a Senate decree recognizing Ariovistus as king and enrolling him as friend
of the Roman people (standard procedure with friendly rulers). Dio
rightly regards this recent grant, made after Ariovistus had established
his dominance over the Aedui and Sequani, as a flaw in Caesar's case
against him.

not . . . the aggressor: Caesar (*BG* 1.33–36) claims to have been obliged to
act against Ariovistus from loyalty to the Aedui and to avert a potential
threat to the Roman province and to Italy, and portrays Ariovistus'
responses to his envoys as an arrogant breach of the recently granted friendship. Dio
summarizes the exchanges, but explains Caesar's actions as driven solely
by his self-interested quest for glory.

34.4   *sent for him*: here and at 38.42.2 Dio implies that Caesar was summoning
Ariovistus to come to him. According to Caesar (*BG* 1.34.1), his envoys
requested Ariovistus to choose a middle ground for their meeting.

should do the travelling: Dio adds liveliness by turning Caesar's indirect-
speech report of Ariovistus' response into direct speech.

34.6 *Vesontio*: modern Besançon. Caesar advanced there up the valley of the Doubs.

35.1 *among Caesar's soldiers*: according to Caesar (*BG* 1.39), the panic started with the inexperienced junior officers, and then spread to the more senior officers and the troops. Dio attributes it to the soldiers, not the officers.

35.2 *did not change his mind*: of the various fears listed here, only the Germans' large bodies and courage are mentioned by Caesar. Scholars differ as to whether the others are Dio's own conjecture or drawn from another source.

35.3 *senior and junior officers*: i.e. Caesar's quaestor, senatorial legates, and equestrian officers (military tribunes and cavalry prefects), as is confirmed by 38.36.4. These officers normally formed a Roman commander's council. On this occasion Caesar included the centurions as well (*BG* 1.40.1), but Dio omits them. Dio adds his own explanation for Caesar's not addressing the whole army.

spoke . . . along the following lines: on this speech's significance, its relationship to Caesar's own version (*BG* 1.40), and its debt to Demosthenes and Thucydides, see Introduction, pp. xx–xxi.

36.2 *quickly be overthrown*: both this sentence and 1.36.8 echo passages in the last address to the Athenians by their leader Pericles (Thucydides 2.60.2–3, 63.3).

36.3 *laws . . . as long as mortal creatures exist*: echoing the Athenian ambassadors' words to the Melians, asserting as a natural law that all mankind rule where they can (Thucydides 5.105.2).

37.4 *misfortune with passive inactivity*: in 38.37.3–4 Dio draws heavily on the Corinthian speakers' characterization of the Athenians at Thucydides 1.70.

37.5 *peoples who came against them*: the three-stage account of Roman expansion in 38.37.5–38.4 echoes Pericles' celebration of the successive extensions of Athenian power by their ancestors, their fathers, and his hearers themselves, in his speech at the funeral of their war dead in 431 (Thucydides 2.36). At 38.37.5 Dio lists peoples of central and southern Italy conquered in the early centuries of the Republic, and mainly in 343–265, in wars recounted in his lost first ten books. However, Roman control was not extended to the foot of the Alps until the early second century. The Opici were supposed early inhabitants of Campania (cf. Zonaras 7.12), sometimes identified with the Oscans. The reference to the repulse of foreign invaders relates mainly to the Gauls who sacked Rome in 390 and continued to invade central Italy intermittently until 225 and to King Pyrrhus of Epirus, who crossed to Italy in support of Tarentum in 280, inflicted defeats on Rome, but was driven out in 275.

38.2 *Sardinia . . . Africa*: these territories had mostly come under Roman control in the years 264–146, covered in Dio's Books 11–21. The Romans' victories in their three wars with Carthage brought them successively Sicily and Sardinia, Spain, and Carthage's former territory in Africa, and they won control of the eastern territories listed through their early second-century wars over Philip V of Macedon, the Seleucid king Antiochus III, and Philip's son Perseus. Control over much of the Spanish hinterland was only gradually established over the second century, and some regions only became provinces later, e.g. Macedonia (146), Asia (133), Bithynia (74).

38.4 *Crete . . . Palestine*: recent acquisitions, recounted in Dio's Books 36–38. Apart from Crete, conquered by Metellus Creticus (see note to 36.17a), and Cyprus, annexed by Cato (see note to 38.30.5), all these eastern territories were brought under control by Pompey. Only Pontus and Syria were made provinces, with the rest being left under friendly rulers. Although Pompey claimed that his campaigns in Iberia and Albania (36.54–37.5.1) made them subject to Rome, lasting control was not established there. By 'both Syrias' Dio means the two provinces into which Syria had been divided by his own time (see note to 37.7a), anachronistic terminology with Caesar as speaker. By 'both Armenias' Dio means respectively Tigranes' kingdom and Lesser Armenia (see note to 36.9.1), formerly part of the kingdom of Pontus, and assigned by Pompey to Deiotarus of Galatia. For the campaigns in Judaea and against the Nabataean Arabs, see 37.15.1–16.4.

39.2 *superior to them in any respect*: for inferiors' jealousy as a recurrent theme in Dio, see note to 36.24.6.

39.3 *or to perish utterly ourselves*: this sentence echoes similar sentiments about the Athenian empire at Thucydides 1.76.1 and 2.63.2–3.

40.1 *plausible reason for doing so*: 38.40.1 is closely modelled on Demosthenes 8.49.

40.3 *always be acquiring more*: 38.40.2–3 echoes Alcibiades' speech in 415 advocating the (ultimately disastrous) Athenian expedition to conquer Sicily (Thucydides 6.18.2–3). Pericles had argued that the Athenians should defend their empire against Peloponnesian attack, but not seek to expand it at the same time. Thucydides portrays Alcibiades as perverting his arguments in support of continued expansion.

40.4 *Epirotes*: here and throughout 38.40.4–7 Dio makes Caesar generalize rhetorically from specific instances. Pyrrhus' invasion was the only Epirote offensive against Rome.

40.5 *Philip was going to invade Italy*: Philip V of Macedon allied with Hannibal in 215, and the alleged threat of a Macedonian invasion was used as an argument for war against him in 200.

40.6 *Carthaginians*: 38.40.6 generalizes from Hannibal, who invaded Italy (by land, not sea) in 218, advanced to Rome itself in 211, but withdrew to Africa in 203 to face Scipio.

40.7 *except once*: the Cimbri invaded northern Italy in 101, but were defeated by Marius at Vercellae.

41.1 *responses to emerging situations*: in 38.41 Dio gives Caesar an effective response to the alleged objection that the war had not been voted. In theory wars had to be voted by the Senate and the popular assembly, but in practice such votes were normally held only before the relatively few wars begun in regions where no provincial commander and army were present. Although Late Republican laws prohibited commanders from otherwise leaving their province, they were permitted to do so in the public interest, and it was not uncommon for them to campaign beyond the provincial boundary (cf. notes to 38.10.1 and 39.56.4). Caesar crossed the boundary of his province of Transalpine Gaul when he crossed the Rhône in pursuit of the Helvetii (*BG* 1.10.5), and he remained beyond it for the rest of the year and after.

41.4 *why did the people send you here?*: the measures granting Caesar his provinces (see note to 38.8.5) had not specified a war, but it would have been generally expected that Caesar would use his five-year command for major warfare.

four legions: for his pursuit of the Helvetii, Caesar brought the three legions stationed in Cisalpine Gaul to join the one already in Transalpine Gaul, along with two others which he had raised himself (*BG* 1.10.3).

41.5 *the subject territory*: i.e. the taxpaying provincials (see note to 38.10.1).

42.2 *his own actions*: in 38.42–44 Dio makes Caesar's case against Ariovistus appear as weak as possible by basing it solely on his response to Caesar's summons, which in Dio's view was issued just to get a war pretext (38.34.3–4).

43.3 *Allobrogian*: a bad error by Dio. The Allobroges, south of the Rhône and in the Roman province (see note to 37.47.1), were quite distinct from Ariovistus and his followers from east of the Rhine.

44.4 *my views are still the same*: another Periclean echo (Thucydides 1.140.1 and 2.61.2).

45.1 *many others of his race we've defeated in the past*: Dio here treats Gauls and Germans as the same Celtic race. Caesar in his speech referred particularly to Marius' victories over the Cimbri and Teutones in 102–101 (*BG* 1.40.5).

45.4 *in no kind of order*: here, as at 38.35.2, Dio draws on stereotypes about the Celts in the Graeco-Roman ethnographic tradition.

46.3 *the Tenth legion will be enough for me*: Dio follows Caesar's own version in finishing the speech with this threat. The Tenth legion may have been the one Caesar took over in Transalpine Gaul (see note to 38.41.4).

47.2 *the same principle*: legions raised by individual commanders were numbered in order of enrolment, but, since legions were kept in existence over extended periods in the Late Republic and indefinitely under the Principate, numbering sequences overlapped, with several legions having the same number. The legions Caesar took over in 58 were numbered VII–X and the additional legions he raised in 58 and 57 XI–XIV.

47.4 *refused to accept any of them*: Caesar (*BG* 1.42–47) gives a detailed account of his meeting with Ariovistus, portraying his behaviour as arrogant and treacherous.

48.1 *encamped close to each other*: the decisive confrontation took place in mid-September in the southern foothills of the Vosges. (The precise location is disputed: see C. Pelling, 'Caesar's Battle-Descriptions and the Defeat of Ariovistus', *Latomus* 40 (1981), 741–66.) Dio broadly follows Caesar's account of the preliminary manoeuvres (*BG* 1.48–51), but his divergences include the Germans' greater success and resulting contempt for the Romans.

48.2 *infantrymen deployed with them*: each cavalryman fought with a supporting infantryman.

48.3 *occupied another position close by*: Ariovistus' moving of his camp (to a position blocking Caesar's supply line) in fact occurred before the cavalry skirmishing. Caesar offered battle on the five following days, and on the sixth established a second camp with two of his six legions. It was this camp that Ariovistus attacked on the following afternoon.

49.1 *the Romans fell to*: Caesar gives only a brief account of the battle, according to which the Roman right was successful in the initial assault and the reinforcing of their left secured the victory (*BG* 1.52). Dio's fuller version, which may combine Caesar's version with another source, includes more detail on the Germans' weaponry and the differences between the two sides' qualities (as earlier at 38.35.2, 45.4–5, 47.5).

50.1 *The Romans . . . shed their spears*: their *pila*, the throwing spears which Roman legionaries discharged in the first phase of battle. Caesar tells us that the rapid engagement in this battle left no time for a volley of *pila*.

BOOK THIRTY-NINE

1.1 *Cornelius Spinther and Metellus Nepos*: P. Cornelius Lentulus Spinther and Q. Caecilius Metellus Nepos. For continuity Dio stays in Gaul for the opening section of his narrative of the year 57, returning to Rome at 39.6.1. His very compressed account of the warfare in Gaul in 57 draws on Caesar's much fuller version (*BG* 2.1–3.6), but with many divergences.

The Belgae: all the tribes living from the Rhine to the Seine and Marne belonged to this larger grouping.

1.2 *some . . . had been allies of the Romans*: this detail is not in Caesar, who stresses the Belgae's isolation (*BG* 1.1.3).

Galba as their leader: he was king of the Suessiones. Caesar's campaign against the Belgae extended Roman control over what is now northern France. By contrast with his cynical judgement of Caesar's motivation against Ariovistus (38.34), Dio accepts Caesar's explanation of this campaign as responding to planned Belgic aggression.

1.3 *informed . . . by the Remi*: Caesar had learnt of the Belgae's plans first from Labienus, whom he had left in command of his army in its winter quarters among the Sequani. Caesar's advance against the Belgae brought him first to the Remi (themselves Belgic), whose principal centre was at Durocortorum (modern Reims).

river Aisne: known in antiquity as the Axona, it ran through the northern part of the territory of the Remi. Caesar's camp, on the northern bank, may have been at the modern Berry-au-Bac.

did not dare to engage the enemy: here, as at 39.2.1, Dio interprets as timidity what Caesar himself portrays as prudent caution. He initially contented himself with cavalry skirmishing against the huge Belgic force, but then drew up for a battle which did not ensue due to each side's reluctance to advance across intervening swampy ground (*BG* 2.7.3–9.2).

1.4 *deserters . . . night*: Caesar does not mention information from deserters or set the engagement at night. He learnt of the Belgic advance against the bridge from Q. Titurius Sabinus, whom he had stationed south of the river to defend it, and the Roman forces attacked as the enemy were fording the river.

2.1 *Aedui had invaded it*: the Aedui invaded the territory of the Bellovaci, western neighbours of the Remi, at Caesar's request. Caesar attributes the Belgae's decision to withdraw not to their losses, but to their failure to achieve anything and shortage of grain.

ignorance of the region: according to Caesar, fear of an ambush.

2.2 *caught up with them*: according to Caesar, he did not command the pursuit himself, but entrusted it to *legati*, and the Belgae's disorderly withdrawal soon became a rout.

some . . . without resistance and some by war: the Suessiones surrendered when Caesar began siege-works, the Bellovaci and Ambiani without further hostilities.

3.1 *to match the Romans*: Caesar says nothing about the Nervii's inferiority or withdrawal, but instead stresses their warlike qualities and determination to resist (*BG* 2.15.3–6).

when . . . from there: there is a short gap in Dio's text here. According to Caesar, the Nervii advanced from their ambush, crossing a river he calls the Sabis (perhaps the Sambre), when his baggage train came into sight and the six legions which had already arrived had begun to fortify a camp above the river.

3.2 *massacred them*: Dio misrepresents Caesar's personal role in the battle. The Roman left wing, which defeated the Atrebates and pursued them across the river, was commanded by Labienus, who then sent back the Tenth legion to relieve the Roman camp. The Roman right was heavily pressed by the Nervii themselves, and Caesar averted defeat there by a display of personal bravery, later much celebrated, but passed over by Dio.

subdue the rest of the Nervii: after the battle, the surviving Nervii sent an embassy to surrender.

4.1 *Cimbri in both descent and spirit*: Caesar (*BG* 2.29.4) says that the Atuatuci were descended from 6,000 Cimbri and Teutones, left behind by the rest to guard herds and other possessions which they could not take on their southern invasion in the late second century.

the strongest they had: perhaps at modern Namur, in southern Belgium.

4.4 *changed their minds*: Caesar claims that the Atuatuci had throughout planned another attack.

all sold into slavery: 53,000, according to Caesar (*BG* 2.33.7). Caesar followed Roman norms in showing leniency to those who surrendered and complied with his orders, e.g. for the handing over hostages and arms, but according subsequent rebels no mercy.

5.1 *by his legates*: Caesar (*BG* 2.34) reports the submission, obtained by P. Crassus, of the Veneti and six other coastal peoples dwelling between the Seine and the Loire (the ancient region of Armorica).

winter quarters: Caesar billeted his army in the Loire region, while he himself, as usual, spent the winter in his provinces south of the Alps.

fifteen days . . . unprecedented honour: before 63, the longest period for which *supplicationes* (see note to 37.36.3) had been voted in thanksgiving for victories was five days. Pompey was voted ten days of *supplicationes* in 63 on the death of Mithridates and again in 62 for bringing all wars to an end. Inflation continued subsequently: see notes to 39.53.2 and 40.50.4.

5.2 *Galba*: Ser. Sulpicius Galba, familiar with the region through his service in Pomptinus' campaign against the Allobroges (37.48.1).

Veragri . . . up to the Alps: Galba received the submission of the Nantuates, on the southern shores of Lake Leman, and the Veragri and Seduni in the upper Rhône valley (the Valais). Caesar had sent him to the region with the Twelfth legion in the hope of securing the route to Italy over the Great St Bernard Pass. Galba established his winter camp among the Veragri, at Octodurus (modern Martigny).

5.3 *some on furlough . . . some . . . by themselves*: Caesar (*BG* 3.2.3) says that Galba's force had been depleted by the stationing of two cohorts among the Nantuates and by the despatch of individuals to seek supplies. Dio's divergence may arise from misunderstanding of the Latin word *commeatus*: Caesar uses it here for 'supplies', but it can also mean 'furlough'.

5.4 *subjugated them*: not mentioned by Caesar.

moved to the territory of the Allobroges: in the Roman province (see note to 37.47.1).

6.1 *Pompey had arranged for Cicero's recall to be voted*: Dio now turns to Rome, narrating events there over the years 57–55 as a block, before returning to Gaul at 39.40.1. He starts by picking up the story of Cicero's recall (begun at 38.30.1–4), continuing it down to his return and its immediate sequel (39.6–11). Cicero's speeches and letters after his return provide further evidence; for discussion, see Tatum, *Patrician Tribune*, 176–93. Dio oversimplifies in crediting the recall solely to Pompey.

6.2 *brought the proposal before the plebs*: an assembly was called for 23 January to vote on a law recalling Cicero, proposed by Q. Fabricius with the support of seven further tribunes.

adultery, . . . Clodius [. . .]: the end of the sentence, missing in Dio's text, may have referred to the Senate meeting convened by Lentulus Spinther on 1 January, at which Pompey and others expressed their support for Cicero's recall. Lentulus' strong backing for Cicero before and throughout his consulship won his fervent gratitude. Cicero regarded Lentulus as 'completely under Pompey's thumb' (*Att.* 3.22.2). Dio is our only source for his personal enmity with Clodius. Here, as before, Dio misstates the formal charge at Clodius' trial in 61 (see note to 37.46.2).

6.3 *Nepos . . . hating Cicero*: Nepos' conduct as tribune for 62 had made him Cicero's enemy, and he was also related to Clodius (see notes to 37.38.2, 42.2, 51.2). However, Dio is wrong to claim that Nepos now opposed Cicero's recall as consul: in the Senate on 1 January, he announced that he would not oppose the Senate's wish. Nepos did, however, help Clodius by frustrating Milo's attempts to prosecute him (see below).

7.2 *Clodius . . . wounded and killed many people*: Dio implies that Clodius arrived while the voting was in progress, Cicero that the assembly never began. In Cicero's account (*Sest.* 75–78, 85), Clodius occupied the Forum overnight with his gangs and the gladiators, and, when Fabricius and his supporters arrived before dawn on 23 January, rioting broke out in which Cicero's brother Quintus barely escaped with his life and 'the Tiber was filled with the bodies of citizens'. If the emendation 'Marcius' for the manuscripts' 'Marcus' is correct, the show for which Clodius' brother, the praetor Ap. Claudius Pulcher, had collected the gladiators was to honour Q. Marcius Rex, who had been married to their sister (36.17.2) and died in 61. On gladiatorial shows, see note to 37.8.1.

7.3 *avoid being convicted for violence*: Milo sought to prosecute Clodius under the Plautian law for violence (*vis*), which had been used earlier against Catiline and his supporters (see notes to 37.31.3, 41.4). He made two attempts in 57, the first around February, the second in November–December. Dio confuses the two, and the details he supplies here in fact relate to Milo's second attempt. Clodius' candidature for the aedileship thus took place after Cicero's return from exile. Milo's first attempted prosecution was thwarted by an edict suspending all judicial proceedings issued by Nepos, Ap. Claudius, and a tribune.

7.4 *chief cause of the delay*: boards of magistrates were elected in rank order. Milo in late 57 was obstructing the election of aediles for 56 to prevent Clodius from getting immunity from prosecution when he entered office, and the lower-ranking quaestors (who were due to enter office on 5 December 57) had thus also not been elected. The jury panel for each case was selected by lot from the overall list of jurors. The ballot was normally administered by the urban quaestors, and no jury ballot had yet been held for Clodius' trial when the quaestors for 57 stepped down on 4 December. Cicero (*QF* 2.1.2–3) reports a Senate meeting at which alternative arrangements for the ballot were proposed without success.

8.2 *Nepos then had a change of heart*: false, since Nepos had not been opposed to Cicero's recall from January. From July he gave it positive support, declaring his reconciliation with Cicero, and joining all the other magistrates except Ap. Claudius and two tribunes in promulgating the law. The tide was turned not by Nepos, but by Pompey's mobilization of public opinion, starting with the Italian towns.

voted their approval: at Senate meetings in early July, decrees demanding a law for Cicero's recall were passed with only Clodius dissenting, and on 4 August the law was passed by the *comitia centuriata* (see Glossary, pp. 283–4), which was biased in favour of the wealthy and only occasionally used for legislation.

9.1 *address both bodies*: Cicero arrived on 4 September to a rapturous reception, addressing the Senate on 5 September and the people on 7 September. Published versions of both speeches survive, but the speech actually delivered on 7 September will have been significantly different, dominated by Pompey's appointment.

9.3 *commissioner of the grain supply . . . proconsul . . . in Italy and abroad for five years*: Cicero describes these events in a letter to Atticus (4.1.5–7) and in his speech *On His House* (5–18), but only Dio mentions the crowd's threats. High grain prices had led to riots from July. On 7 September rioters attacked the theatre, where plays were being performed for the Roman Games (in a temporary structure, as was still necessary: see note to 37.58.4), and then the Senate. Arriving there only when summoned by the crowd and the consuls, Cicero proposed Pompey's appointment, as the crowd demanded. After the Senate meeting Cicero delivered his address to the people. The Senate met again on 8 September to fix the terms of the appointment, which were subsequently ratified by a law carried by the consuls and gave Pompey, as proconsul, complete control over grain supplies throughout the Roman world for five years, with the right to nominate fifteen legates. On Pompey's appointment see F. J. Vervaet, 'No Grain of Salt. Casting a New Light on Pompeius' *cura annonae*', *Hermes* 148 (2020), 149–72.

rule the entire world . . . under Roman sway: an exaggeration (so also Plut. *Pomp.* 49). Pompey had only the same power as the proconsuls commanding provinces (the tribune Messius had unsuccessfully proposed that his power be made greater than theirs).

10.1 *Caesar . . . quite well disposed towards him*: as Cicero later admitted to Lentulus Spinther (*Fam.* 1.9.9, 12), Pompey had got Caesar's agreement for Cicero's recall by securing pledges from his brother for his future conduct.

10.2 *secret book . . . defence of his policies*: later citations show that the title included the word *consilia* ('policies'). Dio may not have good reason to date the book's composition to the period immediately after Cicero's return from exile in 57: letters to Atticus show that he began work on it in 59. The work's allegations included that Crassus had conspired with Catiline in 65 and that both he and Caesar had opposed Cicero's election as consul and supported Catiline's conspiracy in 63. Dio shows no sign of having consulted the work himself. For full discussion, see A. Drummond in T. J. Cornell et al. (eds.), *The Fragments of the Roman Historians* (Oxford, 2013), 1.376–9, 2.765–73, 3.478–82.

10.3 *handed it over to his son*: unlikely. Cicero's son was aged 7 in 57.

11.1 *even though it had been dedicated to Liberty*: for the dedication, see note to 38.17.6. Cicero reports his recovery of the site in a letter to Atticus (4.2). The Senate had asked the College of Pontiffs to rule on the validity of the dedication. At a hearing on 29 September, both Clodius and Cicero addressed the pontiffs; Cicero's speech survives (*On His House*). The pontiffs then ruled that, unless Clodius had been instructed by name by a popular assembly to make the dedication, the site could be returned to Cicero without sacrilege. At this both Cicero and Clodius claimed victory, but at meetings on 1–2 October the Senate took Cicero's side.

11.2 *the time stipulated by ancestral usage*: i.e. a *trinundinum* (see Glossary, p. 288). Such an interval was required between the promulgation and voting of other laws (see note to 36.23.5), but it is uncertain whether Cicero was right to claim (*On His House* 41) that the requirement applied to the *lex curiata* enacting Clodius' adoption as a plebeian (see notes to 37.51.2 and 38.12.2). Dio correctly reports Cicero's objection, but greatly exaggerates its significance. This was only one of several arguments Cicero deployed to deny the validity of Clodius' adoption and so of his whole tribunate, and he anyway insisted that he was not relying on this claim (*On His House* 34–42). He devoted the bulk of the speech to attacking the validity of Clodius' law exiling him and of the dedication itself.

11.3 *With this argument . . . not consecrated or hallowed ground*: the issue in fact turned on the authorization for the dedication. The exile law (38.17.6–7) ordered the dedication, but the pontiffs accepted Cicero's argument that the authorizing law had to name the dedicator: see further W. Stroh, '*De domo sua*: Legal Problem and Structure', in J. Powell and J. Paterson (eds.), *Cicero the Advocate* (Oxford, 2004), 313–70. The decision to restore the site to Cicero was taken by the Senate, not the pontiffs.

rebuild . . . and repair anything . . . damaged: the consuls assessed (ungenerously, in Cicero's view) the rebuilding costs for this house and two others outside Rome at 2,750,000 sesterces.

12.1 *King Ptolemy*: after completing his narrative of Cicero's recall, Dio passes to the Egyptian crisis, giving it extensive treatment as illustrative of corruption at Rome (39.12–16, continued later at 39.55–63). For much of this episode Dio is our chief source. The introductory chronological link ('after this') is misleading: Dio is in fact turning back to earlier developments. Ptolemy XII, nicknamed Auletes ('Flute-player'), had ruled Egypt since 80 without Roman recognition. In 65 Crassus as censor (see note to 37.9.3) had led an attempt to annex it as a province based on the alleged will of an earlier king. In 59 Caesar as consul obtained recognition for Ptolemy through a Senate decree, law, and treaty, according to Suetonius

(*Jul.* 54.3) for a promised bribe of nearly 6,000 talents (= 144,000,000 sesterces) for Pompey and himself. On the disputes over Ptolemy's restoration in 57–54, see K. Morrell, '"Who Wants to Go to Alexandria?" Pompey, Ptolemy, and Public Opinion, 57–56 BC', in C. Rosillo López (ed.), *Communicating Public Opinion in the Roman Republic* (Stuttgart, 2019), 151–74; J. Rich, 'Corruption, Power and an Oracle in the Late Roman Republic: The Restoration of Ptolemy Auletes', in J. Armstrong, A. Pomeroy, and D. Rosenbloom (eds.), *Money, Warfare and Power in the Ancient World: Studies in Honour of Matthew Freeman Trundle* (London, 2024), 219–43.

borrowed: much of it from a Roman banker later defended by Cicero (*For Rabirius Postumus* 4).

12.2 *return of Cyprus from the Romans*: for its annexation, see note to 38.30.5.

12.3 *thrown him out of his kingdom*: Ptolemy's dispute was mainly with the inhabitants of his capital, Alexandria (for their unruliness, see 39.58.2). He reached Rome in late 58 or early 57.

Spinther . . . Cilicia: Lentulus Spinther left Rome for Cilicia before the end of his consulship in 57. Earlier in the year, a decree of the Senate had commissioned him to carry out Ptolemy's restoration.

13.1 *Berenice*: Berenice IV, for whom see further 39.57–58.

14.1 *Marcus Favonius*: the follower of Cato (38.7.1), then absent in Cyprus. Favonius was still only an ex-quaestor, the most junior senatorial rank.

14.3 *into his house*: Ptolemy was staying in Pompey's Alban villa, where Cicero reports him as contracting for loans from Roman creditors (*For Rabirius Postumus* 6).

14.4 *few were convicted*: this is our only evidence for proceedings against subjects of Ptolemy. In 56 Cicero successfully defended two Romans, P. Asicius and M. Caelius, who were accused of involvement in Dio's murder (*For Caelius* 23–24).

15.1 *statue of Jupiter on the Alban Mount*: at the sanctuary of Jupiter Latiaris, on the summit of Monte Cavo, the highest point in the Alban Hills, 21 km (13 miles) south-east of Rome. The Latin Festival, attended by all the magistrates, was held there every year.

15.2 *Sibylline verses*: also known as the Sibylline books, a collection of oracles in Greek verses, attributed to the Sibyl, a legendary priestess, which was kept in the Capitoline temple in the care of the *quindecimviri sacris faciundis* ('fifteen men for performing rituals'), one of the principal priestly colleges. The books were lost in 83 when the temple was destroyed by fire, but a substitute collection was amassed from 76 on from Sibylline sanctuaries in Italy and abroad. When portents occurred, it was customary for the Senate to seek guidance on appropriate expiatory rituals by instructing the *quindecimviri* to consult the books (instead of, or as well as, consulting the *haruspices*: see Glossary, p. 284).

15.3 *rescind all that had been voted about Ptolemy*: no such cancellation was in fact passed (see note to 39.16.1). C. Porcius Cato, a distant cousin of the more famous M. Cato, had been campaigning against Ptolemy and Lentulus Spinther since taking up his tribunate on 10 December.

15.4 *the more insistent the plebs became*: a small gap in the transmitted text leaves the precise sense uncertain.

16.1 *Latin translation was . . . proclaimed*: by a *praeco* (herald), no doubt at another public meeting (*contio*) convened by C. Cato.

   discussion . . . in the Senate: here Dio summarizes proceedings at successive Senate meetings, of which Cicero (himself supporting Lentulus) gives a detailed report in letters to his brother (*QF* 2.2.3) and Lentulus Spinther (*Fam.* 1.1–2, 4). On 14 January the Senate resolved that, in obedience to the oracle, Ptolemy should not be restored 'with a multitude' (i.e. an army), and it rejected Bibulus' proposal of a three-man embassy. At some point the Senate voted that Ptolemy should not be restored at all, but a tribune vetoed the decree (*Fam.* 1.7.4). Pompey throughout avoided making his own preference clear.

16.3 *These developments happened*: i.e. the events narrated in 39.15.1–16.2.

   Lucius Philippus and Gnaeus Marcellinus: L. Marcius Philippus and Cn. Cornelius Lentulus Marcellinus.

   with the goddess: at the celebrated sanctuary of Artemis.

17.1 *The previous year . . . relevance to this history*: having avoided disruption to his Egyptian narrative by continuing it into the new year, Dio now backtracks to 57 for this further detail. He presumably deemed it worth including as yet another instance of the overriding of constitutional convention so frequent in this period (see Introduction, pp. xiv, xxii–xxiii).

   hold the same priesthood at the same time: this ban on two members of the same *gens* (see Glossary, p. 284) belonging to the same priestly college was probably included in Labienus' law of 63, which reinstated elections for the priesthoods (see note to 37.37.1). It is uncertain whether Labienus was the first to introduce the ban or it had been included in Domitius' law of 104 and then lifted by Sulla (see J. A. North, '*Lex Domitia* Revisited', in J. H. Richardson and F. Santangelo (eds.), *Priests and State in the Roman World* (Stuttgart, 2011), 39–61).

17.2 *adopted into the Manlii Torquati*: the consul's son continued to be known (like his father) as P. Cornelius Lentulus Spinther. Cicero (*Sest.* 144) confirms that he was elected augur in 57.

18.1 *Clodius had taken up the post of aedile*: after a long delay (see notes to 39.7.3–4), the aediles for the year were elected on 20 January 56. Dio now (39.18–23) uses Clodius and his conflicts as a linking theme for a sequence of events occurring in the first half of the year.

   instituted proceedings against Milo: rather than using the jury court, Clodius revived the aediles' ancient right to conduct a prosecution in the popular assembly. Hearings were held on 2, 7, and 17 February.

19.1 *One of his schemes . . . as follows*: Dio converts a single incident on 7 February into repeated practice. Plutarch (*Pomp.* 48), probably using the same source, gives examples of Clodius' questions: 'Who's a sex-mad commander? Which man is after another man? Who scratches his head with one finger?' Cicero, who was present, reports the following exchanges (*QF* 2.3.2): ' "Who's starving the people to death?" "Pompey," answered the gang. "Who wants to go to Alexandria?" Answer: "Pompey." "Who do you want to go?" Answer: "Crassus." ' The session ended in a riot.

19.3 *would not allow the lex curiata to be introduced*: a puzzling and perhaps confused statement. This *lex curiata* (not to be confused with the adoption law mentioned at 37.51.2 and 39.11.2) was a measure passed by the *comitia curiata* (see Glossary, p. 283) which was deemed necessary to confer full legitimacy on the higher, and perhaps also the lower, magistrates. It was normally passed soon after the magistrates' entry into office, but in this period was sometimes obstructed by tribunes. Despite Dio's claim, this seems not to have disrupted civil government or the courts.

20.2 *in Latinum subterranean noises were heard*: Cicero, in his speech *On the Response of the Haruspices* (*Har. Resp.* 20), speaks of 'a loud noise with a rumbling' heard in the 'Latinian land' (*ager Latiniensis*, a district on the Tiber's left bank shortly north of Rome). Cicero implies that the *haruspices*' response related just to this portent. He also mentions (*Har. Resp.* 62) an earthquake at Potentia on the east coast of Italy, which had not yet been considered by the Senate and is presumably the one mentioned by Dio. What action was taken about this and the other portents in Dio's list is unknown.

sanctuaries . . . places of residence: 'sacred and hallowed places have been profaned' (*Har. Resp.* 9). The *haruspices* also declared that games and sacrifices had been carelessly performed and polluted, ambassadors killed, and oaths neglected.

20.3 *Clodius began to target Cicero directly*: Clodius dropped the prosecution of Milo, perhaps as a result of his reconciliation with Pompey; for which, see note to 39.29.1.

delivered a speech: to an assembly meeting (*contio*). Cicero replied with *On the Response of the Haruspices*, delivered in the Senate probably in early May 56, blaming Clodius for all the offences listed by the *haruspices*.

attacked the house: Clodius had disrupted the rebuilding work on Cicero's house with an armed gang on 3 November 57. If Dio is right, he now made a second attack.

21.1 *tablets . . . for his exile*: inscribed with the text of the law declaring Cicero an exile (38.17.7). For the publication of laws on bronze, see note to 37.9.1.

21.2 *his brother Gaius*: C. Claudius Pulcher.

22.1 *Cato . . . supported Clodius strongly*: Plutarch (*Cato* 40; *Cic.* 34) shows that Cato's intervention took place at a Senate meeting at which Clodius protested at Cicero's removal of the tablets. It appears that the first time

Cicero had removed just the tablet recording the exile law from the Capitol, but on the repeat he took away those for all Clodius' laws. Cato probably returned from Cyprus in May or June 56. For his assignment there, see further note to 38.30.5; Plut. *Cato* 34–39.

22.2 *could not abide . . . living if his realm was taken away from him*: Ptolemy of Cyprus had been offered the priesthood of Aphrodite at Paphos.

22.4 *money from the royal holdings*: nearly 7,000 talents (= 168 million sesterces), according to Plutarch.

23.1 *praetorship . . . not yet legally eligible*: Cato, now 40, met the age requirement for the praetorship and stood unsuccessfully in the next election (see note to 39.32.1). The proposal may have been that Cato's name should be put to the assembly for approval before it voted on the other candidates.

23.2 *'Porcians'*: after Cato's *gens* (his full name was M. Porcius Cato).

23.3 *records . . . lost at sea*: according to Plutarch, one copy of Cato's accounts had been lost in a shipwreck, the other in a fire at his camp.

24.1 *delay in the distribution of the grain*: Dio now turns from Clodius to Pompey as his narrative focus. Pompey's appointment (see note to 39.9.3) was primarily concerned with the grain supply for Rome, but also involved oversight of the distribution. The slaves of Roman citizens became citizens themselves when freed, and so, if resident in Rome, eligible for the grain dole. Since freedmen still owed services to their former masters, it could thus be to masters' advantage to free them. Pompey's registration of recently freed slaves may have been designed to supplement records of those eligible for the dole. The recent burning of the temple of the Nymphs and records held there by Clodian supporters may have been intended as a counterstroke.

25.1 *Pompey bitterly resented Caesar's increasing strength*: with elaborate reconstruction of Pompey's thinking, Dio here continues themes from his earlier treatment of Caesar's rivalry with Pompey and the latter's unsuccessful attempts to avoid jealousy and retain honour (cf. note to 36.24.6). However, Dio's view of Pompey as now acting against Caesar in concert with Crassus is quite mistaken (see further Introduction, pp. xxvii–xxviii). Caesar had spent winter 57–56 south of the Alps, in his provinces of Cisalpine Gaul and Illyricum. There he had been in close touch with Roman politics, and in April 56 he re-established his alliance with Pompey and Crassus and with it their political dominance. According to Cicero (*Fam.* 1.9.9 ff.), Caesar met Crassus in Ravenna and then Pompey in Luca (modern Lucca), and Cicero himself, under pressure from Pompey, then switched to actively supporting their alliance. Both Clodius and C. Cato also switched from attacking Pompey to supporting him (see notes to 39.28.1, 29.1). Suetonius (*Jul.* 24), Plutarch (*Pomp.* 51; *Caes.* 21; *Crass.* 14; *Cato* 41), and Appian (*BC* 2.17) claim that the three dynasts, meeting in Luca, agreed that Pompey and Crassus should become consuls for 55 and then take provinces, and Caesar's command should be extended for five years, but this may anticipate decisions only reached later.

senatorial delegation . . . money: army pay and ten *legati*, as Cicero's references show (e.g. *Fam.* 1.7.10). These were voted not by the assembly, as
Dio implies, but by the Senate, with Cicero's active support. The pay was
for the four legions raised by Caesar in 58–57. The ten *legati* were the
customary senatorial commission to settle conquered territory (cf. notes
to 36.43.2 and 37.49.5), not (as some scholars argue) additional staff for
Caesar, but in the event they seem not to have been sent. Both proposals
will have been agreed by Pompey at Luca (attested for the money grant
by Plutarch).

25.2 *before the expiration of his command*: as was legally required (see note to
36.1a), the Senate met (probably in June 56) to fix provinces for the consuls for 55 before their election. At this meeting, proposals that Caesar
should be replaced in one or other of his Gallic provinces were easily
defeated, with Cicero delivering his speech *On the Consular Provinces* in
support. Contrary to Dio's claim, this outcome was a victory for the alliance of Pompey, Caesar, and Crassus. A consul could have succeeded
Caesar in Transalpine Gaul, to which he had been appointed by the
Senate, from late 55, but Vatinius' law, under which he held Cisalpine
Gaul, did not allow his supersession there before 1 March 54.

25.4 *had enough of what was familiar*: according to Dio (36.43.4), Caesar had
earlier aimed to bring forward the time when people had 'had enough
of' Pompey.

27.3 *legally prescribed period*: a *trinundinum* (see Glossary, p. 288). Catiline's
candidacy had been disallowed on this ground in 66 (see note to 36.44.3).
Dio is our only source for this objection to Pompey's and Crassus'
candidacies and for most of the resulting developments reported at
39.27.3–30.4.

Marcellinus . . . carried weight: Lentulus Marcellinus, as the consul due to
preside over the elections, was entitled to block candidacies he deemed
invalid.

interrex: see Glossary, p. 285.

28.1 *agents . . . deployed on various pretexts*: including the tribunes C. Cato (cf.
39.15.3–4) and M. Nonius Sufenas, both of whom were prosecuted in 54
over their obstruction of these elections. Like Clodius, C. Cato had been
hostile to Pompey earlier in the year, but now took his side.

28.2 *change their clothing*: adopting mourning dress (see note to 37.43.3).

dragged people in off the streets: these words have been supplied to fill a gap
in the text.

28.3 *games . . . taking place at the time*: the reference may be to the *ludi Romani*
(5–19 September), *ludi Victoriae Sullanae* (26 October–1 November), or
ludi plebeii (4–17 November).

29.1 *Clodius . . . leapt over to Pompey's side*: Clodius' reconciliation with
Pompey was prompted by the dynasts' realignment in April 56 and
announced by him in early May (see notes to 39.20.3, 25.1).

30.2 *in the public interest*: Pompey's and Crassus' responses to Marcellinus are also reported by Plutarch, in a form which makes Pompey still ambivalent about his intentions. Plutarch is inconsistent on whether the incident occurred in the Senate (*Crass.* 15) or the assembly (*Pomp.* 51). If the latter, it may also be the occasion when Marcellinus attacked Pompey's excessive power as a threat to liberty (Valerius Maximus 6.2.5).

30.3 *no election-related business . . . at all*: a puzzling passage. A quorum requirement for a Senate vote on election matters is not attested elsewhere, and the elections were being held up not by the lack of a Senate vote, but by Marcellinus' refusal to accept Pompey and Crassus as candidates.

30.4 *feast . . . on the Capitol*: the *epulum Iovis*, held on 13 November and normally attended by the senators.

Latin Festival: the *feriae Latinae*, an ancient ceremony held on the Alban Mount (see note to 39.15.1) early in the consular year and attended by all the magistrates. As with all festivals, a ritual flaw could necessitate its repetition.

31.1 *appointed consuls after an interregnum*: in January 55.

Lucius Domitius . . . too frightened to carry on: descended from a long line of consuls, L. Domitius Ahenobarbus would in normal circumstances have been certain of election to the consulate this year, the first when he was legally eligible. As praetor in 58, he had attempted to challenge Caesar's acts as consul, and his threats to use the consulship to get Caesar's command terminated were one of the factors leading to the renewal of the alliance between Caesar, Pompey, and Crassus in spring 56. Plutarch (*Pomp.* 52; *Crass.* 15; *Cato* 41–42) tells us that, after the murder of Domitius' torchbearer, the rest of his companions were driven off, with his brother-in-law M. Cato sustaining an arm wound.

31.2 *Publius Crassus . . . brought soldiers . . . for that very purpose*: clearly with Caesar's approval, despite Dio's claim that Pompey and Crassus were acting against Caesar. According to Plutarch, Caesar had agreed at their Luca meeting (see note to 39.25.1) to send troops to support their election. Dio's wording makes P. Crassus a legate, but Caesar's references to him show that he remained an equestrian officer.

32.1 *Cato was not elected praetor*: Plutarch reports that, when the first unit of the *comitia centuriata* (see Glossary, pp. 283–4) voted for Cato, Pompey dissolved the assembly by claiming to have heard thunder, and then used even more bribery to ensure the election of his supporters, including Vatinius.

curule aediles: it was probably now that Cn. Plancius and A. Plotius were elected to this post. Their election was held twice (probably because of the violence) and in 54 led to Plancius' prosecution for corruption. The published version of Cicero's defence speech survives.

33.2 *and the neighbouring territories*: so also Appian (*BC* 2.18). The reference was probably chiefly to the Nabataean Arabs (see notes to 37.15.1–2), whose depredations had been a continuing problem for governors of

Syria following Pompey's departure. The law probably did not commission the governor of Syria to undertake a Parthian war, as some sources claim (see note to 40.12.1).

Spains . . . recent uprising: Spain was administered as two provinces, Hither (Citerior) and Further (Ulterior) Spain to its west. For the recent uprising, see 39.54.

right to make war and peace on whomever they pleased: granted earlier for Pompey's Mithridatic command by the *lex Manilia* (see note to 36.42.4).

33.3 *outrage . . . among Caesar's friends*: Dio's belief that jealousy of Caesar had led Pompey and Crassus to seek consulships and provinces obliges him to implausibly explain the extension of Caesar's command as a belated concession, whereas it was in fact part of a package to which all three had agreed (cf. note to 39.25.1).

three years: other sources show that the five-year command which Caesar had been granted under the *lex Vatinia* (see note to 38.8.5) was now extended for a further five by a law passed by Pompey and Crassus (*lex Pompeia Licinia*). Dio mistakenly amends this, misled by the fact that Caesar's command actually lasted for eight years overall (cf. 44.43.2).

34.1 *resisted them at every turn*: so also Plutarch (*Cato* 43), largely agreeing with Dio's account. Favonius had been Cato's regular supporter from 59 (38.7.1).

34.4 *did not moderate his behaviour*: according to Plutarch, a crowd of listeners accompanied Cato to the Carcer (see notes to 37.50.1 and 38.3.2), so Trebonius released him.

35.1 *private citizens . . . speak before any office-holders*: for magistrates' obligation to give private citizens an opportunity to speak for or against a law, see note to 36.24.4. They could also invite other magistrates to speak, but seem not to have been obliged to do so (cf. 36.30.1). A magistrate could anyway convene his own assembly (*contio*).

35.4 *place where the meeting was to be held*: the Forum, to which the Curia (senate-house) was adjacent.

35.5 *Ninnius*: for his support of Cicero as tribune in 58, see 38.14.1–2, 16.3, 30.3.

declared a celestial omen: claiming to have heard thunder (Plutarch). For thunder or lightning as preventing a voting assembly, see 38.13.4.

36.2 *put the measure relating to Caesar to the vote*: Caesar's command was extended by a law carried by Pompey and Caesar as consuls, but it is unlikely to have been voted through as hastily as Dio implies.

37.1 *penalties for bribery*: the consular law of 63 on electoral corruption (*ambitus*, see note to 37.29.1) continued in force, but Crassus now carried a law (*lex Licinia de sodaliciis*) creating a new offence with a heavier penalty (perhaps lifelong exile) for those who exploited certain associations (*sodalitates*) as a channel for electoral bribery. Plancius was prosecuted under this law (see note to 39.32.1), for which Cicero's speech in his defence provides our main evidence. Also in this year Pompey carried a law modifying the procedure for selecting the overall list of jurors for criminal trials.

by force rather than bribery: other accounts report extensive bribery to secure the election of the consuls' supporters as praetors (see note to 39.32.1).

37.2 *planned to curb personal expenditure*: by proposing a sumptuary law, restricting expenditure on dinners. Seven such laws had been passed from 182 on. This proposal (attested only here) may have been linked to Crassus' law: lavish dinners could bring political advantage, and sumptuary laws had sometimes coincided with laws against electoral corruption. The consuls' legislation will also have been portrayed as fulfilling their claim to have sought the office just in the public interest (see note to 39.30.2).

37.3 *Hortensius . . . greatness of the city*: Dio briefly summarizes Hortensius' Senate speech against the law, in which, like Asinius Gallus in 16 CE (Tacitus, *Annals* 2.33), he will have argued that the growth of Roman wealth and luxury was the natural consequence of empire. Hortensius' fishponds and parks were celebrated, and he was the first Roman to serve peacock at a dinner.

38.1 *Pompey dedicated his theatre*: on 12 August. Permanent stone theatres had previously been prohibited in Rome. The theatre, in the Campus Martius, was surmounted by a temple to Venus Victrix, and to its east lay a portico, with associated structures and gardens, all adorned with artworks. The vast scale of the complex, covering some 45,000 m², hugely surpassed earlier victors' monuments. Other sources for the dedicatory games include Cicero's disdainful eyewitness account (*Fam.* 7.1) and Pliny, *Natural History* 8.20–1, both confirming the spectators' sympathy for the elephants. Dio omits the plays, enhanced by spectacular props. See further Beard, *The Roman Triumph*, 22–31.

38.5 *purification of their bodies*: these stories about elephant behaviour are also reported by *Pliny, Natural History* 8.1–2.

38.6 *Demetrius*: from Gadara (in Syria), and notorious for his wealth and arrogance (Plut. *Pomp.* 2, 40). Only Dio retails the absurd claim that he paid for the theatre.

39.1 *levies of troops*: apparently held in Rome, a relatively rarity in the Late Republic, when legionary recruiting was usually conducted locally in Italian regions.

39.2 *proceedings . . . against the consuls themselves*: obscure. The tribunes may have been exercising their traditional right to assist individuals claiming levy exemption. Dio is our only source for the events reported in 39.39.1–3.

change their clothes as though for a catastrophe: adopting the ploy previously used by their conservative opponents (see note to 39.28.2).

39.4 *happy to stay in Rome himself*: Pompey had no further need for a great campaign, and his unprecedented governorship of his provinces from Rome through *legati* enabled him to combine parity with Caesar and Crassus with oversight of the capital. According to Plutarch (*Crass.* 16), the provinces were allocated in the traditional way by the lot, but the outcome was what each wanted: Syria gave Crassus the opportunity to rival his partners in military glory through victory against Parthia (see note to 40.12.1). Crassus left Rome in mid-November.

39.6 *Capitol . . . celestial omens and other portents*: on the day of their departure, Roman commanders took the auspices before dawn, and then proceeded to Jupiter's temple on the Capitol, where they took a vow for the success of their command (to be fulfilled at their triumph, if granted). Cicero (*On Divination* 1.29–30) says that Ateius made an obstructing announcement (*obnuntiatio*: see note to 38.6.1) of *dirae* (dreadfully unfavourable auspices, presumably unpropitious birds, thunder, or lightning), and that, during his censorship in 50 (40.63), Ap. Claudius Pulcher expelled Ateius from the Senate for 'falsifying the auspices' and so causing Crassus' disaster. Others blamed Crassus' neglect of omens for the disaster. See L. Driediger-Murphy, 'Falsifying the Auspices in Republican Rome', in H. van der Blom, C. Gray, and C. Steel (eds.), *Institutions and Ideology in Republican Rome* (Cambridge, 2018), 183–202.

39.7 *left and crossed the pomerium*: after the vow on the Capitol, departing commanders donned the military cloak (*paludamentum*) and left the city, crossing the *pomerium* (see Glossary, p. 286). Plutarch (*Crass.* 16) supplies further details on Ateius' attempt to imprison Crassus in the Carcer (see note to 37.50.1) and cursing at the *pomerium*. Numerous other sources mention the curses (wrongly doubted by some scholars). Unlike Dio, these sources portray Ateius as seeking to prevent the planned Parthian war.

Crassus met disaster: at Carrhae in 53 (40.12–27).

40.1 *Caesar . . . Marcellinus and Philippus*: Dio reverts to Caesar's campaigns in Gaul, picking up from 39.5.4 and providing a continuous narrative for the years 56 and 55 BCE (39.40–53). Caesar's own account in books 3–4 of his *Gallic War* is Dio's main source.

Veneti, who live by the Ocean: in what is now southern Brittany. In 57 P. Crassus had obtained the submission of the Veneti and other Armorican peoples, with hostages supplied as guarantees (see note to 39.5.1).

hostages by the Romans: P. Crassus, who was wintering with the Seventh legion on the lower Loire, sent two equestrian officers to the Veneti and others to neighbouring peoples to request grain, but these were detained and an embassy was sent to Crassus offering to release them in exchange for the hostages (Caesar, *BG* 3.7–8). Dio wrongly claims that a Roman embassy was sent to demand the officers' release and was detained as well. The mistake perhaps arose through misunderstanding of Caesar's (tendentious) assertion that the officers' detention violated the rights of ambassadors (*BG* 3.9.3, 16.4).

40.3 *Caesar himself marched against the Veneti*: Dio overlooks that Caesar had spent the winter of 57–56 south of the Alps (see notes to 39.5.1, 25.1). He gave instructions for the fleet construction before his return, and may not have reached the territory of the Veneti himself until midsummer.

boats . . . suitable for the tidal . . . Ocean: erroneous—the ships built were oared galleys of the usual Roman type.

40.5 *Decimus Brutus*: D. Iunius Brutus Albinus, then an equestrian prefect. Although advanced by Caesar, he was one of the conspirators against him in 44.

swift ships from the Mediterranean: a bad error. Brutus in fact brought the new fleet built on the Loire and ships supplied by Roman allies south of the Loire. Before his arrival Caesar had merely undertaken land operations against some Venetic strongholds.

the barbarians' contempt . . . brought about their defeat: the battle was probably fought in Quiberon Bay. Dio reproduces some of Caesar's information on the Veneti's ships, but adds the claim that their contempt led to their defeat and diverges on the course of the battle. In Caesar's account (*BG* 3.14–15), the Romans captured several ships while the wind was still blowing by cutting the sail ropes with their scythes and then boarding, and, when the wind dropped, the enemy fleet was at their mercy. Some scholars suppose that Dio was drawing on another source, but his version is better interpreted as his own elaboration for dramatic effect, with echoes of Thucydides' accounts of Greek sea battles, such as the tactics of 'outflanking' and 'breaking through' the enemy line to ram, and the contrast of land and sea fighting styles (39.42.2, 43.5; compare Thucydides 2.83.5, 84.1, 89.8).

42.2 *reliant on oars*: in fact the Venetic ships did not carry oars, depending wholly on sail power (*BG* 3.14.7).

42.3 *sometimes ramming*: according to Caesar (*BG* 3.13.8, 14.4), their stout construction meant that the Venetic ships could not be damaged by Roman ramming.

43.4 *a match for the Romans . . . in determination and bravery*: contradicting Caesar's claim that 'in courage our soldiers were easily superior' (*BG* 3.14.8).

scythes . . . shredded the sails: this tactic occurs much earlier in Caesar's account (see note to 39.40.5).

43.5 *killed the most eminent . . . and sold the rest*: Caesar says (*BG* 3.16) that all the Veneti were concentrated in the same place and surrendered, and that he executed their senators and sold the rest. This must be an exaggeration: the tribe continued in existence. The harsh penalty will have been intended as a deterrent to other rebellions, but Caesar defends it as upholding the rights of ambassadors (cf. note to 39.40.1).

44.1 *Morini and . . . Menapii*: Belgic peoples living on the coast from around modern Boulogne to the Rhine mouth, not reached in the expedition against the other Belgae in 57. The submission of the Veneti, Venelli, and their allies (39.40–43, 45) had re-established Roman control from the Loire to the Seine, leaving Caesar free to move north against these peoples in late summer. Caesar (*BG* 3.28–29) gives a more upbeat account of the campaign than Dio, minimizing Roman casualties and attributing the withdrawal to bad weather and the onset of winter. Two details occurring only in Dio's version are the hut-dwelling and the (topographically inaccurate) mountains.

45.1 *Venelli*: they lived in what is now the Cotentin Peninsula, and were joined in resistance by neighbouring peoples to the south and east. Sabinus' campaign against these peoples and Crassus' campaign in Aquitania took place at the same time as Caesar's against the Veneti, and accordingly follow it in Caesar's narrative, whereas Dio opted instead to finish narrating Caesar's own activity (39.44) before turning to his subordinates. Except in some details, Dio's account of Sabinus' and Crassus' campaigns (39.45–46) closely follows Caesar's own (*BG* 3.17–28).

45.4 *sated with food and drink*: this detail is not in Caesar. The fake deserter claimed that the Romans were going to withdraw that night (*BG* 3.18.4), but there is no need to suppose (as editors have suggested) that this information was included by Dio and lost in a gap in his text.

not even the fire-bearer should survive: a proverbial expression for complete annihilation (perhaps deriving from Spartan armies being accompanied by a fire-bearer carrying sacrificial fire from the altar of Zeus the Leader). Dio is here echoing the language of Herodotus' description (8.6.2) of a Persian plan to destroy the Greek fleet at Artemisium before it could escape.

to burn the Romans alive: according to Caesar, the wood was to fill the ditches surrounding the Roman camp.

45.7 *Gauls . . . boldness*: this ethnographic generalization is taken over from Caesar (*BG* 3.19.6).

46.1 *Publius Crassus*: after commanding the cavalry against Ariovistus in 58, Crassus held independent commands in 57 and 56. He returned to Rome in winter 56 (39.31.2), and joined his father in Syria in 54, dying at Carrhae in 53, probably aged around 30.

Aquitania: the land of the Aquitani, between the Garonne and the Pyrenees. Caesar distinguishes between the Aquitani and the Gauls to their north and east (*BG* 1.1.1–2), and Dio's reference to 'Celtic lands' here appears to relate to those peoples, departing from his normal practice (see note to 39.47.1).

46.2 *their town*: modern Sos.

46.3 *some of the other tribes*: the Vocates and Tarustes.

Sertorius' former troops: the civil-war leader Sertorius had held out in Spain with much native support from 80 until his assassination in 73.

47.1 *two Celtic tribes . . . entered the territory of the Treveri*: here, as usual, Dio uses 'Celt' to refer to peoples dwelling east of the Rhine, called Germans by Caesar and later writers (cf. notes to 38.34.1 and 39.49.2). At 39.47–49 Dio heavily compresses Caesar's account of his dealings with German tribes in 55 BCE (*BG* 4.1–19), with some modifications tending to Caesar's discredit. The Tencteri and Usipetes crossed the lower Rhine into the territory of the Menapii in winter 56/55, and in the spring moved south to the territory of the Treveri and their dependants the Eburones and Condrusi. Caesar's campaign against them and his subsequent Rhine crossing occupied most of summer 55. Dio misdates these events to the preceding winter.

47.2 *finding Caesar there*: Caesar's army had wintered south of the lower Seine, watching over the recently pacified peoples. Caesar himself spent the winter in northern Italy as usual, but hurried back in the spring to deal with the Tencteri and Usipetes.

promised to return . . . and asked for a truce: Caesar (*BG* 4.7–11) reports two visits from the envoys as follows. At the first meeting, he rejected their demand for land in Gaul, but promised to request land for them east of the Rhine from the Ubii, and refused to halt his advance while they consulted their peoples. At the second, when the two forces were only 12 (Roman) miles apart, the envoys promised to withdraw to Ubian territory if the Ubii confirmed the land grant. Caesar (so he claims) refused their request for a three-day truce to seek the Ubii's agreement, but urged that a larger deputation be sent to him the next day, promised meanwhile to advance only 4 (Roman) miles, and instructed his cavalry to avoid hostilities. He alleges that the enemy were only negotiating to gain time until the main body of their cavalry returned from raiding elsewhere. (Dio first mentions their absence at 39.48.3.)

47.3 *small cavalry squadron of his*: Caesar's cavalry in Gaul was provided by his Gallic allies. He tells us (*BG* 4.12) that his cavalry force at this point was much larger than the victorious enemy squadron (5,000 against 800), and it lost seventy-four men.

48.1 *elders . . . younger men*: this contrast in age groups' attitude to war is common in ancient military narratives, but absent from Caesar's account here.

would give them a reply before long: by adding this undertaking, Dio makes the Roman attack clearly treacherous. Caesar's version is that, after the treacherous assault by the enemy cavalry, he decided that further negotiations were out of the question and it was essential to counter-attack the next day (*BG* 4.13). His conduct attracted some criticism at Rome: at the end of the year, when the Senate voted him a *supplicatio* (39.53.2), Cato argued instead that he should be surrendered to the enemy for breaching faith (Plut. *Caes.* 22 and *Cato* 51; App. *Celt.* 18; Suet. *Jul.* 24.3).

48.2 *slaughtered them . . . women and children*: Caesar gives the (certainly exaggerated) figure of 430,000 for the total numbers of the Tencteri and Usipetes, and implies that few survived the massacre. Its location may have been in the Rhine delta, at the confluence of the Waal, its main branch, with the Meuse (as Caesar's manuscripts imply, *BG* 4.15.2), and archaeological traces of the massacre may survive there (N. Roymans, 'Caesar's Conquest and the Archaeology of Mass Violence in the Germanic

Frontier Zone', in A. J. Fitzpatrick and C. Haselgrove (eds.), *Julius Caesar's Battle for Gaul: New Archaeological Perspectives* (Oxford, 2019), 115–25). However, some scholars locate it further south, at the confluence of the Rhine and Moselle (near modern Koblenz).

48.3 *pretext for crossing the river*: Dio reproduces the justifications for the crossing given in Caesar's own account (*BG* 4.16), but adds his desire to win the glory of being the first Roman to cross the Rhine (so also Plut. *Caes.* 22) and that the demand to the Sugambri was a mere pretext, whose rejection Caesar expected (as with Ariovistus, 38.34.5–6).

48.4 *built a bridge*: in ten days. Caesar gives a detailed account of this engineering feat (*BG* 4.17).

48.5 *withdrawn into their strongholds*: 'to uninhabited areas and forests' (Caesar, *BG* 4.18.1).

crossed back within twenty days: after an eighteen-day stay according to Caesar, who presents its achievements in a much more positive light.

49.1 *Raetia*: an Alpine region conquered in 15 BCE, and from the reign of Claudius a province comprising Tyrol and parts of Bavaria and Switzerland. As usual, Dio uses the provinces of his own day for geographical indication.

49.2 *their separate names*: for Dio's distinctive usage of 'Celts', see notes to 38.34.1 and 39.47.1.

50.1 *later, in the consulship of Pompey and Crassus*: not realizing that Caesar's campaign against the Tencteri and Usipetes and crossing of the Rhine took place in 55, Dio marks the year change now. Caesar crossed to Britain in late August, returning in mid-September (Julian dates: see Appendix, p. 162). By making it appear that the expedition was Caesar's only activity in 55, Dio heightens the impression of its futility (cf. 39.53.1).

50.2 *450 stades*: 88 km/55 miles (cf. note to 38.17.7), over twice the true distance. Other ancient estimates are closer, e.g. Caesar's 30 (Roman) miles (= 44 km/28 miles) for his crossing (*BG* 5.2.3).

past almost all Spain as well: other ancient descriptions have the same distortion (e.g. Caesar, *BG* 5.13.2).

50.4 *under Agricola's propraetorship*: as governor of Britain (77–84 CE), Cn. Julius Agricola campaigned as far as northern Scotland. During his command, the island was circumnavigated, first by mutineers and then by his fleet (66.20.1–2; Tacitus, *Agricola* 28, 38). Dio's term reflects Agricola's formal status as governor of one of the emperor's provinces (*legatus pro praetore*, cf. 53.13).

under . . . Severus: repeated at 76[77].12.5. Septimius Severus (emperor 193–211) campaigned beyond the Forth–Clyde line in 208–10, the first Roman commander to do so since Agricola.

51.1 *Morini*: Caesar had failed to subdue them in 56 (39.44), but they now made a voluntary submission as he advanced into their territory for the crossing to Britain (*BG* 4.22).

eager to invade Britain: Caesar (*BG* 4.20) claims that he crossed because Gauls fighting against Rome had regularly received assistance from Britain and he judged that a reconnaissance would be useful. Dio instead, here and at 39.53, attributes the crossing to Caesar's desire for glory (see Introduction, p. xiii). Dio's account of the expedition (39.51–52) agrees with Caesar's much fuller account (*BG* 4.21–38) except on some details.

51.2 *rounded a certain prominent headland*: this detail is not included in Caesar's own account. If, as is usually supposed, Caesar arrived off the cliffs of Dover and then sailed along to land between Walmer and Deal, the headland will be the South Foreland.

51.3 *sent some of the Morini*: not mentioned by Caesar, who instead says that the Britons' embassy was accompanied by the Atrebatan leader Commius, whom Caesar had sent ahead as his emissary, but the Britons had arrested (*BG* 4.27.2–3).

52.2 *killed them all, apart from a few*: according to Caesar (*BG* 4.32.5), only a few Romans were killed.

a number of defeats: not according to Caesar.

52.3 *received only a few*: the new demand was for hostages additional to those received earlier (39.51.3) to be sent on to Caesar in Gaul, but he received them from only two communities (*BG* 4.38.5).

53.1 *quelled the disturbances there*: Caesar mentions the crushing of a rebellion among the Morini and another attempt to conquer the Menapii (*BG* 4.38).

53.2 *festal period of twenty days*: *supplicationes*, decreed by the Senate in response to Caesar's despatch reporting his achievements this year, including the invasions of Germany and Britain, and exceeding the unprecedented fifteen days voted him in 57 (see notes to 37.36.3 and 39.5.1). For Cato's opposition, see note to 39.48.1.

54.1 *uprising in Spain . . . assigned to Pompey*: referring back to 39.33.2. Having not worked it in earlier, Dio awkwardly gives a brief account of the uprising here. Following his consulship in 57, Metellus Nepos governed Hither Spain until replaced by Pompey's legate L. Afranius in 55. His campaign against the Vaccaei and their allies took place in 56. The fighting was in the upland plains around the upper Douro, a region which had sided with Sertorius. The Vaccaei continued to make occasional trouble down to 29.

54.2 *Clunia*: a hilltop town (modern Peñalba de Castro) of the Arevaci, eastern neighbours of the Vaccaei.

55.1 *Ptolemy . . . recovered his kingdom*: at 39.55–63 Dio completes the account of the Egyptian crisis which he had begun at 39.12–16, covering both the restoration of Ptolemy Auletes in 55 and the resulting trials of Gabinius following his return in 54. Dio once again gives the topic extended treatment to illustrate Roman corruption, with an introduction (39.55) leading into the detailed narrative. His account is very hostile to Gabinius, and may exaggerate Pompey's responsibility for the restoration.

rescinded their vote to help him: inaccurate, as at 39.15.3.

55.2 *decrees of the people and the Senate*: in accordance with the published Sibylline oracle, the Senate decreed in January 56 that Ptolemy should not be restored 'with a multitude', but no vote on the matter was passed in the assembly (cf. notes to 39.15.2–16.1).

55.4 *acquittal*: for *maiestas* (treason, see notes to 39.62.2–3).

55.5 *found guilty*: of *repetundae* (extortion, see notes to 39.63.1–5). Dio appears to imply that Gabinius was convicted for extorting 100 million denarii from his province. However, his wording ('myriad myriads') may not have been meant to be taken literally, and the prosecution appears to have focused mainly on the huge bribe Gabinius was alleged to have received from Ptolemy for his restoration. Following his conviction, the sum assessed for restitution was 10,000 talents (= 60 million denarii), the supposed total of the bribe.

56.1 *Gabinius had mistreated Syria*: following his consulship in 58, Gabinius governed Syria (assigned to him under Clodius' law: see note to 38.15.6) from 57 until he was succeeded by Crassus in 54. Cicero gives scathing accounts of his misgovernment in speeches delivered in 57–55, stressing especially the sufferings of the Roman tax-farmers (*publicani*). In fact, Gabinius probably sought to protect the provincials against them.

raiding: only mentioned by Dio (and sometimes mistranslated as piracy). The chief disturbances were in Judaea, where rebellion against Pompey's settlement (see notes to 37.15.2–16.4) was led by escaped members of Aristobulus' family. Gabinius campaigned there in 57–56, first against his son Alexander and then against Aristobulus himself. Josephus' detailed account of his activity there is strongly favourable to Gabinius (*Jewish Antiquities* 14.82–104; *Jewish War* 1.160–78).

56.2 *Mithridates*: Mithridates III of Parthia. Coins show that he may have been co-ruler with Phraates III and was his initial successor, following Phraates' assassination in 58/57. 'Media' here is sometimes thought to mean Greater Media, south of the Caspian Sea and under Parthian rule from the later second century BCE, but more probably refers (as elsewhere in Dio) to the kingdom of Media Atropatene to its north. If so, Mithridates III may be identical with the Mithridates mentioned as its ruler at 36.14.2.

56.3 *letter from Pompey*: other sources report Gabinius being diverted from Parthia to Egypt by Ptolemy's promised bribe, but only Dio mentions Pompey's role. If Pompey did write such a letter, it was doubtless cautiously worded. For Gabinius' long-standing association with Pompey, see notes to 36.23.4 and 38.15.6.

56.4 *not allowed to start wars of their own accord*: Sulla's law on *maiestas* and Caesar's law on *repetundae*, under which Gabinius was prosecuted at his two trials, as well as some earlier laws, prohibited a provincial governor from leaving his province or starting a war on his own authority (Cicero, *Against Piso* 50). However, Gabinius' defence was that he had acted in the public interest (Cicero, *For Rabirius Postumus* 20), and all the laws probably included this exemption (see note to 38.41.1; A. W. Lintott, *Imperium Romanum: Politics and Administration* (London, 1993), 23–7).

the people and the Sibyl: see note to 39.55.2.

56.5 *Sisenna*: Cornelius Sisenna, Gabinius' adopted son. Josephus mentions him as one of Gabinius' subordinate commanders in the war against Aristobulus.

vulnerable to raiders: Josephus tells us that Alexander renewed the rebellion in Judaea during Gabinius' absence in Egypt. On his return Gabinius restored order there by renewed fighting, and also campaigned against the Nabataean Arabs (see note to 37.15.1).

56.6 *arrested Aristobulus . . . sent him to Pompey*: in fact back to official custody in Rome. Josephus shows that Gabinius' campaign against Aristobulus took place before his departure for Egypt.

57.1 *Berenice*: see 39.13.1. She ruled initially with her mother Cleopatra VI Tryphaena. Contrary to the impression given by Dio, her marriages will have been contracted before Gabinius began his expedition.

Seleucus: the later Ptolemies and Seleucids quite often intermarried, and, despite the doubts of Dio and Strabo (17.1.11), Seleucus' claim to royal birth was probably well founded. Strabo says that Berenice had him killed in a few days because of his coarseness.

57.2 *Archelaus . . . living in Syria*: the elder Archelaus was Mithridates' principal general in his first war with Rome, but defected to Rome in 83: he will have been prominent in Dio's account of the period. His son had been made the priestly ruler of Pontic Comana (see note to 36.11.2) by Pompey and was serving with Gabinius in Syria.

57.3 *making out that he had escaped*: Dio's claim that Gabinius connived at Archelaus' flight and speculations as to his motives are implausible. More probably, he slipped away undetected (so Strabo, according to whom he claimed to be the son of Mithridates).

58.1 *Pelusium*: a city at the easternmost mouth of the Nile (modern Tell el-Farama).

58.2 *riots . . . in Alexandria*: founded by Alexander in 331, Alexandria was the royal capital, ethnically diverse and one of the largest cities in the Mediterranean world. Dio is critical of its unruliness again at 66.8.7.

58.3 *handed the kingdom over to Ptolemy*: rumours of Ptolemy's restoration had reached Italy by 22 April 55 (Cic. *Att.* 4.10.1).

59.2 *raiders . . . tax-farmers*: see notes to 39.56.1, 5.

60.1 *insulted Cicero . . . as an exile*: Pompey, who since April 56 (see note to 39.25.1) had been taking care to ensure Cicero's compliance, will not have openly insulted him. Cicero later told Lentulus Spinther (*Fam.* 1.9.20) that, after attacking Gabinius, Crassus had suddenly switched to defending him and abused Cicero when he objected, to which Cicero had responded angrily, but Pompey had insisted on their being reconciled before Crassus left for Syria in November 55. Gabinius himself called Cicero 'exile' in the Senate on 8 October 54 (*QF* 3.2.2).

60.3 *rivals for the consulship*: L. Domitius Ahenobarbus had been a bitter opponent of the alliance of Pompey, Caesar, and Crassus since its formation in 59, and, to protect Caesar, they had been determined to exclude him from the consulship for 55 (see note to 39.31.1). For 54 they had been unable to prevent him from getting a consulship and his brother-in-law Cato a praetorship.

Claudius was related to Pompey: Pompey's eldest son, Cn. Pompeius Magnus, was married to Ap. Claudius Pulcher's daughter. The connection may have been formed as part of the realignments of spring 56, when Appius had been among Caesar's visitors (see note to 39.25.1; J. Tatum, 'The Marriage of Pompey's Son to the Daughter of Ap. Claudius Pulcher', *Klio* 73 (1991), 122–9).

if he created a little confusion: Dio speculates implausibly on Appius' motives, associating him with his brother Clodius' demagoguery and the universal corruption.

60.4 *the Sibylline verses should be consulted*: if Dio's information is accurate, the Senate instructed the *quindecimviri* (see note to 39.15.2) to search in the Sibylline books for guidance on how disregard of their warning against helping an Egyptian king with an army should be punished, but they reported that they had found nothing to the purpose.

61.1 *Tiber . . . burst its banks*: Cicero's report (*QF* 3.5.8) of extensive flooding about the end of October 54, after Gabinius' acquittal at his first trial, probably relates to the same flood. If so, Dio has misdated the flood in placing it before Gabinius' return.

62.1 *entered the city under cover of darkness*: on 27 September 54. Cicero's letters (*QF* 3.1–7; *Att.* 4.17–18) give vivid information on political developments from September until November/December, including Gabinius' return and first trial (for *maiestas*).

62.2 *Cicero accused him with the greatest vehemence*: Cicero in fact refrained from acting as one of Gabinius' prosecutors, from fear of a rupture with Pompey, contenting himself with giving a witness statement for the prosecution.

62.3 *acquitted*: on 23 October, by thirty-eight votes to thirty-two. Cicero blamed the incompetence of the prosecutors, the corrupt jury, and Pompey's lobbying. For the case for the defence, see also note to 39.56.4; R. S. Williams, '*Rei publicae causae*: Gabinius' Defence of His Restoration of Ptolemy Auletes', *Classical Journal* 81 (1985), 25–38.

63.1 *found guilty of them*: for *repetundae* (extortion, see note to 39.55.5). Another indictment against Gabinius, for electoral corruption (*ambitus*), now lapsed.

63.3 *ruined by the floods*: repeated misdating (see note to 39.61.1).

until the second trial was over: Dio assumes that Gabinius' conviction for *repetundae* followed soon after his acquittal for *maiestas*, and still in the year 54. This dating is accepted by most scholars but, in view of Cicero's failure to mention it in his letters of late 54, A. W. Lintott (*Cicero as Evidence* (Oxford, 2008), 246) may be right that the *repetundae* trial could not be held until the second half of 53 (after the delayed election of magistrates).

63.4 *the people were convened outside the pomerium*: in a *contio* (see Glossary, p. 284). Pompey was a proconsul both as grain commissioner (from 57: see note to 39.9.3) and as governor of Spain (from this year: see note to 39.39.4) and so not normally able to cross the *pomerium* (see note to 37.54.1). It was perhaps by special dispensation that Pompey entered the city in early 56 to give evidence for Sestius and Milo (cf. 39.19.1-2). When near the city, he generally stayed in his suburban villa in the northern Campus Martius.

63.5 *defector*: for this charge against Cicero, see note to 36.44.2. Since 58 Cicero had been bitterly hostile to Gabinius because of the latter's role in his exile (cf. 38.15.6–16.6), and it was only under extreme pressure from Pompey that he agreed to be reconciled with Gabinius and defend him in his second trial. Cicero went on to defend the banker C. Rabirius Postumus on a follow-up charge of receiving money extorted by Gabinius, and his published speech at this trial provides important evidence for Gabinius' trials.

brought back by Caesar: during the civil war. Gabinius commanded for Caesar in Illyricum in 48–47, dying there.

64.1 *During this same time*: Dio had continued his account of Gabinius' restoration of Ptolemy and its consequences (39.55–63) into the new consular year. Having already reported one other event at Rome in 54 (the Tiber flood), he now adds two more (39.64–65). In each case he highlights illegalities, so making a fitting close to Book 39, which had featured so much disorder. Despite his stress on corruption in relation to Ptolemy's restoration, Dio omits the other major corruption scandal of the year over the delayed elections (see note to 40.45.1).

baby girl: Julia, Caesar's daughter and Pompey's wife (38.9.1), died in August 54, and the child (sources differ on its sex) survived only a few days. Other sources stress the political implications of the severing of the kinship tie between Pompey and Caesar, as does Dio at 40.44.3.

Campus Martius: an area of public land comprising most of the Tiber floodplain north of the city. The only recent burial there had been that of Sulla in 78, authorized by decree of the Senate. Julia's burial there appears to have been a spontaneous popular demonstration, opposed not only by the consul Domitius but also by tribunes (Plut. *Caes.* 23; *Pomp.* 53). However, a monumental tomb was constructed, and in 44 Caesar's bones were interred there after his cremation nearby (44.51.2).

65.1 *Pomptinus celebrated his triumph over the Gauls*: on 2 November 54. For his campaign against the Allobroges in 62–61 and Ser. Sulpicius Galba's part in it, see 36.47–48. Pomptinus had remained governor of Transalpine Gaul until 59. The Senate may have decreed him a triumph soon after his return in 58, but friends of Caesar had prevented him from holding it by obstructing the law extending his *imperium* for the day of the triumph, without which his *imperium* would lapse when he crossed the *pomerium* (see Glossary, p. 286).

65.2 *before the first hour*: the Roman day, from dawn to sunset, was divided into twelve equal hours, whose length thus varied by the season.

some of the tribunes . . . made trouble . . . during his triumph: in fact it was two praetors (one of them Cato) and a tribune, acting as upholders of constitutional propriety (Cic. *QF* 3.4.6; *Att.* 4.18.3).

BOOK FORTY

1.1 *its seven hundredth year*: various calculations of the foundation date of Rome had been made. Dio follows Varro's dating (widely adopted by his day) to Olympiad year 6.3 (= 754/3 BCE). He includes a similar notice of the 800th anniversary under 47 CE (60[61].29.1), and probably noted all the centenaries in the remaining lost parts of his work.

In Gaul in the same year: Dio now continues the narrative of Caesar's campaigns from 39.53, but confines himself here to the events of a single year, 54 BCE. His account is generally close to Caesar's much fuller version in the fifth book of his *Gallic War*, and divergences are mostly minor, except on the disaster suffered by Sabinus and Cotta against the Eburones (see notes to 40.5–6).

1.2 *At the start of the sailing season*: Cicero's correspondence with his brother (now serving with Caesar) shows that in fact Caesar did not cross to Britain until late July (Julian dating, see Appendix, p. 162). Besides his preparations, he had also been delayed by emergency actions against disaffection in Gaul.

all the hostages they had promised: see note to 39.52.3.

his craving for the island was so strong: Dio again stresses Caesar's desire for Britain (see note to 39.51.1; Introduction, p. xiii), making a characteristic contrast between pretext and real motive. Caesar's own narrative offers no explanation for this year's expedition. The much larger forces deployed show that he was now aiming to bring south-east Britain under Roman control.

1.3 *landed at the same place as before*: see note to 39.51.2.

2.1 *larger army he had come with*: Caesar now brought five of his eight legions and 2,000 cavalry. The previous year he had taken just two legions to Britain.

2.2 *rough stockade*: perhaps at a hill fort at Bigbury, near Canterbury.

inflict a lot of casualties: not according to Caesar, who says that the Britons were driven out of their stronghold with only a few Romans wounded (*BG* 5.9–10).

2.3 *ship enclosure itself*: Caesar had left his ships riding at anchor. Returning to the coast after the storm, he had the ships dragged ashore and a continuous fortification constructed for them and the camp. Unlike Dio, Caesar locates the enemy assault inland, where he had rejoined his main force (*BG* 5.11.7–8).

Cassivellaunus: king of an unknown people north of the Thames.

2.4 *this tactic*: not mentioned in Caesar's account of the fighting (*BG* 5.15–17).

3.2 *the fortress*: Cassivellaunus' own stronghold, some distance north of the Thames, usually identified with the hill fort at Wheathampstead, near St Albans. Cassivellaunus also suffered the desertion of the Trinovantes and other tribes north of the Thames.

those who were attacking the roadstead: four kings in what is now Kent, acting at Cassivellaunus' request.

came to terms: Caesar uses the traditional Roman formulation—they surrendered, and were ordered to give hostages and pay tribute (*BG* 5.22.4).

4.1 *withdrew . . . from the island*: in mid-September.

not to risk losing even that by seeking for more: Dio's preceding sentence is close to Caesar's own explanation of his withdrawal for winter, but he adds a generalizing reflection: having stressed Caesar's desire for Britain, he now represents him as giving up this 'seeking for more', as with Pompey's avoidance of a Parthian war (see note to 37.7.2).

4.2 *When he set out for Italy . . . garrisoned on each of the tribes*: disturbances occurred only in north-east Gaul. Caesar stationed his legions across the region in separate winter quarters. He decided to remain at Samarobriva (modern Amiens) himself until the legions were settled in their camps, and, contrary to Dio's implication, the revolts broke out before he could leave for Cisalpine Gaul.

5.1 *Eburones*: dependants of their neighbours the Treveri, they lived on both sides of the river Meuse north of the Ardennes.

They claimed . . . the truth was: Caesar's account does not discuss the Eburones' motivation, but Dio supplies a characteristic contrast between claims and real reasons.

Sabinus and Cotta: Q. Titurius Sabinus and L. Aurunculeius Cotta had both commanded effectively in 58 and 57 (for Sabinus, see notes to 39.1.4, 45.1). They were now in joint command of the Fourteenth legion (recruited in 57) and five additional cohorts.

5.3 *going to attack the Romans that night*: according to Caesar (*BG* 5.27), Ambiorix claimed that the initial assault had been part of a concerted set of Gallic attacks on the Roman winter camps, and urged the Romans to leave before German reinforcements arrived in two days' time.

Eburonia: the only occurrence of this place name. Caesar later (*BG* 6.32.3–4) calls the site of Sabinus' and Cotta's camp Atuatuca, probably not to be identified with the later Roman town of that name (modern Tongeren).

to some of their comrades who were wintering nearby: either to Q. Cicero's camp among the Nervii or Labienus' among the Remi.

6.1 *taken in by what Ambiorix said*: Caesar (*BG* 5.28–31) portrays the with-drawal as the chaotic outcome of a bitter dispute between the hysterical Sabinus and the upright Cotta, who argued for staying put. Dio instead, surely following a different source, represents the commanders as in agreement and believing that Ambiorix was loyally repaying his debt to Caesar, a claim mentioned by Caesar only in his report of Ambiorix's speech.

set out after nightfall: according to Caesar, at dawn the next day.

6.2 *Ambiorix . . . had not taken part in the attack*: Caesar, however, portrays him as playing a leading part in it.

6.3 *these men's fate*: Caesar's and Dio's versions again diverge. In Caesar's (*BG* 5.33–37), Sabinus loses his nerve and foolishly seeks the meeting with Ambiorix, while Cotta dies after Sabinus, resisting heroically.

7.1 *Nervii*: for their conquest in 57, see 39.3.

Quintus Cicero: the orator's younger brother, praetor in 62, proconsul of Asia 62–58, and Caesar's legate from 54 to 51. Like his brother, he was to die in the proscriptions of 43.

Ambiorix added the Nervii to his army: in what follows, Dio represents Ambiorix as individually responsible for actions which Caesar ascribes to the Nervii collectively.

7.2 *tried to trick Cicero too*: after the failure of the initial attempt to take the camp by assault, leading Nervii unsuccessfully attempted to persuade Cicero to withdraw from their territory, promising safe conduct.

experience he had acquired . . . as an ally of the Romans: probably Dio's error, crediting to Ambiorix the knowledge the Nervii had gained through service with the Romans (so Caesar, *BG* 5.42.2).

palisade: surmounting an earthwork, as in Roman sieges. The Nervii also constructed other Roman-style siege-works.

8.1 *lacked medical supplies . . . food*: details not in Caesar's account. Cicero will in fact have laid in food supplies for the winter.

9.1 *still on the march*: in fact he had not left Samarobriva (see note to 40.4.2).

hastened on his way: with a relief force of two legions. Caesar details the troop redeployments at *BG* 5.46–47.

9.2 *their language . . . clothes*: this detail and Caesar's reason for not sending back the slave are Dio's additions.

9.3 *in Greek*: Caesar says 'in Greek characters' (*BG* 5.48.4), so probably wrote the message in Latin.

9.4 *lodge in a tower*: according to Caesar, the use of a javelin had been his suggestion, and the message remained undetected for two days until spotted by one of Cicero's soldiers.

11.1 *Treveri . . . renewed war . . . at Indutiomarus' instigation*: according to Caesar (*BG* 5.3–4, 26.2, 47, 53.1–2), the leadership of the powerful Treveri, in the Moselle basin, had been contested from the start of the year between the pro-Roman Cingetorix and anti-Roman Indutiomarus; Indutiomarus had instigated the rebellion of the Eburones, and, after their destruction of Sabinus and Cotta's force, had led the Treveri against Labienus' camp, withdrawing after Caesar's defeat of the Nervii.

11.2 *Titus Labienus*: Dio first mentions him in Gaul here, but Labienus was in fact Caesar's principal legate throughout his Gallic command. For his career, see note to 37.26.1.

crushed them: Labienus tricked the Treveri into overconfidence, as Caesar had just done to the Nervii and he himself was to do again to the Treveri in 53 (40.31.3–5). Indutiomarus was killed in this battle, a fact mentioned by Dio only at 40.31.2.

pacify them completely: concern about the possibility of further revolts led Caesar to spend the winter north of the Alps for the first time in his command. The alleged overconfidence about his ability to complete the pacification is Dio's own addition.

12.1 *glory and profit*: earlier sources also give one or both of these as Crassus' motive for his Parthian campaign, and, unlike Dio, rightly suppose that he was planning the campaign from the moment he accepted the governorship of Syria. Plutarch (*Crass.* 17–33) and Dio (40.12–27) provide our only detailed accounts of the campaign.

no grievance . . . against them: other sources insisting that Crassus had no ground for the war include Cicero (*De Finibus* 3.75, written in 45). Some scholars suppose that, like Gabinius (see note to 39.56.2), Crassus was acting in support of Orodes' rival Mithridates III, but Mithridates' defeat and execution had probably taken place before Crassus' arrival.

no vote . . . to undertake the war: it is unlikely that the *lex Trebonia*, under which Crassus had been appointed, had specified the province as Syria and the Parthian war, as some sources claim. However, the law had granted him the right to make war on whom he pleased (see note to 39.33.2).

recently established on the throne: see note to 39.56.2.

12.2 *satrap*: the empire of the Achaemenid Persian kings had been divided into provinces, each governed by a satrap, and this system was continued by their successors, Alexander, the Seleucids, and the Parthians.

Ichniae: south of Carrhae on the river Balikh, a tributary of the Euphrates (other sources call it Ichnae).

13.1 *Nicephorium*: modern Raqqa, on the Euphrates near its confluence with the Balikh.

colonists . . . alongside them: after Alexander's death in 324, his general Seleucus I had become ruler of a vast region extending eastwards from Syria, establishing a dynasty, and he and his successors founded numerous cities across their empire.

13.2 *expelled*: Plutarch says that Crassus plundered the city and sold the inhabitants as slaves. The location of Zenodotium is unknown.

13.3 *There can be no doubt . . . under close guard*: Plutarch too (*Crass.* 17) criticizes Crassus' withdrawal, arguing that he should have continued south, winning over Seleucia-on-Tigris and Babylon. In fact, winter conditions in the region would have been hazardous, and, having established a bridgehead in western Mesopotamia, it was prudent for Crassus to take his main force back to Syria. He devoted much of the winter to financial exactions, including from the temple in Jerusalem.

13.4 *left behind in the region*: according to Plutarch, Crassus left garrisons in the Greek cities totalling 7,000 infantry and 1,000 cavalry.

14.1 *Ctesiphon . . . palace*: the Greek city of Seleucia-on-Tigris, on the west bank above Babylon and below modern Baghdad, had been founded *c.*305 by Seleucus I. Ctesiphon was founded nearby but on the opposite bank by the Parthian kings after their conquest of Mesopotamia, and was used by them as their winter residence.

14.2 *under the Persian kings*: Parthia was a region east of the south-eastern shore of the Caspian Sea, crossing modern Iran and Turkmenistan.

14.3 *Arsaces . . . Arsacids*: Arsaces I established himself as king in Parthia in the mid-third century, and his successors retained 'Arsaces' as the royal name (see note to 36.1.1). Some sources claim that Arsaces I took over Parthia as leader of a nomad war-band from further east. Parthian independence from Seleucid rule was definitively achieved by the early second century.

prospered . . . satrapies: under Mithridates I (*c.*171–138), the Parthians took over all of the eastern part of the Seleucid empire, so extending their rule from the Euphrates to Bactria. Under them, as under the Seleucids, Upper Mesopotamia and Babylonia were each governed by a satrap (see note to 40.12.2).

14.4 *whenever war breaks out between us*: the Parthians inflicted further military humiliation on Rome in 40–36 BCE. Augustus' policy of peaceful coexistence with Parthia was observed until the early second century CE, but Trajan, Lucius Verus, Septimius Severus, and Caracalla each invaded the Parthian empire, resulting in periods of Roman occupation for Mesopotamia. Dio wrote this passage before the overthrow of the Parthian empire by the Persian Artaxerxes *c.*224, briefly noted by Dio at the end of his work (80.3).

15.2 *mounted archers and lancers, mostly armoured*: Dio's wording fails to make it clear that the Parthian cavalry had two components: the 'cataphract' (armoured) cavalry, with both man and horse wearing mail armour and the rider carrying a heavy lance, and the light-armed mounted archers. The Romans had encountered cataphract cavalry in eastern armies before, but the mounted archers, with their distinctive tactic of feigned withdrawal, were a novelty for them.

16.1   *Orodes . . . war on him*: Plutarch (*Crass.* 18) and other sources provide further details on Orodes' embassy. Both this and his troop deployments in fact took place in early 53.

Surenas: not a personal name, but designating the leader of the noble Sūrēn clan, second only to the king in status and vividly described by Plutarch (*Crass.* 21). Although under 30, he had already recovered Seleucia from Orodes' rival Mithridates (see note to 40.12.1). He was accompanied now by a cavalry force of 10,000 of his own vassals, including 1,000 cataphracts, and perhaps also some troops supplied by the satrap Silaces (cf. 40.12.2). Soon after his victory over Crassus, Orodes had Surenas executed.

16.2   *the Armenia that had formerly belonged to Tigranes*: Dio's wording distinguishes the Armenian kingdom from Lesser Armenia (cf. notes to 36.9.1, 45.3; 38.38.4).

Artabazes: Artavasdes II of Armenia (modern scholars follow Latin authors in using this form of the name). Artavasdes succeeded his father in 56 or 55 and reigned until deposed by Antony in 34. According to Plutarch (*Crass.* 19), Artavasdes came to Crassus with 6,000 cavalry, but withdrew after failing to persuade him to invade via Armenia. Orodes deployed his main army to prevent Artavasdes from helping Crassus, leaving Surenas' smaller force to confront Crassus himself. After Crassus' disaster, Artavasdes was reconciled with Orodes, marrying his sister to Orodes' son Pacorus (cf. note to 40.27.3).

16.3   *Seleucia*: see note to 40.14.1. For Crassus' plan to advance to Seleucia and Ctesiphon, see 40.20.3.

17.1   *winter when Gnaeus Calvinus and Valerius Messalla became consuls*: their election and entry into office was in fact delayed until summer 53, as Dio reports at 40.17.2 and 45.1–46.1.

Eagle owls . . . lightning: a similar list is reported in the prodigy collection of Julius Obsequens (63), adding that in expiation a *lustratio* of the city was held, a purificatory procession around the city bounds, decreed especially after eagle owls or wolves had been sighted in the city. Dio reports similar portents in 52, perhaps a duplication (see note to 40.47.2).

17.3   *Zeugma*: modern Belkis (Turkey). Twin towns had been founded there on either side of the Euphrates by Seleucus I, at the crossing point of the main route from Antioch to Edessa. Crassus will have crossed there in 54 as well as 53. Zeugma (so named from its bridge of boats) continued to be the main crossing point from the Roman province of Syria, becoming a legionary base in the first century CE, and Trajan provided a stone bridge. Alexander's crossing point, Thapsacus, was further south.

signs . . . easily comprehensible: Plutarch (*Crass.* 19) and other sources report the portents at Crassus' crossing with minor divergences. As often, Dio makes his firm belief in portents apparent.

18.1 *eagles*: the eagle (*aquila*) was the emblem of a whole legion, to be distinguished from the standard (*signum*) of the individual maniples composing the legion.

18.3 *one of the large standards*: a *vexillum*, the standard of cavalry and some other units, formed of a cloth draped from a crossbar and suspended from a pole. The word derives from *velum*, 'sail'.

18.5 *sacrifices . . . unfavourable*: Plutarch says that Crassus held a lustration of his army, but dropped the sacrificial entrails.

20.1 *Abgar of Osrhoene*: Abgar II. Osrhoene in north-west Mesopotamia had broken away from Seleucid control in the later second century, with Edessa as its capital. Other sources give different identifications of the traitor.

Alchaudonius: see note to 36.2.5.

20.3 *cross over to Ctesiphon*: crossing the Tigris (see note to 40.14.1).

20.4 *Surenas . . . had only a small force*: see note to 40.16.1. Plutarch (*Crass.* 20) tells us that Crassus had seven legions and 4,000 each of cavalry and light-armed troops, but the garrisons left in the Greek cities (see note to 40.13.4) may have been drawn from these forces. Crassus' decision to strike east to confront Surenas' force, criticized by the ancient sources, is defended by some modern scholars.

21.2 *The battle went as follows*: Plutarch's fuller account (*Crass.* 23–7) is less rhetorical and more reliable. Both versions agree in attributing the victory to the combined action of the cataphracts and archers. The battle took place near the river Balikh, south of Carrhae. Ovid (*Fasti* 6.465–8) gives the date as 9 June.

The terrain being . . . wooded: false. Dio replaces the Parthians' concealment devices (described by Plutarch) with a stereotypical ambush.

Crassus . . . the younger: P. Crassus. Following his distinguished service in Gaul in 58–56 (see note to 39.46.1), he joined his father in Syria in winter 54/3, bringing 1,000 Gallic cavalry supplied by Caesar.

21.3 *advanced against them with the cavalry*: Plutarch (*Crass.* 25) gives a much fuller account of P. Crassus' advance and annihilation, more plausibly locating it at a later stage in the battle. On the elder Crassus' orders, his son responded to the encirclement of the main Roman force by breaking out with a mixed force from one of the Roman wings.

23.1 *When he joined the attack on the Romans*: a rear assault by a treacherous ally is a conventional battle feature rightly omitted in Plutarch's account.

24.1 *run out of arrows*: according to Plutarch (*Crass.* 25), the Parthians avoided running out of arrows by providing additional supplies on camels.

25.1 *the Romans who remained inside*: the garrison installed in 54 (see note to 40.13.4). For Carrhae, see note to 37.5.5.

25.3 *Crassus . . . decided to flee as soon as possible*: according to Plutarch (*Crass.* 28–9), Surenas was preparing to besiege Carrhae, having discovered Crassus' presence there.

25.4 *Cassius Longinus, the quaestor*: C. Cassius Longinus, Caesar's future assassin. Cassius was probably elected quaestor for 55, left Rome with Crassus in November 55, and served from 54 as proquaestor. Plutarch represents Cassius as having repeatedly advised against Crassus' errors and now opting to return via Carrhae to Syria with 500 cavalry.

25.5 *gained the mountains with Crassus himself*: according to Plutarch (*Crass.* 29), Crassus was led into marshland by a treacherous local guide, but another detachment under the legate Octavius reached hill country, where Crassus' force later managed to join them.

26.2 *Crassus . . . trusted him completely*: Plutarch (*Crass.* 30–31) differs, claiming that Crassus distrusted Surenas, but was forced by his soldiers to go to meet him.

27.3 *to mock him*: for starting the war from greed (see note to 40.12.1). The molten-gold story is also told by Florus (1.46.10), but not Plutarch. Some sources report that in 88, during his first war with Rome, Mithridates had molten gold poured down the throat of the allegedly corrupt Roman ambassador M.' Aquillius while he was still alive. According to Plutarch (*Crass.* 32–33), Surenas had Crassus' head and hands sent to Orodes' court, where they arrived in time to be used in a performance of Euripides' *Bacchae* at a banquet celebrating Orodes' reconciliation with Artavasdes (cf. note to 40.16.2).

legion out of their own resources: Cicero twice reports Crassus as saying that no one was rich who could not support an army from the income from his property, but in the Elder Pliny's version the reference is to a legion, as for Dio. Some scholars suppose that Crassus was referring to the six legions he raised against Spartacus in 72. Crassus was the richest man of his day until equalled by Pompey.

27.4 *Most . . . escaped*: only a few according to Plutarch (*Crass.* 31), who gives the Romans' losses on the campaign as 20,000 killed and 10,000 captured.

28.1 *Later . . . they also invaded Syria*: probably in 52. Dio provides no year indications in this survey of Parthian activity after the Carrhae victory.

28.2 *take charge of Syria . . . for the longer term*: It was normal for the quaestor to assume command of a province if its governor died. Cassius formed the survivors of Crassus' army (perhaps under 10,000 men) into two legions, and, after repelling the Parthian incursion, crushed a rebellion in Judaea.

28.3 *invaded again with a larger army*: in September 51. Other sources confirm Dio's account of Cassius' repelling of the invasion, especially the letters of Cicero, who governed the neighbouring province of Cilicia from July 51 to July 50. As usual, the Parthian force comprised mainly cavalry.

29.1 *Antigonia*: founded by Antigonus I in 307. Seleucus I had moved most of the inhabitants to Antioch, when he founded it a short distance down the river Orontes in 300, but this passage shows that Antigonia continued to exist.

29.3 *Pacorus . . . did not return to it again*: in fact, Pacorus led a major invasion of Syria in 40–38, duly reported by Dio (48.25 ff.).

30.1 *Bibulus arrived to govern Syria*: he reached Antioch in early October 51.

within five years afterwards: the reference is to Pompey's law on the provinces, passed in 52 (see notes to 40.46.2, 56.1). Dio is wrong to imply that Bibulus' appointment contravened the law. Cicero was appointed to Cilicia and Bibulus to Syria in 51 in accordance with the law, as the two most senior senators who had not held provinces after their consulships in respectively 63 and 59.

30.2 *Bibulus kept the subject territory at peace*: Dio seems unaware that (as Cicero's letters show) the Parthians invaded Syria again in June 50. Like Cassius the previous year, Bibulus thwarted their assault on Antioch by remaining within the walls, and they soon withdrew.

turn the Parthians against one another: Dio is our only evidence for this Parthian civil war. Pacorus was later on good terms with his father, becoming co-ruler. Pacorus' death in 38 obliged Orodes to appoint another son, Phraates IV, as his heir, and in 37 Phraates killed him and took his place.

30.3 *the consulship of Marcus Marcellus and Sulpicius Rufus*: 51 BCE. Dio's ignorance of the invasion in 50 leads him to date the end of the Parthian war to this year. For the election of Marcellus and Sulpicius, see 40.58.2.

31.1 *In that same period . . . only those most worthy of mention*: without marking the year changes (as for Parthia: see note to 40.28.1), Dio now gives what he acknowledges to be a highly selective and compressed account of events in Gaul in the years 53 (40.31–32), 52 (40.33–41), and 51 (40.42–43). Caesar and (for the last book) his continuator Hirtius give a full account of these events in books 6–8 of the *Gallic War*, as before devoting a book to each year.

31.2 *Ambiorix united almost all the region*: the rebellion in north-east Gaul, which had begun in winter 54/3 (40.5–11), continued in 53. Indutiomarus had been killed in Labienus' earlier victory (see note to 40.11.2). Caesar attributes the initiative now to the Treveri (*BG* 6.2.1–2) but, as before (see note to 40.7.1), Dio transfers it to Ambiorix.

Celts: as before (see note to 38.34.1), Dio's term for the Germans.

31.3 *Labienus . . . invaded the territory of the Treveri*: advancing from his winter quarters among the Remi and with his army reinforced from one to three legions. Caesar himself in early 53 brought his army up to ten legions by levying two new legions and obtaining one from Pompey, and by rapid expeditions obtained the submission of the Nervii, Senones, Carnutes, and Menapii. By omitting all this, Dio makes it appear that Caesar was then inactive, and in the following chapter he is consistently critical of Caesar.

convened his troops and addressed them: Caesar (*BG* 6.7.6, 8.3–4) says that Labienus made his deceptive speech 'openly in a council' and briefly addressed the troops later immediately before the battle.

32.2 *won the glory of having crossed the Rhine again*: as on Caesar's first crossing (see notes to 38.48.3–5), Dio represents this as a futile quest for glory. His claim that Caesar withdrew for fear of the Suebi is hardly fair: according to Caesar (*BG* 6.29.1), the Suebi (whom he had identified as the Treveri's allies) withdrew to a remote forest and he thought it unsafe to pursue them there for fear of grain shortage.

destroyed the bridge: not (as Dio appears to suppose) the bridge constructed in 55, but a new bridge built a little upriver (*BG* 6.9.3).

32.3 *Ambiorix was still at large*: he was nearly caught by the Roman cavalry, but continued to evade capture both now and in 51 (*BG* 6.29–31, 8.24). His ultimate fate is unknown.

not . . . involved in the rebellion: another unfair criticism of Caesar. As Dio's own account acknowledged (40.5–6), the Eburones had started the rebellion in winter 54/3, destroying the army of Cotta and Sabinus.

Gauls and Sugambri . . . came for the booty: Dio implies that the Sugambri came by Caesar's invitation, but Caesar claims that the plunder invitation was made only to the Gauls and the Sugambri crossed the Rhine to join in at their own initiative (*BG* 6.34–35).

32.4 *attacked the Romans as well*: in fact just a single legion, stationed at Atuatuca (see note to 40.5.3) under Q. Cicero to guard the baggage, while the remaining nine legions were deployed in three detachments to annihilate the Eburones.

33.1 *the Gauls rose up again*: early in 52 BCE. Dio gives only the briefest sketch of developments before the siege of Avaricum, fully narrated by Caesar at *BG* 7.1–15.

Arverni . . . Vercingetorix: the Arverni, who occupied modern Auvergne, had contested the primacy of Gaul with the Aedui to their east. They had been at peace with the Romans since their defeat in 121. Vercingetorix now rebelled successfully against the current Arvernian leadership and rapidly brought all the tribes of western Gaul into his anti-Roman coalition.

killed all the Romans . . . in their towns or countryside: Caesar mentions a massacre of Romans only by the Carnutes at Cenabum (modern Orléans), before the Arverni joined the rebellion.

33.2 *invasion of Arvernian territory*: Caesar took them by surprise by crossing the Cevennes through deep snow with recently levied troops.

34.1 *captured one of their towns, Avaricum*: modern Bourges. The Bituriges had in fact rapidly joined the rebels, after the Aedui failed to help them resist. The Arverni then attacked the neighbouring Boii, but Caesar, having rejoined his legions, diverted them by a campaign in which he took Cenabum and other towns and then laid siege to Avaricum. Caesar narrates the siege at length (*BG* 7.16–28), whereas Dio focuses on a few details.

34.2 *supposed besiegers . . . under siege*: Dio here echoes the Athenian commander Nicias' letter describing his force's plight at Syracuse (Thucydides 7.11.4). Vercingetorix, camped some way from the town, concentrated on disrupting the Romans' foraging, while the defenders obstructed the siege-works.

34.3 *winter having set in*: a chronological confusion. Caesar tells us that he left Avaricum, a few days after its capture, 'when winter was nearly over' (*BG* 7.32.1). Dio picturesquely exaggerates the effect of the storm.

34.4 *for all that they had suffered during the siege*: and for the massacre at Cenabum (see note to 40.33.1), according to Caesar (*BG* 7.28.4).

slaughtering all the inhabitants: according to Caesar, only 800 escaped out of 40,000.

35.1 *the river*: the Allier (ancient Elaver), a tributary of the Loire. The latter formed the boundary between the Aedui and the Arverni.

35.3 *constructed rafts*: Dio perhaps envisages a pontoon bridge resting on rafts. Caesar in fact had one of the destroyed bridges rebuilt (*BG* 7.35.4).

35.4 *Gergovia*: the principal settlement of the Arverni. Such fortified hilltop towns (*oppida*) served as regional power centres throughout central and southern Gaul. Gergovia's site has been identified as the volcanic plateau of Merdogne, south of Clermont-Ferrand and 360 metres above the plain which it overlooks, and excavations have revealed traces of Caesar's camps. See M. Reddé, 'Recent Archaeological Research on Roman Military Engineering Works of the Gallic War', in Fitzpatrick and Hazelgrove (eds.), *Julius Caesar's Battle for Gaul*, 91–112, at 94–8.

wasted effort: Caesar interweaves his accounts of his siege of Gergovia and of the developments leading to the Aedui's revolt (*BG* 7.36–53), giving the impression that it was only the risk of wider rebellion which led him to abandon the siege. Dio separates the two themes and places more stress on the futility of the siege.

36.1 *occupied all the surrounding high ground*: Vercingetorix placed the contingents from the various rebel communities in camps on the plateau around the town.

36.4 *control of a part of it*: early in the siege Caesar seized a lower hill (identified as the hill of La Roche Blanche) at the foot of the plateau on which the town stood and stationed two of the six legions he had with him there, linking it to the main camp by a double trench.

36.5 *men he left behind suffered badly*: see note to 40.37.3.

raised the siege: Dio omits the assault staged by Caesar immediately before the withdrawal, apparently with the limited aim of capturing some of the enemy camps. Two legions pressed on to attack the town itself, but were driven back with heavy losses (*BG* 7.44–51).

37.3 *accompanied them himself with the cavalry*: in fact Caesar sent the cavalry ahead to meet the force of 10,000 Aedui being brought by Litaviccus (his spelling), following himself with four legions. He returned early the next morning, but in his absence the two legions left in the camp under C. Fabius had suffered badly from enemy attacks (*BG* 7.40–41).

38.1 *since the Romans . . . would punish them*: a small gap in the transmitted text leaves the precise sense uncertain.

38.2 *Noviodunum*: an Aeduan town on the Loire, probably modern Nevers.

38.3 *foiled by the Loire and turned against the Lingones*: this and the following sentences are inaccurate summaries of events recounted by Caesar at *BG* 7.55–66. Vercingetorix tried to prevent Caesar from crossing the Loire, but Caesar got his army across by fording and then advanced to the territory of the Senones, where Labienus' army rejoined him. The Lingones in fact remained loyal, like their neighbours the Remi. For Caesar's march to their territory, see note to 40.39.1.

38.4 *Labienus seized the island in the Seine*: when setting out against the Arverni with six legions (40.35.1), Caesar had despatched Labienus with the remaining four legions against the Senones and the Parisii to their north. Labienus took Mediosedum (modern Melun), on an island in the Seine, and then advanced along the river against Lutetia (modern Paris), the capital of the Parisii and also on an island. On learning of Caesar's withdrawal from Gergovia and the revolt of the Aedui, Labienus withdrew to rejoin Caesar, defeating an enemy force on the way. Dio's references to a victory and multiple crossings relate to this success.

39.1 *Vercingetorix . . . marched against the Allobroges*: in the Roman province (see note to 37.47.1). Vercingetorix did not march against them with his main force, but sent a contingent from the neighbouring tribes against them and another against the Helvii, also in the province. Contrary to Dio's implication, these and the subsequent developments took place after Labienus' campaign and junction with Caesar.

intercepted him in the territory of the Sequani: in fact, in that of their neighbours the Lingones, near modern Dijon.

39.2 *The Romans had so little hope of survival*: Dio exaggerates their plight for dramatic effect. Like Plutarch (*Caes.* 26), he does not make it clear that only cavalry took part in the battle. Trusting in their superiority, Vercingetorix deployed his cavalry in three contingents against the front and both flanks of the Roman marching column, but the Roman cavalry held their own against each contingent, and, after the German auxiliaries reached the top of a ridge, the enemy were routed.

the Celts who were fighting for the Romans: before he left the Senones' territory Caesar had obtained cavalry and light infantry from the German tribes across the Rhine who had come to terms.

39.3 *Insatiable . . . physical strength*: 'Celtic' ethnic stereotyping added by Dio.

inside Alesia . . . under siege: after his defeat, Vercingetorix withdrew west to Alesia (Mont Auxois, above modern Alise-Sainte-Reine), a hilltop *oppidum* of the Mandubii. Recognizing that the site could only be taken by blockade, Caesar surrounded it by a circumvallation 10 Roman miles long and subsequently constructed an outer defensive circuit (the contravallation) to protect his army from the Gallic relieving force. Excavation has revealed extensive traces of the Roman siegeworks, summarized by Reddé, 'Roman

Military Engineering Works' (cited in note to 40.35.4), 98–106. Caesar gives a detailed account of the siege (*BG* 7.68–89).

40.4 *died . . . shut out by both sides*: Caesar merely states that he refused to admit the non-combatants whom the defenders had expelled (*BG* 7.78.5). Dio spells out what he presumes to have been Caesar's motives and the victims' grim fate.

reinforcements: Caesar claims that they totalled 8,000 cavalry and 250,000 infantry.

with the help of [. . . .]: a small number of words has dropped out of the transmitted text, and we have supplied the words 'they were repulsed'. Dio's reference to help may relate to the Romans' German auxiliaries, who once again played a decisive part (*BG* 7.80.6; cf. Dio 40.39.2–3).

40.5 *tried to get . . . into the town by night*: the relief force was seeking not to get through to the town, but to overwhelm the Roman besiegers by breaking through the contravallation into their camps. Dio oversimplifies the complex obstacles which the Romans had constructed, and seems mistakenly to envisage this night assault as made chiefly with cavalry.

40.6 *defeated, along with the defenders . . . from the town*: this final attack consisted of simultaneous assaults at multiple points on the Roman walls by the relief force and from the town. Fighting was particularly intense at a weak point in the Roman defences identified by the enemy, and Caesar claims that only his personal intervention there saved the day. After this defeat, the survivors of the relief force fled and the defenders in Alesia submitted to Caesar. Caesar spared the Aeduan and Arvernian prisoners, but distributed the rest as plunder to his troops.

41.1 *Vercingetorix . . . hoped to be pardoned by him*: Caesar (*BG* 7.89) merely says that Vercingetorix was (with his own agreement) handed over to him as he sat before the Roman camp. Dio's more dramatic version derives from another source or sources, and has some similarities with those of Plutarch (*Caes.* 27) and Florus (1.45.6). However, only Dio claims that Vercingetorix had formerly been Caesar's friend, hoped for mercy, and met instead with reproach.

41.3 *put him to death*: in September 46. Only Dio mentions Vercingetorix's execution (also at 43.19.4).

42.1 *won over some . . . others he subjugated . . . in battle*: the Aedui and Arverni submitted in late 52. Unrest continued among many other Gallic communities during 51, but was suppressed everywhere by the end of the year. Maintaining the selectivity announced at 40.31.1, Dio gives details only on the crushing of the Belgic revolt, of which Caesar's continuator Hirtius gives a full account at *BG* 8.6–23. He thus passes over other campaigns by Caesar and his legates, particularly in south-west Gaul, where the siege of Uxellodunum (in the Dordogne) broke the final resistance.

Commius . . . their leader: the Belgic tribes now in revolt were the Bellovaci, the Atrebates, and their immediate neighbours, and leadership was provided jointly by the Bellovacan Correus and by Commius. Following their conquest in 58, Caesar had appointed the loyal Commius as king of the Atrebates, and he had performed valuable service for Caesar in Britain in 55–54. However, in 52 he defected and played a leading part in the great rebellion.

42.3   *slaughtered huge numbers of them*: Dio's account of the fighting at 40.42.1–3 is markedly different from Hirtius' more reliable version. Hirtius does report the rebels' use of fire to cover their withdrawal to a different position, but the decisive Roman victory (in which Correus was killed) followed later.

43.2   *wounded by one of the Romans*: Hirtius (*BG* 8.23), probably correctly, puts this incident earlier, in winter 53/2, and portrays it as an abortive Roman attempt to assassinate Commius.

   that he should never come within sight of any Roman: so also Hirtius (*BG* 8.48.9). Dio's 'as some report' may indicate that he was here using both Hirtius and another source. Commius subsequently escaped to south-east Britain, where he founded a kingdom which included Atrebates who had settled there.

43.3   *tribute*: payable by all Caesar's new conquests except favoured tribes and fixed at a total of 40 million sesterces (Suet. *Jul.* 25.1).

44.1   *the consulship of Lucius Paullus and Gaius Marcellus*: L. Aemilius Paullus and C. Claudius Marcellus. There were no disturbances in Gaul in this year. Having taken his account of Roman dealings with Parthia and in Gaul down to this point, Dio now turns back to developments in Rome in 53–50 BCE, picking up from 39.65 and opening with a brief outline (40.44) showing how these events led up to the outbreak of civil war.

   The term was now at an end: Caesar's command had been extended for five years (not three, as Dio supposed) in 55 BCE (see note to 39.33.3). The date it was due to expire remains controversial (see note to 40.59.3).

44.2   *extension . . . in Spain for a further five years*: see note to 40.56.2.

   the child: see note to 39.64.1.

44.3   *at the mercy of Pompey and his other enemies*: see notes to 40.60.1, 62.3.

45.1   *Calvinus and Messalla were appointed consuls*: Cn. Domitius Calvinus and M. Valerius Messalla Rufus. Their delayed entry into office was already mentioned at 40.17.1–2. Cicero's letters give detailed information on the failure to elect consuls for the following year in the second half of 54. Pompey and Caesar initially supported the two other candidates, C. Memmius and M. Aemilius Scaurus. Memmius and Calvinus made a bribery deal with the consuls of 54, promising to remove impediments to their taking up their provinces if elected, but in August Memmius revealed the deal in the Senate and an abortive attempt was made to set up a tribunal. All four candidates were later charged with bribery, and the elections continued to be obstructed. Dio's account at 40.45.2–5 is our main evidence for the continuing delay in 53 until Calvinus and Messalla were at last elected as consuls for the year in July (Dio) or August (Appian, *BC* 2.19).

45.2 *thrown into the prison*: the Carcer (see note to 37.50.1). The Senate itself had no power of imprisonment, and Pompey, currently just a proconsul, could hardly have carried this out (as Dio perhaps implies) in 53.

grandson of Sulla and a tribune: Q. Pompeius Rufus' same-named grand-father had been Sulla's colleague as consul in 88 and had married his son to Sulla's daughter. Dio is wrong that Pompeius Rufus delayed the election of Calvinus and Messalla as tribune, since his tribunate was in fact in 52 (so rightly 40.49.1, 55.1). If he did obstruct their election, he will have been acting as a private citizen. However, Dio may have misdated action taken by Pompeius Rufus after his entry into office on 10 December 53 against the election of consuls for 52.

45.3 *auspices . . . refusing to favour the interreges*: after the outgoing consuls left office at the end of December 54, a succession of *interreges* (see note to 39.27.3) were appointed to conduct the consular elections. Dio had earlier blamed the continuing failure to hold the elections mainly on 'auguries and celestial signs' (40.17.2). The distinction that he draws here between unfavourable auspices and obstruction by tribunes obscures the fact that one of the obstructing tribunes' main tactics was probably obnuntiation (i.e. reporting inauspicious signs: see note to 38.6.1).

games . . . organized by them, not the praetors: the elections of consuls, praetors, curule aediles, and quaestors were conducted by the consuls in this rank order (cf. note to 39.7.4), and so the failure to elect consuls for 53 had also prevented these lower magistracies from being filled. However, the tribunes and aediles of the plebs were elected in the plebeian assembly under the presidency of the tribunes, and so men had been elected to these posts for 53, entered office at the normal time, and discharged some of the functions of the vacant magistracies, including the presidency of the *ludi Apollinares* on 6–13 July, normally held by the urban praetor.

45.4 *Favonius*: the loyal associate of Cato. Favonius' imprisonment by Rufus must date to 52, when Rufus held this power as tribune, and this was prob-ably also the year of his aedileship.

military tribunes . . . as in the past: in many years between 444 and 367 BCE between three and eight military tribunes with consular power (in modern discussions usually called consular tribunes) were said to have been appointed in place of consuls. Dio had given an account of this institu-tion, preserved in summary by Zonaras 7.19.4–5. The proposal in 53 was presumably intended to allow all four consular candidates to be appointed.

45.5 *Pompey should be made dictator*: from 54 Pompey had remained in Italy, governing Spain through his *legati* and spending most of his time near Rome (see notes to 39.39.4, 63.4). A dictatorship for Pompey to resolve the electoral crisis had been mooted in 54 and in 53 was promoted especially by the tribune C. Lucilius Hirrus, a cousin of Pompey, with opposition from Cato (Plut. *Pomp.* 54). On the office of dictator, see note to 36.34.1.

46.1 *Pompey . . . made arrangements for the consuls to be elected*: that Pompey
helped to ensure the election is confirmed by Plutarch, but how this was
achieved is unclear. Pompey was probably not formally offered a dictatorship, as Dio appears to imply.

as though . . . mourning a great catastrophe: in adopting mourning dress in
response to election delay, the consuls (and no doubt the Senate, following their lead) were following the precedent set in 56. For this dress
change, see notes to 38.14.7 and 39.28.2.

46.2 *command abroad before five years had passed*: this Senate decree could not
take effect until confirmed by the law carried through the assembly by
Pompey in 52 (see notes to 40.30.1, 56.1). The measure was a radical
change from the existing system under which consuls and praetors taking
provincial commands left for their provinces shortly before or shortly
after the end of their year of office. The proposal may have been intended
both to check corruption by preventing those elected from recovering
electoral expenditure from their profits as provincial governors and to
serve wider aims such as improving the process of assigning provinces to
governors and the quality of provincial governance. See Morrell, *Pompey,
Cato and the Governance of the Empire* (Oxford, 2017), 200–36; D. Rafferty,
Provincial Allocations in Rome, 123–52 BCE (Stuttgart, 2019), 133–51.

46.3 *prefect of the city*: an official appointed to take responsibility for the city of
Rome during the Latin Festival, when all the magistrates were absent on
the Alban Mount (see note to 39.30.4).

no government at all: as in the previous year (see note to 40.45.3), tribunes
and aediles of the plebs were elected and took office at the normal time.

47.1 *market . . . on the first day of January*: market days (*nundinae*) occurred on
an eight-day cycle. It was held to be ill-omened for a market day to fall on
the kalends of January, as had happened in 78, the year of Lepidus' rebellion. The coincidence could be avoided by inserting an additional day,
balanced by subtracting a day later, as happened in 41 (48.33.4).

47.2 *an eagle owl . . . through the air*: Dio may here be repeating the similar
portents he had given for 53 BCE (see note to 40.17.1), perhaps an acci-
dental duplication in his notes, but one which helped him to build up
a list of portents presaging the momentous domestic events of 52.

47.3 *demolish their temples*: these Egyptian cults had become popular at Rome
during the first century BCE, when a shrine is attested on the Capitol.
This measure of 53 BCE followed action against them taken in 58, and
demolition of their shrines was ordered again in 48 (42.26.2). Dio will
have found this report in an earlier historian but added his own interpretation of the decree as a portent.

47.4 *established their temples outside the pomerium*: a temple to Isis and Sarapis
was decreed in 43 (47.15.4), but may never have been built. Augustus
banned Egyptian rites within the *pomerium* in 28, and Agrippa in 21
extended the ban a mile outside (53.2.4; 54.6.6). Tiberius too took action

against the cults, but they were favoured by later emperors. A major sanctuary with temples to Isis and Sarapis was established in the Campus Martius (so outside the *pomerium*) by the mid-first century CE, if not before.

48.1 *the elections could not be held*: there were three candidates for the consulships of 52—Milo, Metellus Scipio (see notes to 40.51.2–3), and P. Plautius Hypsaeus. Milo, whose prospects were strongest (despite the opposition of his former friend Pompey), wanted the elections held as soon as possible, while his rivals preferred delay. The violence was mainly between supporters of Milo and of Clodius, now standing for the praetorship: these men had been bitter opponents and political gang leaders since Milo's tribunate in 57. As in the previous year (see note to 40.45.3), the plebeian officers for 52 had been elected as normal, and three of the tribunes were hostile to Milo, namely T. Munatius Plancus Bursa, Q. Pompeius Rufus (see note to 40.45.2), and C. Sallustius Crispus (Sallust, the future historian). From the start of the year Plancus blocked the appointment of an *interrex* to hold the elections. Dio's narrative of events from this electoral crisis up to the trial of Milo (40.48–54) can be supplemented and corrected from the detailed and accurately researched account given by Asconius in his commentary on Cicero's *For Milo* (Asconius 30–56), whose sources include the *Acta*, the public record of the daily business of the Senate and the Roman people instituted by Caesar as consul in 59. Dio's version also includes some information omitted by Asconius. On these events, see J. T. Ramsey, 'How and Why Was Pompey Made Sole Consul in 52 BC?', *Historia* 65 (2016), 298–324; T. J. Keeline's edition and commentary of Cicero, *Pro Milone* (Cambridge, 2021), 6–22.

48.2 *Milo . . . went on to kill him*: on 18 January, just beyond Bovillae, about 18 km (11 miles) south-east of Rome. Milo was on his way back from his home town Lanuvium, Clodius on his way to Aricia. Milo's prosecutors claimed that he planned an ambush, intending to kill Clodius, and Cicero in his defence counterclaimed that Clodius ambushed Milo. However, Asconius, Dio, and other later sources must be right that the encounter was an accident. A brawl broke out between their retinues in which Clodius was wounded (Dio oversimplifies in speaking of Milo himself as the wounder). Clodius was taken into a nearby inn, but Milo's men then attacked the inn and killed Clodius. Asconius, like Dio, claims that Milo ordered this, thinking that it would be more dangerous to leave Clodius alive.

48.3 *the news reached Rome towards evening*: Clodius' body was brought back to his house in Rome soon after nightfall, and a mourning crowd converged there.

49.2 *dressed it*: Clodius' body had been placed on the Rostra naked with its wounds on view. The crowd's leader in the move to the senate-house and the cremation was Sex. Cloelius, a public scribe and long-standing associate of Clodius.

49.3 *at the ninth hour*: on the Roman day, see note to 39.65.2. The ninth hour at Rome on 19 January 52 BCE (= 9 December 53 BCE, Julian) ran from approximately 1.40 to 2.25 p.m.

funeral banquet: relatives of prominent individuals quite often feasted the Roman people after their death, usually not until some time after the funeral, but in this case the arrangements were made by the crowd and its leaders.

49.5 *the Senate . . . on the Palatine*: perhaps in the temple of Jupiter Stator, on the northern slope of the Palatine Hill. The meeting probably took place on the same day as the burning of the senate-house, as Dio implies.

an interrex should be chosen: previously blocked by Plancus (see note to 40.48.1). The crowd demanded that the appointee, M. (or M.') Aemilius Lepidus, should hold the elections straight away. He refused, since custom prohibited the first *interrex* appointed from doing so, and his house was then besieged by the crowd in the hope of getting Milo's opponents elected. Once Milo resumed canvassing, his opponents' supporters reverted to blocking the elections.

see that it suffered no harm: the Senate's emergency 'last decree', last passed in 63 and 62 BCE (see notes to 37.31.2, 43.3). In the absence of consuls, the Senate addressed the decree to such officers as were available to act. Asconius (34) confirms Dio's account of the decree's wording, but shows that Dio dated it too soon (his next sentence betrays confusion). The decree was prompted by continuing violence between the supporters of Milo and his opponents and was probably passed on or soon after 1 February. However, the electoral impasse continued.

showed himself in public: Milo returned to Rome on the night of 19 January (Asconius 33).

50.1 *entrust him with recruiting fresh troops*: Asconius shows that Pompey was given this instruction at the same time as the passage of the 'last decree'.

change their dress: assuming military cloaks (*saga*), as at a similar moment in 63 (see note to 37.33.3).

50.2 *outside the pomerium, near his theatre*: in the Curia Pompeii, a dedicated meeting place for the Senate which Pompey had constructed in the portico adjacent to his theatre (see note to 39.38.1). The meeting had to be held outside the *pomerium* to allow the proconsul Pompey to attend (see note to 39.63.4).

50.3 *Curia Hostilia . . . named after Sulla*: the original senate-house, near the Forum, was attributed to Tullus Hostilius, Rome's supposed third king. Sulla, probably from 81, reconstructed it on a larger scale to accommodate his expanded Senate. It was customary for restoration and rebuilding to be entrusted to descendants of the original builder. However, Faustus' rebuilt Curia was soon replaced by the Curia Julia on a different site, projected by Caesar and completed by Augustus.

50.4 *sixty days of sacrifices for them*: *supplicationes* (see note to 37.36.3). Caesar had been voted fifteen days of *supplicationes* in 57 and twenty in 55 (see notes to 39.5.1, 53.2), and was voted a further twenty at the end of 52 following his defeat of Vercingetorix. Dio's 'sixty days' may be intended as a rounded-up figure for the total voted to Caesar before the civil wars. (He will have been voted a *supplicatio* in 60 following his Spanish command, but surely for fewer than five days.)

Pompey . . . to him alone: an intercalary month (see Appendix, p. 162) was inserted in 52 BCE after 24 February. On the twenty-fourth day of the intercalary month (so fifty-eight days after Clodius' murder), the Senate's decree that Pompey should be sole consul was passed and Pompey was elected by an assembly convened by the current *interrex*. Bibulus' proposal was supported by his father-in-law and fellow conservative Cato. The election of a sole consul was unprecedented and also involved dispensing Pompey from the legal ten-year interval between consulships. It enabled magistrates to take office and trials to be held without giving Pompey the greater power of the dictatorship.

50.5 *designed to please the Senate*: Dio had earlier portrayed Caesar as gradually winning over the plebs from Pompey (see note to 36.43.2). Here, as often, Dio misrepresents the Senate as a monolithic bloc. Pompey's sole consulship marked the rapprochement with the conservative grouping led by Cato which eventually led to his breach with Caesar, but for the time being the two remained on good terms.

51.1 *avoid the jealousy it would entail*: for Dio's recurrent theme of Pompey's wish to avoid jealousy, see note to 36.24.6.

Caesar would be foisted upon him as his colleague: Suetonius (*Jul.* 26.1) confirms that tribunes argued for Caesar's being elected as Pompey's colleague, but this was not a realistic prospect, since Caesar was now fully occupied with Vercingetorix's revolt.

51.2 *when the laws permitted*: having been consul in 59, Caesar would have been eligible to stand again in 49 for the consulship of 48. At some point he may have considered standing in 50 for the consulship of 49, but this would have required a dispensation from the legal ten-year interval (cf. note to 40.50.4).

even if he was absent from Rome: Pompey induced all ten tribunes to carry a law dispensing Caesar from the legal requirement to present his candidature in person within the city. The law was probably passed in March 52, despite opposition from Cato and his associates. This exemption would ensure that Caesar would not be required to forgo his triumph in order to stand for election, as had happened in 60 (see note to 37.54.1). It would also enable him to retain his army (if permitted) until taking up the consulship, and this became the nub of the dispute leading to the civil war (see note to 40.60.1).

chose as his colleague Quintus Scipio, his father-in-law: Q. Caecilius Metellus Scipio Nasica. Dio misleadingly gives the impression that Pompey proceeded rapidly to take a colleague. In fact, the senatorial decree under which he had been elected permitted him to take a colleague only after at least two months had elapsed since his entry into office (Plut. *Pomp.* 54), so enabling progress to be made first with reforming legislation and trials, and in the event Scipio was not appointed until July. Dio's ordering of the remaining events of the year is thematic rather than chronological.

51.3 *bore the name of Metellus as well*: both Scipio's natal and his adoptive family were among the most eminent noble Roman families (as were his mother's family, the Licinii Crassi). His father, P. Cornelius Scipio Nasica, had not progressed beyond the praetorship, but before him stretched consuls in four successive generations. Scipio's adoptive father, Q. Caecilius Metellus Pius, consul with Sulla in 80 and then co-commander with Pompey against Sertorius, was one of a long series of Metellan consuls.

married his daughter to Pompey: according to Plutarch, after his election as sole consul. After Julia's death, Pompey had declined Caesar's offer of another marriage connection. Cornelia, Scipio's daughter, was the widow of P. Crassus, who had died with his father at Carrhae.

spared prosecution: see note to 40.53.2.

52.1 *Pompey's laws*: Asconius (36–39) and other sources provide further details of Pompey's laws on the courts. Two days after entering office, Pompey proposed two laws in the Senate, one on violence (*vis*, not mentioned by Dio) and the other on electoral corruption (*ambitus*), and these were passed by the popular assembly around 18 March. Both laws provided for stiffer penalties than the existing laws for these offences and streamlined procedure. The violence law related just to the killing of Clodius and the ensuing burning of the senate-house and attack on the house of the *interrex* Lepidus. The other law had general, retrospective application to cases of electoral corruption, but probably continued in force only for a limited period. The procedural changes appear also to have applied to the other jury courts, as Dio implies, but only for a limited period. Three days were allowed for the examination of witnesses and just one day for the prosecution and defence speeches and the jury vote.

selection of jurors ... to be made: Pompey personally selected a panel of 360 jurors. Before the final speeches, eighty-one jurors were selected by lot, chosen as before (see note to 38.8.1) equally from senators, *equites*, and *tribuni aerarii*. After the speeches, each side rejected five jurors from each order, leaving fifty-one to vote.

52.2 *character witnesses*: 'praisers' (*laudatores*) commonly gave evidence as to the excellence of defendants' character, either in person or in writing, with sometimes as many as ten appearing. Pompey's ban on the practice was short-lived.

52.3 *granted a pardon*: Dio is our only source for this provision. Earlier *ambitus* laws had offered pardon for successful prosecutors who had themselves been convicted of the offence, perhaps on more generous terms than this law.

53.1 *Plautius Hypsaeus ... rival ... for the consulship*: Plautius had been Pompey's quaestor in the East and Pompey had warmly supported him for the consulship (Asconius 35), but now abandoned him.

53.2 *Scipio . . . never came to court*: other sources mention only one prosecutor of Scipio, identified by Appian (*BC* 2.24) as C. Memmius, seeking pardon for his conviction for *ambitus* in his campaign for the consulship for 53 (see note to 40.45.1). Pompey made such pressing appeals to the jurors that the prosecution abandoned the case.

Milo . . . was found guilty: Asconius shows that Milo's was the first case to be dealt with in this series of trials for violence and electoral corruption, a fact which Dio appears to overlook. Milo was found guilty of the murder of Clodius under Pompey's new law on violence on 8 April. Dio is wrong to state that Milo was not charged with corruption: he was indicted under Pompey's *ambitus* law as well, and found guilty on this charge in absence on 9 April, and a few days later he was also convicted of corruption and violence under earlier laws.

53.3 *a few . . . were wounded and killed*: Dio may not have meant to suggest that the suppressed riot described here took place at Milo's trial, and in fact it cannot have done so, since Asconius (40–2) shows that no violence occurred there after Pompey took up position at the court with a guard from the second day. The incident appears to be the same as the one described by Appian (*BC* 2.24) as occurring at a trial of M. Aemilius Scaurus (for *ambitus* as a candidate for the consulship of 53, see note to 40.45.1). This may be the correct context, with Scaurus' trial occurring later in 52. However, other evidence (Cicero, *On Duties* 1.138; Asconius 32) may show that Scaurus' trial and conviction occurred before he sold his house to Clodius in late 53. If so, the suppressed riot may have occurred at one of the other trials of 52, perhaps that of Sex. Cloelius (see note to 40.55.1).

54.1 *those convicted of Clodius' murder included Milo*: only Milo is known to have been convicted in connection with the murder. Milo's associate M. Saufeius, alleged to have led the assault on the tavern and the ensuing killing of Clodius, was prosecuted for violence under both Pompey's law and the earlier Plautian law, but each time narrowly acquitted, with Cicero leading the defence (Asconius 55).

54.2 *contrary to custom*: soldiers normally did not appear within the *pomerium* except on the day of a triumph. At the start of his surviving speech *For Milo* Cicero refers to 'this new form of a new court'.

muttered a few faint and awkward words: as the sole defence advocate to speak on the final day, Cicero had been assigned the full three hours permitted (40.52.2). All sources agree that his speech fell below his usual standards. However, Cicero managed to utter much more than the few words implied by Dio and Plutarch (*Cic.* 35), since Asconius (41–2) and others report that the text of the speech actually delivered was available in their day. Plutarch, like Dio, asserts that it was the sight of Pompey and his troops which unnerved Cicero, whereas Asconius attributes it to barracking by Clodius' supporters. Both their heckling and Cicero's awareness of Pompey's hostility to Milo probably played a part.

The speech . . . in circulation today: the surviving speech *For Milo*, judged both in antiquity and today as perhaps Cicero's best.

54.3 *the following story*: attested only by Dio.

Massilia: modern Marseilles.

54.4 *he pushed hard and often for his return*: not otherwise attested. Milo was excluded from Caesar's recall of exiles at the start of the civil war. In 48 he joined M. Caelius Rufus (who had been his chief supporter among the tribunes of 52) in an uprising against Caesar in which both were killed.

55.1 *Rufus and Plancus . . . for the burning of the senate-house*: Pompeius Rufus and Munatius Plancus were indicted and convicted under Pompey's law on violence after their term as tribunes ended on 9 December 52, probably in early 51. Sex. Cloelius had been convicted on the same charge soon after Milo.

55.2 *in contravention of his own laws*: see note to 40.52.2. Cato prevented Pompey's testimony being read out by clapping his hands over his ears (Plut. *Cato* 48) and/or by reciting the clause in his law banning such evidence (Valerius Maximus 6.2.5).

right to eliminate five jurors from those . . . going to serve: in fact, five from each of the three orders from which juries were composed (see note to 40.52.1).

55.4 *just as poorly as . . . when defending Milo*: probably Dio's own mistaken guess. In 51 Pompey was again just a proconsul and so unable to attend the court. Plancus' conviction was a victory for Cicero in what was his only prosecution except against Verres in 70.

set them against each other again: Pompey and Cicero in fact remained on good terms.

56.1 *all candidates had to present themselves . . . before the assembly*: this was just one provision of a general law on the duties of magistrates (*de iure magistratuum*), passed by Pompey as part of a programme of constitutional reform. This clause of the law (the only one known) restated the existing legal requirement that those standing for office should present their candidature in person within the *pomerium* (see note to 37.54.1). Dio is wrong to say that the requirement had become obsolete, and to speak of it as requiring presence 'before the assembly', since voting in the elections took place outside the *pomerium*, on the Campus Martius.

until five years had passed: also as part of his reform programme, Pompey now passed a law through the assembly on provincial commands (*lex Pompeia de provinciis*), giving effect to the Senate decree passed in late 53 prescribing an interval of at least five years between holding a consulship or praetorship and a provincial governorship (see notes to 40.30.1, 46.2). The law made it possible for Caesar to be replaced in Gaul earlier than would have been possible under the previous law, and so has sometimes been thought to have been intended against him. However, it also lifted the ban on tribunes vetoing the Senate's votes on consular provinces, which enabled his supporters to block moves against him in 51–50. The law continued in effect only until the outbreak of civil war in 49, but the interval between magistracy and governorship was reimposed by Augustus in 27 BCE.

56.2 *take Spain for a further five years*: on top of the five years' command of the Spanish provinces granted by the *lex Trebonia* in 55 (39.33.2). So also 40.44.2, but Plutarch (*Pomp.* 55) says that the extension was for four years. According to Appian (*BC* 2.24), it was granted by decree of the Senate. Pompey's command had previously been due to expire at the same time as Caesar's, but he was now due to retain it for several more years.

as had been voted: by the Law of the Ten Tribunes (see note to 40.51.2).

56.3 *adding a rider to the law*: Suetonius (*Jul.* 28.3) says that Pompey forgot in this law to exempt Caesar from the ban on candidature in absence and corrected the mistake after the law had been engraved on bronze and deposited in the treasury. This probably implies that the correction was not made until the law had been passed, in which case it would have been invalid. Dio's version is best taken as implying that the correction was made after the law had been promulgated, but before it was voted on, and this is more likely. Corrections of laws at this stage (requiring a fresh promulgation of the corrected version) were not uncommon: for instances, described by Dio in the same way, see 36.39.4 and 37.50.1.

57.1 *repealed Clodius' law about the censors*: for the law, see note to 38.13.2.

57.3 *no one . . . wanted to be a censor any more*: Dio's judgement is refuted by his later notice about the censors elected in 50 (40.63): two eminent nobles were elected, and one, Ap. Claudius Pulcher, made vigorous use of his powers of expulsion.

58.1 *Cato did not want to hold office*: so also Plutarch (*Cato* 49), reflecting later idealizing of Cato, but as a Roman noble he would have been keen to hold the highest office. Dio wrongly portrays him as now opposed to Pompey as well as Caesar. Along with other senatorial conservatives, Cato was aiming to turn Pompey against Caesar and destroy him.

58.2 *Marcus Marcellus and Sulpicius Rufus were elected*: M. Claudius Marcellus and Ser. Sulpicius Rufus. Sulpicius was the leading jurist (legal expert) of his time. He had stood unsuccessfully for the consulship of 62 (see note to 37.29.1).

58.3 *Cato courted no one's favour*: ostentatiously abstaining from normal canvassing. Plutarch supplies more details.

59.1 *a partisan of Pompey*: misleading. Marcellus was acting as a hard-line conservative, aligned with Cato and Bibulus.

numerous measures against him: Marcellus challenged the citizen status of the colony Caesar had founded at Novum Comum (modern Como), provocatively having one of its councillors flogged.

a successor . . . before the due time: a range of sources provide details of the gathering crisis over Caesar's replacement in 51–50, notably the letters sent by M. Caelius Rufus to Cicero (absent as governor of Cilicia) reporting on events in Rome (*Fam.* 8.1–14). Recent discussions include Pelling, *Plutarch, Caesar* (Oxford, 2011), 283–306; Morstein-Marx, *Julius Caesar*, 258–320. Marcellus argued that Caesar should be replaced early because he had finished the war (Suet. *Jul.* 28.2). Senatorial discussion of the issue was repeatedly postponed over summer 51, but at some point Marcellus' proposal may have been voted down (so Hirtius, *BG* 8.53).

59.2 *Pompey . . . kept watch on the city*: with his third consulship in 52 over, Pompey reverted in 51 to proconsul. As in 54–53, he continued to govern Spain through his *legati* and spent most of his time in his suburban villa in the northern Campus Martius, with occasional absences elsewhere in Italy. He was able to attend the Senate only when it was convened outside the *pomerium* for his benefit (see notes to 39.63.4, 40.45.5).

59.3 *return to Rome as a private citizen*: Caelius gives a detailed report of a Senate meeting on 29 September 51 (*Fam.* 8.8.4–9), at which it was decreed that the Senate should decide on the consular provinces as a top priority from 1 March 50, and further decrees ensuring that Caesar would be replaced then were passed but vetoed. At this meeting Pompey said that he could not without injustice decide on Caesar's province before 1 March, but after that date would have no hesitation. This evidence suggests that for him to be replaced before 1 March 50 would have been a breach of the law passed in 55 giving Caesar a five-year extension to his command (*lex Pompeia Licinia*). What further definition, if any, the law had given to the terminal date of his command has been much disputed. Dio wrongly believed that it had added three years to the previously assigned five-year command (see note to 39.33.3) and so speaks here of Caesar's term as expiring in 50 BCE. Dio envisages Pompey as working covertly against Caesar from 52 on (cf. 40.50.5, 63.1). More probably, he was gradually drawn by senatorial hardliners into adopting a position which Caesar would find unacceptable.

59.4 *He accordingly arranged*: that Pompey was behind these elections is probably Dio's groundless conjecture.

Marcellus: C. Claudius Marcellus was cousin to the Marcelli who were consuls in 51 and 49. Of a great noble family, all three now acted as hardline opponents of Caesar. This Marcellus was married to Octavia, granddaughter of Caesar's sister and sister of the future emperor Augustus.

Curio: C. Scribonius Curio, brilliant but raffish, had supported Clodius in his trial in 61 and was now married to his widow Fulvia. However, like his same-named father (consul in 76), he had been opposed to the alliance of Pompey, Caesar, and Crassus, and on good terms with Cicero from 59 on.

60.1 *afraid of falling into the clutches of his enemies*: Caesar claimed that the right to stand in absence granted him in 52 by the Law of the Ten Tribunes (see note to 40.51.2) entitled him to proceed directly from his command to the consulship, and that he would not be safe if he gave up his army and provinces while Pompey retained his (cf. note to 40.62.3). It is usually supposed that he was concerned above all with the risk of being prosecuted and convicted if he had a period as a private citizen, but against this see Morstein-Marx, *Julius Caesar*, 259–69.

enrolled additional soldiers: probably Dio's conjecture. The 'twenty-two cohorts from recent levies' who joined Caesar early in his advance into Italy in 49 (Caesar, *BG* 1.18.5) were probably those raised in 52 in the Roman province of Transalpine Gaul to defend it against Vercingetorix's forces (*BG* 7.65.1).

60.3 *paid off all his debts*: that Caesar won over Curio with a huge bribe is asserted by many later sources, but doubted by e.g. E. S. Gruen, *The Last Generation of the Roman Republic* (Berkeley and Los Angeles, 1974), 473–4.

60.4 *slaves, if they had any kind of influence with their masters*: Suetonius has similar wording (*Jul.* 27).

61.2 *many outrageous proposals*: early in his tribunate Curio proposed a measure relating to the Campanian land (cf. notes to 38.1.4, 7.3) and another under which travellers would be taxed on their accompanying slaves. He also proposed the annexation of the kingdom of Numidia either then or after his switch to overt support of Caesar.

62.1 *a practice . . . adopted when it was appropriate*: see Appendix, p. 162. The insertion of an intercalary month was in fact necessary in 50, when the Roman calendar was running over a month ahead.

62.3 *put forward all sorts of proposals . . . unlikely to be accepted*: Caelius' letters (*Fam.* 8.6.5; 8.11.3) report that in February, because he had not got his way about intercalation, Curio suddenly changed sides, speaking in favour of Caesar and proposing a law for a road-building commission and another about the grain distributions, and in April he abandoned his other proposals to concentrate on resisting Caesar's replacement.

everyone in arms should . . . dismiss their legions: from March 50 on (cf. note to 40.59.3), the consul C. Marcellus attempted to get a senatorial decision for Caesar's replacement, but was blocked by Curio's vetoes, and this stalemate continued for the rest of the year. Around June the Senate voted down a proposal that pressure be brought to bear on Curio to drop his veto. Curio repeatedly offered on Caesar's behalf that he would give up his army, if Pompey did so too. In August Caelius claimed that 'Pompey is determined not to allow Caesar to be elected consul unless he hands over his army and provinces, but Caesar is convinced that he cannot be safe if he leaves his army' (*Fam.* 8.14.2).

63.2 *Lucius Paullus*: L. Aemilius Paullus. Caesar is said to have won Paullus' neutrality (App. *BC* 2.26) or support (Plut. *Caes.* 29; *Pomp.* 58) by a bribe of 1,500 talents (= 36 million sesterces) with which he began building the magnificent Basilica of Paullus on the north side of the Forum. The building replaced the Basilica Fulvia, with which Paullus had a family connection, and was completed and dedicated by Paullus' son in 34.

Appius Claudius and Piso were made censors then: L. Calpurnius Piso had been consul in 58, Ap. Claudius Pulcher in 54. For their marriage connections with respectively Caesar and Pompey, see notes to 38.9.1 and 39.60.3. They were elected censors in June–July 50, but abdicated when the civil war broke out.

63.3 *he . . . expelled a great many equites and senators*: taking advantage of the repeal of his brother Clodius' law limiting censors' power of demotion (38.13.2; 40.57.1), Claudius exercised it more actively than any censor since those of 70.

63.4 *all the sons of freedmen*: a few freedmen's sons had long gained entry to the Senate, but this was frowned on, and one senator is known to have been expelled by the censors of 70 on this ground. See further S. Treggiari, *Roman Freedmen during the Late Republic* (Oxford, 1969), 54–62.

Sallustius Crispus, the historian: known to us as Sallust. As tribune in 52, he had been active against Milo alongside Pompeius Rufus and Plancus (see note to 40.48.1) but, unlike them, had escaped prosecution. Claudius' ground for expelling him is uncertain (immorality according to a hostile source). As a Caesarian supporter he reached the praetorship in 46 and governed an African province, but, after being charged with extortion, he withdrew from public life to write history. The only other individual known to have been expelled by Claudius is C. Ateius Capito, whom he alleged to have falsified auspices against Crassus as tribune in 55 (see note to 39.39.6).

63.5 *Curio was threatened with expulsion*: Claudius' attempt to expel Curio and his and Marcellus' subsequent actions against him are mentioned only by Dio (40.63.5–64.4).

64.4 *the majority voted to let him off*: Dio anachronistically gives the impression that Curio was put on trial before the Senate, a function which it only acquired under Augustus. Probably the consul Marcellus was trying to get the Senate to take action to prevent Curio from continuing to veto Caesar's replacement. Appian (*BC* 2.30–1) and Plutarch (*Pomp.* 58–59) instead describe the votes taken at this point (probably early December) as being on Curio's proposal that both Caesar and Pompey should give up their armies: Marcellus divided the question, and the Senate passed a motion that Caesar should give up his army, and rejected a motion that Pompey should give up his; Curio then put the motion that both should give up their armies, which was passed by 370 votes to 22, so exposing the hardliners' limited support. Probably both this account and Dio's are historical, with the votes on Curio's proposal and against action against him perhaps all taking place at the same meeting. All three authors agree that Marcellus' entrusting of the two legions to Pompey followed very soon after the Senate's votes: they may have occurred on the same or the next day.

Pompey, who was in the outskirts of the city: see note to 40.59.2.

the protection of the city . . . two citizen legions: Marcellus was acting as though the Senate had passed its 'last decree' against Caesar, as it did early in 49 (see note to 40.66.5). According to Appian, he used a rumour that Caesar was marching on Rome to justify his action, and had first sought senatorial approval, thwarted by Curio.

65.1 *given him . . . for use in his campaign*: Pompey had sworn in the men in Caesar's province of Cisalpine Gaul as consul in 55, but the legion had not been mustered, and in winter 54–53, following the rebellion of the Eburones, Pompey loaned it to Caesar, who levied two further legions at the same time, so more than making good the losses sustained in the revolt (Caesar, *BG* 6.1).

66.1 *as though for use against the Parthians*: Dio is wrong to dismiss the Parthian scare as a pretext invented by Pompey. Syria had been garrisoned just by two weak legions since the Carrhae disaster in 53 (see note to 40.28.2). When (in April 50) the Senate decreed that the two legions should be sent, a major Parthian invasion of Syria was expected. The Parthians invaded in June, but soon withdrew (see note to 40.30.2), and news that the immediate Parthian threat was over will have reached Rome by August.

66.2 *Cornelius Lentulus and Gaius Claudius . . . the next year's consuls*: L. Cornelius Lentulus Crus and C. Claudius Marcellus (brother of the consul of 51). They had been elected as anti-Caesarians, defeating Caesar's former legate Ser. Sulpicius Galba.

66.3 *before they took up office*: for the powers allowed to magistrates elect, including the issuing of edicts, see 55.6.5; F. Pina Polo, 'The Political Role of the *cónsules designati* at Rome', *Historia* 62 (2013), 420–52.

66.5 *he set out to join Caesar*: new tribunes came into office on 10 December, of whom M. Antonius and Q. Cassius Longinus were Caesar's supporters. From 1 January 49, when the new consuls entered office, events moved rapidly to civil war: Dio describes this process at 41.1–5; other accounts include Caesar's own (*Civil War* 1.1–11). On 1 January Curio brought a letter from Caesar to the Senate, reiterating his demand that he and Pompey should both lay down their commands. After debate, the Senate responded by voting that Caesar should dismiss his army before a certain date or be considered to be acting against the Republic. Antonius and Cassius vetoed this decree, and threats were then made against them at this and subsequent meetings. On 7 January the Senate passed its 'last decree' (see note to 37.31.2) and Antonius and Cassius fled to Caesar. A few days later, probably on the night of 10–11 January, Caesar left Ravenna in his province of Cisalpine Gaul, crossed the river Rubicon, which marked the boundary of the province, and advanced to Ariminum, en route for Rome. (Some sources make much of the Rubicon crossing, but Dio, like Caesar himself, leaves it unmentioned.) Peace negotiations took place in late December or early January and again in late January to no avail, despite significant concessions from Caesar.

GLOSSARY

aedile the third most senior of the Roman annual magistrates. There were four
aediles, two curule (elected by the whole Roman people) and two plebeian
(elected by the plebs). The aediles' responsibilities included the administration,
fabric, and grain supply of the city of Rome, and putting on public games.
Tenure of the aedileship was not required for the higher offices of praetor and
consul, but a successful aedileship (and particularly lavish spending on games)
could enhance a man's electoral prospects for those offices.

agrarian law a law providing for the distribution of public land in allotments to
Roman citizens as individual settlers.

assemblies see *COMITIA*, *CONTIO*.

augur a member of the college of augurs, one of the most prestigious Roman
priestly colleges. Their special expertise was in divination.

censor one of two magistrates who had traditionally been elected every five
years for a maximum term of eighteen months. They conducted the census of
Roman citizens, registering them, their property, and dependants; revised the
lists of senators and *equites*, excluding those they deemed unworthy; and
carried out a general supervision of public morals. They also leased out
contracts for tax collection and public works. The office held great prestige
and was normally held by ex-consuls. Censors were elected in 70 for the first
time since 86/5, and acted with great severity, expelling a record sixty-four
senators. Censors were elected in 65, 64, 61, 55, and 50, but all resigned with
their work uncompleted.

colony a settlement of Roman citizens, given land grants either in an existing
community or as a new community. Under the emperors existing cities were
sometimes given the status of a *colonia* as an honorific title.

comitia assemblies of adult male Roman citizens summoned in groups by
a magistrate for voting. Such assemblies met for elections, to pass laws, and for
some criminal trials (although in the Late Republic most trials were held in jury
courts: see *quaestio*). Notice of a *TRINUNDINUM* had to be given before a voting
assembly could be held.

The *comitia curiata* was the oldest form of assembly, but was retained only to
pass a law (*lex curiata*) on certain formal matters, such as adoption (see note to
38.51.2) and conferring full legitimacy on certain magistrates (see note to 39.19.3).
Voting was by the thirty *curiae*, but these were represented only by lictors.

In tribal assemblies voting was by the thirty-five local tribes (four for the city of
Rome, thirty-one rural). The assembly for the whole Roman people (*comitia
tributa*) was convened by consuls or praetors to pass laws and for some elections.
The assembly for the PLEBEIANS alone (*concilium plebis*) was convened by
tribunes to pass *plebiscita*, to elect tribunes and aediles of the plebs, and for some
trials. Tribal assemblies voted in various locations, often the Forum.

The centuriate assembly (*comitia centuriata*) was convened by consuls on the
Campus Martius chiefly for the election of consuls and praetors, but was

occasionally used for legislation, as for the recall of Cicero (see note to 39.8.2), and for capital trials, as against Rabirius (see note to 37.28.1). Voting was by 193 centuries, most of which were distributed across the five wealth classes, and there was a strong wealth bias. The *proletarii*, whose property was below the fifth-class census rating, voted in a single century.

consul the chief annual magistrate of the Roman state. The two consuls held office as colleagues and gave their names to the year. In the Late Republic consuls were elected in or after July of the preceding year, entered office on 1 January, spent their year in Rome as heads of the civil government, and then, if they wished, went out to govern a province as proconsul. Consuls normally had to be at least 42 years old and to have served as praetor at least three years earlier.

contio an informal public meeting convened by a consul, praetor, aedile, or tribune to hear speeches by the convening officer or by others at his invitation. Such meetings took place before laws were voted on and at other times when the convening officer saw fit. The pre-voting hearings of assembly trials were also called *contiones*. *Contiones* were often held in the Forum, but were also held in other locations, both within and outside the POMERIUM.

eques, equites member(s) of the equestrian order, the second order of Roman society after the Senate. The word *eques* literally means 'horseman', and is often translated as 'knight'. The *equites* had formed the original Roman cavalry, but by the Late Republic the cavalry were provided by non-Roman auxiliaries, and *equites* served in the army only as officers and on a commander's staff. All freeborn Roman citizens with property worth at least 400,000 sesterces qualified as *equites*, unless they were members of the Senate. Of those so qualified, 1,800 were enrolled by the censors in the eighteen equestrian centuries of the centuriate assembly (see COMITIA) and could retain their membership unless expelled by later censors as unworthy (see 38.13.2; 40.57.1–2). Gaius Gracchus in 123 had transferred jury membership for the criminal courts from senators to *equites*; repeated changes had been made in the following years, but under the *lex Aurelia*, passed in 70 (see note to 38.8.1), juries were composed of equal numbers of senators, *equites*, and *tribuni aerarii* (see QUAESTIO). The *lex Roscia*, passed in 67, reserved the first fourteen rows at the theatre for the *equites* (36.42.1). While many *equites* were just landowners, some had commercial interests (forbidden to senators), and the PUBLICANI were leading *equites* and influential within the order. See further C. Davenport, *A History of the Roman Equestrian Order* (Cambridge, 2019).

fasces see LICTORS.

gens (plural *gentes*), 'lineage', a Roman kinship grouping. All members of a *gens* shared a common *nomen* (see Appendix, p. 161). Some aristocratic *gentes* shared common cult and customs. *Gentes* may have had greater importance in early Rome.

haruspices Etruscan diviners sometimes summoned by the Senate to explain portents and to make recommendations for the appeasing of the divine anger of which the portents were held to be a sign.

imperium the supreme power, involving command in war and the interpretation and execution of law, which belonged in the Late Republic chiefly to consuls, praetors, proconsuls, and propraetors, and to dictators when appointed (see note to 40.34.1).

interrex   when both consuls left office without successors appointed, the patrician senators selected one of their number in turn to serve as *interrex*, each for a period of five days, to supervise the election of consuls.

legate   a senator acting as a senior assistant to a Roman commander, sometimes conducting independent operations in command of part of his army.

legion   the principal unit of the citizen element of Roman armies. In the Late Republic legions comprised ten cohorts, each subdivided into six centuries. A full-strength legion may have numbered 5,000 or more, but legions were often below this strength.

lex   (plural *leges*) a law passed by the COMITIA. Laws passed by the plebeian assembly were strictly known as *plebiscita*, but by the *lex Hortensia* of 287 these were made binding on the whole Roman people, and were also often called *leges*. A law had first to be formally promulgated—that is, the text read out and posted publicly—and an interval of a TRINUNDINUM then had to elapse before a vote. Speeches for and against the law might be made at a CONTIO during this period, and such a *contio* was also held immediately before the vote. Laws were known by the *nomen* of the proposer (see 38.7.6; Appendix, p. 161).

lictors   attendants of senior magistrates. A consul had twelve, a praetor six. Each lictor carried *fasces*, a bundle consisting of an axe and some long rods tied together with red straps; the axe and the rods symbolized the right to inflict capital and corporal punishment respectively, though the axe was omitted in Rome itself in recognition of citizens' right of appeal (*provocatio*).

magistrate   the holder of a Roman public office (technically, however, tribunes of the plebs were not magistrates). They are listed in T. R. S. Broughton's *The Magistrates of the Roman Republic*, 3 vols. (1951–2, 1986).

'**new man**'   *novus homo*, the first man of his family to reach the Senate.

noble   *nobilis*, a son or direct descendant of a consul through the male line. Most consuls were *nobiles*.

patricians   members of a select group of Roman *gentes*, who in the Early Republic had monopolized the priesthoods and magistracies. By the end of the fourth century this monopoly had been ended with a few minor exceptions (e.g. INTERREX). Only fourteen patrician *gentes* survived by the Late Republic, and the only patrician families to hold consulships in 69–49 were the Aemilii Lepidi (66, 50), Cornelii Lentuli (57, 56, 49), Claudii Pulchri (54), Iulii Caesares (64, 59), Sulpicii Rufi (51), and Valerii Messallae (61, 53).

plebeians   see PLEBS.

plebiscita   see LEX.

plebs   the name for the non-privileged mass of Roman citizens. The individual members of the plebs were the plebeians. Originally the plebs comprised all non-patricians. However, after the fourth century, when the patrician monopoly of office was broken, many of the great noble families were plebeian. The word plebs came to be used for humbler citizens, and by at least the reign of Augustus for all those not senators or *equites*. Dio usually uses the Greek word *plēthos* (and sometimes also *okhlos* or *homilos*) for the Latin *plebs*, reserving *dēmos* for the Latin *populus* (the whole citizen body).

pomerium the sacred boundary of the city of Rome. In the Late Republic it roughly corresponded to the line of the so-called Servian Wall, except that the Aventine hill was excluded. See further PROCONSUL.

pontiff *pontifex* (plural *pontifices*), a member of the College of Pontiffs, one of the most prestigious Roman priestly colleges. They had wide-ranging religious responsibilities, advising on correct procedure and performing some rituals themselves.

praetor the second most senior of the Roman annual magistrates. In the Late Republic there were eight praetors each year; the city praetor (*praetor urbanus*) handled civil suits between citizens, the foreign praetor (*praetor peregrinus*) handled civil suits between citizens and non-citizens, and the remaining six praetors each presided over one of the permanent criminal courts. After their year of office, praetors regularly went out to govern a province as proconsul or propraetor. The normal minimum age for the praetorship was 39.

proconsul the governor of a province holding the command after his consulship. The title was also given to some ex-praetors governing a province and to private citizens given special provincial commands (like Pompey against the pirates and against Mithridates). Proconsuls retained their *IMPERIUM* until their return to Rome, but lost it when they crossed the *POMERIUM*, unless entering in a triumph, when their *imperium* was extended for the day.

promulgation the reading out and posting of a law (see *LEX*).

province *provincia*, a word originally denoting a sphere of responsibility assigned to a magistrate or promagistrate, but subsequently used also for a territory regularly assigned to a Roman governor. Each year the Senate decreed which provinces were to continue under their existing governors and which were to be assigned to consuls or praetors, who then drew lots for them. In the Late Republic consuls and praetors normally went out to their provinces shortly before or shortly after the end of their term of office. For Pompey's modification of this system in 52 BCE, see notes to 40.46.2, 56.1. After Pompey's reorganization of the East, the provinces regularly assigned to governors were Further Spain, Nearer Spain, Transalpine Gaul, Cisalpine Gaul (i.e. northern Italy), Sicily, Sardinia, Africa, Macedonia, Asia, Bithynia–Pontus, Cilicia, and Syria.

publicani contractors for public services and works, and for tax collection (see CENSORS). The *publicani* were organized in companies, whose directors were leading *equites*.

quaestio (plural *quaestiones*) jury courts, the main form of criminal jurisdiction in the Late Republic. Such courts were sometimes established as special measures for particular occasions, and there were also standing courts established by laws for particular offences. The first standing court was established in 149 for *repetundae* (extortion by senators from Roman allies). Standing courts were subsequently established for other offences including *ambitus* (electoral corruption), *maiestas* (treason), *peculatus* (embezzlement), and *vis* (violence).

The presidency of each court was held annually either by a praetor or by a specially appointed president (*iudex quaestionis*).

quaestor the most junior of the Roman annual magistrates. Under a law passed by Sulla as dictator in 81 the number of quaestors was increased to twenty, and the quaestorship, with a minimum age of 30, conferred membership of the Senate and was a requirement for election to the higher magistracies. Two quaestors served at Rome as the urban quaestors: their primary responsibility was for the running of the state treasury (the *aerarium*), but they also had some other administrative functions, for example for jury ballots (39.7.4). Two quaestors served as assistants for the consuls, and some were given assignments in Italy, but the majority were assigned to provincial governors as assistants, sometimes continuing as proquaestors after their year of office. Provincial quaestors' main responsibilities were financial, but they also undertook military duties, and, in the event of the governor's death, took over as acting governor (so C. Cassius Longinus after Crassus' death: 40.28–29).

Senate the supreme council of the Roman state, consisting of all ex-magistrates (except those expelled as unworthy by the censors). As dictator, Sulla had substantially increased the Senate and ordained that the most junior magistracy, the quaestorship, should henceforth confer membership, and in the last years of the Republic the number of senators may have approached 600. The Senate's formal role was to advise the magistrates, but in practice its decrees (*senatus consulta*) determined most aspects of government. The Senate's main meeting place was the senate-house (Curia: see note to 40.50.3), but it often met elsewhere, always in a temple. In debates senators spoke in the order of their last magistracy. The most senior, the ex-consuls, spoke first and usually carried the most weight, although a few more junior senators achieved prominence, for example Cato.

tribune (of the plebs) one of ten annual officers elected by the plebeian assembly. The office, closed to patricians, had been created in the fifth century to protect the interests of the plebeians against the patricians. They were empowered to defend individuals' persons and property, to convene and put resolutions to the plebeian assembly, and to veto any public business. After the fourth century, when conflict between the two orders ceased, the tribunate came to be held by rising politicians, like the magistracies, and acquired the right to convene the Senate. However, the popular origins of the office were not forgotten, and many tribunes used it to promote popular causes. Sulla as dictator imposed heavy limitations on the office, but the tribunes recovered their right to stand for other offices in 75 and Pompey and Crassus as consuls in 70 passed a law restoring their full powers. The tribunes entered office not on 1 January (like consuls and praetors), but on 10 December.

tribuni aerarii originally responsible for collecting a wealth tax (*tributum*) from Roman citizens and paying legionary soldiers from the proceeds. By the Late Republic, their function had long been obsolete, but they remained in existence, probably as a subgroup of the EQUITES, and under the *lex Aurelia* of 70 supplied one-third of each criminal jury.

trinundinum   the required period of notice (probably three market days, so seventeen days or more) between the announcement of elections or PROMULGATION of a law and the voting assembly.

Vestals   the six priestesses of Vesta, the Roman goddess of the hearth. Required to maintain strict sexual purity during their minimum of thirty years' service, their chief responsibility was the tending of the undying fire in Vesta's temple, and their other responsibilities included the annual rite of the Bona Dea (see notes to 37.35.4, 45.1).

INDEX OF PROPER NAMES

References to Dio are to book (bold type), chapter, and section. Bold letters indicate the maps as follows: A—Central Rome (p. xli); B—The East (pp. xlii–xliii); C—Gaul (p. xliv).

American Literature

British and Irish Literature

Children's Literature

Classics and Ancient Literature

Colonial Literature

Eastern Literature

European Literature

Gothic Literature

History

Medieval Literature

Oxford English Drama

Philosophy

Poetry

Politics

Religion

The Oxford Shakespeare

A complete list of Oxford World's Classics, including Authors in Context, Oxford English Drama, and the Oxford Shakespeare, is available in the UK from the Marketing Services Department, Oxford University Press, Great Clarendon Street, Oxford OX2 6DP, or visit the website at www.oup.com/uk/worldsclassics.

In the USA, visit www.oup.com/us/owc for a complete title list.

Oxford World's Classics are available from all good bookshops.

An Anthology of Elizabethan Prose
Fiction

Early Modern Women's Writing

Three Early Modern Utopias (Utopia;
New Atlantis; The Isle of Pines)

FRANCIS BACON   **Essays**
The Major Works

APHRA BEHN   **Oroonoko and Other Writings**
The Rover and Other Plays

JOHN BUNYAN   **Grace Abounding**
The Pilgrim's Progress

JOHN DONNE   **The Major Works**
Selected Poetry

JOHN FOXE   **Book of Martyrs**

BEN JONSON   **The Alchemist and Other Plays**
The Devil is an Ass and Other Plays
Five Plays

JOHN MILTON   **The Major Works**
Paradise Lost
Selected Poetry

EARL OF ROCHESTER   **Selected Poems**

SIR PHILIP SIDNEY   **The Old Arcadia**
The Major Works

SIR PHILIP and   **The Sidney Psalter**
MARY SIDNEY

IZAAK WALTON   **The Compleat Angler**